Reading STREET

Program Authors

Peter Afflerbach

Camille Blachowicz

Candy Dawson Boyd

Elena Izquierdo

Connie Juel

Edward Kame'enui

Donald Leu

Jeanne R. Paratore

P. David Pearson

Sam Sebesta

Deborah Simmons

Alfred Tatum

Sharon Vaughn

Susan Watts Taffe

Karen Kring Wixson

PEARSON

Glenview, Illinois • Boston, Massachusetts
Chandler, Arizona • Upper Saddle River, New Jersey

We dedicate Reading Street to
Peter Jovanovich.

His wisdom, courage,
and passion for education
are an inspiration to us all.

Accelerated Reader

PEARSON

ISBN-13: 978-0-328-46992-5
ISBN-10:   0-328-46992-0
2 3 4 5 6 7 8 9 10 V064 14 13 12 11 10
CC1

Any Path, Any Pace

"Welcome to Reading Street! Bienvenidos too."

PEARSON

Find Your Place on Reading Street!

Who said so?

The Leading Researchers,

Program Authors

Peter Afflerbach, Ph.D.
Professor
Department of Curriculum and
Instruction
University of Maryland at
College Park

**Camille L. Z. Blachowicz,
Ph.D.**
Professor of Education
National-Louis University

Candy Dawson Boyd, Ph.D.
Professor
School of Education
Saint Mary's College of California

Elena Izquierdo, Ph.D.
Associate Professor
University of Texas at El Paso

Connie Juel, Ph.D.
Professor of Education
School of Education
Stanford University

Edward J. Kame'enui, Ph.D.
*Dean-Knight Professor of
Education and Director*
Institute for the Development of
Educational Achievement and
the Center on Teaching and Learning
College of Education
University of Oregon

Donald J. Leu, Ph.D.
*John and Maria Neag Endowed
Chair in Literacy and Technology
Director, The New Literacies
Research Lab*
University of Connecticut

Jeanne R. Paratore, Ed.D.
Associate Professor of Education
Department of Literacy and
Language Development
Boston University

P. David Pearson, Ph.D.
Professor and Dean
Graduate School of Education
University of California, Berkeley

Sam L. Sebesta, Ed.D.
Professor Emeritus
College of Education
University of Washington, Seattle

Deborah Simmons, Ph.D
Professor
College of Education and
Human Development
Texas A&M University

Alfred W. Tatum, Ph.D.
*Associate Professor and Director
of the UIC Reading Clinic*
University of Illinois at Chicago

Sharon Vaughn, Ph.D.
*H. E. Hartfelder/Southland
Corporation Regents Professor
Director, Meadows Center for
Preventing Educational Risk*
University of Texas

Susan Watts Taffe, Ph.D.
Associate Professor in Literacy
Division of Teacher Education
University of Cincinnati

Karen Kring Wixson, Ph.D.
Professor of Education
University of Michigan

Consulting Authors

Jeff Anderson, M.Ed.
Author and Consultant
San Antonio, Texas

Jim Cummins, Ph.D.
Professor
Department of Curriculum,
Teaching and Learning
University of Toronto

Lily Wong Fillmore, Ph.D.
Professor Emerita
Graduate School of Education
University of California, Berkeley

Georgia Earnest García, Ph.D.
Professor
Language and Literacy Division
Department of Curriculum
and Instruction
University of Illinois at
Urbana-Champaign

George A. González, Ph.D.
Professor (Retired)
School of Education
University of Texas-Pan American,
Edinburg

Valerie Ooka Pang, Ph.D.
Professor
School of Teacher Education
San Diego State University

Sally M. Reis, Ph.D.
*Board of Trustees Distinguished
Professor*
Department of Educational
Psychology
University of Connecticut

Jon Scieszka, M.F.A.
*Children's Book Author
Founder of GUYS READ
Named First National Ambassador
for Young People's Literature 2008*

Grant Wiggins, Ed.D.
Educational Consultant
Authentic Education
Concept Development

Lee Wright, M.Ed.
Pearland, Texas

Practitioners, and Authors.

Consultant

Sharroky Hollie, Ph.D.
Assistant Professor
California State University
Dominguez Hills, CA

Teacher Reviewers

Dr. Bettyann Brugger
*Educational Support Coordinator—
Reading Office*
Milwaukee Public Schools
Milwaukee, WI

Kathleen Burke
K–12 Reading Coordinator
Peoria Public Schools, Peoria, IL

Darci Burns, M.S.Ed.
University of Oregon

Bridget Cantrell
District Intervention Specialist
Blackburn Elementary School
Independence, MO

**Tahira DuPree Chase,
M.A., M.S.Ed.**
*Administrator of Elementary
English Language Arts*
Mount Vernon City School District
Mount Vernon, NY

Michele Conner
Director, Elementary Education
Aiken County School District
Aiken, SC

Georgia Coulombe
*K–6 Regional Trainer/
Literacy Specialist*
Regional Center for Training and
Learning (RCTL), Reno, NV

Kelly Dalmas
Third Grade Teacher
Avery's Creek Elementary, Arden, NC

Seely Dillard
First Grade Teacher
Laurel Hill Primary School
Mt. Pleasant, SC

Jodi Dodds-Kinner
Director of Elementary Reading
Chicago Public Schools, Chicago, IL

Dr. Ann Wild Evenson
District Instructional Coach
Osseo Area Schools, Maple Grove, MN

Stephanie Fascitelli
Principal
Apache Elementary, Albuquerque
Public Schools, Albuquerque, NM

Alice Franklin
*Elementary Coordinator, Language
Arts & Reading*
Spokane Public Schools, Spokane, WA

Laureen Fromberg
Assistant Principal
PS100 Queens, NY

Kimberly Gibson
First Grade Teacher
Edgar B. Davis Community School
Brockton, MA

Kristen Gray
Lead Teacher
A.T. Allen Elementary School
Concord, NC

Mary Ellen Hazen
State Pre-K Teacher
Rockford Public Schools #205
Rockford, IL

Patrick M. Johnson
Elementary Instructional Director
Seattle Public Schools, Seattle, WA

Theresa Jaramillo Jones
Principal
Highland Elementary School
Las Cruces, NM

Sophie Kowzun
*Program Supervisor, Reading/
Language Arts, PreK–5*
Montgomery County Public Schools
Rockville, MD

David W. Matthews
Sixth Grade Teacher
Easton Area Middle School
Easton, PA

Ana Nuncio
Editor and Independent Publisher
Salem, MA

Joseph Peila
Principal
Chappell Elementary School
Chicago, IL

Ivana Reimer
Literacy Coordinator
PS100 Queens, NY

Sally Riley
Curriculum Coordinator
Rochester Public Schools
Rochester, NH

Dyan M. Smiley
Independent Educational Consultant

Michael J. Swiatowiec
Lead Literacy Teacher
Graham Elementary School
Chicago, IL

Dr. Helen Taylor
Director of English Education
Portsmouth City Public Schools
Portsmouth, VA

Carol Thompson
Teaching and Learning Coach
Independence School District
Independence, MO

Erinn Zeitlin
Kindergarten Teacher
Carderock Springs Elementary School
Bethesda, MD

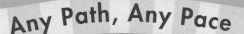

Any Path, Any Pace

v

UNIT 6

Putting It Together

In this Teacher's Edition Unit 6, Volume 2

In the **First Stop** on Reading Street

GO Digital!

See It!

- **Big Question Video**

- **Concept Talk Video**

- **Envision It! Animations**

- **Sing With Me Animations**

Hear It!

- **Sing With Me Animations**

- **eReaders**

- **Grammar Jammer**

- **Leveled Reader Database**

Do It!

- **Story Sort**

- **Letter Tile Drag and Drop**

UNIT 1

All Together Now

Volume 1

Carol Roth
The Little School Bus
Illustrated by Pamela Paparone

WEEK 1 • The Little School Bus

WEEK 2 • We Are So Proud! Realistic Fiction

WEEK 3 • Plaidypus Lost Realistic Fiction

Volume 2

WEEK 4 • Miss Bindergarten Takes a Field Trip with Kindergarten Animal Fantasy

WEEK 5 • Smash! Crash! Fantasy

WEEK 6 • Dig Dig Digging Nonfiction

UNIT 2

Look at Us!

Volume 1

Volume 2

UNIT 3

Changes All Around Us

Volume 1

Volume 2

Let's Go Exploring

Volume 1

Volume 2

UNIT 5

Going Places

Volume 1

WEEK 1 • Max Takes the Train Animal Fantasy.........7–104

Differentiated Instruction **SI** **OL** **A** **ELL** ....DI•1–DI•17

WEEK 2 • Mayday! Mayday! Nonfiction.................105–210

Differentiated Instruction **SI** **OL** **A** **ELL** ....DI•18–DI•34

WEEK 3 • Trucks Roll! Rhyming Nonfiction.......................211–310

Differentiated Instruction **SI** **OL** **A** **ELL** ....DI•35–DI•51

Volume 2

WEEK 4 • The Little Engine That Could
Classic Fantasy 311–414

Differentiated Instruction **SI** **OL** **A** **ELL** ....DI•52–DI•68

WEEK 5 • On the Move! Nonfiction 415–512

Differentiated Instruction **SI** **OL** **A** **ELL** ....DI•69–DI•85

**WEEK 6 • This Is the Way We Go to
School** Informational Fiction..513–615

Differentiated Instruction **SI** **OL** **A** **ELL** ....DI•86–DI•102

Customize Literacy...CL•1–CL•31

Putting It Together

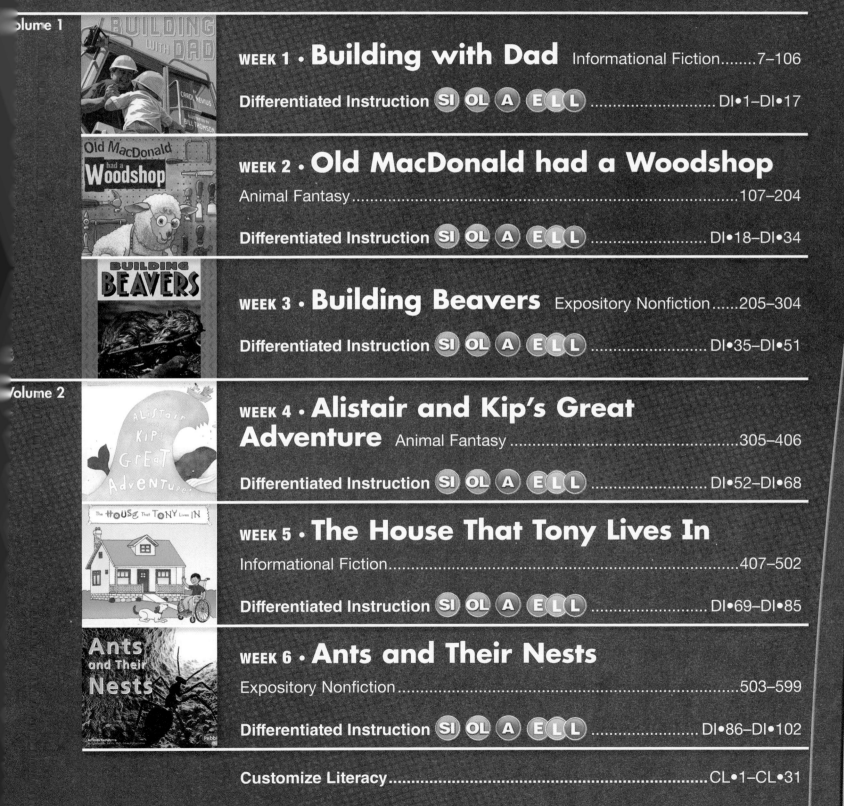

Skills Overview

Key

T Tested

🎯 Target Skill

Building with Dad
Informational Fiction pp. 59–73

Old MacDonald had a Woodshop
Animal Fantasy pp. 160–171

		Building with Dad	Old MacDonald had a Woodshop
Get Ready to Read	**Question of the Week**	How is a school built?	What tools do you need to build things?
	Amazing Words	*groundbreaking, trenches, foundation, welding, waterproof, gleaming*	*saw, drill, hammer, screwdriver, file, chisel*
	Phonemic Awareness	**T** 🎯 /a/ **T** 🎯 /i/	**T** 🎯 /o/
	Phonics	**T** 🎯 /a/ Spelled *Aa* **T** 🎯 /i/ Spelled *Ii* Review /y/ Spelled *Yy*; /kw/ Spelled *Qu*	**T** 🎯 /o/ Spelled *Oo* Review /a/ Spelled *Aa*; /i/ Spelled *Ii*
	High-Frequency Words	**T** *here, do, little, with, what*	**T** *where, is, go, that, come*
Read and Comprehend	**Comprehension**	🎯 **Skill** Compare and Contrast Review Draw Conclusions	**T** 🎯 **Skill** Character Review Plot
Language Arts	**Writing**	List	Song
	Conventions	Pronouns *I* and *me*	Prepositional Phrases
	Vocabulary	Compound Words	Location Words
	Speaking/Listening	Recite Language	Discuss Fact and Opinion

The Big Question

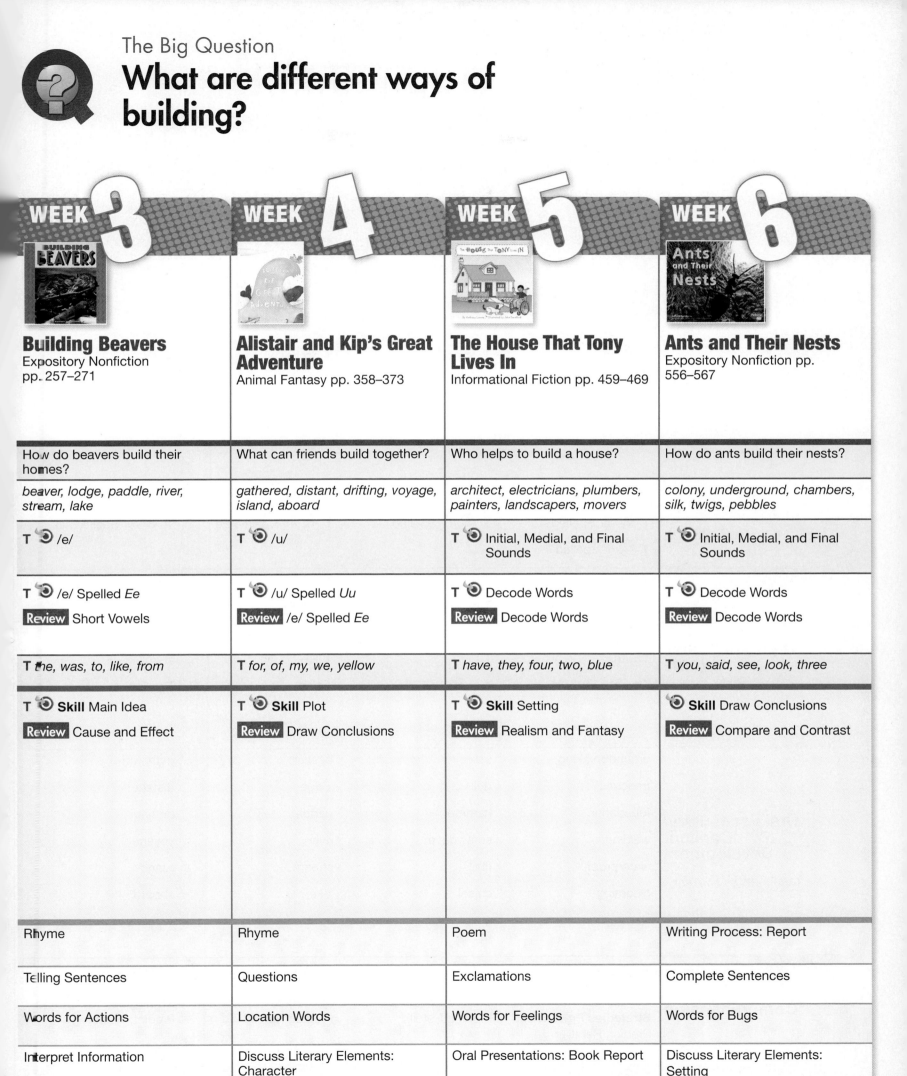

What are different ways of building?

WEEK **3**	WEEK **4**	WEEK **5**	WEEK **6**
Building Beavers Expository Nonfiction pp. 257–271	**Alistair and Kip's Great Adventure** Animal Fantasy pp. 358–373	**The House That Tony Lives In** Informational Fiction pp. 459–469	**Ants and Their Nests** Expository Nonfiction pp. 556–567
How do beavers build their homes?	What can friends build together?	Who helps to build a house?	How do ants build their nests?
beaver, lodge, paddle, river, stream, lake	*gathered, distant, drifting, voyage, island, aboard*	*architect, electricians, plumbers, painters, landscapers, movers*	*colony, underground, chambers, silk, twigs, pebbles*
T /e/	**T** /u/	**T** Initial, Medial, and Final Sounds	**T** Initial, Medial, and Final Sounds
T /e/ Spelled *Ee* **Review** Short Vowels	**T** /u/ Spelled *Uu* **Review** /e/ Spelled *Ee*	**T** Decode Words **Review** Decode Words	**T** Decode Words **Review** Decode Words
T *the, was, to, like, from*	**T** *for, of, my, we, yellow*	**T** *have, they, four, two, blue*	**T** *you, said, see, look, three*
T **Skill** Main Idea **Review** Cause and Effect	**T** **Skill** Plot **Review** Draw Conclusions	**T** **Skill** Setting **Review** Realism and Fantasy	**Skill** Draw Conclusions **Review** Compare and Contrast
Rhyme	Rhyme	Poem	Writing Process: Report
Telling Sentences	Questions	Exclamations	Complete Sentences
Words for Actions	Location Words	Words for Feelings	Words for Bugs
Interpret Information	Discuss Literary Elements: Character	Oral Presentations: Book Report	Discuss Literary Elements: Setting

Monitor Progress
Make Data-Driven Decisions

Data Management
- Assess
- Diagnose
- Prescribe
- Disaggregate

Classroom Management
- Monitor Progress
- Group
- Differentiate Instruction
- Inform Parents

Don't Wait Until Friday!

SUCCESS PREDICTOR	WEEK 1	WEEK 2	WEEK 3	WEEK 4
Phonemic Awareness	T /a/ T /i/	T /o/	T /e/	T /u/
Phonics	T /a/ Spelled *Aa* T /i/ Spelled *Ii*	T /o/ Spelled *Oo*	T /e/ Spelled *Ee*	T /u/ Spelled *Uu*
High-Frequency Words	T here T do T little T with T what	T where T is T go T that T come	T the T was T to T like T from	T for T of T my T we T yellow
Oral Vocabulary/ Concept Development (assessed informally)	groundbreaking trenches foundation welding waterproof gleaming	saw drill hammer screwdriver file chisel	beaver lodge paddle river stream lake	gathered distant drifting voyage island aboard
Comprehension	T **Skill** Compare and Contrast **Strategies** Preview and Predict; Retell	T **Skill** Character **Strategies** Preview and Predict; Retell	T **Skill** Main Idea **Strategies** Preview and Predict; Retell	T **Skill** Plot **Strategies** Preview and Predict; Retell

Phonemic Awareness · Sound-Spelling · Word Reading · Retelling

Key

T Tested

⟳ Target Skill

WEEK 5

T ⟳ Initial, Medial, and Final Sounds

T ⟳ Decode Words

T have
T they
T four
T two
T blue

architect

electricians

plumbers

painters

landscapers

movers

T ⟳ **Skill** Setting

Strategies Preview and Predict; Retell

WEEK 6

T ⟳ Initial, Medial, and Final Sounds

T ⟳ Decode Words

T you
T said
T see
T look
T three

colony

underground

chambers

silk

twigs

pebbles

T ⟳ **Skill** Draw Conclusions

Strategies Preview and Predict; Retell

GO Digital!

See It!
- **Big Question Video**
- **Concept Talk Video**
- **Envision It! Animations**
- **Sing with Me Animations**

Hear It!
- **Sing with Me Animations**
- **eReaders**
- **Grammar Jammer**
- **Leveled Reader Database**

Do It!
- **Story Sort**
- **Letter Tile Drag and Drop**

UNIT 6

Assessment and Grouping
for Data-Driven Instruction

4-Step Plan for Assessment
1 Diagnose and Differentiate
2 Monitor Progress
3 Assess and Regroup
4 Summative Assessment

STEP 1 Diagnose and Differentiate

Baseline Group Tests

Diagnose

To make initial grouping decisions, use the Baseline Group Test, the Texas Primary Reading Inventory (TPRI), or another initial placement test. Depending on students' ability levels, you may have more than one of each group.

Differentiate

If... student performance is **SI** **then...** use the regular instruction and the daily Strategic Intervention small group lessons.

If... student performance is **OL** **then...** use the regular instruction and the daily On-Level small group lessons.

If... student performance is **A** **then...** use the regular instruction and the daily Advanced learners small group lessons.

Small Group Time

SI Strategic Intervention

- Daily small group lessons provide more intensive instruction, more scaffolding, more practice, and more opportunities to respond.
- Reteach lessons in the *First Stop* provide more instruction of target skills.
- Leveled readers, decodable readers, and other weekly texts build background and provide practice for target skills and vocabulary.

OL On-Level

- Explicit instructional routines teach core skills and strategies.
- Daily On-Level lessons provide more practice and more opportunities to respond.
- Independent activities provide practice for core skills.
- Student Readers and Get Set, Roll! Readers provide additional reading and practice core skills and vocabulary.

A Advanced

- Daily Advanced lessons provide instruction for accelerated learning.
- Independent Leveled Readers provide additional reading tied to lesson concepts and skills.

Additional Differentiated Learning Options

Reading Street Response to Intervention Kit

- Focused intervention lessons on the five critical areas of reading: phonemic awareness, phonics, vocabulary, comprehension, and fluency

My Sidewalks on Reading Street

- Early Reading Intervention

STEP 2 Monitor Progress

Don't Wait Until Friday

Use these tools during lesson teaching to **monitor student progress.**

- **Skill and Strategy** instruction during reading

- **Don't Wait Until Friday** boxes to check letter and sound fluency, word reading, retelling, and oral vocabulary

- **Weekly Assessment** on Day 5 to check phonics, high-frequency words, and comprehension

- **Reader's and Writer's Notebook** pages at point of use

Weekly Phonics and High-Frequency Words Assessment

Weekly Comprehension Assessment

STEP 3 Assess and Regroup

Use these tools during lesson teaching to **assess and regroup.**

- **Weekly Assessments** Record results of weekly assessments for phonics and high-frequency words to track student progress.

- **Unit Benchmark Assessment** Administer this assessment to check progress of unit skills.

- **Regroup** We recommend the first regrouping to be at the end of Unit 2. Use weekly assessment information and Unit Benchmark Assessment performance to inform regrouping decisions. Then regroup at the end of each subsequent unit.

Unit 1 Reading Chart in First Stop

Group					
Baseline Group Test →	Regroup Units 1 and 2 →	Regroup Unit 3 →	Regroup Unit 4 →	Regroup Unit 5 →	**End of Year**
Unit 1 Weeks 1–6	Unit 2 Weeks 7–12	Unit 3 Weeks 13–18	Unit 4 Weeks 19–24	Unit 5 Weeks 25–30	Unit 6 Weeks 31–36

Outside assessments, such as DRA, TPRI, and DIBELS, may recommend regrouping at other times during the year.

STEP 4 Summative Assessment

Use these tools after lesson teaching to **assess students.**

- **Unit Benchmark Assessments** Use to measure a student's mastery of unit skills.

- **End-of-Year Benchmark Assessment** Use to measure a student's mastery of program skills covered in all six units.

Unit and End-of-Year Benchmark Assessments

Assessment and Grouping • **xix**

Concept Launch

Understanding By Design

Grant Wiggins, Ed. D.
Reading Street Author

"A big idea may be thought of as a *linchpin*. The linchpin is the device that keeps the wheel in place on an axle. Thus, a linchpin is one that is essential for understanding. Without grasping the idea and using it to 'hold together' related content knowledge, we are left with bits and pieces of inert facts that cannot take us anywhere."

Putting It Together

Reading Street Online
www.ReadingStreet.com

• Big Question Video
• Envision It! Animations
• Story Sort

THE BIG ?

What are different ways of building?

UNIT 6

Small Group Time
Flexible Pacing Plans

Small Group Time

Sometimes you have holidays, programs, assemblies, or other interruptions to the school week. This plan can help you make Small Group Time decisions if you have less time during the week.

SI OL A

5 Day Plan

DAY 1	• Phonemic Awareness • Phonics • Reading Practice
DAY 2	• Phonemic Awareness • Phonics • Reading Practice
DAY 3	• Phonemic Awareness/ Phonics • Leveled Reader
DAY 4	• Phonemic Awareness • Reading Practice
DAY 5	• Phonics • Reading Practice

4 Day Plan

DAY 1	• Phonemic Awareness • Phonics • Reading Practice
DAY 2	• Phonemic Awareness • Phonics • Reading Practice
DAY 3	• Phonemic Awareness/ Phonics • Leveled Reader
DAY 4	• Phonemic Awareness • Reading Practice

3 Day Plan

DAY 1	• Phonemic Awareness • Phonics • Reading Practice
DAY 2	• Phonemic Awareness/ Phonics • Leveled Reader
DAY 3	• Phonemic Awareness • Reading Practice

ELL

5 Day Plan

DAY 1	• Frontload Concept • Phonemic Awareness/ Phonics • Comprehension
DAY 2	• Comprehension • Vocabulary
DAY 3	• Phonemic Awareness/ Phonics • Conventions

DAY 4	• Phonemic Awareness/
	  Phonics
	• Concepts and Oral
	  Language

DAY 5	• Language Workshop • Writing

4 Day Plan

DAY 1	• Frontload Concept • Phonemic Awareness/ Phonics • Comprehension
DAY 2	• Comprehension • Vocabulary
DAY 3	• Phonemic Awareness/ Phonics • Conventions
DAY 4	• Language Workshop • Writing

3 Day Plan

DAY 1	• Frontload Concept • Phonemic Awareness/ Phonics • Comprehension
DAY 2	• Phonemic Awareness/ Phonics • Conventions
DAY 3	• Language Workshop • Writing

Alistair and Kip's
Great Adventure

This Week's ELL Overview

ELL Handbook

- Maximize Literacy and Cognitive Engagement
- Research Into Practice
- Full Weekly Support for Every Selection

Allistair and Kip's Great Adventure
  - Routines to Support Instruction

- Transfer Activities
- Professional Development

Daily Leveled ELL Notes

ELL notes appear throughout this week's instruction and ELL Support is on the DI pages of your Teacher's Edition. The following is a sample of an ELL note from this week.

English Language Learners

Beginning Connect Sound-Spelling Native Spanish speakers may have difficulty distinguishing /v/ and /b/. Have children observe the difference in how the two sounds are formed. Then read pairs of words and have them distinguish which pairs sound the same and different: *ban/ban, ban/van, van/van, berry/very, very/berry.*

Intermediate High-Frequency Words Remind children that *my* and *we* are words they can use to talk about themselves. Help children list other words they can use to talk about themselves, such as *I, me,* and *us.*

Advanced High-Frequency Words Have children tell what words in their home languages are used for the words *for, my, of, we,* or *yellow.* If they are struggling with one of the words, have them write the word in English and in their home language to help them make the connection.

Advanced High High-Frequency Words Remind children that the word *yellow* is a color word. Have them name other words for colors that they know in English, such as *red, blue,* and *green.* Help children write each color word using a crayon of that color to help them connect the word with the color.

ELL by Strand

The ELL lessons on this week's Support for English Language Learners pages are organized by strand. They offer additional scaffolding for the core curriculum. Leveled support notes on these pages address the different proficiency levels in your class. See pages DI•63–DI•68.

ELL Guy
Dr. Jim Cummins

The Three Pillars of ELL Instruction

ELL Strands	Activate Prior Knowledge	Access Content	Extend Language
Vocabulary p. DI•65	Frontload Vocabulary	Provide Scaffolding	Practice
Reading Comprehension p. DI•65	Provide Scaffolding	Set the Scene	Frontload Vocabulary
Phonics, Spelling, and Word Analysis pp. DI•63, DI•66–DI•67	Frontload Words with Initial and Medial /u/	Isolate Initial and Medial /u/	Review /e/
Listening Comprehension p. DI•64	Prepare for the Read Aloud	First Listening	Second Listening
Conventions and Writing pp. DI•66, DI•68	Provide Scaffolding/ Introduce and Model	Practice	Leveled Practice Activities/ Leveled Writing Activities
Concept Development p. DI•63	Read the Concept Literacy Reader	Read the Concept Literacy Reader	Develop Oral Language

This Week's Practice Stations Overview

Six Weekly Practice Stations with Leveled Activities can be found at the beginning of each week of instruction. For this week's Practice Stations, see pp. 312–313.

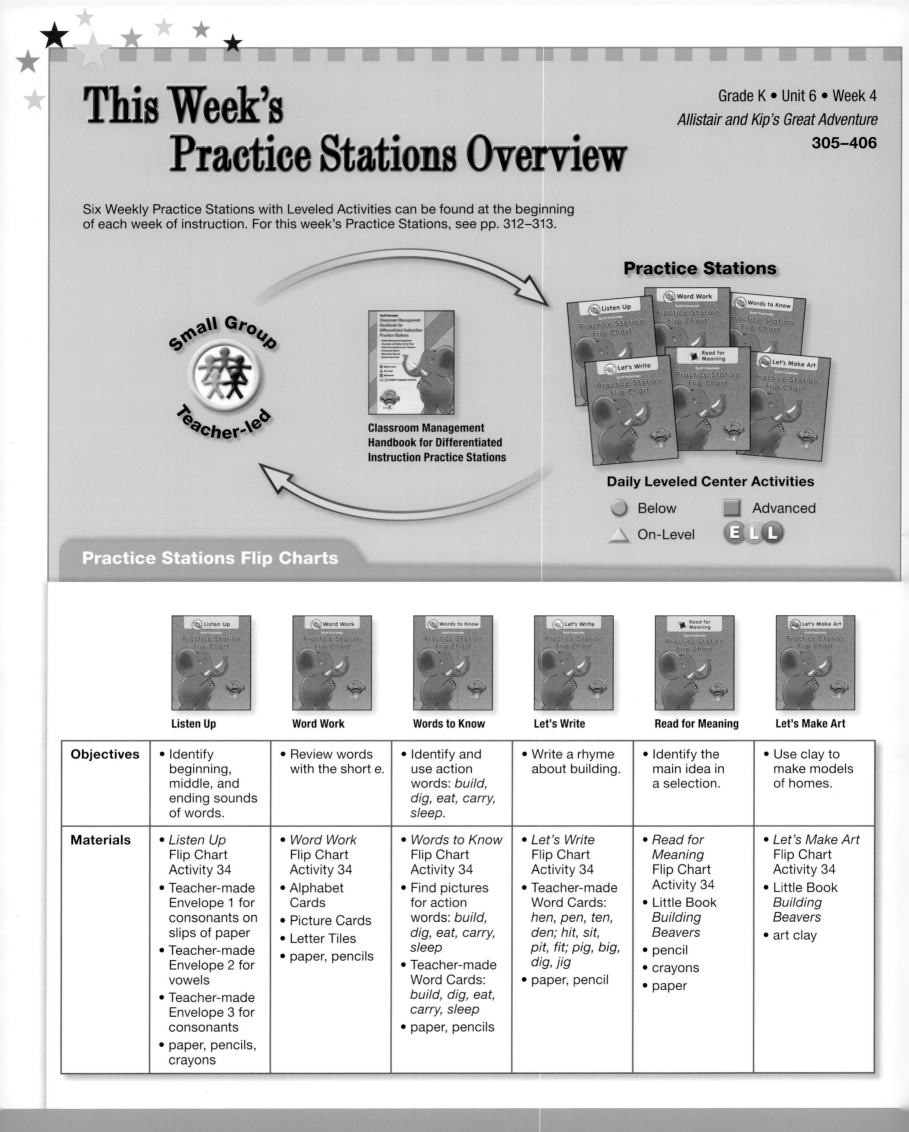

Small Group / Teacher-led

Classroom Management Handbook for Differentiated Instruction Practice Stations

Practice Stations

Daily Leveled Center Activities

○ Below   ▢ Advanced

△ On-Level   **ELL**

Practice Stations Flip Charts

	Listen Up	Word Work	Words to Know	Let's Write	Read for Meaning	Let's Make Art
Objectives	• Identify beginning, middle, and ending sounds of words.	• Review words with the short *e*.	• Identify and use action words: *build, dig, eat, carry, sleep.*	• Write a rhyme about building.	• Identify the main idea in a selection.	• Use clay to make models of homes.
Materials	• *Listen Up* Flip Chart Activity 34 • Teacher-made Envelope 1 for consonants on slips of paper • Teacher-made Envelope 2 for vowels • Teacher-made Envelope 3 for consonants • paper, pencils, crayons	• *Word Work* Flip Chart Activity 34 • Alphabet Cards • Picture Cards • Letter Tiles • paper, pencils	• *Words to Know* Flip Chart Activity 34 • Find pictures for action words: *build, dig, eat, carry, sleep* • Teacher-made Word Cards: *build, dig, eat, carry, sleep* • paper, pencils	• *Let's Write* Flip Chart Activity 34 • Teacher-made Word Cards: *hen, pen, ten, den; hit, sit, pit, fit; pig, big, dig, jig* • paper, pencil	• *Read for Meaning* Flip Chart Activity 34 • Little Book *Building Beavers* • pencil • crayons • paper	• *Let's Make Art* Flip Chart Activity 34 • Little Book *Building Beavers* • art clay

This Week on Reading Street!

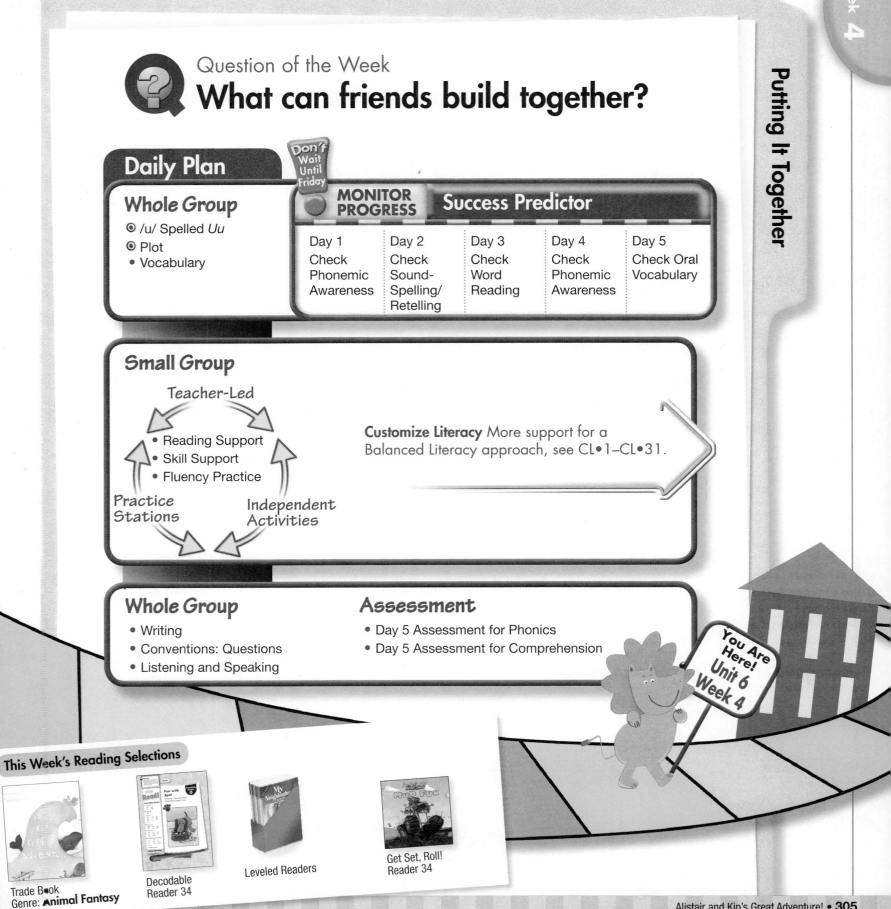

Question of the Week
What can friends build together?

Daily Plan

Don't Wait Until Friday

Whole Group
- /u/ Spelled *Uu*
- Plot
- Vocabulary

MONITOR PROGRESS | **Success Predictor**

Day 1	Day 2	Day 3	Day 4	Day 5
Check Phonemic Awareness	Check Sound-Spelling/ Retelling	Check Word Reading	Check Phonemic Awareness	Check Oral Vocabulary

Small Group

Teacher-Led
- Reading Support
- Skill Support
- Fluency Practice

Practice Stations

Independent Activities

Customize Literacy More support for a Balanced Literacy approach, see CL•1–CL•31.

Whole Group
- Writing
- Conventions: Questions
- Listening and Speaking

Assessment
- Day 5 Assessment for Phonics
- Day 5 Assessment for Comprehension

You Are Here! Unit 6 Week 4

This Week's Reading Selections

Trade Book Genre: Animal Fantasy

Decodable Reader 34

Leveled Readers

Get Set, Roll! Reader 34

Resources on Reading Street!

	Build Concepts	Phonemic Awareness and Phonics	Vocabulary
Whole Group	Talk With Me/ Sing With Me	Student Edition, pp. 72–73 — Student Edition, p. 76	Student Edition p. 77 — Student Edition p. 88
Go Digital	• Concept Talk Video • Sing with Me Animations	• eReaders	
Small Group and Independent Practice	Practice Station Flip Chart — Leveled Readers	Practice Station Flip Chart — Decodable Reader 34 — Leveled Readers Get Set, Roll! Reader 34	Practice Station Flip Chart — Student Edition p. 77
Go Digital	• eReaders	• eReaders • Letter Tile Drag and Drop	
Customize Literacy	• Leveled Readers	• Decodable Reader	• High-Frequency Word Cards
Go Digital	• Concept Talk Video • Big Question Video • eReaders	• eReaders	• Sing with Me Animations

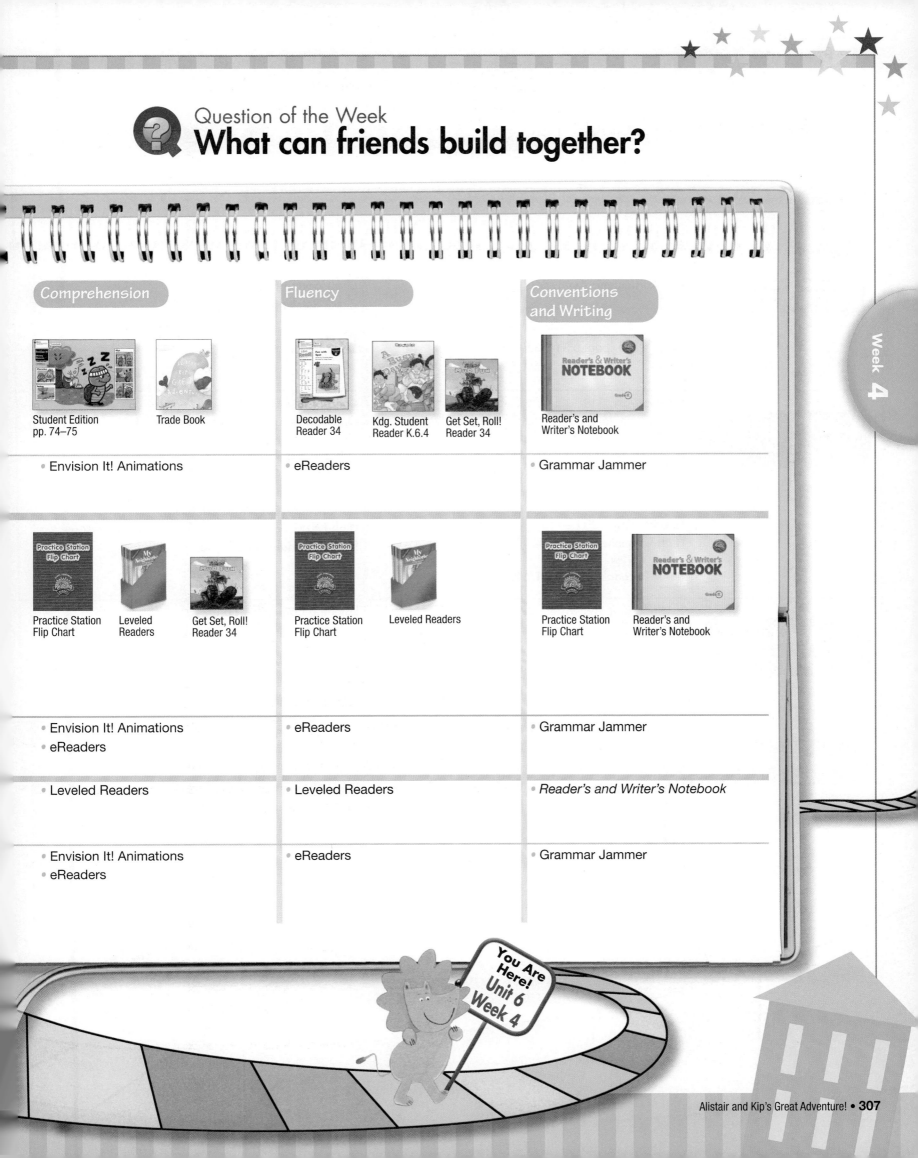

Question of the Week
What can friends build together?

Comprehension	Fluency	Conventions and Writing
Student Edition pp. 74–75 Trade Book	Decodable Reader 34 Kdg. Student Reader K.6.4 Get Set, Roll! Reader 34	Reader's and Writer's Notebook
• Envision It! Animations	• eReaders	• Grammar Jammer
Practice Station Flip Chart Leveled Readers Get Set, Roll! Reader 34	Practice Station Flip Chart Leveled Readers	Practice Station Flip Chart Reader's and Writer's Notebook
• Envision It! Animations • eReaders	• eReaders	• Grammar Jammer
• Leveled Readers	• Leveled Readers	*Reader's and Writer's Notebook*
• Envision It! Animations • eReaders	• eReaders	• Grammar Jammer

Week 4

You Are Here! Unit 6 Week 4

My 5-Day Planner for Reading Street!

MONITOR PROGRESS
Don't Wait Until Friday

	Check Phonemic Awareness **Day 1** pages 314–329	**Check Sound-Spelling** **Check Retelling** **Day 2** pages 330–347
Get Ready to Read	**Concept Talk,** 314 **Oral Vocabulary,** 315 *gathered, distant, drifting, voyage, island, aboard* **Phonemic Awareness,** 316–317 ◉ Initial and Medial /u/ **Phonics,** 318–319 ◉ /u/ Spelled *Uu* **Handwriting,** 320 Letters *U* and *u* **High-Frequency Words,** 321 Review *for, my, of, we, yellow* **READ Decodable Story 34,** 322–323	**Concept Talk,** 330 **Oral Vocabulary,** 331 *gathered, distant* **Phonemic Awareness,** 332–333 ◉ Initial and Medial /u/ **Phonics,** 334–335 ◉ /u/ Spelled *Uu* **Handwriting,** 336 Words with *Uu* **High-Frequency Words,** 337 *for, my, of, we, yellow* **READ Decodable Reader 34,** 338–339
Read and Comprehend	**Listening Comprehension,** 324–325 ◉ Plot	**Listening Comprehension,** 340 ◉ Plot **READ Trade Book—First Read,** 340 *Alistair and Kip's Great Adventure!* **Retell,** 341 **Think, Talk, and Write,** 342
Language Arts	**Conventions,** 326 Questions **Writing,** 327 Wonderful, Marvelous Me! **Daily Handwriting,** 327 Letters *U* and *u* **Listening and Speaking,** 328 Discuss Literary Elements – Character **Wrap Up Your Day,** 328 **Extend Your Day!,** 329	**Conventions,** 343 Questions **Writing,** 344 Respond to Literature **Daily Handwriting,** 344 Letters *U* and *u* **Vocabulary,** 345 Location Words **Wrap Up Your Day,** 346 **Extend Your Day!,** 347

You Are Here! Unit 6 Week 4

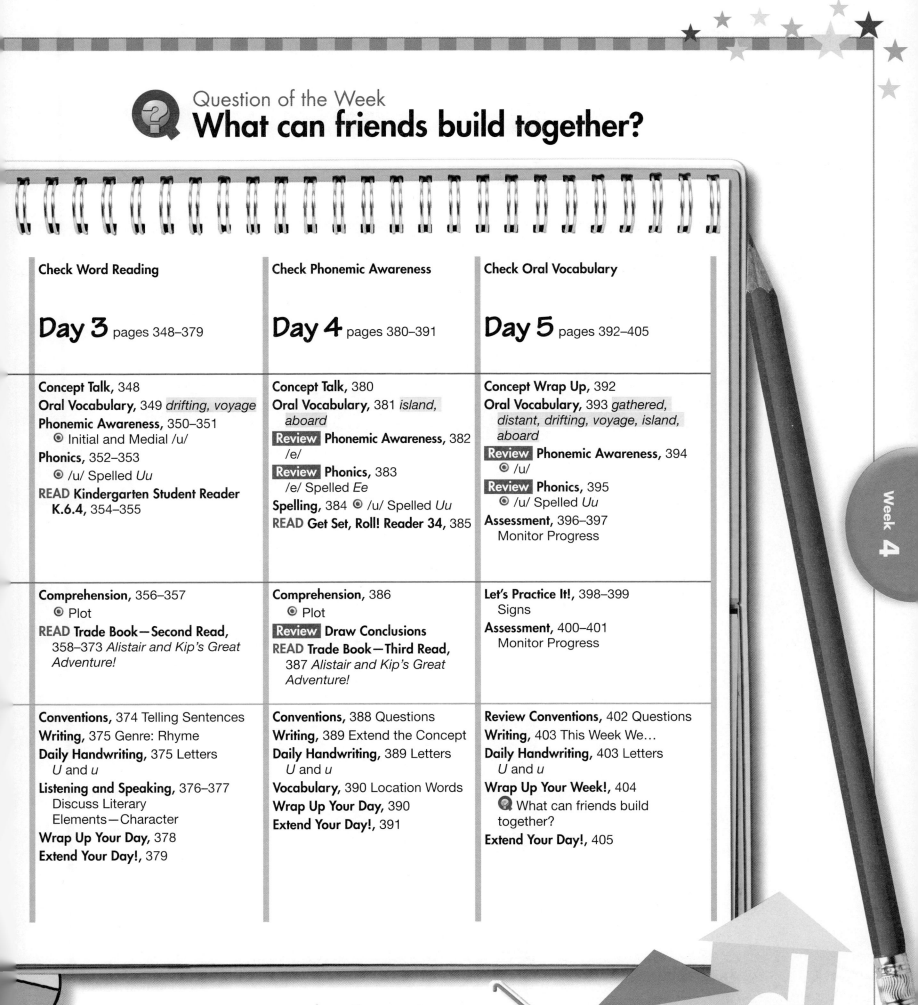

Question of the Week
What can friends build together?

Check Word Reading	Check Phonemic Awareness	Check Oral Vocabulary
Day 3 pages 348–379	**Day 4** pages 380–391	**Day 5** pages 392–405
Concept Talk, 348 **Oral Vocabulary,** 349 *drifting, voyage* **Phonemic Awareness,** 350–351 ◉ Initial and Medial /u/ **Phonics,** 352–353 ◉ /u/ Spelled *Uu* **READ Kindergarten Student Reader K.6.4,** 354–355	**Concept Talk,** 380 **Oral Vocabulary,** 381 *island, aboard* Review **Phonemic Awareness,** 382 /e/ Review **Phonics,** 383 /e/ Spelled *Ee* **Spelling,** 384 ◉ /u/ Spelled *Uu* **READ Get Set, Roll! Reader 34,** 385	**Concept Wrap Up,** 392 **Oral Vocabulary,** 393 *gathered, distant, drifting, voyage, island, aboard* Review **Phonemic Awareness,** 394 ◉ /u/ Review **Phonics,** 395 ◉ /u/ Spelled *Uu* **Assessment,** 396–397 Monitor Progress
Comprehension, 356–357 ◉ Plot **READ Trade Book—Second Read,** 358–373 *Alistair and Kip's Great Adventure!*	**Comprehension,** 386 ◉ Plot Review **Draw Conclusions** **READ Trade Book—Third Read,** 387 *Alistair and Kip's Great Adventure!*	**Let's Practice It!,** 398–399 Signs **Assessment,** 400–401 Monitor Progress
Conventions, 374 Telling Sentences **Writing,** 375 Genre: Rhyme **Daily Handwriting,** 375 Letters *U* and *u* **Listening and Speaking,** 376–377 Discuss Literary Elements—Character **Wrap Up Your Day,** 378 **Extend Your Day!,** 379	**Conventions,** 388 Questions **Writing,** 389 Extend the Concept **Daily Handwriting,** 389 Letters *U* and *u* **Vocabulary,** 390 Location Words **Wrap Up Your Day,** 390 **Extend Your Day!,** 391	**Review Conventions,** 402 Questions **Writing,** 403 This Week We… **Daily Handwriting,** 403 Letters *U* and *u* **Wrap Up Your Week!,** 404 What can friends build together? **Extend Your Day!,** 405

Week 4

Grouping Options for Differentiated Instruction
Turn the page for the small group time lesson plan.

Planning Small Group Time on Reading Street!

SMALL GROUP TIME RESOURCES

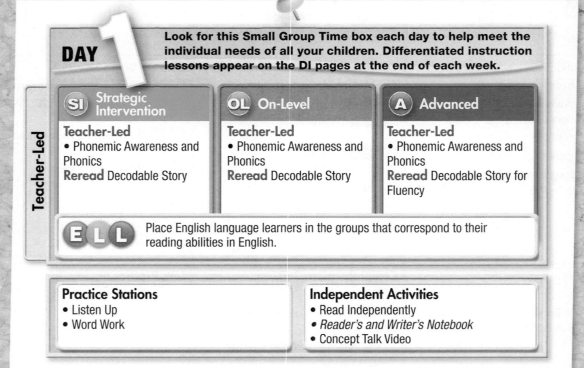

DAY 1

Look for this Small Group Time box each day to help meet the individual needs of all your children. Differentiated instruction lessons appear on the DI pages at the end of each week.

Teacher-Led

SI Strategic Intervention

Teacher-Led
• Phonemic Awareness and Phonics
Reread Decodable Story

OL On-Level

Teacher-Led
• Phonemic Awareness and Phonics
Reread Decodable Story

A Advanced

Teacher-Led
• Phonemic Awareness and Phonics
Reread Decodable Story for Fluency

ELL Place English language learners in the groups that correspond to their reading abilities in English.

Practice Stations
• Listen Up
• Word Work

Independent Activities
• Read Independently
• *Reader's and Writer's Notebook*
• Concept Talk Video

ELL

ELL Poster 34

		Day 1
SI	Strategic Intervention	**Phonemic Awareness and Phonics,** DI•52 **Reread** Decodable Story 34, DI•52
OL	On-Level	**Phonemic Awareness and Phonics,** DI•57 **Reread** Decodable Story 34, DI•57
A	Advanced	**Phonemic Awareness and Phonics,** DI•60 **Reread** Decodable Story 34 for Fluency, DI•60
ELL	English Language Learners	DI•63–DI•64 Frontload Concept Phonemic Awareness and Phonics Comprehension Skill

You Are Here! Unit 6 Week 4

Reading Street Response
to Intervention Kit

Practice Station
Flip Chart

Reading

Reading Street Leveled
Practice Stations Kit

Question of the Week
What can friends build together?

SI Strategic Intervention

Decodable
Reader

Listen to Me Reader

Concept Literacy Reader

Get Set, Roll! Reader

OL On-Level

Kindergarten
Student Reader

Get Set, Roll! Reader

Decodable Reader

A Advanced

Independent
Reader

Decodable Reader

Week 4

Small Group Weekly Plan

Day 2	Day 3	Day 4	Day 5
Phonemic Awareness and Phonics, DI•53 **Reread** Decodable Reader 34, DI•53	**Phonemic Awareness and Phonics,** DI•54 **Read** Concept Literacy Reader K.6.4, DI•54	**Phonemic Awareness and Phonics,** DI•55 **Read** Get Set, Roll! Reader 34, DI•55	Phonics Review, DI•56 **Read** Listen to Me Reader K.6.4, DI•56
Phonemic Awareness and Phonics, DI•57 **Reread** Decodable Reader 34, DI•57	**Phonemic Awareness and Phonics,** DI•58 **Read** Kindergarten Student Reader K.6.4, DI•58	**Review Phonics and High-Frequency Words** **Read** Get Set, Roll! Reader 34, DI•59	Phonics Review, DI•59 **Reread** Leveled Books, DI•59
Phonics and Spelling, DI•60 **Reread** Decodable Reader 34 for Fluency, DI•60	**Read** Independent Reader K.6.4 or Kindergarten Student Reader K.6.4, DI•61	**Read** Get Set, Roll! Reader 34 or **Reread** Kindergarten Student Reader K.6.4, DI•62	Fluency and Comprehension, DI•62 **Reread** Independent Reader for Fluency, DI•62
DI•65 Comprehension Skill Frontload Vocabulary	DI•66 Review Phonemic Awareness and Phonics Scaffold Conventions	DI•67 Review Phonemic Awareness and Phonics Revisit Concept and Oral Language	DI•68 Language Workshop Writing

Practice Stations for Everyone on Reading Street!

Listen Up!
Beginning, middle, and ending sounds

Objectives
• Identify beginning, middle, and ending sounds in words

Materials
• *Listen Up!* Flip Chart Activity 34
• Teacher-made envelope 1 containing all consonants on separate slips of paper except *q* and *x*
• Teacher-made envelope 2 containing all vowels on separate slips of paper
• Teacher-made envelope 3 containing all consonants on separate slips of paper except *c, h, j, q, v, w,* and *y*
• paper, pencils, crayons

Differentiated Activities

⬤ Draw a letter from the envelopes one at a time and place the letters on the table. Say the sound you learned for each letter in order. Do the letters make a word you know?

▲ Draw a letter from the envelopes one at a time and place the letters on the table. Say the sound you learned for each letter in order. Do the letters make a word you know? What letter could you change to make a word?

◼ Draw a letter from the envelopes one at a time and place the letters on the table. Say the sound you learned for each letter in order. Do the letters make a word you know? What letter could you change to make a word? Keep a list of the words you spell.

Word Work
/e/ spelled *Ee*

Objectives
• Review words with the short *e*.

Materials
• *Word Work* Flip Chart Activity 34
• Alphabet Cards
• Picture Cards
• Letter Tiles
• paper, pencils

Differentiated Activities

⬤ Look for Picture Cards with /e/ in the middle. Use the Letter Tiles to build one of the words. Look at the back of the Picture Card if you need help.

▲ Find Picture Cards with /e/ in the middle. Did you find hen? Use Letter Tiles to build *hen*. Change the *h* to *p*. Say the new word.

◼ Find Picture Cards with /e/ in the middle. Use Letter Tiles to build one of the words. Change the beginning or the ending sound to make new words. Write three new words on your paper.

Technology
• Letter Tile Drag and Drop

Words To Know
Action words

Objectives
• Identify and use action words: *build, dig, eat, carry, sleep*

Materials
• *Words to Know* Flip Chart Activity 34
• Find pictures (or take quick digital photos and print out) for action words: *build, dig, eat, carry, sleep,* and five other actions.
• Teacher-made word cards for *build, dig, eat, carry, sleep*
• paper, pencils

Differentiated Activities

⬤ Choose pictures that show the actions: *build, dig, eat, carry,* and *sleep.* Say the name for each picture.

▲ Match pictures and word cards that show the action words: *build, dig, eat, carry,* and *sleep.*

◼ Match the pictures and word cards that show *build, dig, eat, carry,* and *sleep.* Write sentences that use the words *build, dig, eat, carry,* and *sleep.* Underline the action words that you use.

You Are Here! Unit 6 Week 4

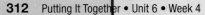

Key

Below-Level Activities

On-Level Activities

Advanced Activities

Practice Station
Flip Chart

Use this week's materials from the Reading Street Leveled Practice Stations Kit to organize this week's stations.

Let's Write!
Rhyme

Objectives
• Write a rhyme about building.

Materials
• *Let's Write!* Flip Chart Activity 34
• Teacher-made word cards: *hen, pen, ten, den; hit, sit, pit, fit; pig, big, dig, jig*
• paper, pencil

Differentiated Activities

⬤ Sort the word cards into rhyming groups. Use a set of rhyming words to make up a two-line rhyme about building something.

△ Sort the word cards into rhyming groups. Use a set of rhyming words to write a four-line rhyme about building something.

▢ Sort the word cards into rhyming groups. Use one or more sets of rhyming words to make up a rhyme about building something. Write it on your paper.

Read For Meaning
Main idea

Objectives
• Identify the main idea in a selection.

Materials
• *Read for Meaning* Flip Chart Activity 34
• Little Book *Building Beavers*
• pencil
• crayons
• paper

Differentiated Activities

A **main idea** tells the most important part, or the big idea of a book.

⬤ Read your book. Think about the big idea. Point to pictures and words that tell about the big idea.

△ Read your book. Point to pictures and words that tell about the big idea. Draw a picture or write a sentence that tells the big idea.

▢ Read your book. Think about the most important part. Write a sentence that tells the main idea.

Let's Make Art!

Objectives
• Use clay to make models of homes.

Materials
• *Let's Make Art!* Flip Chart Activity 34
• Little Book *Building Beavers*
• art clay

Differentiated Activities

⬤ Look at the pictures in your Little Book. Use the clay to show what a beaver's home looks like.

△ Look at the pictures in your Little Book. Use the clay to show what a beaver's home looks like. Use some of the clay to show what your home looks like.

▢ Look at your Little Book. Use the clay to show what a beaver's home looks like. Think of another animal. Use some of the clay to show what that animal's home looks like.

Week 4

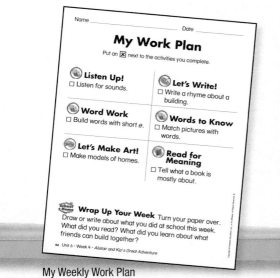

Name _____ Date _____

My Work Plan
Put an ☒ next to the activities you complete.

Listen Up!
☐ Listen for sounds.

Let's Write!
☐ Write a rhyme about a building.

Word Work
☐ Build words with short *e*.

Words to Know
☐ Match pictures with words.

Let's Make Art!
☐ Make models of homes.

Read for Meaning
☐ Tell what a book is mostly about.

Wrap Up Your Week Turn your paper over. Draw or write about what you did at school this week. What did you read? What did you learn about what friends can build together?

Unit 6 • Week 4 • *Alistair and Kip's Great Adventure*

My Weekly Work Plan

Objectives

- Share information and ideas about the concept.

Today at a Glance

Oral Vocabulary
gathered, distant, drifting, voyage, island, aboard

Phonemic Awareness
◉ Initial and Medial /u/

Phonics
◉ /u/ Spelled *Uu*

Handwriting
U and *u*

High-Frequency Words
for, my, of, we, yellow

Comprehension
◉ Plot

Conventions
Questions

Writing
Wonderful, Marvelous Me!

Listening and Speaking
Discuss Literary Elements—Character

TRUCKTOWN on Reading Street

Start your engines!

Display p. 21 of *Truckery Rhymes*.

- Read aloud "Rub-a-Dub-Dub" and track the print.
- Reread the rhyme and have children chime in as they wish.
- Ask children to identify the rhyming words. (*dub, tub; who, you; be, three*)

Truckery Rhymes

Concept Talk

 Question of the Week

What can friends build together?

Introduce the concept

To build concepts and to focus their attention, tell children that this week they will talk, sing, read, and write about **things that friends build together.** Track each word as you read the question of the week.

Play the CD that features children talking about what they want to build using a large cardboard box. What would you and your friends build using the large box? Would it be real or make-believe?

 Background Building Audio

ROUTINE Activate Prior Knowledge **Team Talk**

1. **Think** Have children think for a minute about what they know about friends playing and building together.

2. **Pair** Have pairs of children discuss the question of the week. Remind them to take turns speaking. Have children use complete sentences in their discussions about friends.

3. **Share** Call on a few children to share their ideas with the group. Guide discussion and encourage elaboration with prompts such as: What do you and your friends like to build or make together?

Routines Flip Chart

Anchored Talk

Develop oral language

Display Talk with Me Chart 34A. What do you see in the pictures? Point to the first picture. What is this boy pointing to? He is pointing to something far away. Something far away can be called *distant*. Point to the people boarding the airplane. These people are climbing *aboard* the airplane. That means they are getting on the plane. Where do you think they are going?

We are going to learn six new Amazing Words this week. Listen as I say each word: *gathered, distant, drifting, voyage, island, aboard.* Have children say each word as you point to the picture.

Display Sing with Me Chart 34B. Tell children that they are going to sing a song about having an adventure. Read the title. Have children describe the illustration. Sing the song several times to the tune of "Take Me Out to the Ball Game." Listen for the Amazing Words: *gathered, distant, drifting, voyage, island, aboard.* Have children stand up and sing with you.

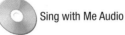 Sing with Me Audio

Talk with Me/Sing with Me Chart 34A

Let's Go Have an Adventure

Let's go have an adventure,
A voyage out to sea.
I've gathered together everything.
It's all aboard, so what else should we bring?
Oh, look a tropical island,
A distant coconut tree.
There'll be sun, waves, and lots of fun
Drifting on the open sea!

Talk with Me/Sing with Me Chart 34B

ELL **Preteach Concepts** Use the Day 1 instruction on ELL Poster 34 to assess and build background knowledge, develop concepts, and build oral vocabulary.

ELL Poster 34

gathered	distant
drifting	voyage
island	aboard

Differentiated Instruction

SI Strategic Intervention

Build Background Display Sing with Me Chart 34B and discuss the illustration with children. Ask them if this song is about a real or make-believe adventure at sea. Help them connect the song with the word *fantasy*.

 **ELL**

English Language Learners

Build Background Use the pictures on Talk with Me Chart 34A to help children understand words such as *distant* and *island*.

ELL Support Additional ELL support and modified instruction is provided in the *ELL Handbook* and in the ELL Support lessons on pp. DI•63–68.

Objectives

◎ Learn initial and medial /u/.

• Identify words with initial and medial /u/.

• Discriminate words with initial /u/.

• Blend phonemes to say words.

Check Phonemic Awareness

! **SUCCESS PREDICTOR**

My Skills Buddy, pp. 72–73

Phonemic Awareness
↻ Initial and Medial /u/

Teach

Today we are going to review a sound. Listen carefully: /u/ /u/ /u/. Say it with me: /u/ /u/ /u/. **Display the** *up* **Picture Card.** *Up* begins with /u/; /u/, *up.* **What sound does** *up* **begin with? Display the** *drum* **Picture Card.** This is a *drum.* The middle sound in *drum* is /u/. **What is the middle sound in** *drum?* **Repeat the routine with the** *umbrella* **and** *duck* **Picture Cards.**

Picture Card

Model

Have children look at the picture on pp. 72–73 of *My Skills Buddy.* Let's look for words that begin like *up.* I see a kangaroo *unlocking* a door. I hear /u/ at the beginning of *unlock.* The first sound in *unlock* is /u/. What other things do you see that begin with that sound?

Guide practice

As children name example words from the picture, guide them in stating that /u/ is the beginning sound. Discuss some of the bulleted items on p. 72 of *My Skills Buddy.* Save the other bulleted items for Day 2.

Corrective feedback

If... children have difficulty naming words that begin with /u/, **then...** say *unlock* again, stretching the beginning sound—/u/ /u/ /u/, *unlock.*

Discriminate sounds

Listen to these words: *ugly, under, untie.* Do they begin the same? **(yes)** I will say some words. I want you to point up if you hear /u/ at the beginning of the word. Listen carefully: *umpire* **(point)**, *until* **(point)**, *ask, ink, us* **(point)**, *under* **(point)**, *ox, act.*

Repeat the routine for medial /u/. Have children pretend to beat on a drum for each word with /u/ in the middle: *duck, sun, bed, fish, mud, cap, pup, pet, dust, pond, fun.*

Corrective feedback

If... children cannot discriminate initial or medial /u/, **then...** have them enunciate /u/ as they say *umbrella.*

When you say /u/, the middle of your tongue is in the middle of your mouth. Your mouth and cheeks are relaxed. **Have children say /u/ words and feel the position of the mouth and tongue.**

Blend phonemes

I will say the sounds in a word. I want you to blend the sounds to make a word. I will do the first ones with you. Listen carefully. The sounds are /t/ /u/ /b/. Say them with me: /t/ /u/ /b/. Now let's blend the sounds: /t/ /u/ /b/, *tub.* The word is *tub.* **Continue blending phonemes with the following words:** *pat, fib, hum, dress, sun, drum, spot, rug, dust, sand.*

> **Don't Wait Until Friday**
>
> **MONITOR PROGRESS**   ↻ **Check Phonemic Awareness   Short /u/**
>
> Say *bus* and *fan.* Have children identify the word that has /u/ in the middle. Continue using the following word pairs: *club, wig; duck, men; pot, jump; plum, yell; stuck, back; truck, girl.*
>
> **If...** children cannot discriminate medial /u/,
>
> **then...** use the small-group Strategic Intervention lesson, p. DI•52, to reteach /u/.
>
> | **Day 1** | **Day 2** | **Day 3** | **Day 4** | **Day 5** |
> |---|---|---|---|---|
> | Check Phonemic Awareness | Check Sound-Spelling/ Retelling | Check Word Reading | Check Phonemic Awareness | Check Oral Vocabulary |
>
> *Success Predictor*

Differentiated Instruction

SI Strategic Intervention

Support Phonemic Awareness
Have children look around the classroom for things that have initial or medial /u/. Have them say the name of each item they find, enunciating the short *u.*

Teacher Tip

Oral blending exercises prepare children to decode words. If children have difficulty blending individual sounds in words, have them blend onset and rime first.

English Language Learners
Support Phonemic Awareness
Have children say *cut, jump, up, pulled,* and *fun.* Tell them that these are /u/ words they will read in this week's story, *Alistair and Kip's Great Adventure!* Then have them make up phrases or sentences using the words.

Objectives

- Recognize uppercase *U* and lowercase *u*.
- ◎ Associate the sound /u/ with the spelling *u*.
- Blend and read words with /u/.

Skills Trace

◉ **Short *u* Spelled *Uu***

Introduce U5W3D1; U5W4D1; U6W4D1

Practice U5W3D2; U5W3D3; U5W4D2; U5W4D3; U6W4D2; U6W4D3

Reteach/Review U5W3D5; U5W4D4; U5W4D5; U5W5D4; U6W4D5

Assess/Test Benchmark Assessment U5; U6

KEY:
U=Unit   W=Week   D=Day

Phonics—Teach/Model
◉ /u/ Spelled *Uu*

Teach
Display p. 22 of *Trucktown ABCs.* Point to *Uu.* What are the names of these letters? What is the sound we learned for *Uu? Under* begins with *u.* Point out and identify uppercase *U* and lowercase *u* in the book.

Model
Write *duck* and *luck* on the board. Point to the *u* in *duck.* When I see this letter, I think of the sound /u/. This word is *duck.* Where do you hear /u/ in *duck*? Yes, /u/ is in the middle of *duck.* Point to *luck.* This word has /u/ too. I know that when I see a *u,* the sound may be /u/. This word is *luck.* Where do you hear /u/ in *luck*?

Guide practice
Display Phonics Songs and Rhymes Chart 34. Teach children the song "Oh, Where, Oh, Where Can the Dog-Walker Stop?" sung to the tune of "Oh, Where, Oh, Where Has My Little Dog Gone?" Play the CD and sing the song several times. When children are familiar with the song, ask them to identify words with /u/, /e/, /o/, /a/, and /i/.

🔘 Phonics Songs and Rhymes Audio

On their own
Have children use their "hand binoculars" to look around the room and find examples of uppercase *U* and lowercase *u.* Repeat the activity for *Aa, Oo, Ee,* and *Ii.*

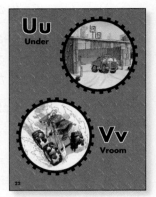

TruckTown ABCs

Phonics Songs and Rhymes Chart 34

Blend Words

Review To review sound-spellings, use Alphabet Cards *Bb, Gg, Hh, Ll, Mm, Oo, Ss,* and *Ww* and the *bat, goat, hen, ladybug, moose, otter, seal,* and *wolf* Picture Cards to practice previously taught letters. Then use this routine for sound-by-sound blending to have children blend new words.

ROUTINE Sound-by-Sound Blending

① **Connect** Write the letter *b.* What is the sound for this letter? The sound is /b/. Say it with me: /b/ /b/ /b/. When you see this letter in a word, what sound will you say?

② **Model** Write *bus* on the board.

- Touch under the letter *b:* What is the sound for this letter? Say it with me: /b/ /b/ /b/. Repeat the routine for *u* and *s.*

- Let's blend the sounds together. Listen as I blend the sounds: /b/ /u/ /s/. Say it with me: /b/ /u/ /s/, *bus.* Now say it without me.

- Listen as I use *bus* in a sentence: *I ride a bus to school.* Say it with me. Then have children use *bus* in their own sentences.

③ **Guide Practice** Continue the routine established in step 2 with the words below:

| Gus | will | hug | mom | pal | Wes | hot | bug |

Children should successfully read these words before reading Decodable Story 34 on pp. 439–440 of *Reader's and Writer's Notebook.*

Corrective Feedback If children have trouble reading a word, model blending the sounds to read the word. Then have children say it with you.

Routines Flip Chart

Objectives
- Write *U* and *u.*
- Learn high-frequency words.

Handwriting

Introduce

Write *Uu* on the board. Words that begin with /u/ are written with an uppercase *U* or a lowercase *u.* Which letter is uppercase *U?* Which letter is lowercase *u?*

Model uppercase *U*

Write the name *Ursula* on the board. Point to the uppercase *U.* This is the uppercase *U.* We use uppercase letters to begin sentences and for the first letter in a name. Watch as I trace the uppercase *U* with my finger. Follow the stroke instructions pictured below.

Guide practice

Have children write the uppercase *U* in the air. Use your finger to make an uppercase *U* in the air. Now write it on your hand.

Model lowercase *u*

Point to the lowercase *u* in *Ursula.* This is a lowercase *u.* Watch as I trace a lowercase *u* with my finger. Write another lowercase *u* on the board following the stroke instructions. Again, have children write *u* in the air and on their hands.

Guide practice

Have children use their Write-On Boards to write a row each of uppercase *U* and lowercase *u.*

D'Nealian™   Ball and Stick

More practice

Use *Reader's and Writer's Notebook,* pp. 437, 438, for additional practice with initial and medial *u.*

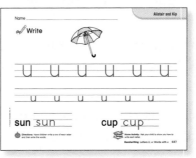

Reader's and Writer's Notebook, p. 437

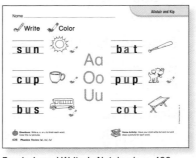

Reader's and Writer's Notebook, p. 438

High-Frequency Words

Introduce

Use the routine below to teach high-frequency words *for, my, of, we,* and *yellow.*

Nondecodable Words

1. **Say and Spell** Some words we must learn by remembering the letters rather than saying the sounds. We will say and spell the words to help learn them. **Write *for* on the board.** This is the word *for.* It has three letters. The letters in *for* are *f, o,* and *r.* **Have children say and spell the word, first with you and then without you.**

2. **Demonstrate Meaning** I can use the word *for* in lots of sentences. Here is one sentence: *I am late for the bus.* Now you use the word in a sentence.

Repeat the routine with the words *my, of, we,* and *yellow.*

Routines Flip Chart

Academic Vocabulary

Write the following on the board:

plot	**question**
location	**telling sentence**
rhyme	**character**
draw conclusions	**sign**

Point to the list. This week we are going to learn these important words. They are tools for learning. As we work this week you will hear them many times. **Read the words.** Preteach the Academic Vocabulary at point-of-use by providing a child-friendly description, explanation, or example that clarifies the meaning of each term. Then ask children to restate the meaning of the Academic Vocabulary in their own words.

Differentiated Instruction

SI Strategic Intervention

High-Frequency Words If children are having difficulty reading the high-frequency words, have them practice naming each letter in the words and then reading the words.

English Language Learners

High-Frequency Words Remind children that *my* and *we* are words they can use to talk about themselves. Help children list other words they can use to talk about themselves, such as *I, me,* and *us.*

Decodable Story 34
/u/ Spelled *Uu* and High-Frequency Words

Review Review the previously taught high-frequency words by having children read each word as you point to it on the Word Wall.

the	was	a	go

Read Decodable Story 34

Display Decodable Story 34. Today we will read a story about Gus and his bus ride. What is the title of the story? **Point to the title of the story.** The title of the story is *Gus and the Bug.* What sound do you hear in the middle of *Gus?* We will read lots of words that have /u/ in this story. **Have children read Decodable Story 34 on pp. 439–440 in** *Reader's and Writer's Notebook.*

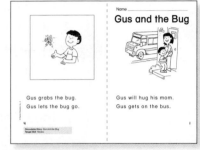

Reader's and Writer's Notebook, pp. 439–440

Use the routine for reading decodable books to read Decodable Story 34.

ROUTINE Reading Decodable Books

1. **Read Silently** Have children whisper read the story page by page as you listen in.

2. **Model Fluent Reading** Have children finger point as you read a page. Then have children reread the page without you.

3. **Read Chorally** Have children finger point as they chorally read the page. Continue reading page by page, repeating steps 1 and 2.

4. **Read Individually** Have children take turns reading aloud a page.

5. **Reread and Monitor Progress** As you listen to individual children reread, monitor progress and provide support.

6. **Reread with a Partner** Have children reread the story page by page with a partner.

Routines Flip Chart

Small Group Time

| **DAY 1** | Break into small groups after reading the Decodable Story and before the comprehension lesson. |

Teacher-Led

SI Strategic Intervention	**OL On-Level**	**A Advanced**
Teacher-Led Page DI•52	Teacher-Led Page DI•57	Teacher-Led Page DI•60
• Phonemic Awareness and Phonics	• Phonemic Awareness and Phonics	• Phonemic Awareness and Phonics
• **Reread** Decodable Story 34	• **Reread** Decodable Story 34	• **Reread** Decodable Story 34 for Fluency

ELL Place English language learners in the groups that correspond to their reading abilities in English.

Practice Stations
• Visit the Listen Up! Station
• Visit the Word Work Station

Independent Activities
• Read independently
• Concept Talk Video
• *Reader's and Writer's Notebook*

English Language Learners
Frontload Decodable Story
Before children read *Gus and the Bug,* review /a/, /i/, /o/, /u/, and /e/ words with the *hat, six, fox, jug,* and *pen* Picture Cards.

Objectives
◎ Identify and describe plot.

Skills Trace
◎ **Plot**
Introduce U3W2D1; U3W4D1;
U5W4D1; U6W4D1
Practice U3W2D2; U3W2D3;
U3W2D4; U3W4D2; U3W4D3;
U3W4D4; U5W4D2; U5W4D3;
U5W4D4; U6W4D2; U6W4D3;
U6W4D4
Reteach/Review U3W2D5;
U3W4D5; U3W6D4; U4W2D4;
U5W1D4; U5W4D5; U6W2D4;
U6W4D5
Assess/Test Benchmark
Assessment U5; U6
KEY:
U=Unit W=Week D=Day

My Skills Buddy, pp. 74–75

Listening Comprehension
◎ Plot

Introduce

A story is made up of events that happen one after another. The events that happen at the beginning, in the middle, and at the end of the story are the **plot** of the story. All stories have a plot. Good readers pay attention to the plot because it helps them to understand the story.

Have children turn to pp. 74–75 in *My Skills Buddy* and look at the pictures on the right side. Remind children of the story "The Tortoise and the Hare." Help me tell what happens in this story. Guide children as they describe the pictures.

- What happens in the beginning? (Hare and Tortoise start out on a race.)
- What happens in the middle? (Hare takes a nap; Tortoise passes him.)
- What happens at the end? (Tortoise beats Hare to the finish line.)

Model

Tell children that you will read a story about building a shelter in the wild. Read **"A Home for the Night"** and model identifying plot events.

Think Aloud In the beginning of the story, Mom, Liz, and Lou have been hiking all day and decide to spend the night near a lake. In the middle, they make a shelter out of branches and a rock.

Guide practice

After reading, ask children questions about plot.

- How do Mom, Liz, and Lou use leaves and grass in their shelter? (They pile them on the branches to keep out cold and rain.)
- What happens at the end of the story? (Mom, Liz, and Lou make a fire.)
- What steps do they take to make the fire? (They dig a pit, fill it with stones, and put in wood for a fire.)

More practice

Display and page through *Mayday! Mayday!* with children. What happens at the beginning of this selection? (The sailors get stuck in a storm.) What happens in the middle? (The Coast Guard members rescue the sailors.) What happens at the end? (The Coast Guard and the sailors return to the Coast Guard base.)

Connect to everyday life

Tell me about what you do after school. What happens first, next, and at the end?

Differentiated Instruction

A **Advanced**

Support Comprehension
Display *Goldilocks and the Three Bears.* Have children tell you what happened in the beginning, in the middle, and at the end of the story.

Academic Vocabulary

plot a series of related events at the beginning, middle, and end of a story; the action of a story

English Language Learners
Oral Comprehension To prepare English learners for the Read Aloud, use the modified Read Aloud in the ELL Support lesson on p. DI•64.

A Home for the Night

Mom, Liz, and Lou were backpacking in the mountains. Late in the afternoon, they came to a clearing by a lake.

"This is a good place to make our camp," said Mom.

Liz, Mom, and Lou knew what to do. Mom cut tree branches and leaned them against a tall, wide rock, with the pointed ends stuck into the ground. Liz and Lou piled leaves and grass on top of the branches to keep out the cold and the rain.

Mom dug a pit in the ground. Liz put stones in the pit while Lou gathered wood. In the center of the pit, Mom laid twigs and bark and leaned bigger sticks of wood together like a tipi. Now Lou, Liz, and Mom had a warm fire and a cozy shelter for the night.

Conventions
Questions

Teach questions

A question is a special kind of sentence. Like all sentences, a question begins with a capital, or uppercase, letter. A question does not end with a period. A question ends with a question mark. **Write a question mark on the board.**

Model

AlphaBuddy has a question for you. **Have AlphaBuddy hold up the** *zebra* **Picture Card and say:** I have never seen this animal before. What animal is it? **Invite a child to answer his question.**

AlphaBuddy just asked a question. What did AlphaBuddy ask? **Write the question** *What animal is it?* **on the board.**

Guide practice

Let's ask AlphaBuddy some questions now. **Invite children to ask simple questions. Restate the children's questions:** AlphaBuddy, Paulette wants to know: What is your favorite color?

Remember, a question is a sentence that asks something. It begins with a capital letter and ends with a question mark. Let's write some questions for AlphaBuddy on the board.

I would like to know where AlphaBuddy lives. I will write this question. **Write the following question on the board.**

> **Where do you live?**

When we write a question, we use a capital letter for the first word. The capital letter in this question is *W.* The question ends with a question mark. **Circle the uppercase** *W* **and the question mark. Write another question, such as** *when do you sleep,* **without proper capitalization or end punctuation. Have children fix the errors.**

Team Talk Pair children and have them ask each other questions about themselves.

Daily Fix-It

Use the Daily Fix-It for more conventions practice.

Writing
Wonderful, Marvelous Me!
I'll Tell You a Story…

Introduce Talk with children about why people tell stories. Stories can be about real things or about make-believe things. Why do you think we tell stories? Why do you think we like to listen to stories? I think we like to share our imagination and we like to hear what other people can imagine. We all have such wonderful, marvelous imaginations! Encourage children to share their thoughts about stories they have read and stories they can imagine.

Model Today we're going to write a make-believe story about friends playing and building together. I'm going to close my eyes and use my imagination. I have a story in my mind about two friends named Kari and Marcus. Kari's mom and dad buy a new refrigerator, and they give Kari the box it comes in. The box is huge! Draw a picture of a girl labeled *Kari* and a boy labeled *Marcus.* Between them, draw a box that is twice as big as they are. Kari and Marcus don't see a box—they see a robot, waiting to be built! Add a face and arms to the box. Kari and Marcus spend hours turning the box into their new robot friend, and then the three of them play for hours!

Guide practice Encourage children to help you come up with more ideas for your story. Write down their ideas and draw pictures when appropriate.

Independent writing Now you're going to tell a story about friends playing and building together. Close your eyes and use your wonderful, marvelous imagination. What friends do you see? What do the friends do or build? Have children write or dictate and illustrate their stories.

Daily Handwriting

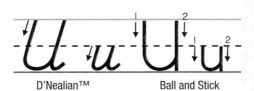

D'Nealian™   Ball and Stick

Write *Uma* and *tug* on the board. Review correct letter formation of uppercase *U* and lowercase *u*.

Have children write *Uma* and *tug* on their Write-On Boards. Remind them to use proper left-to-right and top-to-bottom progression and proper spacing between letters when writing *U* and *u*.

Write Guy
Jeff Anderson

The Sunny Side

I like to look for what's *right* in childrens' writing rather than focusing on things I can edit or fix. Most children don't write flawlessly—who does? However, they will learn what they are doing well if we point it out.

Academic Vocabulary

question a sentence that asks something and ends with a question mark

Daily Fix-It

where is the little bug
Where is the little bug?

This week's practice sentences appear on Teacher Resources DVD-ROM.

Writing Routine

Day 1 Wonderful, Marvelous Me!

Day 2 Respond to Literature

Day 3 Genre Writing

Day 4 Extend the Concept

Day 5 This Week We…

Objectives

- Practice discussing characters.
- Face the speaker when listening.
- Speak loudly and clearly.
- Take turns when speaking.

Listening and Speaking
Discuss Literary Elements—Character

Teach

When we talk about a story, we need to be good listeners and speakers. When I am a listener, I face the speaker. When I am the speaker, I talk loudly and clearly.

Model

All stories have characters. Characters are the people or animals in the story. They can be real people and animals, or they can be make-believe. The characters in *Old MacDonald had a Woodshop* were animals. See if you can tell what the characters are like just by listening. **Read** *Old MacDonald had a Woodshop,* **giving each character as much personality as possible.** Were they real or make-believe animals? They were make-believe animals. Animals don't really use tools to build things.

Guide practice

Organize children into small groups. Have them discuss the characters in a story you've read. Refer children to the Rules for Listening and Speaking on pp. 1–2 of the *Reader's and Writer's Notebook*. Remind them to face the speaker when listening and to speak loudly and clearly when it is their turn to speak.

Name _____

🟢 Listening Rules

1. Face the person who is speaking.
2. Be quiet while someone is speaking.
3. Pay attention to the speaker.
4. Ask questions if you don't understand.

Reader's and Writer's Notebook, p. 1

Wrap Up Your Day

✔ **Comprehension** Have children think of the last time they played at a friend's house. What did you do at the beginning, in the middle, and at the end of the day?

✔ **Oral Language** Today we talked about building shelters. What kind of shelter can you build quickly in nature?

✔ **Homework Idea**
Send home the Family Times Newsletter
Let's Practice It!
TR DVD•67–68.

Preview DAY 2

Tomorrow we will read about two friends who build a boat together.

Extend Your Day!

Social Studies
Safe Building

Materials: pictures of wood planks, hammer, nails, paint, fabric, and rope

Brainstorm Building Tools Display the pictures and talk with children about what each picture shows. Ask children to identify how the items in the pictures are related. Guide children to understand that all of the items can be used to build or make things. Brainstorm a list of building materials and record them on the left side of a T-chart.

Think Safety Talk with children about how each item can be used properly and safely. On the right side of the chart, write or draw a safety tip for using each tool. Tell children that they should always ask a grown-up before using a building tool.

Building Tool	Safety Tip
wood	Wear gloves.
hammer	Wear glasses.
nails	Get Mom or Dad.
paint	Paint outside.
fabric	Get help cutting.
rope	Wear gloves.

Have children choose a tool and draw a picture of themselves using it safely.

Phonics
Rhyme Chains

Make Rhyming Words Say a CVC, CCVC, or CVCC word, such as *went.* Go around the room and have each child say a word that rhymes with your word. Continue until no one can think of another rhyming word. Write the last rhyming word on the board. Change the vowel or the final consonant(s) to make a new word, and begin the rhyming chain again.

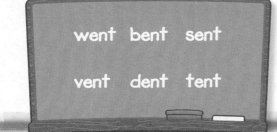

went   bent   sent

vent   dent   tent

Conventions
Clue Questions
Materials: Picture Cards

Ask Questions About Picture Cards Display 10 to 12 Picture Cards. Invite a child to secretly choose a card and give the class a clue in the form of a question. For example, a child might choose the *zebra* Picture Card and then ask, "Which card has black and white on it?" The child continues to ask questions about the card until another child figures out what the secret card is. Continue until many children have turns.

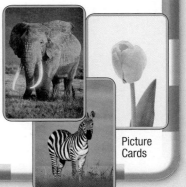

Picture Cards

Objectives
- Discuss the concepts to develop oral language.
- Build oral vocabulary.

Today at a Glance

Oral Vocabulary
gathered, distant

Phonemic Awareness
◉ Initial and Medial /u/

Phonics
◉ /u/ Spelled *Uu*

Handwriting
Words with *Uu*

Comprehension
◉ Plot

Conventions
Questions

Writing
Respond to Literature

Vocabulary
Location Words

TRUCKTOWN on Reading Street

Start your engines! Display p. 21 of *Truckery Rhymes.* Point to "Rub-a-Dub-Dub." Who remembers which trucks are in this rhyme? Yes, the Fire and Rescue trucks—the Pumper, the Hook and Ladder, and Rita! Let's read the rhyme together. Now have a child point to the rhyming words as the class reads the rhyme again.

Truckery Rhymes

Concept Talk

Question of the Week

❓ **What can friends build together?**

Build concepts

Write the question of the week on the board and track the print as you read it aloud. Have children answer the question in complete sentences and speak loudly and clearly. To reinforce the concept and focus children's attention, display Talk with Me/Sing with Me Chart 34B. Tell children that they are going to sing about friends having an adventure together.

💿 Sing with Me Audio

Listen for Amazing Words

The Amazing Words *gathered* and *distant* are in the song "Let's Go Have an Adventure." Have children describe the characters in the illustration. Sing the song several times to the tune of "Take Me Out to the Ball Game." Ask children to sing along with you. Have them pretend to row a boat when they hear *gathered* and *distant.*

ELL Reinforce Vocabulary Use the Day 2 instruction on ELL Poster 34 to reinforce the meanings of high-frequency words.

Let's Go Have an Adventure

Let's go have an adventure,
A voyage out to sea.
I've gathered together everything.
It's all aboard, so what else should we bring?
Oh, look a tropical island,
A distant coconut tree.
There'll be sun, waves, and lots of fun
Drifting on the open sea!

Talk with Me/Sing with Me Chart 34B

ELL Poster 34

Oral Vocabulary
Amazing Words

Teach Amazing Words

Amazing Words Oral Vocabulary Routine

1 Introduce the Word When people or things are grouped together in one place, they are *gathered*. What's our new Amazing Word for when people or things are grouped together? Say it with me: *gathered*.

2 Demonstrate Provide examples to show meaning. *I gathered the apples together in one basket.*

Repeat steps 1 and 2.

Introduce the Word *Distant* means far away. What's our new Amazing Word for far away? Say it with me: *distant*.

Demonstrate *The sun is distant from Earth.*

3 Apply Tell children to use *gathered* and *distant* in complete sentences. Have them draw a picture to illustrate each word.

Routines Flip Chart

Use Amazing Words

To reinforce the concept and the Amazing Words, have children supply the appropriate Amazing Word for each sentence.

The dogs _____ together at the park. (gathered)

We saw a bird nest in a _____ tree. (distant)

gat
drifti
island

**Differen
Instructio**

A Advanced

Sentence Produc
children to use both
and *distant* in the sar
Then have them illustra
sentence with one pictu

English Language Learners
Amazing Words Explain to children that the word *gathered* is a verb for the past. Tell them that if they want to use the verb for now, they should use the word *gather*.

Objectives
◎ Practice initial and medial...
• Blend phonemes to say...

Phonemic Awareness
🎯 Initial and Medial /u/

...olate /u/

Display the *up* Picture Card. This sign points *up*. *Up* begins with /u/. Which way does this sign point? What sound does *up* begin with?

Picture Card

Model

Display the *bus* Picture Card. This is a *bus*. Listen as I say the sounds: /b/ /u/ /s/, *bus*. I hear /u/ in the middle of the word: /b/ /u/ /s/. Say it with me: /b/ /u/ /s/; /u/ is in the middle. Let's try some more. Continue with the following words: *buzz, cub, cut, dust, fuss, jump, mud, snug, tub, tuck.*

Picture Card

Guide practice

Have children look at the picture on *My Skills Buddy* pp. 72–73. Remember, we saw a kangaroo unlocking a door in the picture. *Unlock* begins with /u/. Now let's look for things in the picture that have /u/ in the middle. Discuss with children those bulleted items on p. 72 not discussed on Day 1.

My Skills Buddy, pp. 72–73

Corrective feedback

If... children cannot discriminate initial and medial /u/, **then...** have them enunciate /u/ as they segment short *u* words.

Listen as I segment a word: /m/ /u/ /g/. Say it with me: /m/ /u/ /g/. What sound do you hear in the middle? I hear /u/ in the middle. Continue with the following words: *cut, hum, tub, tug.*

On their own Display Phonics Songs and Rhymes Chart 34, "Oh, Where, Oh, Where Can the Dog-Walker Stop?" Remind children of the tune: "Oh, Where, Oh, Where Has My Little Dog Gone?" Have them sing the song with you several times. We're going to listen to the song again. Listen for words with /u/. Clap your hands when you hear /u/ in the middle of a word. We can do it together the first time. Repeat the routine to identify words with /e/, /o/, /a/, and /i/.

Review **Blend Phonemes** Listen to the sounds in this word: /b/ /u/ /g/. Say them with me: /b/ /u/ /g/. Now I will blend the sounds together to say the word: /b/ /u/ /g/, *bug*. Now you try it with me: /b/ /u/ /g/, *bug*. Continue the blending routine with the words *band, cot, jug, rip,* and *well*.

Oh, Where, Oh, Where Can the Dog-Walker Stop?

Oh, where, oh, where can the
   dog-walker stop?
She must duck out of the rain!
It's a bit of bad luck
When it drips on her pup,
But her wet pet does not complain!

Oh, here, oh, here is good place to stop—
Very cozy, quiet, and warm!
Just snuggle your pup
And fix him all up!
Sit back and enjoy the fine storm!

Phonics Songs and Rhymes
Chart 34

Physic
children
go with "
Can the D
Encourage
specific mov
medial vowel,
for /a/, stepping
/e/, putting their
hips for /i/, noddin
for /o/, and jumping
Have children perfor
movements for the cla

English Language Learners
Support Phonemic Awareness
In many languages, short vowel sounds may not exist or may only have approximations. English language learners may have a hard time hearing the differences in these sounds. Provide additional phonemic awareness activities to help children hear and pronounce words with short vowel sounds.

DAY **2** Get Re**d**y

Objectives
◎ Practice /u/ spelled Uu.
• Blend /u/ words.

•view

Check Sound-S
SUCCESS PR

Phonics—Teach/Model
🎯 /u/ Spelled *Uu*

/u/Uu Point to the *umbrella* on the *Uu* Alphabet Card. What is this? What sound does *umbrella* begin with? *Umbrella* begins with /u/. **Write *umbrella* on the board and point to the letter *u*.** The letter for /u/ is *u*. What letter does *umbrella* begin with?

Alphabet Card

Model

Display the *tub* Picture Card. What is this? Say the sounds in *tub* with me: /t/ /u/ /b/, *tub*. Where do you hear /u/ in *tub*? I hear /u/ in the middle. Do you?

Write *tub* on the board. Point to each letter as you say the sound: /t/ /u/ /b/, *tub*. Continue the routine with the following words: *fun, cup, sun, gust, buck, plum, rug.*

Guide practice

Have children open *My Skills Buddy* to p. 76. Have them point to the first red arrow under the word *must*. Which direction does this arrow move? Which direction do you move when you read? **Children should respond *left to right*. Put your finger on the red arrow below the *m*.** Say the sound that *m* stands for: /m/. **Continue with the letters *u*, *s*, and *t*.** Now run your finger from left to right along the blue arrow as you blend the letters quickly to read the word *must*. **Repeat with the word *fun*. Have children work with a partner to blend the rest of the words on the page. Explain that when you add the letter *c* to the word *up*, you make the word *cup*.**

Picture Card

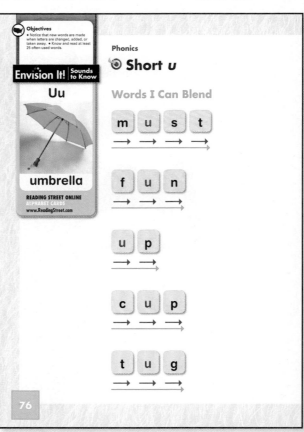

My Skills Buddy, p. 76

Blend   Use the following routine to review blending *u* words.

ROUTINE   **Sound-by-Sound Blending**

(1) Connect Write the letter *u*. What is the sound we learned for this letter? The sound is /u/. Say it with me: /u/ /u/ /u/. When you see this letter in a word, what sound will you try?

(2) Model Write the word *pup* on the board.

- Point to *p*. What is the sound for this letter? Say it with me: /p/ /p/ /p/. Repeat the routine for *u* and the second *p*.

- Let's blend the sounds together. Listen as I blend the sounds: /p/ /u/ /p/. Say it with me: /p/ /u/ /p/. Now say it without me.

- Listen as I use *pup* in a sentence: *He is a playful pup.* Say it with me. Have children use *pup* in a sentence.

(3) Guide Practice Continue the routine established in step 2 with these words:

| run | fun | up | mud | tug | pot | jump |

Have children successfully read all of the words before reading Decodable Reader 34 on pp. 78–85 of *My Skills Buddy.*

Corrective Feedback Model blending the sounds to read the word. Then have children say it with you.

Routines Flip Chart

Don't Wait Until Friday

MONITOR PROGRESS   ⟳ **Check Sound-Spelling** /u/ Spelled *Uu*

Have children write the letters *Uu* on a blank card. I am going to read some words. When you hear a word with /u/, hold your *Uu* card up in the air. Say: *up, beg, nut, pet, bath, bunch, frog, fib, run, hunt, drop, sad, tusk, dull, dish.*

If... children cannot discriminate /u/ words,

then... use the small-group Strategic Intervention lesson, p. DI•53, to reteach /u/.

Continue to monitor children's progress using other instructional opportunities during the week so that children can be successful with the Day 5 Assessment.

Day 1	Day 2	Day 3	Day 4	Day 5
Check Phonemic Awareness	Check Sound-Spelling/ Retelling	Check Word Reading	Check Phonemic Awareness	Check Oral Vocabulary

Success Predictor

ELL

English Language Learners
Support Phonics Display the *Aa* Alphabet Card. Ask children to name the sound and then the letter name. Repeat the routine with the *Ee, Ii, Oo,* and *Uu* Alphabet Cards.

335   Sound-Spelling   **Success Predictor**

Objectives
- Write *U* and *u*.
- Read high-frequency words.

view

Handwriting
Write Words with *Uu*

Write *Uncle Bud* on the board. This is the name *Uncle Bud.* I use an uppercase *U* for the first letter in *Uncle.* Watch me make an uppercase *U.* Write another uppercase *U* on the board using the instructional strokes indicated in the model. There is another *u* in the name *Uncle Bud.* It is in the middle of the name *Bud.* It is a lowercase *u.* Watch me make a lowercase *u.* Write another lowercase *u* on the board using the proper instructional strokes.

D'Nealian™   Ball and Stick

Guide practice

Have children use their Write-On Boards to make a row of uppercase *U* and a row of lowercase *u.* Circulate around the room, assisting children as necessary. Have children then write the following words: *pup, fun, mud, tug, hug, jump.*

High-Frequency Words

Model reading

Have children turn to p. 77 of *My Skills Buddy*. Read the high-frequency words *for, my, of, we,* and *yellow* together. Then have children point to each word and read it themselves. Read the sentences on the *My Skills Buddy* page together to read the new high-frequency words in context.

Team Talk Pair children and have them take turns reading each of the sentences aloud.

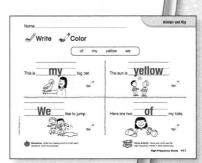

High-Frequency Words

Words I Can Read

| for |
| my |
| of |
| we |
| yellow |

Sentences I Can Read

1. That gift is for me.
2. My mom got it for me.
3. It is a big box of hats.
4. We like to dress up.
5. The yellow hat is best.

77

My Skills Buddy, p. 77

On their own

Use *Reader's and Writer's Notebook,* p. 441, for additional practice with this week's high-frequency words.

Reader's and Writer's Notebook, p. 441

Objectives
- Read decodable text.
- Read high-frequency words.

Decodable Reader 34
/u/ Spelled *Uu* and High-Frequency Words

Review Review the previously taught high-frequency words. Have children read each word as you point to it on the Word Wall.

is	my	a	for	the
of	I	with	what	we

Have children turn to Decodable Reader 34, *Fun with Spot,* on p. 78 of *My Skills Buddy*. Today we will read a story about a dog named Spot. Point to the title. The title of this story is *Fun with Spot*. What is the title? Point to the name of the author. The author's name is Cassandra Belton. What does the author do? The illustrator's name is Joseph Green. What does the illustrator do?

Use the routine for reading decodable books to read Decodable Reader 34.

My Skills Buddy, pp. 78–85

Make connections After children read *Fun with Spot*, have them make connections between the ideas in the story and other texts they have read. What other stories about pets have they read? How do the pets' actions in those stories compare with Spot's actions in *Fun with Spot*?

Reading Decodable Books

1. **Read Silently** Have children whisper read the book page by page as you listen in.

2. **Model Fluent Reading** Have children finger point as you read a page. Then have children reread the book without you.

3. **Read Chorally** Have children finger point as they chorally read the page. Continue reading page by page, repeating steps 1 and 2.

4. **Read Individually** Have children take turns reading aloud a page.

5. **Reread and Monitor Progress** As you listen to individual children reread, monitor progress and provide support.

6. **Reread with a Partner** Have children reread the book page by page with a partner.

Routines Flip Chart

Small Group Time

DAY 2 Break into small groups after reading the Decodable Reader and before the comprehension lesson.

(SI) Strategic Intervention	(OL) On-Level	(A) Advanced
Teacher-Led Page DI•53 • Phonemic Awareness and Phonics • **Reread** Decodable Reader 34	**Teacher-Led** Page DI•57 • Phonemic Awareness and Phonics • **Reread** Decodable Reader 34	**Teacher-Led** Page DI•60 • Phonics and Spelling • **Reread** Decodable Reader 34 for Fluency

ELL Place English language learners in the groups that correspond to their reading abilities in English.

Practice Stations	**Independent Activities**
• Visit the Word Work Station • Visit the Words to Know Station	• Read independently • Background Building Audio • *Reader's and Writer's Notebook*

Differentiated Instruction

(SI) Strategic Intervention

Frontload Decodable Reader
Before children read *Fun with Spot,* have volunteers model the actions run, dig, tug, sip, sit, hug, and jump.

English Language Learners

Frontload Decodable Reader
Before children read *Fun with Spot,* review short vowels using the *ant, egg, inch, ox,* and *up* Picture Cards.

Listening Comprehension
◎ Plot

Review

Envision It!

Have children turn to pp. 74–75 of *My Skills Buddy.* A story is about things that happen one after another. The things that happen at the beginning, in the middle, and at the end of a story are called the **plot.** Good readers pay attention to the plot so they can follow what happens in the story.

My Skills Buddy, pp. 74–75

First Read—Trade Book
Alistair and Kip's Great Adventure!

Concepts of print

Display the cover of *Alistair and Kip's Great Adventure!* Explain that the printed words tell us the title of the story and who wrote and illustrated it.

Preview and predict

Think Aloud

The title of this book is *Alistair and Kip's Great Adventure!* Tell me what you see on the cover. I see a big wave with a small boat on top. What do you think this book will be about? Let's read to find out.

Use illustrations

Take children on a picture walk through the book. Have children tell about what they see in each illustration.

Introduce genre

An animal fantasy is a make-believe story about animal characters. The animals in the story do things that animals can't do in real life.

Set purpose

Remind children of the question of the week: *What can friends build together?* Have children listen as you read to see what the friends in this story build.

Model

Read *Alistair and Kip's Great Adventure!* with expression for enjoyment.

DAY 2
Read for enjoyment

DAY 3
Reread using Develop Vocabulary notes

DAY 4
Reread using Guide Comprehension notes

Retell

Check retelling

Envision It!

Have children turn to p. 86 of *My Skills Buddy*. Walk through the retelling boxes as children retell *Alistair and Kip's Great Adventure!* Let's retell what happens in the first box—the beginning of the story. Alistair and Kip measure, cut, hammer, and glue as they build their boat. Let's retell what happens in the next box. Continue with the rest of the boxes. After children retell the story as a group, have them draw a picture to retell a favorite part of the story. Have them write or dictate a word or sentence to go with their picture.

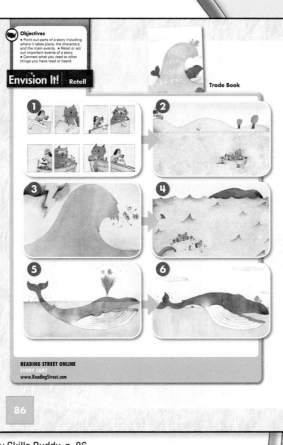

My Skills Buddy, p. 86

Top-Score Response A top-score response describes events in sequence with details.

Differentiated Instruction

SI Strategic Intervention

Build Background Ask children to think about things they like to do or build with their friends. Ask about a time they have used their imaginations to have a wild adventure. Then tell them that this is what Alistair and Kip do in the story they will listen to.

Retelling Plan

☑ **Week 1** Assess Advanced students.

☑ **Week 2** Assess On-Level students.

☑ **Week 3** Assess Strategic Intervention students.

☑ **This week assess Advanced students.**

☐ **Week 5** Assess On-Level students.

☐ **Week 6** Assess Strategic Intervention students.

Don't Wait Until Friday

MONITOR PROGRESS Check Retelling

If... children have difficulty retelling the story,

then... go through the story one page at a time, and ask children to tell what happens in their own words.

Day 1	Day 2	Day 3	Day 4	Day 5
Check Phonemic Awareness	Check Sound-Spelling/ Retelling	Check Word Reading	Check Phonemic Awareness	Check Oral Vocabulary

Success Predictor

Think, Talk, and Write

Discuss concept

We're learning about what friends can build together.

• What do you like to do with your friends?

• What have you built or made?

• Would you like to build a boat with your friends? Why or why not?

Confirm predictions

Have children recall their predictions before you read *Alistair and Kip's Great Adventure!*

• What did you think the selection would be about?

• Was your prediction correct?

Have children turn to p. 87 of *My Skills Buddy*. Read the questions and directives and have children respond.

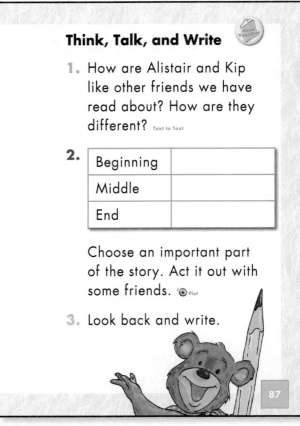

My Skills Buddy, p. 87

Think, Talk, and Write

1. How are Alistair and Kip like other friends we have read about? How are they different? Text to Text

2.

Beginning	
Middle	
End	

Choose an important part of the story. Act it out with some friends. ◎ Plot

3. Look back and write.

Text to text

1. How are Alistair and Kip like other friends we have read about? How are they different? Are they more like the friends in *Old MacDonald had a Woodshop* or the friends in *Farfallina and Marcel?* Why?

◎ Plot

2. Let's make a chart like this and fill it in. What happens at the beginning of the story? (Alistair and Kip build a boat.) What happens in the middle of the story? (A wave tips their boat.) What happens at the end of the story? (A whale brings them home.) Choose an important part of the story and act it out with some friends.

Look back and write

3. Let's look back at our story and write about it. We remember that Alistair and Kip had to do a lot of work to build their boat. Listen for all they had to do to build their boat. Read pp. 6–9 of *Alistair and Kip's Great Adventure!* Now let's write our ideas. Discuss with children the steps Alistair and Kip took. Record their responses on chart paper. (Possible responses: They gathered wood, paint, cloth, rope, a hammer, and nails. They measured, cut, hammered, and glued. They put the boat in water and cast off.)

Conventions
Questions

Review
Remind children of what they learned about questions.
A question is a sentence that asks something. A question begins with a capital letter, just like all sentences. We put a question mark at the end of a question.

Guide practice
Display p. 3 of *Alistair and Kip's Great Adventure!* At the start of *Alistair and Kip's Great Adventure!* Alistair has nothing to do. How does he feel? Write the question on the board.

> **How does he feel?**

Why did I use a capital *H* at the beginning of the question? Why did I put a question mark at the end? What is the answer to this question? **(bored)** What other questions can we ask about the story? Have children suggest questions. Write these on the board. Have children direct you on capitalization and end punctuation. Circle the capital letter and question mark in each question.

On their own
Use *Reader's and Writer's Notebook*, p. 442, for more practice with questions.

Daily Fix-It
Use the Daily Fix-It for more conventions practice.

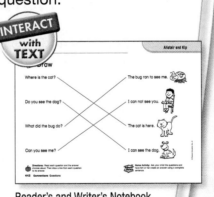

Reader's and Writer's Notebook, p. 442

Differentiated Instruction

A Advanced
Think, Talk, and Write Have children imagine that they are playing with Alistair and he says he is bored. What would they suggest doing together? Have children act out a scene between Alistair and Kip in which they try to decide what to do.

Daily Fix-It

i see a bug in the rug
I see a bug in the rug.

This week's practice sentences appear on Teacher Resources DVD-ROM.

ELL

English Language Learners
Support Conventions In Spanish, an upside-down question mark goes at the beginning of questions. Children who have literacy skills in Spanish may put this additional question mark before questions. Explain that English questions only get a question mark at the end.

Objectives

- Write sentences about the plot of the story.
- Write *U* and *u*.
- Identify and use words for locations.

Writing
Respond to Literature

Discuss Discuss *Alistair and Kip's Great Adventure!* Have children recall events in the story. List their responses on a chart.

Model Identify the event that happened first in the story. Write a complete sentence about the event on the board.

> **Alistair and Kip make a boat.**

Guide practice Have children dictate more sentences about the events on the board, choosing events from the list in the order they happened in the story.

Independent writing Have children write or dictate their own sentences about *Alistair and Kip's Great Adventure!* or copy one of the sentences the class wrote together. Then have children illustrate their sentences.

Daily Handwriting

Write *Uri* and *cup* on the board. Review correct letter formation of upper-case *U* and lowercase *u*.

D'Nealian™   Ball and Stick

Have children write *Uri* and *cup* on their Write-On Boards. Remind them to use proper left-to-right and top-to-bottom progression and proper spacing between letters when writing *U* and *u*.

Vocabulary
Location Words

Model

Have children turn to p. 88 of *My Skills Buddy.* Use the first Vocabulary bullet on the page to guide the discussion. Direct children to the first picture. This is a *hospital. A hospital* is a place where doctors and nurses care for sick or injured people. Direct children to the next picture. This is a *bank. A bank* is a place that keeps and loans money. Direct children to the third picture. This is a *grocery store. A grocery store* is a place that sells food and things for the house. Direct children to the last picture. This is a *laundromat. A laundromat* is a place where you can pay to wash your clothes. The words we learned about all name locations, or places where something can be found.

My Skills Buddy, p. 88

Guide practice

Ask questions about locations and have children point to the correct picture in their *My Skills Buddy* and say the location name.

- Where would you go to buy food?
- Where would you go if you cut your finger and needed stitches?
- Where would you go if you wanted to wash your clothes?
- Where would you go if you wanted to put your money in a safe place?

On their own

Set up four stations around the room and label them *Hospital, Bank, Grocery Store,* and *Laundromat.* Have children take turns visiting each station and acting out what they would do at that location.

Differentiated Instruction

SI Strategic Intervention

Build Vocabulary Review the vocabulary words *school, library, post office,* and *park* with children. Then page through *Miss Bindergarten Takes a Field Trip* and help children recall the different locations the children in the story visited.

Academic Vocabulary

location where something can be found

English Language Learners

Survival Vocabulary As children learn the words for *hospital, bank, grocery store,* and *laundromat,* help them learn or practice the English phrase "I need to go to the..." Tell them they can follow this with any location, such as hospital or bathroom.

Objectives
• Review skills learned and practiced today.

Wrap Up Your Day

✔ **Concept Talk** Today we talked about two friends who built a boat together. Where did they go in their boat?

✔ **Phonemic Awareness** Listen to this sentence. Jump when you hear /u/ words: *Gus and his puppy had fun in the sun.*

✔ **Vocabulary Skill** Have children describe a hospital, bank, grocery store, or laundromat, using the location word in their description. What is it like? Why do people go there?

✔ **Homework Idea** Ask children to tell a family member what happened at the beginning, in the middle, and at the end of their day today.

Preview DAY 3

Tomorrow we will reread the story about Alistair and Kip.

Extend Your Day!

Social Studies
Building Boats

Materials: pictures of a powerboat, a sailboat, and a rowboat; craft sticks; glue; tissue paper; markers

Compare Boats Show a picture of a powerboat, a sailboat, and a rowboat. Powerboats have engines like cars. The engines move them quickly through the water. Sailboats are moved by the wind. They use pieces of fabric called sails to catch the wind. People in rowboats use paddles or oars to move their boats through the water.

Display p. 5 of *Alistair and Kip's Great Adventure!* Point to and name each boat on the page. Identify a sail and a mast for children. Then discuss with them how the boats on the page are alike and different.

- How are a sloop and a ketch alike? (They both have more than one sail.)
- How are they different? (The sloop has one mast and the ketch has two.)
- How are the dory and kayak different from the other boats? (They aren't sailboats.)

Build a Boat Have children use craft sticks and glue to build the base and mast of a sailboat. Then have them use tissue paper to make a sail. Encourage them to decorate their boats with markers.

Literature
Unique Characters

Materials: drawing tools, scissors, craft sticks, glue

Create a Story Puppet Have children create their own unique story character. Ask them to draw a detailed picture of their character. Have children carefully cut around the drawing and glue it to a stick. Tell them to choose a name and age for their character, tell what kind of character it is (person or animal), and tell what the character likes to do. Invite children to display their character creations and tell the class about their puppets. Let children pair up to create a story with their characters.

Comprehension
Plot

Identify Plot Write what happened at the beginning, in the middle, and at end of the story *The Little Engine That Could* in random order on the board.

The clown asks other trains to help them over the mountain.
A little blue engine helps the train over the mountain, puffing, "I think I can."
The train full of toys and food can't get over the mountain.

Read through the sentences with children and have them write 1, 2, and 3 to indicate the order in which the events happen.

Objectives

- Share information and ideas about the concept.
- Build oral vocabulary.

Today at a Glance

Oral Vocabulary
drifting, voyage

Phonemic Awareness
◉ Initial and Medial /u/

Phonics
◉ /u/ Spelled *Uu*

Comprehension
◉ Plot

Conventions
Telling Sentences

Writing
Rhyme

Listening and Speaking
Discuss Literary Elements—Character

TRUCKTOWN on Reading Street

Start your engines! Display p. 21 of *Truckery Rhymes.* Do you know the original "Rub-a-Dub-Dub"? Recite it first, and then have children say it with you:

> Rub-a-dub-dub, three men in a tub,
> And who do you think were there?
> The butcher, the baker, the
> candlestick maker;
> And all of them gone to the
> fair.

Truckery Rhymes

Concept Talk

Question of the Week

What can friends build together?

Write the question of the week on the board. Read the question as you track the print. Talk with children about what they have made or built with their friends. Remind children to speak clearly and to take turns speaking.

Listen for Amazing Words

Let's Sing Display Sing with Me Chart 34B. Remind children that yesterday they sang "Let's Go Have an Adventure" and listened for the words *gathered* and *distant.* Today we are going to listen for the Amazing Words *drifting* and *voyage.* Sing the song several times to the tune of "Take Me Out to the Ball Game." Have children sing along with you. Have them pretend to drift or float when they say the Amazing Word *drifting* or *voyage.*

Let's Go Have an Adventure

Let's go have an adventure,
A voyage out to sea.
I've gathered together everything.
It's all aboard, so what else should we bring?
Oh, look a tropical island,
A distant coconut tree.
There'll be sun, waves, and lots of fun
Drifting on the open sea!

Talk with Me/Sing with Me Chart 34B

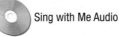 Sing with Me Audio

Oral Vocabulary
Amazing Words

Amazing Words

gathered	distant
drifting	voyage
island	aboard

Teach Amazing Words

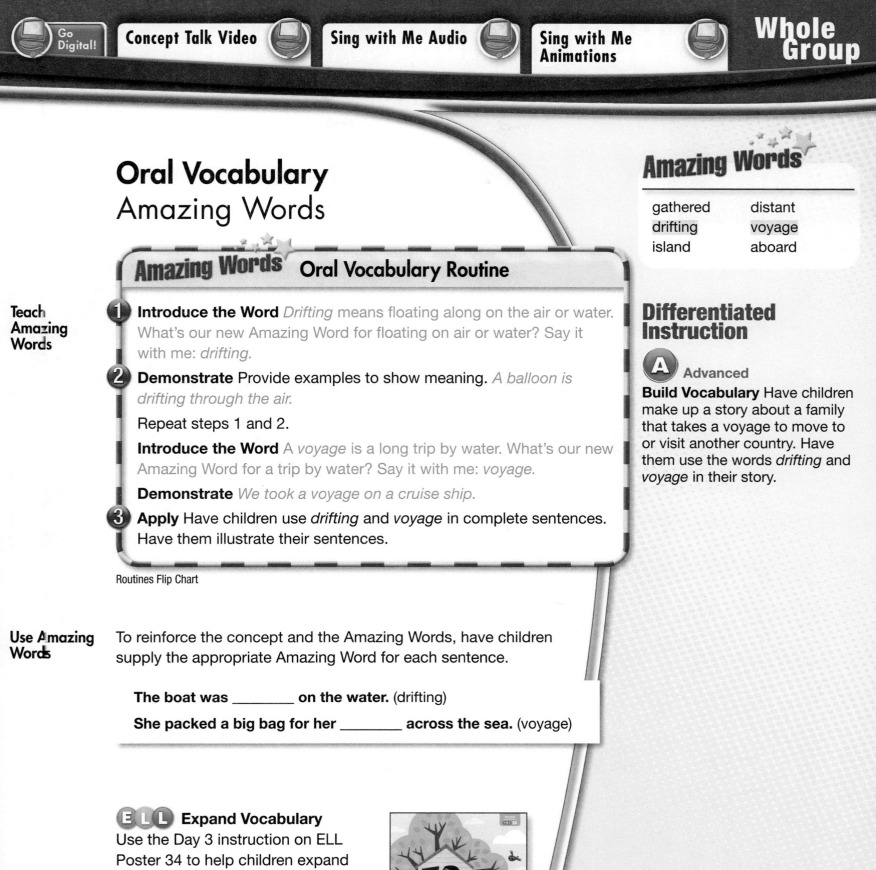

Amazing Words Oral Vocabulary Routine

1 **Introduce the Word** *Drifting* means floating along on the air or water. What's our new Amazing Word for floating on air or water? Say it with me: *drifting.*

2 **Demonstrate** Provide examples to show meaning. *A balloon is drifting through the air.*

Repeat steps 1 and 2.

Introduce the Word *A* voyage *is a long trip by water.* What's our new Amazing Word for a trip by water? Say it with me: *voyage.*

Demonstrate *We took a voyage on a cruise ship.*

3 **Apply** Have children use *drifting* and *voyage* in complete sentences. Have them illustrate their sentences.

Routines Flip Chart

Differentiated Instruction

A **Advanced**

Build Vocabulary Have children make up a story about a family that takes a voyage to move to or visit another country. Have them use the words *drifting* and *voyage* in their story.

Use Amazing Words

To reinforce the concept and the Amazing Words, have children supply the appropriate Amazing Word for each sentence.

The boat was _____ on the water. (drifting)

She packed a big bag for her _____ across the sea. (voyage)

E L L **Expand Vocabulary**
Use the Day 3 instruction on ELL Poster 34 to help children expand vocabulary.

 Poster 34

E L L

English Language Learners
Visual Support Use the pictures on Talk with Me Chart 34A to help children complete the Amazing Word sentences.

Objectives

◎ Isolate initial and medial /u/.
- Discriminate initial and medial /u/.
- Count syllables.

Phonemic Awareness
Initial and Medial /u/

Review

Initial /u/ Display the *umbrella* Picture Card. Listen as I say this word: *umbrella.* What is the first sound in *umbrella?* Say it with me: /u/ /u/ /u/, *umbrella.* Today we will hear /u/ in the beginning and in the middle of words.

Practice medial /u/

Use the *gum* Picture Card to isolate medial /u/. This is *gum.* I hear /u/ in the middle of the word. The /u/ is in the middle of *gum.* Continue the routine with the *bus, duck,* and *mug* Picture Cards.

Picture Card

Discriminate sounds

What is the first sound in the word *bed?* The first sound in *bed* is /b/. What is the last sound in *bed?* The last sound in *bed* is /d/. Repeat the routine with the following words: *tin, hall, peg, mad, wax, nod, jab, such.*

On their own

Display the Picture Cards used in this activity: *bus, duck, gum, mug, umbrella.* Have children choose one of the pictures to draw. Have them tell whether the word has /u/ at the beginning or in the middle.

Picture Card

Blend sounds

Listen as I say the sounds in a word. I want you to blend the sounds and tell me the word. I'll do the first one with you. **Display the *drum* Picture Card.** This is a *drum.* The sounds in the word *drum* are /dr/ /u/ /m/, *drum.* Say it with me: /dr/ /u/ /m/, *drum.* **Write *drum* on the board. Continue the routine with the** *bus, duck, gum, jug, mug, rug, sun,* **and** *tub* **Picture Cards. Then mix the cards and ask children to place the picture next to the word.**

Corrective feedback

If... children cannot blend sounds into words,
then... have them practice blending onset and rime of familiar decodable words, and then blend those words sound by sound.

Count syllables

Listen to the word I say. Tell me how many syllables you hear. The word is *adventure.* I hear three syllables. Say it with me: *ad-ven-ture.* Do you hear three syllables? **Continue the routine with the following words:** *Alistair, Tuesday, morning, home, suddenly, another, island, whale, tomorrow.*

Phonics—Teach/Model
 /u/ Spelled *Uu*

Review **/u/Uu** Display the *Uu* Alphabet Card and point to the umbrella. What sound do you hear at the beginning of *umbrella?* What letter spells that sound? Point to the letters *Uu.* What is the sound we learned for this letter? What are the names of these letters?

Review **Letter Names and Sounds** Use Alphabet Cards to review the following letter names and sounds: *Aa, Ee, Ff, Ii, Jj, Kk, Ll, Mm, Nn, Oo, Ss, Tt, Xx.*

Blend sounds Write the word *fun* on the board. Point to each letter as you say the sound: /f/ /u/ /n/. When I blend these sounds together, I make the word *fun.* Say the sounds with me: /f/ /u/ /n/. Now blend the sounds together: /f/ /u/ /n/, *fun.* Repeat the blending routine with *Jen, Max, set, mom, Sam,* and *milk.*

More practice Use *Reader's and Writer's Notebook,* p. 443, for additional practice with /u/.

Alphabet Card

Reader's and Writer's Notebook, p. 443

Review

Sound-Spelling Display the *Bb* Alphabet Card. What sound do you hear at the beginning of *baby*? What letter spells that sound? Yes, the letter *b* spells /b/. Review the following sounds and letters with Alphabet Cards: *Dd, Ff, Jj, Mm, Nn, Pp, Ss.*

Review

High-Frequency Words Write *for* on the board. This is the word *for.* What is this word? Continue the routine with *my, of, we,* and *yellow.*

Alphabet Card

Don't Wait Until Friday

MONITOR PROGRESS   Check Word Reading   High-Frequency Words

Write *for, my, of, we,* and *yellow* on the board. Have children take turns reading the words.

Practice reading these words from Kindergarten Student Reader K.6.4, *A Busy Day.*

| sun | fun | dump | buns | us | Bud | jump |

If... children cannot read the high-frequency words,
then... write the words on cards for them to practice at home.

If... children cannot blend sounds to read the words,
then... provide practice blending the words in chunks, /s/ -un.

If... children can successfully blend sounds to read the words,
then... have them read Kindergarten Student Reader K.6.4, *A Busy Day.*

Day 1	Day 2	Day 3	Day 4	Day 5
Check Phonemic Awareness	Check Sound-Spelling/ Retelling	Check Word Reading	Check Phonemic Awareness	Check Oral Language

Success Predictor

Differentiated Instruction

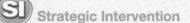 **Strategic Intervention**

High-Frequency Words Have children use the high-frequency words in sentences to show that they understand the words and their meanings.

English Language Learners

High-Frequency Words Remind children that the word *yellow* is a color word. Have them name other words for colors that they know in English, such as *red, blue,* and *green.* Help children write each color word using a crayon of that color to help them connect the word with the color.

Word Reading

Success Predictor

Objectives
- Read /u/ words.
- Read high-frequency words.

Kindergarten Student Reader K.6.4
↻ /u/ Spelled *Uu* and High-Frequency Words

Review | Review the previously taught high-frequency words. Have children read each word as you point to it on the Word Wall.

look	we	go	they	for	she	with	are

Teach rebus words | Write the word *raccoon* on the board. This is the word *raccoon*. Name the letters with me: *r, a, c, c, o, o, n, raccoon*. Look for the word *raccoon* in the story we read today. Repeat the routine for the words *owls* and *baker*. There will be pictures above these words to help you read them.

Read Kindergarten Student Reader K.6.4 | Display Kindergarten Student Reader K.6.4. Today we are going to read a new book. Point to the title of the book. The title of this book is *Max and Jen: A Busy Day.* It was written by Katherine Ramirez. It was illustrated by Nan Brooks.

Use the reading decodable books routine to read the Kindergarten Student Reader.

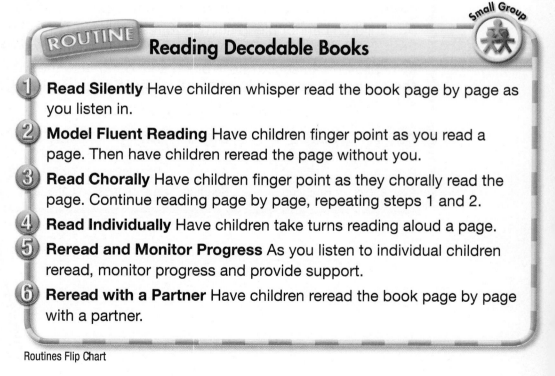

ROUTINE Reading Decodable Books *Small Group*

1. **Read Silently** Have children whisper read the book page by page as you listen in.

2. **Model Fluent Reading** Have children finger point as you read a page. Then have children reread the page without you.

3. **Read Chorally** Have children finger point as they chorally read the page. Continue reading page by page, repeating steps 1 and 2.

4. **Read Individually** Have children take turns reading aloud a page.

5. **Reread and Monitor Progress** As you listen to individual children reread, monitor progress and provide support.

6. **Reread with a Partner** Have children reread the book page by page with a partner.

Routines Flip Chart

Jen and Max look at the sun set.
The sun sets, and we go to bed.
We had fun.

2

Little Raccoon and his mom get up.
They will look for cans to dump.
They will have fun.

3

Six little owls get up.
They will look at the raccoons
in the cans.
Six little owls will have fun.

4

Kindergarten Student Reader K.6.4

Sam the baker gets up.
She will fix the buns for us.
Sam will have fun.

5

Bud gets up.
He will get the milk to us.
We will have milk with the buns.

6

The sun gets up.
Jen and Max jump up.
They will have fun!

7

The raccoons and owls are in bed.
Sam is in bed.
Bud is in bed.
They had fun!

8

Differentiated Instruction

SI Strategic Intervention

Access Content Ask children to tell what a sunset is and what it means to say *the sun sets.* Show pictures of a raccoon and explain how raccoons go out at night looking in garbage cans and other places to find things to eat.

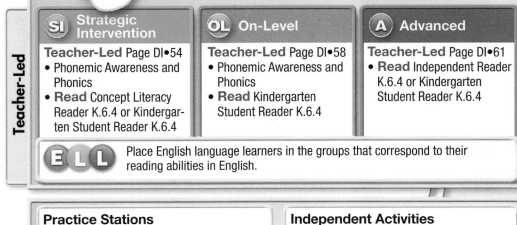

Small Group Time

DAY 3 Break into small groups to read the Kindergarten Student Reader before the comprehension lesson.

Teacher-Led

SI Strategic Intervention

Teacher-Led Page DI•54
- Phonemic Awareness and Phonics
- **Read** Concept Literacy Reader K.6.4 or Kindergarten Student Reader K.6.4

OL On-Level

Teacher-Led Page DI•58
- Phonemic Awareness and Phonics
- **Read** Kindergarten Student Reader K.6.4

A Advanced

Teacher-Led Page DI•61
- **Read** Independent Reader K.6.4 or Kindergarten Student Reader K.6.4

ELL Place English language learners in the groups that correspond to their reading abilities in English.

Practice Stations
- Visit the Words to Know Station
- Visit the Let's Write! Station

Independent Activities
- Read independently
- Audio Text of Trade Book
- *Reader's and Writer's Notebook*

Objectives
- Recall and retell a story.
- Practice plot.

Comprehension

Retell the story

Have children turn to p. 86 of *My Skills Buddy* and use the retelling boxes to retell the story *Alistair and Kip's Great Adventure!*

Envision It!

Think Aloud Direct children to the first retell box. This part of the story tells about Alistair and Kip building their boat. Tell me what we learn about next.

Continue reviewing the retelling boxes and having children retell the story.

My Skills Buddy, p. 86

Review

Plot Display illustrations in *Alistair and Kip's Great Adventure!* Remind children that things happen at the beginning, in the middle, and at the end of the story.

- What happens at the beginning of the story? (Alistair and Kip build a boat.)

- What happens in the middle of the story? (A wave tips their boat and they go under water.)

- What happens at the end of the story? (A whale brings Alistair and Kip home.)

More practice

Use *Reader's and Writer's Notebook*, p. 444, for additional practice with plot.

Reader's and Writer's Notebook, p. 444

Second Read—Trade Book
Alistair and Kip's Great Adventure!

Reread *Alistair and Kip's Great Adventure!* Follow the Day 3 arrow beginning on p. 358 and use the Develop Vocabulary notes to prompt conversations about the story.

Have children use the Amazing Words *gathered, distant, drifting, voyage, island,* and *aboard* to talk about the story.

DAY 2
Read for enjoyment

DAY 3
Reread using Develop Vocabulary notes

DAY 4
Reread using Guide Comprehension notes

Differentiated Instruction

SI Strategic Intervention

Frontload Main Selection
Remind children that *Alistair and Kip's Great Adventure!* is an animal fantasy. Page through several pages of the book and have children identify the main characters, Alistair and Kip. Then remind them that an animal fantasy is a make-believe story about animal characters doing things that animals cannot really do.

Develop Vocabulary

DAY 3

Distancing

How is Alistair feeling? (bored)

- Alistair is feeling bored. What do you do when you are bored?

Expand Vocabulary bored

It was Tuesday morning.
Alistair was bored.

Trade Book, p. 3

Guide Comprehension

DAY 4

Open-ended

When does this story happen?
(Tuesday morning)

- The story happens on Tuesday morning. Tuesday is a day of the week. What are the other days of the week?

Recall

Alistair and Kip are trying to think of things to do. Which one is Alistair? Which one is Kip? **(Alistair is the cat. Kip is the dog.)**

- Alistair is a cat and Kip is a dog. Can a cat and a dog really talk to each other and build boats together? Why or why not?

Trade Book, pp. 4–5

Wh- question

What do these pictures show? **(boats)**

- These are pictures of different kinds of sailboats and boats you paddle. Which boats have sails?

Develop Vocabulary, continued

DAY 3

Wh- question

What do Alistair and Kip gather? (wood, paint, cloth, rope, hammer, nails)

- They gather wood, paint, cloth, rope, a hammer, and nails. What do you think they will make with all of these building supplies?

Develop Vocabulary wood, paint, cloth, rope, nails, glued

Alistair knew just what to do.

He and Kip gathered wood and paint

and cloth and rope

and hammer and nails. And then they went to work.

They measured, cut, hammered, and glued.

Before they knew it . . .

Trade Book, pp. 6–7

Guide Comprehension, continued

DAY 4

Inferential

What is Kip wearing as he hammers? (glasses and a hard hat)

- Kip is wearing glasses and a hard hat. Why do you think he is wearing them?

Wh- question

Why does Kip have to jump into the boat?
(Alistair has already cast off.)

- Alistair has already cast off, and the boat is drifting away from the shore. Do you think Alistair would leave without Kip?

Extend Vocabulary cast off

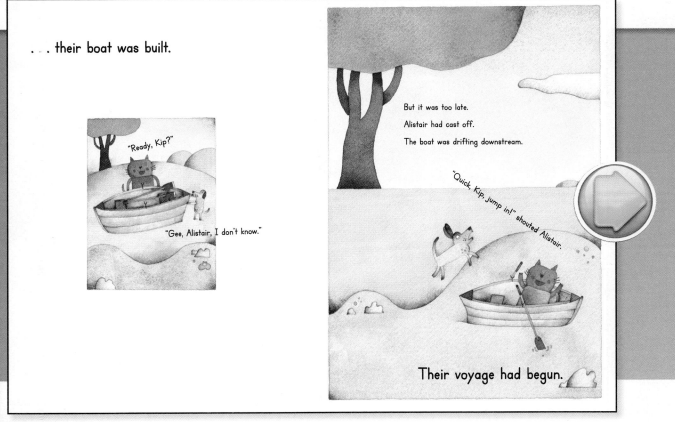

. . . their boat was built.

"Ready, Kip?"

"Gee, Alistair, I don't know."

But it was too late.
Alistair had cast off.
The boat was drifting downstream.

"Quick, Kip, jump in!" shouted Alistair.

Their voyage had begun.

Trade Book, pp. 8–9

Inferential

How do you think Alistair feels about going on an adventure in the boat? (excited; he looks happy and excited in the picture.)

- Alistair is excited to start their adventure. Do you think Kip is as excited as Alistair? Why or why not?

Develop Vocabulary, continued

DAY 3

Distancing

Where do Alistair and Kip row?
(down the creek, to the river, and
into the bay)

• They start in a small stream
  called a creek. Then they go into
  a larger river. Finally, they get to an
  opening into the sea called a bay.

Have you ever seen a bay?

Extend Vocabulary creek, bay

Trade Book, pp. 10–11

Guide Comprehension, continued

DAY 4

Inferential

Do you think that Alistair and Kip
are really taking a boat they built
out to sea? Why or why not? (No;
a cat and a dog can't build a boat
and take it out to sea. This is a
make-believe story.)

Recall

Wha animal do you see swimming near their boat? (a whale)

- There is a whale swimming near their boat. What do you think they will ask the whale?

... and out to sea.

They were a long way from home.

Trade Book, pp. 12–13

Distancing

Where are Alistair and Kip now? (in the sea, a long way from home)

- They are a long way from home. How do you feel when you are a long way from home?

Develop Vocabulary, continued

DAY 3

Distancing

What happens to Alistair and Kip's boat? (a wave tips them over)

- A wave hurled their boat through the air. That means it threw the boat very hard. Have you ever hurled a ball? Have you hurled anything else?

Extend Vocabulary hurled

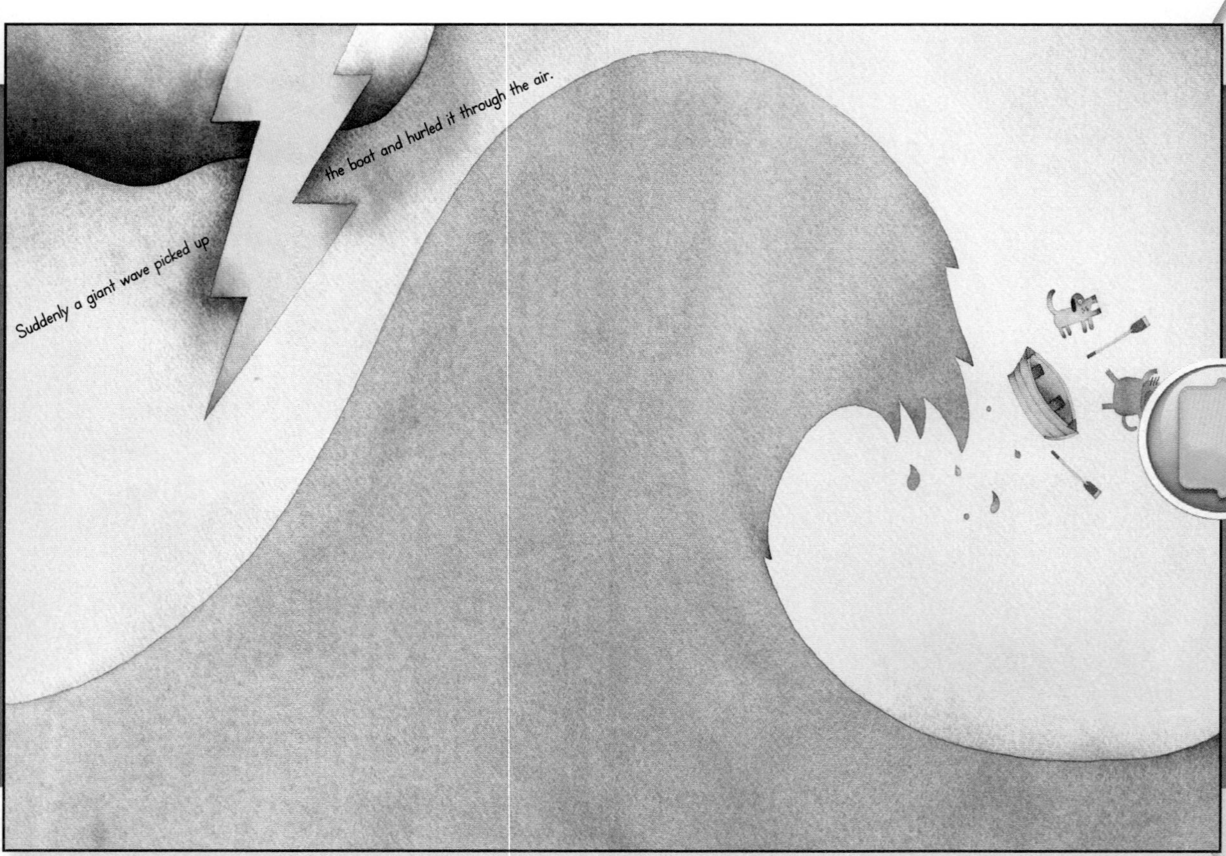

Suddenly a giant wave picked up the boat and hurled it through the air.

Trade Book, pp. 14–15

Guide Comprehension, continued

DAY 4

Open-ended

What is the yellow streak in the sky? (lightning)

- It is a lightning bolt. What kind of weather goes with lightning?

Open-ended

What animals do you see with Alistair and Kip? (sharks, fish, crab, octopus)

- We see sharks, fish, a crab, and an octopus. Where do all of these animals live?

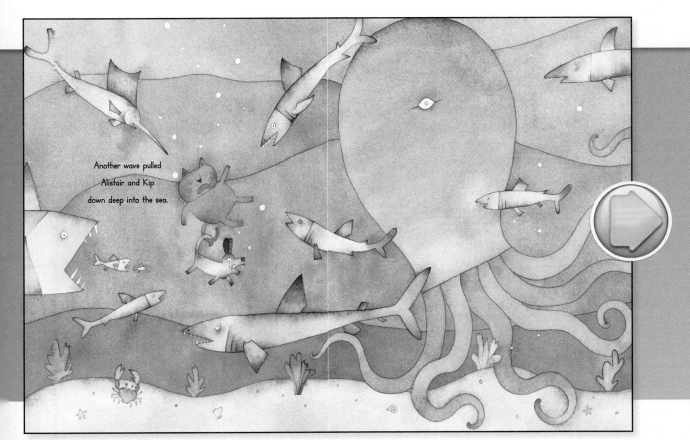

Trade Book, pp. 16–17

Inferential

Where does the wave take Alistair and Kip?
(deep into the sea)

- The wave takes them deep into the sea! How do you think they feel?

Develop Vocabulary, continued

DAY 3

Distancing

What are Alistair and Kip doing?
(swimming up)

- They are swimming to the surface,
  or top, of the water. I bet they are
  happy they know how to swim. Do
  you know how to swim?

Trade Book, pp. 18–19

Guide Comprehension, continued

DAY 4

Recall

What do they see? (an island)

- Alistair and Kip think they see an
  island. What is it really?

Distancing

Where are Alistair and Kip now? (on the whale's back, on an island)

- They are on the whale's back, but they think it is an island. What do you think a whale's skin would feel like?

Trade Book, pp. 20–21

Open-ended

What do you think goes boom? (I think the whale may have smacked his tail on the water and it made a loud noise.)

Develop Vocabulary, continued

DAY 3

Distancing

How do you think Alistair and Kip feel right now? (scared)

- They probably feel scared. Tell me about a time you felt scared.

Trade Book, pp. 22–23

Guide Comprehension, continued

DAY 4

Open-ended

Where are Alistair and Kip now? (in the air)

- They are in the air, on top of the whale's spout. Whales breathe through a hole in the top of their heads. When they breathe out, a big spout of air and water comes out! What do you use to breathe?

Recall

Who is scared now? (the whale)

- The whale gets scared by Alistair and Kip yelling. Do you think Alistair and Kip are still scared?

Trade Book, pp. 24–25

Wh- question

What question do you see on this page? Look for a question mark to help you find it. ("Well, why didn't you say so?")

- "Well, why didn't you say so?" is a question. How do you know it's a question?

Develop Vocabulary, continued

Recall

DAY 3

What happened to Alistair and Kip's boat earlier in the story? **(It broke.)**

- The wave broke the boat. How are they getting home now?

Trade Book, pp. 26–27

Guide Comprehension, continued

DAY 4

Monitor and Fix Up

Do you remember where Alistair and Kip have to go to get home? **This might be a difficult question for children.** When you don't remember the setting of a story, you can go back and reread to find out. If you reread, you learn that they got to the sea by going through the creek, the river, and the bay. They will have to go through all of these places again to get home.

Distancing

How many boats do you see in the pictures?
(three)

- There is a large powerboat, a sailboat, and a small rowboat. Have you ever seen a boat up close?

They rode through the bay,

to the river,

and up the creek . . .

Trade Book, pp. 28–29

Inferential

Why does the whale look so big in the creek?
(A whale is too big to fit in a creek.)

- A creek is very small and a whale is very, very big. This whale is probably having a hard time fitting in the creek. Look at the picture. How do you think the whale feels?

Develop Vocabulary, continued

Inferential

DAY 3

Do you think Alistair and Kip use their imaginations in this story? Why or why not? (Yes. They couldn't really take a boat they built out to sea and have this great adventure; they just pretend that they did.)

. . . all the way home.

"Good-bye and thank you!" said Alistair.

Trade Book, pp. 30–31

Guide Comprehension, continued

Distancing

DAY 4

Why does Alistair say thank you? (He is happy the whale took them home.)

- He is thankful that the whale brought them home. What makes you thankful?

Inferential

What does Alistair want to do tomorrow?
(build an airplane)

- Alistair wants to build an airplane. How do you think Kip feels about that?

Continue with **DAY 3**

Conventions p. 374

"That was **fun,** Kip.
Tomorrow let's build an airplane!"

Trade Book, p. 32

Plot

What happens at the beginning, in the middle, and at the end of this story? (First, Alistair and Kip build a boat and take it through the creek, river, and bay to the sea. Then a big wave tips their boat over and they go underwater. Finally, a whale takes them all the way home.)

Skip to **DAY 4**

Conventions p. 388

Objectives
- Review telling sentences.
- Write a rhyme.

Conventions
Telling Sentences

Review   Write these sentences on the board:

> **My favorite color is blue.**
>
> **I like to paint.**

Remind children of what they learned about telling sentences. A sentence that tells you something is called a telling sentence. It begins with a capital letter and ends with a period. **Point to the first sentence.** Listen to this sentence: *My favorite color is blue.* This is a telling sentence. It tells you my favorite color. **Point to the second sentence.** Listen to this sentence: *I like to paint.* This is a telling sentence. It tells you what I like to do. **Underline the capital letter at the start of each sentence.** Both sentences start with a capital letter. **Circle the period at the start of each sentence.** They both end with a period. They are telling sentences.

Guide practice   Write these sentences on the board. Have children read them with you.

> **We can see the bug.**
>
> **Can you see the bug?**

Which one is a telling sentence? How do you know? What information does it tell you? **Repeat with the following sentences:** *I am not tall. Are you tall? Is she on the rug? She is on the rug.*

Team Talk Pair children and have them take turns using telling sentences that tell about themselves.

On their own   Use *Reader's and Writer's Notebook*, p. 445, for more practice with telling sentences.

Daily Fix-It   Use the Daily Fix-It for more conventions practice.

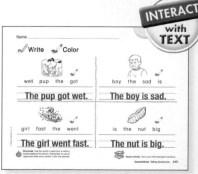

Reader's and Writer's Notebook, p. 445

Writing
Rhyme

Teach

A rhyme is like a short poem. It is a few words or a sentence that sounds like a song. Like a poem, a rhyme has rhythm, like clapping to a beat. The words at the ends of the lines rhyme.

Model

Write the following rhyme on the board.

> **In the morning when I get up,**
>
> **I run outside with my little _____.** (pup)
>
> **We play in rain or in bright sun.**
>
> **Whatever the weather, we have _____.** (fun)

Have children suggest words with /u/ to fill in the blanks as you read the rhyme. Then read the completed rhyme together.

Guide practice

Now let's write our own poem about *Alistair and Kip's Great Adventure!* Let's think of words that rhyme with *Kip.* I know the word *trip* rhymes with *Kip.* Let's write a rhyme using the words *Kip* and *trip.* Write the following rhyme on the board, read it aloud, and complete it with children.

> **Alistair and Kip**
>
> **Take a boat _____.**
>
> **A whale saves the day**
>
> **And takes them all the _____.**

 INTERACT with TEXT

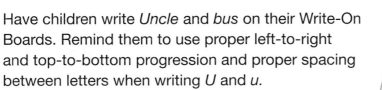

Reader's and Writer's Notebook, p. 446

Independent writing

Have children turn to p. 446 of *Reader's and Writer's Notebook.* Have them copy the poem about Alistair and Kip's trip and then draw a picture to go with it.

Daily Handwriting

Write *Uncle* and *bus* on the board. Review correct letter formation of uppercase *U* and lowercase *u.*

D'Nealian™   Ball and Stick

Have children write *Uncle* and *bus* on their Write-On Boards. Remind them to use proper left-to-right and top-to-bottom progression and proper spacing between letters when writing *U* and *u.*

Differentiated Instruction

SI Strategic Intervention

Support Conventions Remind children that a period is used at the end of most sentences, including telling sentences. If the sentence is a question, a question mark is used instead.

Academic Vocabulary

telling sentence a group of words that tells something and ends with a period

rhyme a short poem with a pattern of similar sounds at the ends of the lines

Daily Fix-It

will you cut the bun
<u>W</u>ill you cut the bun<u>?</u>

This week's practice sentences appear on Teacher Resources DVD-ROM.

ELL

English Language Learners
Support Writing Pair English learners with children for whom English is the home language and have pairs write together.

Objectives
• Practice discussing characters.
• Face the speaker when listening.
• Ask the speaker questions to clarify information.
• Speak loudly and clearly.

Listening and Speaking
Discuss Literary Elements
Character

Review

Remind children that when they listen, they should focus their attention on the speaker and ask questions if they don't understand something. When they speak, they should speak loudly and clearly.

Model

Have children turn to p. 89 of *My Skills Buddy.* I see a picture from *Max Takes the Train.* Let's talk about the characters in that story. Characters are the people or animals in a story. Display *Max Takes the Train.* Page through the book and help children recall the characters Max, Ruby, and Uncle Bunny. Use the Listening and Speaking bullets on p. 88 of *My Skills Buddy* to guide the discussion.

Listening and Speaking

Discuss Literary Elements
Character

Be a good listener!

89

My Skills Buddy, p. 89

Independent practice Display *Alistair and Kip's Great Adventure!* Have pairs of children work together to discuss the characters in the story. What do we learn about Alistair and Kip in the story? What do we learn about the whale? What events in the story show you what they are like? Are these characters real or make-believe? Refer children to their Rules for Listening and Speaking from pp. 1–2 of the *Reader's and Writer's Notebook.* Remind children to face their partner when listening and to ask questions if they don't understand something. When speaking, they should speak loudly and clearly.

Reader's and Writer's Notebook, pp. 1–2

Be a Good Listener

1. Face the speaker who is speaking.
2. Be quiet while someone is speaking.
3. Pay attention to the speaker.
4. Ask questions if you don't understand.

Differentiated Instruction

SI Strategic Intervention

Support Characters If children cannot remember the characters in a story after looking at the pictures, then page through the book with them. Point to an important character and remind children how that character played a part in key events in the story.

Academic Vocabulary

character a person, animal, or personified object in a story

Objectives
- Review skills learned and practiced today.

Wrap Up Your Day

✔ **Concept Talk** Today we talked about animals that Alistair and Kip meet on their adventure. What animals do they meet in the sea?

✔ **Respond to Literature** Today we read about Max and Jen. What did the animals and people do while Max and Jen were sleeping?

✔ **Conventions** Have children use the words *who, what, where, when,* and *why* to ask questions.

✔ **Homework Idea** Have children write words that rhyme with *nut, bug,* and *up.*

Preview DAY 4

Tomorrow we will read about what happens at night in the country.

Extend Your Day!

Science
Night Versus Day

Materials: chart paper, writing and painting tools, painting paper

Discuss Differences Between Night and Day
Display Kindergarten Student Reader K.6.4, *Max and Jen: A Busy Day.* Remind children that this story tells about what happens at night after Max and Jen go to sleep. Take a picture walk through the story and point out changes in the sky, such as the setting sun and the moon and stars.

Talk with children about how the sky changes at night and during the day. Ask them to name things we see in the sky during the day and things we see in the sky at night. Write their responses in a chart under columns labeled *Night Sky* and *Day Sky.* Circle the names of objects visible in both the day and the night sky.

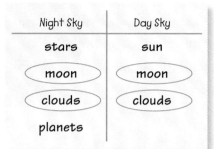

Night Sky	Day Sky
stars	sun
moon	moon
clouds	clouds
planets	

Paint the Night and Day Skies Have children fold a large sheet of painting paper in half. Have them paint the daytime sky on one half of the paper and the nighttime sky on the other half. Then have children label the objects in their paintings.

Math
Water Ways

Materials: cup, pitcher, bucket, drawing paper and tools

Compare Sizes Display the cup, pitcher, and bucket, each filled with water. Which one holds the most water? (the bucket) Which one holds the least water? (the cup)

Make Connections Label the cup *creek,* the pitcher *river,* and the bucket *sea.* Explain to children that creeks, rivers, and the sea hold different amounts of water. Help children draw the conclusion that a creek is much smaller than a river, which is much smaller than the sea.

Phonics
Vowel Substitution

Materials: letter tiles or cards

Make Words Provide each child with a set of letter tiles. Write a word on the board and have children spell it with their tiles. Tell them to substitute the beginning consonant(s), ending consonant(s), or the vowel to make a new word. Invite children to write their new words on the board and to read them to the class. Use these words as starting words: *stop, flap, hand, camp, bend, mask, past.*

flap

flip   clap   map   flop

flag   tap   flat

Objectives
* Discuss the concept to develop oral language.

Today at a Glance

Oral Vocabulary
island, aboard

Phonemic Awareness
Initial and Medial /e/

Phonics
/e/ Spelled *Ee*
Spell Words

Comprehension
◉ Plot

Conventions
Questions

Writing
Extend the Concept

Vocabulary
Location Words

Trucktown on Reading Street

Start your engines!

* Display "Rub-a-Dub-Dub" and lead the group in saying the rhyme a few times.
* Have the group clap the rhythm as they recite the rhyme.
* When children master the rhythm, have them march around the room as they say the rhyme.

Truckery Rhymes

Concept Talk

Question of the Week

What can friends build together?

Build concepts

Write the question of the week on the board. Read the question as you track the print. Tell children to respond in complete sentences. Display Sing with Me Chart 34B.

Listen for Amazing Words

We are going to sing this song again. Listen for the Amazing Words *island* and *aboard.* Sing the song several times with children to the tune of "Take Me Out to the Ball Game." Have them stand up when they hear the Amazing Word *island* or *aboard.*

🔊 Sing with Me Audio

E L L **Produce Oral Language** Use the Day 4 instruction on ELL Poster 34 to extend and enrich language.

Let's Go Have an Adventure

Let's go have an adventure,
A voyage out to sea.
I've gathered together everything.
It's all aboard, so what else should we bring?
Oh, look a tropical island,
A distant coconut tree.
There'll be sun, waves, and lots of fun
Drifting on the open sea!

Talk with Me/Sing with Me
Chart 34B

E L L Poster 34

Oral Vocabulary
Amazing Words

Amazing Words

gathered	distant
drifting	voyage
island	aboard

Teach Amazing Words

Amazing Words   Oral Vocabulary Routine

1. **Introduce the Word** A piece of land with water all around it is called an *island*. What's our new Amazing Word for land with water all around it? Say it with me: *island*.

2. **Demonstrate** *Hawaii is an island.*

   Repeat steps 1 and 2.

   Introduce the Word When people get on a ship, train, bus, or airplane, they get *aboard*. What's our new Amazing Word for getting on? Say it with me: *aboard*.

   Demonstrate *The conductor said, "All aboard!" to tell everyone to get on the train.*

3. **Apply** Have children use *island* and *aboard* in sentences. Then have them illustrate their sentences.

Routines Flip Chart

Use Amazing Words

To reinforce the concept and the Amazing Words, have children supply the appropriate Amazing Word for each sentence.

We climbed _____ the ship from the dock. (aboard)

We could see an _____ from our ship. (island)

Differentiated Instruction

A **Advanced**

Build Background Have children use a world map or globe to find several islands. Help them identify the islands they locate.

English Language Learners
Build Vocabulary Explain to children that the word *aboard* sounds similar to the words *a board,* meaning one piece of wood. Tell them they may need to listen to the context of the sentence to help them understand if a speaker is using the word *aboard* or the words *a board*.

Phonemic Awareness
Initial and Medial /e/

Picture Card

Review

Display the *egg* Picture Card. This is an *egg. Egg* begins with /e/. What is this? What sound does it begin with? Display the *net* Picture Card. This is a *net.* The middle sound in *net* is /e/. Continue the routine with the *bed, elephant, jet, elbow, and tent* Picture Cards. Have children identify and locate /e/.

Display the *bed* Picture Card. I will read two words. Tell me which word has the same middle sound as *bed: jam, bet. Bet* has /e/ in the middle, like *bed.* Repeat the routine with the following sets of words: *pet, dog; pan, web; top, bell; brick, test.*

Picture Card

Corrective feedback

If... children cannot discriminate /e/,
then... have them say /e/ several times, /e/ /e/ /e/.
When you say /e/, the front of your tongue is in the middle of your mouth and your lips and cheeks are relaxed. Have children practice saying /e/, and then repeat the discrimination activity.

Picture Card

Phonics
/e/ Spelled *Ee*

Review

Display the *Ee* Alphabet Card. This is an *escalator.* *Escalator* begins with /e/. What letter spells /e/? Yes, the letter *e.*

Write the word *sell* on the board. Help me blend this word. Listen as I say each sound: /s/ /e/ /l/. Say it with me: /s/ /e/ /l/. Now let's blend the sounds together to read the word: /s/ /e/ /l/, *sell.* What is the word? (*sell*) Let's try one more. Write *ten* on the board and repeat the routine.

Alphabet Card

Differentiated Instruction

SI Strategic Intervention

Support Phonemic Awareness
If children struggle to segment a word into individual phonemes, help them first segment the word into onset and rhyme. Then help them break the rhyme into individual phonemes.

Don't Wait Until Friday

MONITOR PROGRESS | **Check Phonemic Awareness**

Phoneme Segmentation I will say a word. Then I want you to tell me the sounds in that word.

| sat | lap | pet | beg | sip | did |
| not | top | hot | fun | mud | bat |

If... children cannot segment the sounds,
then... use the small-group Strategic Intervention lesson, p. DI•55, to reteach segmentation skills.

Continue to monitor children's progress using other instructional opportunities during the week so that they can be successful with the Day 5 Assessment. See the Skills Trace on p. 318.

| Day 1 | Day 2 | Day 3 | Day 4 | Day 5 |
| Check Phonemic Awareness | Check Sound-Spelling/ Retelling | Check Word Reading | Check Phonemic Awareness | Check Oral Vocabulary |

Success Predictor

Phonemic Awareness

Success Predictor

Spelling
↻ /u/ Spelled *Uu*

> ### ROUTINE Spell Words
>
> Spell words ① **Review Sound-Spellings** Display the *Gg* Alphabet Card. This is a *goose. Goose* begins with /g/. What is the letter for /g/? (*g*) Continue the routine with the following Alphabet Cards: *Cc, Ff, Hh, Pp, Rr.*
>
> ② **Model** Today we are going to spell some words. Listen to the three sounds in *rug:* /r/ /u/ /g/.
>
>
>
> - What is the first sound in *rug?* (/r/) What is the letter for /r/? (*r*) Write *r* on the board.
> - What is the middle sound you hear? (/u/) What is the letter for /u/? (*u*) Write *u* on the board.
> - What is the last sound you hear? (/g/) What is the letter for /g/? (*g*) Write *g* on the board.
> - Point to *rug.* Help me blend the sound of each letter together to read this word: /r/ /u/ /g/. The word is *rug.* Repeat with the word *tub.*
>
> ③ **Guide Practice** Now let's spell some words together. Listen to this word: /k/ /u/ /p/. What is the first sound in *cup?* (/k/) What is one letter we learned for /k/? (*c*) Write *c* on the board. Now you write *c* on your paper. What is the middle sound in *cup?* (/u/) What is the letter for /u/? (*u*) Write *u* on the board. Now you write *u* on your paper. What is the last sound in *cup?* (/p/) What is the letter for /p/? (*p*) Write *p* on the board. Now you write *p* on your paper. Now we can blend the sound of each letter together to read the word: /k/ /u/ /p/. What is the word? (*cup*) Continue spell and blend practice with the following words: *pan, pig, hum, cost.*
>
> ④ **On Your Own** I am going to say a word. I want you to write it on your paper. Remember, first, say the word slowly in your head and then write the letter for each sound. Listen carefully: *bun.* Give children time to write the word. How do you spell the word *bun?* Listen to the sounds: /b/ /u/ /n/. The first sound is /b/. What is the letter for /b/? Did you write *b* on your paper? What is the letter for /u/? Did you write *u* on your paper? What is the letter for /n/? Did you write *n* on your paper? Name the letters in *bun. Bun* is spelled *b, u, n.* Continue the activity with the following words: *pan, cost, hug, hum, pig.*

Routines Flip Chart

Get Set, Roll! Reader 34
🎯 Practice /u/ Spelled *Uu*

Review

Review the high-frequency words *is, look, the, go, for, what, a, he, see,* and *have.* Have children find each word on the Word Wall.

Read Get Set, Roll! Reader 34

Today we will read a book about a muddy puddle. Point to the title of the book. What is the title of the book? (*Mud Fun*) We will read some words with /u/ in this book.

Use the routine for reading decodable books found in the Routines Flip Chart to read Get Set, Roll! Reader 34.

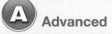

Get Set, Roll! Reader 34

Differentiated Instruction

A Advanced

Use Sentence Frames Have children complete the sentence frame *I like mud because...* or *I don't like mud because....* Have them use their personal experiences with getting muddy to explain their answers.

Small Group Time

DAY 4 Break into small groups to read the Get Set, Roll! Reader before the comprehension lesson.

Teacher-Led

SI Strategic Intervention	**OL** On-Level	**A** Advanced
Teacher-Led Page DI•55	**Teacher-Led** Page DI•59	**Teacher-Led** Page DI•62
• Phonemic Awareness and Phonics	• Review Phonics and High-Frequency Words	• **Read** Get Set, Roll! Reader 34 or **Reread** Kindergarten Student Reader K.6.4
• **Read** Get Set, Roll! Reader 34	• **Read** Get Set, Roll! Reader 34	

ELL Place English language learners in the groups that correspond to their reading abilities in English.

Practice Stations	**Independent Activities**
• Visit the Let's Write Station	• Read independently
• Visit the Read for Meaning Station	• Audio Text
	• *Reader's and Writer's Notebook*

English Language Learners

Frontload Reader Take a picture walk with children to preview the reader before starting the routine.

Objectives
- ◎ Practice plot.
- • Review and practice draw conclusions.

Comprehension
↻ Plot

Practice plot

Envision It!

Have children turn to the Literary Elements picture on pp. 74–75 of *My Skills Buddy*. As you look at the pictures on the right side, remind children that what happens at the beginning, in the middle, and at the end of a story is the plot.

My Skills Buddy, pp. 74–75

Team Talk Pair children and have them take turns describing the plot in a story you have read this year, identifying the beginning, the middle, and the end.

Draw Conclusions

Review

Direct children to the Draw Conclusions picture on pp. 114–115 of *My Skills Buddy.*

After we read a story, we think about what we have read. We use what we know and what we just read to make up our minds about what happened in the story. This is called drawing conclusions. Good readers draw conclusions to help them understand what happened in the story.

- • Look at the girl in the picture. What is she holding? **(a present)**
- • Why do you think she is smiling? **(She is happy to have the present.)**
- • How did you draw that conclusion? **(I already know that people smile when they are happy. She must be happy because she has a present.)**

More practice

For more practice with draw conclusions, use *Reader's and Writer's Notebook,* p. 447.

Reader's and Writer's Notebook, p. 447

Triple Day Read!

Third Read—Trade Book
Alistair and Kip's Great Adventure!

Guide comprehension

Display *Alistair and Kip's Great Adventure!* Let's use what we know and what we read to draw conclusions about *Alistair and Kip's Great Adventure!* Reread p. 32.

- What does Alistair suggest they do tomorrow? (build an airplane)

- How do you think Kip feels about this? (He is not happy. He is scared.)

- Why do you think so? (He has very wide eyes in the picture. I know that people usually look that way when they are shocked or scared. I think he is scared about having another crazy adventure like they had today.)

Reread *Alistair and Kip's Great Adventure!* Return to p. 358. Follow the Day 4 arrow and use the Guide Comprehension notes to give children the opportunity to gain a more complete understanding of the story.

DAY **2**
Read for enjoyment

DAY **3**
Reread using Develop Vocabulary notes

DAY **4**
Reread using Guide Comprehension notes

Differentiated Instruction

SI Strategic Intervention

Practice Draw Conclusions
If children struggle with drawing a conclusion about Kip's reaction, provide a simple classroom example. Pretend to "accidentally" drop a book on the floor and then act as though you are startled. Connect your reaction to Kip's reaction.

Academic Vocabulary

draw conclusions arrive at decisions or opinions after thinking about facts and details and using prior knowledge

ELL

English Language Learners
Professional Development
Use Prior Knowledge
According to Dr. Jim Cummins of the University of Toronto: "In reading, we construct meaning by bringing our prior knowledge of language and of the world to the text. The more we already know about the topic in the text, the more of the text we can understand. Our prior knowledge enables us to make inferences about the meaning of words and expressions that we may not have come across before."

Conventions
Questions

Review | Remind children of what they learned about questions. A question is a sentence that asks something. It begins with a capital letter and ends with a question mark. I want to know the time. I will ask a question: *What time is it?* Write the question on the board. My question begins with a capital *W* and ends with a question mark. Circle the *W* and the question mark.

Guide practice | Tell children that you are thinking of an animal and they are to ask *yes* or *no questions* in order to guess the animal. Guide children to ask broad questions, such as: *Does the animal have four legs? Does the animal live on land? Does the animal have fur?*

Write children's questions on the board. Write some of the questions without proper capitalization or end punctuation and have children correct your mistakes. Answer questions and continue until children guess the animal.

On their own | Use *Reader's and Writer's Notebook,* p. 448, for more practice with questions.

Daily Fix-It | Use the Daily Fix-It for more conventions practice.

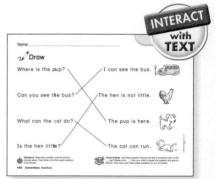

Reader's and Writer's Notebook, p. 448

Writing
Extend the Concept: Text to Self

Discuss our imaginations

We just read a story about friends that use their imagination to have an adventure on a boat. Like Alistair and Kip, you and your friends have great imaginations too.

Ask children to think about things they like to pretend with their friends. Talk about their most creative or their favorite make-believe adventures.

Guide practice

Use children's contributions to the discussion to write sentences.

> **Alissa goes to the moon.**
>
> **Raul is a racecar driver.**
>
> **Jada fixes sick pets.**
>
> **Amar swims in the ocean.**

Encourage each child to contribute a sentence. Have children read the sentences with you.

Independent writing

Have children copy and illustrate a sentence about make-believe adventures from the board. Encourage children to act out their sentences when appropriate.

Daily Handwriting

Write *Uma* and *sun* on the board. Review correct letter formation of uppercase *U* and lowercase *u*.

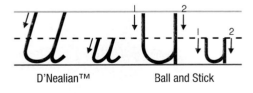

D'Nealian™   Ball and Stick

Have children write *Uma* and *sun* on their Write-On Boards. Remind them to use proper left-to-right and top-to-bottom progression and proper spacing between letters when writing *U* and *u*.

Differentiated Instruction

SI Strategic Intervention

Support Writing Remind children to begin sentences with an uppercase letter and end them with a period or question mark.

Daily Fix-It

put the bug in the box
Put the bug in the box.

This week's practice sentences appear on Teacher Resources DVD-ROM.

Vocabulary
Location Words

Teach

Write the words *hospital, bank, grocery store,* and *laundromat* on the board. Point to each word as you read it. These words tell about locations, or places where things can be found. Have children turn to p. 88 of *My Skills Buddy*. Point to the picture of the hospital. Which location is this? Repeat for the other three pictures. Then use the last three Vocabulary bullets on the page to guide a discussion about locations.

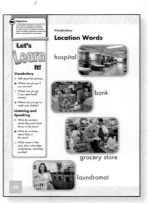

My Skills Buddy, p. 88

Team Talk Pair children and have them take turns using the location words *hospital, bank, grocery store,* and *laundromat* in sentences.

Wrap Up Your Day

✔ **Oral Language** Sing "Let's Go Have an Adventure" with me. Clap when you hear an Amazing Word—*gathered, distant, drifting, voyage, island, aboard*.

✔ **Phonemic Awareness** I am going to read a sentence. Clap when you hear /e/ words: *Do not get dressed in bed or on a sled*.

✔ **Homework Idea** Have children write a question they would like to ask Alistair or Kip.

Preview

DAY 5

Tell children that tomorrow they will review some of the books and stories they have read this week.

Extend Your Day!

Social Studies
Where Am I?

Materials: chart paper or Graphic Organizer 4, writing and drawing tools

Play a Guessing Game Tell children you will describe what is done in different places and they are to guess the location. Provide clues about what is done in a hospital, bank, grocery store, and laundromat.

Conduct a Survey Create a T-chart or use Graphic Organizer 4. Under *Location,* write the names of the places you described in the game. Survey children to find out how many have visited each place in the past. Complete the survey, and then count the tally marks next to each location and write this number on the chart.

Location	Children
hospital	|| = 2
bank	ЖН | = 6
grocery store	ЖН ЖН = 10
laundromat	ЖН || = 7

Tell About Locations Have children tell about the information in the chart. Then have them draw and label a picture of themselves in one of the locations they have visited.

Phonemic Awareness
Vowel Sort

Materials: short vowel Picture Cards, index cards

Distinguish Short Vowel Sounds Write *a, e, i, o,* and *u* on index cards. Place the index cards in a row on the table. Select the short vowel Picture Cards and place them in a stack on the table. Have children sort the Picture Cards by placing each one under the appropriate letter for its vowel sound.

Comprehension
Create a Plot

Materials: paper, writing and coloring tools, Big Book *One Little Mouse,* Trade Books *Mayday! Mayday!* and *The Little Engine That Could*

Illustrate a Plot Help children recall the plots of recently read stories. Remind them that stories have a beginning, a middle, and an end. Arrange children in groups of three. Have one child in each group tell what happens at the beginning of a selected story. The second and third children tell what happens in the middle and at the end. Ask each child to draw and label a picture of his or her part of the story.

Objectives
- Review the concepts.
- Build oral vocabulary.

Today at a Glance

Oral Vocabulary
gathered, distant, drifting, voyage, island, aboard

Phonemic Awareness
◉ Initial and Medial /u/

Phonics
◉ /u/ Spelled *Uu*

Comprehension
◉ Plot

Conventions
Questions

Writing
This Week We…

Check Oral Vocabulary
! SUCCESS PREDICTOR

TRUCKTOWN on Reading Street

Start your engines!

- Display "Rub-a-Dub-Dub" and lead the group in saying the rhyme a few times.
- Have half the group recite the rhyme while the other half acts it out.
- Then have the groups change roles.

Truckery Rhymes

Concept Wrap Up

Question of the Week

 What can friends build together?

Listen for Amazing Words

Write the question of the week on the board. Track the print as you read it to children. Have them use the Amazing Words in their responses (*gathered, distant, drifting, voyage, island, aboard*) and answer in complete sentences. Display Sing with Me Chart 34B. Let's sing "Let's Go Have an Adventure." I want you to listen for the Amazing Words we learned this week. Remind children that the words *gathered, distant, drifting, voyage, island,* and *aboard* are in the song. Sing the song several times to the tune of "Take Me Out to the Ball Game." Have children pretend to saw wood each time they hear an Amazing Word. Then discuss whether the friends in the song had a real or a make-believe adventure at sea.

 Sing with Me Audio

Let's Go Have an Adventure

Let's go have an adventure,
A voyage out to sea.
I've gathered together everything.
It's all aboard, so what else should we bring?
Oh, look a tropical island,
A distant coconut tree.
There'll be sun, waves, and lots of fun
Drifting on the open sea!

Talk with Me/Sing with Me Chart 34B

ELL Check Concepts and Language Use the Day 5 instruction on ELL Poster 34 to monitor children's understanding of the lesson concept.

ELL Poster 34

Oral Vocabulary
Amazing Words

Amazing Words

gathered   distant
drifting   voyage
island   aboard

Review | **Let's Talk** Display Talk with Me Chart 34A. We learned six new Amazing Words this week. Let's say the Amazing Words as I point to the pictures on the chart. Point to each picture and give children the chance to say the appropriate Amazing Word before offering it.

Have children supply the appropriate Amazing Word.

I see an _____ in the middle of the sea. (island)

The scientist takes a long _____ to get to Antarctica. (voyage)

The girl _____ her toys together. (gathered)

The bird is _____ in the wind. (drifting)

The children race to a _____ tree. (distant)

Everyone gets _____ the ship at the same time. (aboard)

Talk with Me/Sing with Me Chart 34A

It's Friday

MONITOR PROGRESS   Check Oral Vocabulary

Demonstrate Word Knowledge Monitor the Amazing Words by asking the following questions. Have children use the Amazing Word in their answer.

- **What is it called when people get on a train?** (aboard)
- **What can you call something that is far away?** (distant)
- **What piece of land has water on all sides?** (island)
- **What is another word for floating on air or water?** (drifting)
- **What trip takes place on water?** (voyage)
- **What verb tells about things grouped in one place?** (gathered)

If... children have difficulty using the Amazing Words,

then... reteach the words using the Oral Vocabulary Routine on the Routines Flip Chart.

Day 1	Day 2	Day 3	Day 4	Day 5
Check Phonemic Awareness	Check Sound-Spelling/ Retelling	Check Word Reading	Check Phonemic Awareness	Check Oral Vocabulary

Success Predictor

Differentiated Instruction

A **Advanced**

Amazing Words Have children make up a short story that uses all of the Amazing Words.

Objectives
◎ Review initial and medial /u/.
◎ Review /u/ spelled *Uu*.

Phonemic Awareness Review
/u/

Isolate initial and medial /u/

Display the *umbrella* Picture Card. What is the beginning sound in *umbrella*? Say the word with me: /u/ /u/ /u/, *umbrella*. Continue to review initial /u/ with the following words: *up, us, umpire, under.*

Display the *duck* Picture Card. What is the middle sound in *duck*? Say it again: *duck.* The middle sound in *duck* is /u/. Continue to review medial /u/ with the words *truck, cup, mug,* and *Gus.*

Picture Card

Discriminate medial /u/, /e/, and /a/

Give each child cards with an umbrella, egg, and apple drawn on them, or make photocopies of the *umbrella, egg,* and *apple* Picture Cards. I am going to read some words. When you hear /u/ in a word, hold up the *umbrella* card. When you hear /e/ in a word, hold up the *egg* card. When you hear /a/ in a word, hold up the *apple* card. Read the following words; hold up a card to model the first word for children: *ant, bug, bed, cat, hen, Gus, duck, ten, sand, smell, rust, pup.*

Picture Card

eReaders

Phonics Review
/u/ Spelled *Uu*

Teach /u/Uu

Display the *Uu* Alphabet Card. This is an *umbrella*. What sound do you hear at the beginning of *umbrella*? What letter spells that sound?

High-frequency words

Write the word *for* on the board. This is the word *for*. What is this word? Repeat the routine with *my, of, we,* and *yellow.*

Apply phonics to familiar text

Have children reread one of the books specific to the target letter sounds. You may wish to review the decodable words and high-frequency words that appear in each book prior to rereading.

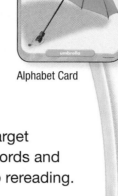

Alphabet Card

Decodable Reader 34
My Skills Buddy, p. 78

Kindergarten Student
Reader K.6.4

Get Set, Roll!
Reader 34

Differentiated Instruction

SI Strategic Intervention

Support Handwriting Have children use Decodable Reader 34, Kindergarten Student Reader K.6.4, or Get Set, Roll! Reader 34 to find a word with initial or medial /u/. Have them copy the word on a sheet of paper or on their Write-On Boards. Then have children read the word.

Small Group Time

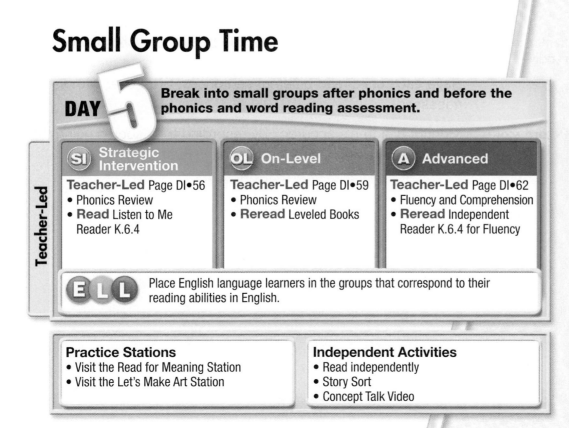

DAY 5

Break into small groups after phonics and before the phonics and word reading assessment.

Teacher-Led

SI Strategic Intervention

Teacher-Led Page DI•56
• Phonics Review
• **Read** Listen to Me Reader K.6.4

OL On-Level

Teacher-Led Page DI•59
• Phonics Review
• **Reread** Leveled Books

A Advanced

Teacher-Led Page DI•62
• Fluency and Comprehension
• **Reread** Independent Reader K.6.4 for Fluency

ELL Place English language learners in the groups that correspond to their reading abilities in English.

Practice Stations
• Visit the Read for Meaning Station
• Visit the Let's Make Art Station

Independent Activities
• Read independently
• Story Sort
• Concept Talk Video

Assess
⊚ Read words with /u/.
• Read high-frequency words.
• Read sentences.

Assessment
Monitor Progress

/u/ Spelled Uu

Whole Class Provide each child with a sheet of paper folded to make twelve boxes (four rows across and three rows down). Say the word *drum*. Tell children to listen carefully and write the letters in the word in the top row of boxes. Repeat with the words *bugs* and *just*.

MONITOR PROGRESS   **Check Word and Sentence Reading**

If... children cannot complete the whole-class assessment,
then... use the Reteach lesson in *First Stop*.

If... you are unsure of a child's grasp of this week's skills,
then... use the assessment below to obtain a clearer evaluation of the child's progress.

/u/ Spelled Uu and high-frequency words

One-on-One To facilitate individual progress monitoring, assess some children on Day 4 and the rest on Day 5. While individual children are being assessed, the rest of the class can reread this week's books and look for words with /u/.

Word reading

Use the word lists on reproducible p. 397 to assess each child's ability to read with /u/. We're going to read some words. I'll read the first word, and you read the rest. The first word is *bump*, /b/ /u/ /m/ /p/. For each child, record any decoding problems.

Sentence reading

Use the sentences on reproducible p. 397 to assess each child's ability to read words in sentences. Have each child read two sentences aloud. Have each child read different sentences. Start over with sentence one if necessary.

Record scores

Monitor children's accuracy by recording their scores using the Word and Sentence Reading Chart for this unit in *First Stop*.

Name _____

Read the Words

bump	☐	said	☐
sun	☐	drum	☐
look	☐	must	☐
hut	☐	club	☐
rug	☐	with	☐
green	☐	bun	☐

Read the Sentences

1. Nat must go to the club.

2. They sat on the rug with Bud.

3. "I did not bump the hut," said Bill.

4. Go and have fun in the sun.

5. She just got a bib for Gus.

Note to Teacher: Children read each word. Children read two sentences.

Scoring for Read the Words: Score 1 point for each correct word.

Short *u* (*bump, sun, hut, rug, drum, must, club, bun*) _____ / __7__

High-Frequency Words (*look, green, said, with*) _____ / __5__

MONITOR PROGRESS
- Review short *u*
- Review high-frequency words

Objectives
- Recognize signs.
- Identify what signs mean.
- Discuss the purpose for signs.

My Skills Buddy, pp. 90–91

Let's Practice It!
Signs

Teach

Today you will listen to a story about a woman's trip to the library. She uses traffic signs to help her drive through town. **Review the features of signs with children.**

- Signs have letters, words, or pictures.
- People use signs to get information.
- Signs help people be good citizens.

Have children turn to pp. 90–91 of *My Skills Buddy.* I am going to read a story about a woman driving through town. Look at the pictures. Trace the woman's route through the picture as I read. Why might it be important to listen to this story? (to learn about signs) Read the text of "Going to the Library." As you read, direct children to look at the appropriate part of the picture and to follow the woman's route.

Guide practice

Discuss the features of signs with children and the bulleted text on p. 90 of *My Skills Buddy.*

- Signs have letters, words, or pictures. Look at the red sign. What word is written on it? **(stop)**
- People use signs to get information. What information does Taneesha get from the speed limit sign? **(It tells her how fast she is allowed to go on this street.)**
- Signs help people be good citizens. When Taneesha sees the sign for the school crossing, she slows down. How is this being a good citizen? **(She is being safe by driving slowly around children. This keeps the kids safe.)**

Read Aloud

Going to the Library

Taneesha is driving to the library. As you listen to the directions, trace Taneesha's route with your finger. Watch out for signs along the way. At the first corner, with the traffic light, Taneesha will turn left. *Can she turn right here? How do you know?* Next, Taneesha will drive up the street past the gas station and the grocery store. *How fast can she go on this street? What tells you that?* Then Taneesha will stop at the next corner and then turn right. *Why does she stop before she turns?* As Taneesha drives down the street, she will pass a school. *How does she know there is a school? What should she do?* Next, Taneesha will cross the railroad tracks. *What tells her about the railroad tracks? Why does she need to know about them?* Finally, Taneesha will see the library. It is a yellow building with a drop box for books.

Objectives
◎ Review plot.

Assess
◉ Identify plot.

Comprehension Assessment
Monitor Progress

Review | **Plot** Things happen at the beginning, in the middle, and at the end of a story. These events are the plot of the story. Good readers notice what happens at the beginning, in the middle, and at the end of a story because it helps them understand the story.

Read "Night in the Country" | Today we will read a story about nighttime in the country. As I read, listen to the details in the story that help you understand what the story is all about. When I finish, I will ask you to tell me what happened at the beginning, in the middle, and at the end of the story. Read "Night in the Country" on p. 81 of the *Read Aloud Anthology*.

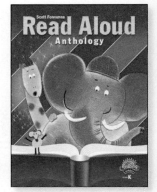

Read Aloud Anthology

Check plot | After you read, ask children to outline the plot of the story.

- What happens at the beginning of the story? (We find out what people and animals do at night in the country.)

- What happens in the middle of the story? (We hear the sounds of the animals at night in the country.)

- What happens at the end of the story? (We hear the birds waking the people up to tell that night is over, and the animals go to sleep.)

Corrective feedback | **If...** a child cannot identify the plot,
then... reteach plot using the Reteach lesson in *First Stop*.

Assess plot | Use the blackline master on p. 401. Make one copy for each child. Have children cut out the pictures and glue them onto another sheet of paper in the correct story order to show the plot.

Name _____

Plot

Show the beginning, middle, and end of "Night in the Country."

Note to Teacher: Have children cut out the boxes and glue them onto another sheet of paper in the correct story order.

Reproducible Page. See also Assessment Handbook. © Pearson Education, Inc.

Objectives
- Review questions.
- Write a song.

Conventions
Questions

Review Remind children of what they learned about questions. A question is a sentence that asks something. A question begins with a capital letter and ends with a question mark. Write *What do you want to do?* on the board. Read the question aloud. What is this question asking? I am asking a friend what she wants to do. I begin my question with a capital letter and end it with a question mark.

Model Display the cover of *Alistair and Kip's Great Adventure!* Who do you see on the cover of this book? I see Alistair and Kip on top of a big wave. I see the whale under the wave.

Guide practice Display the covers of several recently read books. Have children ask each other questions about the illustrations on the covers of the books. Write at least one question for each book on the board.

On their own Ask children to copy a question from the board and draw a picture to answer it. Remind them to begin their question with a capital letter and end it with a question mark.

Daily Fix-It Use the Daily Fix-It for more conventions practice.

Writing
This Week We...

Review Display *Alistair and Kip's Great Adventure!,* Sing with Me Chart 34B, Phonics Songs and Rhymes Chart 34, Decodable Reader 34 from *My Skills Buddy,* Kindergarten Student Reader K.6.4, and Get Set, Roll! Reader 34. This week we learned about things that friends build together. We read new books, and we sang new songs. Which book or song was your favorite?

Team Talk Pair children and have them take turns telling which book or song was their favorite and why.

Model writing a song Teach children this song to the tune of "Skip to My Lou."

> **Build, build, what can we build?**
> **Build, build, what can we build?**
> **Build, build, what can we build?**
> **What can we build together?**

Guide practice I am going to write a verse about what Alistair and Kip built. Write the new verse on the board and sing it with the children.

> **Boat, boat, they built a boat.**
> **Boat, boat, they built a boat.**
> **Boat, boat, they built a boat.**
> **Alistair and Kip built a boat.**

Help children write more verses about the story.

On their own Have children illustrate one line from a verse and label it with the line. Gather the illustrations for a class book.

Daily Handwriting

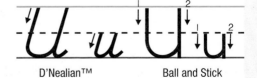

D'Nealian™   Ball and Stick

Write *Uri* and *pup* on the board. Review correct letter formation of uppercase *U* and lowercase *u.*

Have children write *Uri* and *pup* on their Write-On Boards. Remind them to use proper left-to-right and top-to-bottom progression and proper spacing between letters.

Differentiated Instruction

SI Strategic Intervention

Support Writing Remind children that a song should have rhythm. As they suggest words for a new verse, help them establish a rhythm by clapping to the beat. If children need additional help feeling the rhythm, have them march to the beat.

Daily Fix-It

Can sam fix the box
Can <u>S</u>am fix the box<u>?</u>

This week's practice sentences appear on Teacher Resources DVD-ROM.

 ELL

English Language Learners

Poster Preview Prepare children for next week by using Week 5 ELL Poster number 35. Read the Poster Talk-Through to introduce the concept and vocabulary. Ask children to identify and describe objects and actions in the art.

Objectives
- Review weekly concept.
- Review plot.

Wrap Up Your Week!

 Question of the Week

What can friends build together?

Illustrate plot

This week we talked about things that friends build and make together.

- Make a story map like the one shown and fill it with children's responses about the story "Night in the Country."
- Have children draw their favorite event from the story map.
- Have children write or dictate a phrase or sentence about their pictures.
- Help children arrange the pictures to show the order of story events.

Story Map: "Night in the Country"
Characters
Setting
Beginning
Middle
End

Amazing Words

You've learned
| 0 | 0 | 6 |
words this week!

You've learned
| 2 | 0 | 4 |
words this year!

Next Week's Question

Who helps to build a house?

Discuss next week's question. Guide children in making connections between make-believe building and real building.

Preview **NEXT WEEK**

Tell children that next week they will read about a boy named Tony who moves into a new house.

Extend Your Day!

Science
Whale of a Tale

Materials: map of the United States, large mural paper cut into the shape of a whale, paint

Discuss Whales Remind children that one of the main characters in *Alistair and Kip's Great Adventure!* was a whale. A whale called the blue whale is the largest animal that has ever lived on Earth. It is larger than elephants, and it is even larger than any dinosaur that ever lived! It is about as long as two school buses. The blue whale is also the loudest animal on Earth. It makes a very loud whistling sound. **Display a U.S. map and point to the Gulf of Mexico.**

If a whale whistled in the Gulf of Mexico near Florida, you might hear it all the way in Texas!

Make a Mural Review different events in *Alistair and Kip's Great Adventure!* with children. Assign small groups of children key events from the story. Then display a large sheet of mural paper in the shape of a whale. Have children put themselves in order from the first story event at the whale's tail to the last story event at the whale's head. Then ask them to paint their scene on the whale's body. Display the completed mural in the classroom.

Math
Nuts and Bolts

Materials: 8 long bolts, 8 matching nuts, 3 small bags, paper sorting mat with 8 squares

Building Background Knowledge We learned about a lot of tools used to build. Explain that nuts and bolts are also common building materials.

More or Fewer? Give 3 groups of children a bag with differing numbers of nuts and bolts to share. Each group should lay the nuts and bolts side by side in the squares on the mat. The group should compare the number of each item and give a comparison statement.

Comprehension
Sequence

Materials: Trade Book *Alistair and Kip's Great Adventure!*

Dramatize the story Walk through the illustrations in *Alistair and Kip's Great Adventure!* Have children describe what the characters are doing. Then ask small groups of children to dramatize these activities. For example, for pp. 6–7, have children pretend to gather materials and use them to build a boat. Continue the drama activity with pp. 8–9, 10–11, 14–15, 20–21, 24–25, and 32. Encourage children to think about how Alistair (a cat) and Kip (a dog) might move and talk.

Weekly Assessment

Use the whole-class assessment on pages 396–397 and 400–401 in this Teacher's Edition to check:

✓ ⊚ **Short** *u* **Spelled** *Uu*

✓ ⊚ **Comprehension Skill** *Plot*

✓ **High-Frequency Words**

Teacher's Edition, Day 5

Managing Assessment

Use the Assessment Handbook for:

✓ **Observation Checklists**

✓ **Record-Keeping Forms**

✓ **Portfolio Assessment**

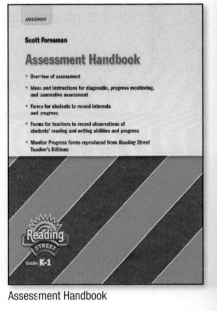

Assessment Handbook

Teacher Notes

Small Group Time

Pacing Small Group Instruction

5 Day Plan

DAY 1
• Phonemic Awareness/ Phonics
• Decodable Story 34

DAY 2
• Phonemic Awareness/ Phonics
• Decodable Reader 34

DAY 3
• Phonemic Awareness/ Phonics
• Concept Literacy Reader K.6.4 or Kindergarten Student Reader K.6.4

DAY 4
• Phonemic Awareness/ Phonics
• Get Set, Roll! Reader 34

DAY 5
• Phonics Review
• Listen to Me Reader K.6.4

3 or 4 Day Plan

DAY 1
• Phonemic Awareness/ Phonics
• Decodable Story 34

DAY 2
• Phonemic Awareness/ Phonics
• Decodable Reader 34

DAY 3
• Phonemic Awareness/ Phonics
• Concept Literacy Reader K.6.4 or Kindergarten Student Reader K.6.4

DAY 4
• Phonemic Awareness/ Phonics
• Get Set, Roll! Reader 34

3 Day Plan: Eliminate the shaded box.

 **Strategic Intervention** **DAY 1**

Phonemic Awareness•Phonics

■ **Isolate /u/** Display the *jug* Picture Card. This is a jug. Jug has /u/ in the middle. Say it with me: /j/ /u/ /g/, jug. Repeat with *bug* and *rug*.

■ **Connect /u/ to *Uu*** I am going to say three words. I want you to tell me which word has /u/. Listen carefully: *mug, pan, dish.* Which word has /u/? *Mug* has /u/. *Pan* and *dish* do not have /u/. Write the letters *Uu* on the board. The letter *u* can stand for /u/ in words. Continue discriminating /u/ with the following sets of words: *sun, trap, pet; stop, step, run; sink, tub, sip.*

Decodable Story 34

■ **Review** Review the previously taught high-frequency words by writing each word on the board and having children read the word with you.

the	with	was	a	go

If... children have difficulty reading the words,
then... say a word and have children point to the word. Repeat several times, giving assistance as needed.

■ **Read** Have children read *Gus and the Bug* orally. Then have them reread the story several times individually.

Reader's and Writer's Notebook, pp. 439–440

Objectives
• Identify the common sounds that letters represent.
• Read at least 25 high-frequency words from a commonly used list.

Go Digital! eReaders

SI *Strategic Intervention*

DAY 2

Phonemic Awareness•Phonics

■ **Discriminate /u/** Display Phonics Songs and Rhymes Chart 34. Sing the song "Oh, Where, Oh, Where Can the Dog-Walker Stop?" to the tune of "Oh, Where, Oh, Where Has My Little Dog Gone?" with children. Ask them to jump when they hear /u/ words.

■ **Recognize *Uu*** Ask children to name words that begin with /u/*Uu*. List the words on the board as they say them. Have children echo read the list of words. Then ask children to take turns circling *u* in the words on the board.

Decodable Reader 34

■ **Review** Review the high-frequency words by writing *is* on the board. This is the word *is*. What word is this? Continue with the following words: *for, I, we, my, the, with, a, of, what.*

> **If...** children have difficulty reading the words,
> **then...** say a word and have children point to the word. Repeat several times, giving assistance as needed.

■ **Read** Display the cover of *Fun with Spot* on p. 78 of *My Skills Buddy*. Ask a volunteer to read the first page of the story. Have children tell what Spot can do. Continue through the story in this manner.

My Skills Buddy

More Reading
Use Leveled Readers or other text at children's instructional level.

Small **Group Time**

Phonemic Awareness•Phonics

■ **Isolate /u/** Display the *bus* Picture Card. This is a *bus.* Do you hear /u/? Say it with me: /b/ /u/ /s/, *bus. Bus* has /u/ in the middle. Repeat with *bug* and *fun.*

■ **Connect /u/ to Uu** Display the *cup* Picture Card. This is a *cup. Cup* has /u/ in the middle. Write the letters *Uu* on the board. The letter *u* can stand for /u/ in words. Say it with me: /k/ /u/ /p/, *cup.* When you hear a word that has /u/, I want you to pretend to drink something from a cup. Use the following words: *cut, sun, bat, mud, tag, tub.*

■ **Blend Sounds** Write *fun* on the board. Have children blend the sound of each letter to read the word. Repeat the routine with the words *sun, mud,* and *us.*

■ **Review High-Frequency Words** Write *for* on the board. Have volunteers say the word and use it in a sentence. Continue with the word *my, of, we,* and *yellow.*

■ To practice phonics and high-frequency words, have children read Kindergarten Student Reader K.6.4. Use the instruction on pp. 354–355.

For a complete lesson plan and additional practice, see the **Leveled Reader Teaching Guide**.

Concept Literacy Reader K.6.4

■ **Preview and Predict** Display the cover of the Concept Literacy Reader K.6.4. Point to the title of the book. The title of the book is *What Can We Make Together?* What do you think the book is about? Have children tell about the picture and what they think the book might be about.

■ **Set a Purpose** We talked about the title of the book. Let's read the book to learn about things we can make with friends. Have children read the Concept Literacy Reader.

■ **Read** Provide corrective feedback as children read the book orally. During reading, ask them if they are able to confirm any of the predictions they made prior to reading.

If... children have difficulty reading the book individually,

then... read a sentence aloud as children point to each word. Then have the group reread the sentences as they continue pointing to the words.

■ **Retell** Have children retell the content as you page through the book. Help them identify what the book is about. Also call attention to what materials the friends use to make things.

Concept Literacy Reader K.6.4

Objectives
• Identify the common sounds that letters represent.
• Predict what might happen next based on the title.
• Retell important facts in a text, heard or read.

SI *Strategic Intervention*

DAY **4**

Phonemic Awareness•Phonics

■ **Segmenting** Say *gum.* I hear three sounds in *gum,* /g/ /u/ /m/. How many sounds do you hear in *cup?* What are they? (three, /k/ /u/ /p/) Continue with *mud, fun, plum, cub,* and *junk.*

■ **Make Letter Cards** Give each child two index cards. Have children write the letter *Uu* on one of the index card and draw objects or animals with /u/ on the remaining index card. Have children show their cards, name the letters and pictures, and place them in a pocket chart. When finished, review all the words.

Get Set, Roll! Reader 34

■ **Review** Review the following high-frequency words with children prior to reading the story: *is, look, the, go, what, a, he, see, have.*

■ **Read** Display Get Set, Roll! Reader 34, *Mud Fun.* Today we will read a new story about a muddy puddle. Point to the title of the story. The title of the story is *Mud Fun.* Look at the cover and think about the title. What do you think this story will be about? Can you have fun in a muddy puddle?

> **If...** children have difficulty reading the story individually, **then...** read a sentence aloud as children point to each word. Then have the group reread the sentences as they continue pointing to the words.

Get Set, Roll! Reader 34

■ **Reread** Use echo reading of Get Set, Roll! Reader 34 to model fluent reading. Use your oral reading to model for children where to pause, when to change pitch, and which words to stress. Then have children reread orally three to four times, or until they can read with few or no mistakes.

More Reading

Use Leveled Readers or other text at children's instructional level.

Objectives
- Identify the common sounds that letters represent.
- Read at least 25 high-frequency words from a commonly used list.
- Predict what might happen next based on the cover.

Small Group Time

More Reading

Use Leveled Readers or other text at children's instructional level.

Phonics Review

■ **Seek and Say** Write the letters *Aa, Ee, Ii, Oo,* and *Uu* on index cards so that you have one per child. Distribute the cards and review the sounds children have learned for the letters. Hold up each card as you say its sound. These are the sounds we learned for these letters: /a/ for *Aa*, /e/ for *Ee*, /i/ for *Ii*, /o/ for *Oo*, and /u/ for *Uu*. Have children look around the room for an object with their sound. For example, a child with the *Aa* card may find a *bat* or a *hat*. When all of the children have identified objects for their sounds, have them say the sound and name the item.

Listen to Me Reader K.6.4

■ **Preview and Predict** Display the cover of the book. The title of this story is *We Get Up!* It is written by Marilyn Fenlon. It is illustrated by Erin Eitter Kono. What do you think the man doing? What time of day is it? Tell me what you think this story will be about.

Listen to Me Reader K.6.4

■ **Teach Rebus Words** Write the word *newspaper* on the board. This is the word *newspaper.* Say the letters with me: *n, e, w, s, p, a, p, e, r, newspaper.* A newspaper tells a reader information. Most newspapers are printed everyday. There are pictures and comics in newspapers too. This word *newspaper* is in the story we will read today. There will be a picture above the word to help us read it.

■ **Set a Purpose** Review children's ideas. Point out that after they read, they will know more about people who work at night. Tell children that you will read the story with them. Follow along with your finger as I read. Then we will take turns reading this page. Repeat this routine through all of the pages. Guide children to decode words.

■ **Reread for Fluency** Use echo reading of Listen to Me Reader K.6.4 to model reading fluently. Use your oral reading to model for children when to pause, when to change pitch, and which words to stress. Then have children reread orally three to four times, or until they can read with few or no mistakes.

Objectives
• Identify the common sounds that letters represent.
• Predict what might happen next based on the cover.

OL On-Level **DAY 1**

Phonemic Awareness•Phonics

■ **Isolate /u/** Display the *drum* Picture Card. *This is a drum. Drum has /u/. Say it with me: /dr/ /u/ /m/, drum. Repeat with* jug *and* bus.

■ **Connect /u/ to Uu** Display the *tub* Picture Card. *This is a tub. Tub has /u/ in the middle. Say it with me: /t/ /u/ /b/, tub. What letter stands for /u/?* Write *Uu* on the board. *The letter u can stand for /u/ in words. When I say a word that has /u/, I want you to pretend to wash your hair like you are in a bathtub.* Use the following words: *nut, pup, big, vet, mud, fox, up.*

Objectives
• Identify the common sounds that letters represent.

Pacing Small Group Instruction 20–30 mins.

5 Day Plan	
DAY 1	• Phonemic Awareness/ Phonics • Decodable Story 34
DAY 2	• Phonemic Awareness/ Phonics • High-Frequency Words • Decodable Reader 34
DAY 3	• Phonemic Awareness/ Phonics • Kindergarten Student Reader K.6.4
DAY 4	• Get Set, Roll! Reader 34
DAY 5	• Phonics Review

OL On-Level **DAY 2**

Phonemic Awareness•Phonics

■ **Listen for /u/** Tell children you will tell them a story and they should listen for /u/. When you say a word with /u/, children should put their hands on their feet, walk like a duck, and repeat the word. Tell a simple story, emphasizing /u/ words and pausing to give children a chance to walk like a duck and repeat the word. *Gus sees the bus. Gus runs to the bus. Wait, bus! Gus jumps onto the bus, but—uh-oh—the bus is stuck! It is stuck in the mud! Get the truck! The truck tugs the bus from the mud! Good job, truck!* Write several of the story sentences on the board. Circle the *u*'s. *A sound we have learned for Uu is /u/.*

■ **High-Frequency Words** Display the following word cards: *for, my, of, we, yellow.* Say the word *for* and select a child to point to the word. Have children say the word and use it in a sentence. Continue with the other words.

Objectives
• Identify the common sounds that letters represent.
• Read at least 25 high-frequency words from a commonly used list.

3 or 4 Day Plan	
DAY 1	• Phonemic Awareness/ Phonics • Decodable Story 34
DAY 2	• Phonemic Awareness/ Phonics • High-Frequency Words • Decodable Reader 34
DAY 3	• Phonemic Awareness/ Phonics • Kindergarten Student Reader K.6.4
DAY 4	• Get Set, Roll! Reader 34

3 Day Plan: Eliminate the shaded box.

More Practice

For additional practice with this week's phonics skills, have children reread the Decodable Story (Day 1) and the Decodable Reader (Day 2).

Small Group Time

OL On-Level   DAY **3**

Phonemic Awareness•Phonics

■ **Discriminate /u/** Draw six rugs on the board. Collect twelve Picture Cards, including the following: *tub, up, umbrella, jug, drum, bus.* Mix the cards and display them one at a time. Have a child name the picture. If the name has /u/, have the child write lowercase *u* in one of the rugs.

■ **Recognize *Uu*** Write uppercase and lowercase *Uu* on the board. Name the letter as you write it several times. The sound we learned for *Uu* is /u/. Then give each child two chenille sticks, one larger than the other, to form into the shape of uppercase and lowercase *Uu.*

Kindergarten Student Reader K.6.4

■ **Preview and Predict** Display the cover of the book. The title of this story is *Max and Jen: A Busy Day.* What do you think this story will be about?

■ **Review Rebus Words** Write the word *raccoon* on the board. This is the word *raccoon.* Name the letters with me: r, a, c, c, o, o, n, *raccoon.* A raccoon is an animal with stripes on its tail. Repeat with the words *owls* and *baker.* The words *raccoon, owls,* and *baker* are in the story we will read today. There will be a picture above the word to help you read it.

Kindergarten Student Reader K.6.4

■ **Set a Purpose** Review the list of things children think might happen in the story. Remind children they will read to find out about Max and Jen's busy day.

■ **Read** Have children follow along as they read the story with you. After reading p. 2, ask children to tell when Max and Jen go to bed. Continue with each page.

- • What do raccoons do at night?
- • Why does the baker get up early?
- • What kind of job does Bud have?

■ **Summarize** Have children retell the story to a partner and tell when Max and Jen get up.

■ **Text to Self** Help children make personal connections to the story as they tell about what they do to get ready for bed.

Objectives
- • Identify the common sounds that letters represent.
- • Predict what might happen next based on the title.
- • Make connections to own experiences.

OL On-Level   DAY 4

Get Set, Roll! Reader 34

■ **Review** Review the words *have, see, he, a, what, for, go, the, look,* and *is* by writing each word on the board and saying the word with children. Then give clues to a word and have children tell which word it is.

■ **Read** Display Get Set, Roll! Reader 34, *Mud Fun.* Point to the title of the story. *Mud Fun* is the title of the story. The story is about a muddy puddle. We can read all the words in this story. Look at the cover of the story. What do you think this story is about? Let's read to find out.

Objectives
- Read at least 25 high-frequency words from a commonly used list.
- Predict what might happen next based on the cover.

More Reading
Use Leveled Readers or other text at children's instructional level to develop fluency.

OL On-Level   DAY 5

Phonics Review

■ **Make the Letter** Provide children with materials such as chenille sticks, yarn, string, uncooked spaghetti, cotton swabs, straws, craft sticks, or twigs. Tell them they will be sculpting letters. Name an object and have children sculpt the letter for the initial sound. For example, if you say *apple,* children should use the materials to make the letters *Aa.* Have children identify the initial letters of these words: *up, insect, egg, October, under.* Use these words for medial sounds: *fun, slim, bed, cat, dot.*

Objectives
- Isolate the initial sound in spoken one-syllable words.
- Identify the common sounds that letters represent.

Small Group Time

Pacing Small Group Instruction

5 Day Plan

DAY 1	• Phonemic Awareness/ Phonics • Decodable Story 34
DAY 2	• Phonics • Spelling • Decodable Reader 34
DAY 3	• Independent Reader K.6.4 or Kindergarten Student Reader K.6.4
DAY 4	• Get Set, Roll! Reader 34 or Kindergarten Student Reader K.6.4
DAY 5	• Fluency • Comprehension

3 or 4 Day Plan

DAY 1	• Phonemic Awareness/ Phonics • Decodable Story 34
DAY 2	• Phonics • Spelling • Decodable Reader 34
DAY 3	• Independent Reader K.6.4 or Kindergarten Student Reader K.6.4
DAY 4	• Get Set, Roll! Reader 34 or Kindergarten Student Reader K.6.4

3 Day Plan: Eliminate the shaded box.

More Practice

For additional practice with this week's phonics skills and to develop fluency, have children reread the Decodable Story (Day 1) and the Decodable Reader (Day 2).

A — Advanced — **DAY 1**

Phonemic Awareness•Phonics

■ **Send the Message!** Have children form a line and tell them you are going to play a game called "Send the Message!" Tell children to listen closely so that they pass the message on correctly. Think of a three-letter word, such as *tub*, and whisper the letters *t, u, b* to the first child in line. That child should then whisper the letters to the next child. Play continues until the last child hears the whispered letters and sounds out the word. Then say the word you spelled for the first child to see if any letters were changed as the message was sent. Repeat the activity with other words, such as *red, pin, hug, hop,* and *sat.*

Objectives
• Identify the common sounds that letters represent.

A — Advanced — **DAY 2**

Phonics•Spelling

■ **Identify /u/** Write the words *hop, skip,* and *jump* on the board. Ask volunteers to read the words. Then ask children to identify the word that has /u/. Underline the letter *u* in *jump.* Continue with the following sets of words: *bug, dog, cat; glass, cup, drink.*

■ **Spell Sounds** Give each child the following letter tiles: *b, d, h, l, m, p, s, t, u.* Listen to the sounds in the word *drum:* /dr/ /u/ /m/, *drum.* What are the letters for /dr/? They are *d* and *r.* Place your *d* and *r* tiles in front of you. Continue with the remaining sounds. Then have children blend the sounds to read the word. Then have children spell *bus, hut, tub,* and *plum.*

Objectives
• Identify the common sounds that letters represent.
• Use letter-sound correspondences to spell consonant-vowel-consonant (CVC) words.

A Advanced

DAY 3

For a complete lesson plan and additional practice, see the **Leveled Reader Teaching Guide**.

Independent Reader K.6.4

■ **Practice High-Frequency Words** Write the previously taught high-frequency words on the board. Have volunteers say each word and use it in a sentence.

a	I	for	said	go	we	have	you	here

■ **Activate Prior Knowledge** Remind children that a club hut is place where children can meet to play games and eat snacks. We read a book about a club hut made out of blankets and tin cans. Have you ever made a club hut? What did you use to make it? Encourage children to discuss what they know about club huts.

The Box
By Madeline Boskey
Illustrated by Jeff Hopkins

Independent
Reader K.6.4

■ **Plot** Display the cover of *The Box.* Have children tell what happens in the beginning, the middle, and the end.

■ **Reread for Fluency** After rereading with children, model reading fluently for them. I am going to read this book aloud. I will read the words with no mistakes. I want you to read it aloud with me. Try to read the words just as I do.

• Use echo reading of Independent Reader K.6.4 to model reading fluently. Use your oral reading to model for children where to pause, when to change pitch, and which words to stress. Then have children reread orally three to four times, or until they can read with few or no mistakes.

■ For more practice with phonics and high-frequency words and to develop fluency, have children read Kindergarten Student Reader K.6.4. Use the instruction on pp. 354–355.

Objectives
• Read at least 25 high-frequency words from a commonly used list.
• Identify elements of a story including key events.

More Reading
Use Leveled Readers or other text at children's instructional level.

Small Group Time

More Reading

Use Leveled Readers or other text at children's instructional level.

A Advanced **DAY 4**

Kindergarten Student Reader K.6.4

■ **Revisit Rebus Words** Write *owls* on the board. This is *owls*. Name the letters with me: *o, w, l, s, owls.* Owls are birds that are awake at night. Repeat the routine with *raccoon* and *baker*. These words are in our story today. There will be a picture above the word to help us read it.

■ **Reread** Use Kindergarten Student Reader K.6.4 to practice reading fluently.

■ **Text to World** Ask children to think about nighttime. How is the night sky different from the sky during the day?

■ **Read** Have children read Get Set, Roll! Reader 34, *Mud Fun.* Use the instruction on p. 385.

Kindergarten Student Reader K.6.4

Objectives
- Read at least 25 high-frequency words from a commonly used list.
- Make connections to the larger community.

A Advanced **DAY 5**

Fluency•Comprehension

■ **Reread for Fluency** Use the Independent Reader K.6.4 to model reading fluently for children. I am going to read this selection aloud. I will read the words with no mistakes. I want you to read it aloud with me. Try to read the words just as I do.

■ **Comprehension** After children have finished reading, have them retell what happens in the selection. Then have children write or draw a picture that shows what the children do at the end of the story.

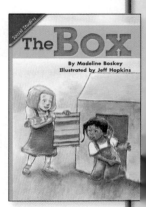

Independent Reader K.6.4

Objectives
- Read at least 25 high-frequency words from a commonly used list.
- Identify elements of a story including key events.

Concept Development

■ **Read the Concept Literacy Reader** To build background and vocabulary, read *What Can We Make Together?* pausing to discuss each page. Model sentence patterns and vocabulary that describe the objects on the page. The children make a tent. What do they use to make the tent? On a second reading, invite children to talk about the pictures on each page. Have you ever made a tent?

■ **Develop Oral Language** Revisit *What Can We Make Together?* Have children sing the following song with you to the tune of "Row, Row, Row Your Boat":

> Make, make, make a boat,
> Save a spot for me.
> Sailing, sailing, sailing, sailing,
> Across the shiny sea!

Repeat the song with other pages from the story.

Phonemic Awareness/Phonics

■ **Frontload Words with Initial and Medial /u/** Have children look at the illustration on pp. 72–73 of *My Skills Buddy.* This is a baseball field. Have you ever played baseball? Do you hit in baseball? Do you catch in baseball? Do you run in baseball? Repeat the word *run.* What sound does *run* have in the middle? *Run* has /u/ in the middle; /u/, *run.* Then use this chant to introduce picture words with /u/ in the middle:

> On the field, they have fun.
> *Fun* is filled with /u/.
> On the field, there is sun.
> *Sun* is filled with /u/.
> (Have children point to the sun.)

Make up a chant for other words in the picture that have /u/ in the middle, including *bunny, hug, bug, cut, bun,* and *cup.* Then include words that start with /u/, including *umpire, umbrella, up,* and *under.*

■ **Connect /u/ to *Uu*** Display the word *tug.* This word is *tug:* /t/ /u/ /g/, *tug.* Say the word with me. Have children write the word *tug* and circle the letter that stands for /u/. Write and read the following sentence: *Bud runs up the steps.* Point to the letter *u* in *Bud.* What letter is this? Repeat with *runs* and *up.*

Content Objective
• Develop content knowledge related to building with friends.

Language Objectives
• Understand and use grade-level content area vocabulary.

• Recognize the sounds of English.

Concept Literacy Reader K.6.4

Daily Planner

DAY 1	• Concept Development • Phonemic Awareness/ Phonics • Listening Comprehension
DAY 2	• Comprehension • Vocabulary
DAY 3	• Phonemic Awareness/ Phonics • Conventions
DAY 4	• Phonemic Awareness/ Phonics • Concepts and Oral Language
DAY 5	• Language Workshop • Writing

Support for English Language Learners

Content Objective
• Understand plot.

Language Objective
• Learn and use academic vocabulary.

My Skills Buddy, pp. 74–75

Listening Comprehension: Plot

■ **Frontload Vocabulary** Discuss the illustrations on pp. 74–75 in *My Skills Buddy* to frontload vocabulary. What characters do you see in the pictures? (a turtle, or tortoise, and a rabbit, or hare) Have you ever seen a tortoise walk? Is it fast or slow? (slow) How about a hare? (fast) Which could you catch? (I could catch a tortoise.) If the tortoise and the hare had a race, who would win? (the hare) Look at the big picture. What is the hare doing? (sleeping) The hare is sure that he will win the race. He is so sure that he's taking a nap. What is the tortoise doing? (walking) Who do you think will win the race?

■ **Provide Scaffolding** Point to the illustrations on p. 75. Explain that the plot is the main part of the story. Help children understand what is happening in each picture. In the first picture, they are having a race. In the second picture, we see the hare fall asleep. In the third picture, we see the tortoise win the race. This is the plot of this story. Support your words with gestures.

■ **Prepare for the Read Aloud** The modified Read Aloud below prepares children for listening to the oral reading "A Home for the Night" on p. 325.

A Home for the Night

Mom, Liz, and Lou hike. Late in the day, they come to an open area.

"This is a good place to camp," Mom says.

Mom, Liz, and Lou get to work. Mom cuts tree branches off. She puts them in the ground to make a tent. Liz and Lou put leaves and grass on top of the branches. This will keep out the cold and the rain.

Mom digs a hole in the ground. She calls the hole a pit. Liz puts rocks in the pit. Lou gathers wood. Mom takes the wood and puts it in the pit. It makes a nice campfire. Now they will be cozy and warm all night.

■ **First Listening** Write the title of the Read Aloud on the board. This is about Mom, Liz, and Lou building a campsite. They use different materials to make things. After reading, ask children to recall the events. What do they build first. What do they work on after that?

■ **Second Listening** Who is building a place to sleep? (Mom, Liz, and Lou) Why are they building a shelter? (to stay warm and dry) In the story, Mom, Liz, and Lou use material from the area to build a place to spend the night. That is the main part of the story. What is another name for the main part of a story? (the plot)

Objectives
• Understand the main points of spoken language ranging from situations in which contexts are familiar to unfamiliar. • Demonstrate English comprehension by employing inferential skills commensurate with content area needs.

Comprehension

- **Provide Scaffolding** Display *Alistair and Kip's Great Adventure!* Lead a detailed picture walk through the story, naming what you see in the illustrations and describing what is happening. Use gestures and facial expressions to convey meaning. Focus on the following:

  - **Set the Scene** Use the cover of the Trade Book to help children understand that this story takes place in the sea. A lot of animals live in the sea. What are some animals that live in the sea? (whales, fish, octopus, squid, sharks)

  - **Frontload Vocabulary** As you lead the picture walk, use the illustrations to introduce unfamiliar words in the text. Look at the picture on page 9. The story says, "Their *voyage* had begun." What do you think the word *voyage* means? (trip, journey) Where does this voyage begin? (in a boat in a stream) Include some of the following words from the story: *creek* (p. 10); *hurled* (p. 14); *island* (p. 19); *airplane* (p. 32).

Vocabulary: Location Words

- **Frontload Vocabulary** Have children turn to p. 88 of *My Skills Buddy.* Location words are the names of places where you can go. Talk about each picture, using the location words *hospital, bank, grocery store,* and *laundromat.* For example, point to the picture of the hospital. This is a hospital. People come here when they are sick or hurt. Sometimes, ambulances bring people to the hospital. Have children talk about the other pictures using the location words.

- **Provide Scaffolding** Write the words *hospital, bank, grocery store,* and *laundromat* on the board. Read the words aloud with children. These are places. They are called location words. Point to the answer. Where do you go to clean your clothes? (laundromat) Say a sentence using the location word and have children repeat the sentence: I clean my clothes at the *laundromat.* Repeat with the other location words.

- **Practice** Write the following sentence frames on the board: *There is food at the ____. There are clothes at the ____. There are beds at the ____. There is money at the ____.* Read each sentence aloud and have children say the word that completes it. Then write each word on the line. Now copy these words on your own paper. Watch children to make sure they are spelling the words correctly.

Content Objective
- Develop background knowledge.

Language Objective
- Learn and use location words.

Use Learning Strategies
Remind children that if they have trouble with action words, they can ask other children for help.

Trade Book

Support for English Language Learners

Content Objective
• Use learning strategies.

Language Objectives
• Connect /u/ and *Uu*.
• Use questions.

Transfer Skills

Pronouncing /u/ Speakers of Spanish may have trouble distinguishing between different vowel pronunciations in English, since each vowel has only one sound in Spanish. Help children practice the sounds of *u* by having them say word pairs such as *put, putt* and *bush, but.*

Use Learning Strategies

In *Alistair and Kip's Great Adventure!* after Alistair and Kip get their supplies together they "get to work." Explain to children that "get to work" is an expression. It does not mean that you go to your job. It means that you begin to get something done.

Phonemic Awareness/Phonics

■ **Isolate Initial and Medial /u/** Say *up,* and then model segmenting sounds by saying /u/ /p/. Emphasize the initial sound in the word. Repeat with *under* and *untie.* Help children identify the initial sound in each word. Then say *mud,* and model segmenting sounds by saying /m/ /u/ /d/. Emphasize the medial sound in the word. Repeat with *put* and *sub.* Help children identify the medial sound in each word.

■ **/u/ Spelled *Uu*** Write the words *ump, mug,* and *sub* on the board. As you read them aloud, track the sounds and letters with your fingers. Help children recognize that these words all begin with /u/ or have /u/ in the middle.

Conventions: Questions

■ **Provide Scaffolding** Direct children to p. 8 of *Alistair and Kip's Great Adventure!* Read the following sentence from the story: *Ready, Kip?* This is a question. A question asks us something. In this sentence, Alistair is asking Kip if he is ready. A question always ends with a question mark.

■ **Practice** Write the following sentences on the board: *How was the game? The game was great.* Read the sentences aloud to the class. Which sentence is a question (the first one) The first sentence asks us something. It ends in a question mark. It is a question. The second sentence tells us something. It ends with a period. It is not a question.

Leveled LS Support

Beginning/Intermediate Write the following sentence frame on the board: *What is your favorite _____?* Have children finish the question and ask another child.

Advanced/Advanced-High Have children ask each other questions about what they had for lunch. Write some of the questions on the board.

Objectives
• Internalize new academic language by using and reusing it in meaningful ways in speaking activities that build concept and language attainment. • Develop repertoire of learning strategies commensurate with grade-level learning expectations. • Decode (sound out) words using a combination of skills.

Phonemic Awareness/Phonics

■ **Review /e/** To review /e/, read the following sentence aloud:

Ed went to bed under the red blanket.

Have children repeat the sentence after you. Then have them pronounce the word with /e/ at the beginning: /e/ /d/, *Ed.* What sound does *e* make? Yes, it makes /e/. Repeat for all the words with /e/ in the middle.

■ **/e/ Spelled *Ee*** Write the letters *Ee.* What are these letters? Yes, they are uppercase *E* and lowercase *e.* Use word tiles to form these words: *bed, egg, men, step, elk, get.* Model reading each word, isolating /e/. Show all the sound-letter correspondences (for example, /b/ /e/ /d/ = *bed*).

Concepts and Oral Language

■ **Revisit Talk with Me Chart 34A** Display the chart. Have children describe the objects and ideas in the photos. Then say a sentence for each picture. After that, ask a question about each Amazing Word. *What is all around an island?* (water)

■ **Develop Oral Language** Introduce language patterns that help describe the pictures on Talk with Me Chart 34A. Describe the things or ideas in each picture with synonyms for the Amazing Words. Then replace the synonyms with the Amazing Words. The mountain is far away. It is *distant.* Have children repeat your sentences. The boat is pulling away from the shore. The boat is *drifting.* Repeat with the rest of the Amazing Words.

 Leveled LS Support

Beginning Have children point to each picture on the chart and use the Amazing Word to describe the picture.

Intermediate With your assistance, have children use the Amazing Words in a sentence unrelated to the picture on the Talk with Me Chart.

Advanced/Advanced-High Encourage children to use their prior knowledge about the Amazing Words to think of examples for each.

Content Objectives
• Develop oral language.
• Use learning strategies.

Language Objectives
• Spell consonant blends.
• Learn English language patterns.

Use Learning Strategies
Work with children to create a two-column chart. Label one column *Land* and the other column *Sea.* Say events from the story *Alistair and Kip's Great Adventure!* such as *Alistair and Kip build a boat,* and have children respond whether it takes place on land or at sea. Then write the sentence in the correct column.

Talk with Me Chart 34A

Objectives
• Use accessible language and learn new language in the process.   • Use visual support to enhance and confirm understanding of increasingly complex and elaborated spoken language.

Alistair and Kip's Great Adventure!   **DI•67**

Support for English Language Learners

Content Objectives

- Understand *Alistair and Kip's Great Adventure.*
- Understand plot.

Language Objectives

- Share your opinion through speaking and writing.
- Write using grade-level vocabulary.

Monitor and Self-Correct

Remind children that if they don't know how to say a word, they can ask the teacher for help.

Home Language Support

Invite children to share ideas in their home languages before creating their sentences.

E L L English Language Learners

Language Workshop: Share Opinions

■ **Introduce and Model** Turn to p. 13 of *Alistair and Kip's Great Adventure!* and point to the sea. Alistair and Kip have gone on an adventure. They have gone to the sea. Have you ever been to the sea? Would you like to go to the sea? If you could go on an adventure anywhere, would you go to the sea? What you think is called your *opinion.* Everyone has an opinion. Your opinion may be different from mine. That's OK. Opinions are not right or wrong. They are just our thoughts.

■ **Practice** Think about the places you want to visit to have an adventure. Do you want to go somewhere that is warm or cold? Do you want to go to a place with a lot of people or not very many? Where would you go if you could go anywhere right now? How would you get there? List answers in a T-chart with columns labeled *Place* and *Transportation.* After writing all the choices, read back the list of places children want to visit. Restate that there is no right or wrong choice.

Writing: Share Opinions

■ **Prepare for Writing** We shared our opinions about where we want to go and how we would get there. Now let's write about our opinions. Have each child fold a piece of paper in half to create two sections.

■ **Create Sentences About Opinions** Have children copy this sentence frame at the bottom of the first section: *I want to go to _____.* Have them copy this sentence frame at the bottom of the second section: *I would get there by _____.* Have children draw where they would go in the first section and how they would get there in the second section. Have them complete the sentence frames. When children finish their sentences, have them read their sentences to a partner several times.

Leveled LS Support

Beginning Provide the sentence frame in each section, and have children dictate or write words to complete the sentences.

Intermediate Guide children in writing words to complete the sentences.

Advanced/Advanced-High Encourage children to write their sentences on their own. You might also have children help less-proficient partners complete their sentences.

Objectives

- Express opinions ranging from communicating single words and short phrases to participating in extended discussions on a variety of social and grade-appropriate academic topics. • Write using a variety of grade-appropriate sentence lengths in increasingly accurate ways as more English is acquired.

The House That
Tony Lives In

This Week's ELL Overview

ELL Handbook

- Maximize Literacy and Cognitive Engagement
- Research Into Practice
- Full Weekly Support for Every Selection

  The House That Tony Lives In
  - Routines to Support Instruction

- Transfer Activities
- Professional Development

Daily Leveled ELL Notes

ELL notes appear throughout this week's instruction and ELL Support is on the DI pages of your Teacher's Edition. The following is a sample of an ELL note from this week.

English Language Learners

Beginning Reinforce High-Frequency Words Make two sets of word cards for high-frequency words *have, they, four, two,* and *blue.* Have children take turns turning cards up two at a time to find matches.

Intermediate Access Content Have children identify the pet on each page, using first the English word and then their native language equivalent. Have children pantomime the action words associated with each pet in the story.

Advanced High-Frequency Words After the Team Talk activity, have children continue to work in pairs to check understanding. Have one child read one of the sentences aloud while another child makes a simple drawing to illustrate the sentences.

Advanced High Vocabulary Development Walk children through *Fun in the Sun.* Have them find the *sun, net,* and *pig* in the story. Display a word card for each of these words and have a child match each card with an appropriate picture.

ELL by Strand

The ELL lessons on this week's Support for English Language Learners pages are organized by strand. They offer additional scaffolding for the core curriculum. Leveled support notes on these pages address the different proficiency levels in your class. See pages DI•80–DI•85.

ELL Guy
Dr. Jim Cummins

— The Three Pillars of ELL Instruction —

ELL Strands	Activate Prior Knowledge	Access Content	Extend Language
Vocabulary p. DI•82	Frontload Vocabulary	Provide Scaffolding	Practice
Reading Comprehension p. DI•82	Provide Scaffolding	Set the Scene	Frontload Vocabulary
Phonics, Spelling, and Word Analysis pp. DI•80, DI•83–DI•84	Frontload Consonant and Vowel Sounds	Review Initial, Medial, and Final Sounds	Review Identifying Sounds in Words
Listening Comprehension p. DI•81	Prepare for the Read Aloud	First Listening	Second Listening
Conventions and Writing pp. DI•83, DI•85	Provide Scaffolding/ Introduce and Model	Practice	Leveled Practice Activities/ Leveled Writing Activities
Concept Development p. DI•80	Read the Concept Literacy Reader	Read the Concept Literacy Reader	Develop Oral Language

This Week's Practice Stations Overview

Six Weekly Practice Stations with Leveled Activities can be found at the beginning of each week of instruction. For this week's Practice Stations, see pp. 414–415.

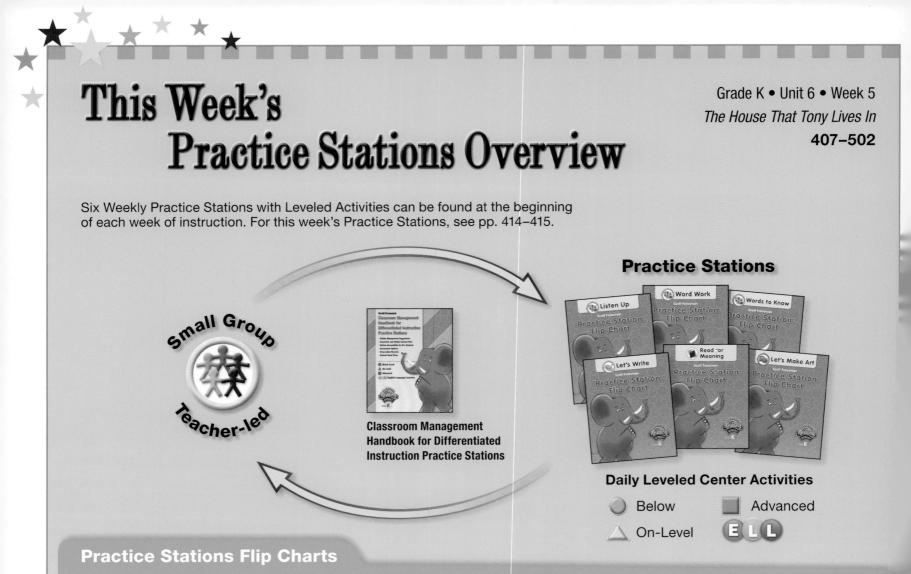

Small Group Teacher-led

Classroom Management Handbook for Differentiated Instruction Practice Stations

Practice Stations

Daily Leveled Center Activities

⬤ Below   ◼ Advanced

▲ On-Level   🅔🅛🅛

Practice Stations Flip Charts

	Listen Up	Word Work	Words to Know	Let's Write	Read for Meaning	Let's Make Art
Objectives	• Identify beginning, middle, and ending sounds of words.	• Review and build words with short *u*.	• Identify and use words for locations: *hospital, bank, grocery store, laundromat.*	• Write a rhyme about people who build houses.	• Identify and describe story plot.	• Use paint to show two friends building together.
Materials	• *Listen Up* Flip Chart Activity 35 • Picture Cards • paper, pencils	• *Word Work* Flip Chart Activity 35 • Alphabet Cards • Picture Cards: *bus, drum, gum, jug, mug, nut, rug, sun* • Letter Tiles • paper, pencils	• *Words to Know* Flip Chart Activity 35 • Find pictures for: *hospital, bank, grocery store, laundromat* • Teacher-made Word Cards: *hospital, bank, grocery store, laundromat* • paper, pencils, crayons	• *Let's Write* Flip Chart Activity 35 • Picture Cards • crayons, paper, pencil	• *Read for Meaning* Flip Chart Activity 35 • Trade Book *Alistair and Kip's Great Adventure* • pencil, crayons, paper	• *Let's Make Art* Flip Chart Activity 35 • art paper • finger paint

This Week on Reading Street!

Putting It Together

Question of the Week
Who helps to build a house?

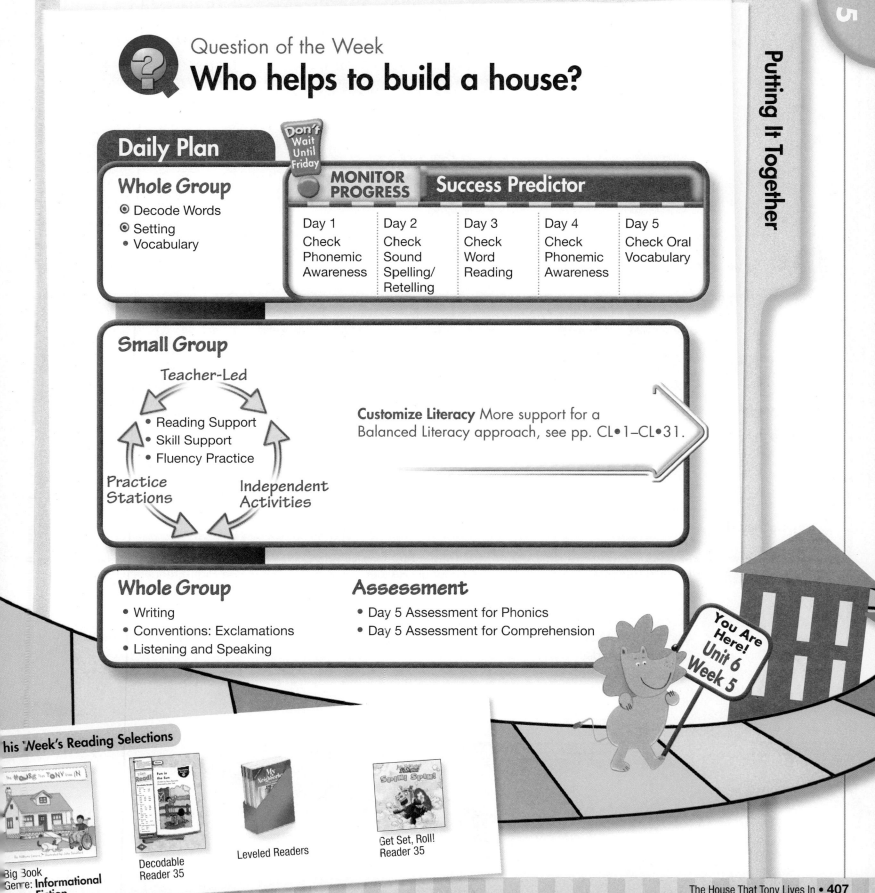

Daily Plan

Don't Wait Until Friday

Whole Group

- ⊙ Decode Words
- ⊙ Setting
- • Vocabulary

MONITOR PROGRESS	Success Predictor			
Day 1 Check Phonemic Awareness	Day 2 Check Sound Spelling/ Retelling	Day 3 Check Word Reading	Day 4 Check Phonemic Awareness	Day 5 Check Oral Vocabulary

Small Group

Teacher-Led
- • Reading Support
- • Skill Support
- • Fluency Practice

Practice Stations

Independent Activities

Customize Literacy More support for a Balanced Literacy approach, see pp. CL•1–CL•31.

Whole Group

- • Writing
- • Conventions: Exclamations
- • Listening and Speaking

Assessment

- • Day 5 Assessment for Phonics
- • Day 5 Assessment for Comprehension

You Are Here! Unit 6 Week 5

This Week's Reading Selections

Big Book Genre: Informational Fiction

Decodable Reader 35

Leveled Readers

Get Set, Roll! Reader 35

Resources on Reading Street!

	Build Concepts	Phonemic Awareness and Phonics	Vocabulary
Whole Group	Talk With Me/ Sing With Me	Student Edition pp. 92–93 Student Edition p. 96	Student Edition p. 97 Student Edition p. 108
Go Digital	• Concept Talk Video • Sing with Me Animations	• eReaders	
Small Group and Independent Practice	Practice Station Flip Chart Leveled Readers	Practice Station Flip Chart Decodable Reader 35 Leveled Readers Get Set, Roll! Reader 35	Practice Station Flip Chart Student Edition p. 97
Go Digital	• eReaders	• eReaders • Letter Tile Drag and Drop	
Customize Literacy	• Leveled Readers	• Decodable Reader	• High-Frequency Word Cards
Go Digital	• Concept Talk Video • Big Question Video • eReaders	• eReaders	• Sing with Me Animations

Question of the Week
Who helps to build a house?

Week 5

Comprehension	Fluency	Conventions and Writing
Student Edition pp. 94–95	Decodable Reader 35	Reader's and Writer's Notebook
Big Book	Kdg. Student Reader K.6.5	
	Get Set, Roll! Reader 35	
• Envision It! Animations	• eReaders	• Grammar Jammer
Practice Station Flip Chart	Practice Station Flip Chart	Practice Station Flip Chart
Leveled Readers	Leveled Readers	Reader's and Writer's Notebook
Get Set, Roll! Reader 35		
• Envision It! Animations	• eReaders	• Grammar Jammer
• eReaders		
• Leveled Readers	• Leveled Readers	• Reader's and Writer's Notebook
• Envision It! Animations	• eReaders	• Grammar Jammer
• eReaders		

You Are Here! Unit 6 Week 5

My 5-Day Planner for Reading Street!

Don't Wait Until Friday — MONITOR PROGRESS

	Check Phonemic Awareness **Day 1** pages 416–431	Check Sound-Spelling Check Retelling **Day 2** pages 432–449
Get Ready to Read	**Concept Talk,** 416 **Oral Vocabulary,** 417 *architect, electricians, plumbers, painters, landscapers, movers* **Phonemic Awareness,** 418–419 ◉ Initial, Medial, and Final Sounds **Phonics,** 420–421 ◉ Decode Words **Handwriting,** 422 Write Words **High-Frequency Words,** 423 Review *have, they, four, two, blue* **READ Decodable Story 35,** 424–425	**Concept Talk,** 432 **Oral Vocabulary,** 433 *architect, electricians* **Phonemic Awareness,** 434–435 ◉ Initial, Medial, and Final Sounds **Phonics,** 436–437 ◉ Decode Words **Handwriting,** 438 Write Words **High-Frequency Words,** 439 *have, they, four, two, blue* **READ Decodable Reader 35,** 440–441
Read and Comprehend	**Listening Comprehension,** 426–427 ◉ Setting	**Listening Comprehension,** 442 ◉ Setting **READ Big Book—First Read,** 442 *The House That Tony Lives In* **Retell,** 443 **Think, Talk, and Write,** 444
Language Arts	**Conventions,** 428 Exclamations **Writing,** 429 Wonderful, Marvelous Me! **Daily Handwriting,** 429 Write Words **Listening and Speaking,** 430 Oral Presentation—Book Report **Wrap Up Your Day,** 430 **Extend Your Day!,** 431	**Conventions,** 445 Exclamations **Writing,** 446 Respond to Literature **Daily Handwriting,** 446 Write Words **Vocabulary,** 447 Words for Feelings **Wrap Up Your Day,** 448 **Extend Your Day!,** 449

You Are Here! Unit 6 Week 5

Who helps to build a house?

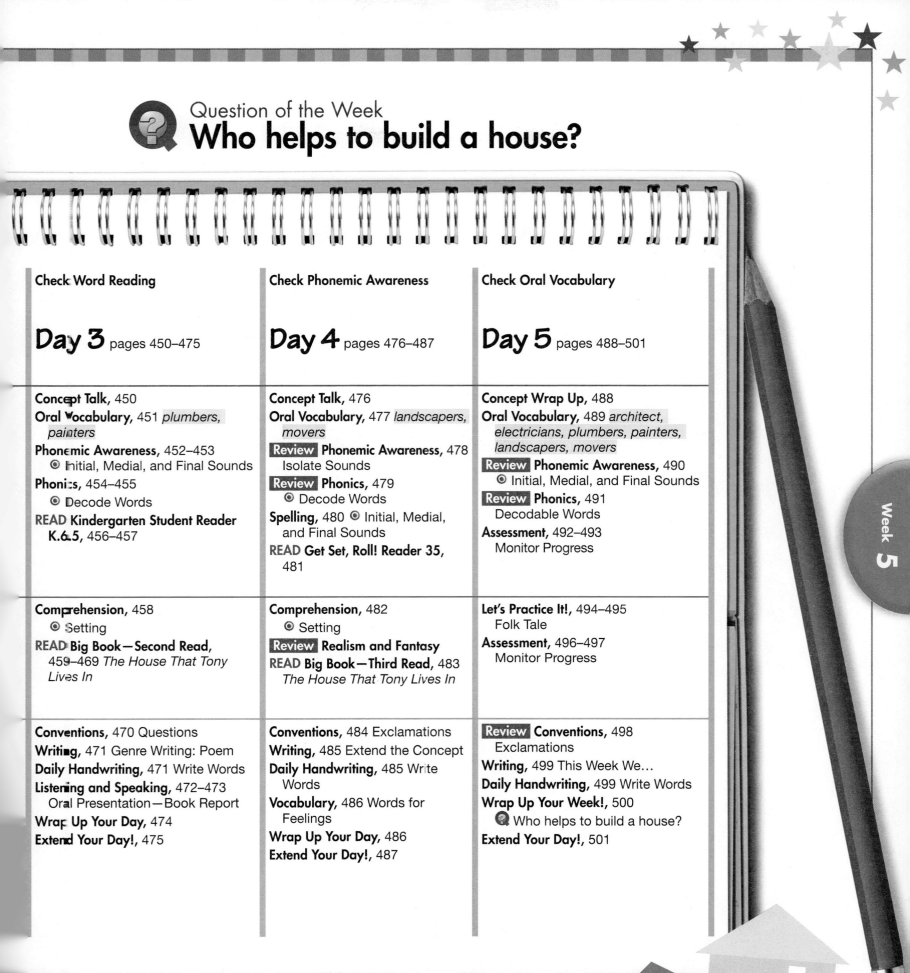

Check Word Reading	Check Phonemic Awareness	Check Oral Vocabulary
Day 3 pages 450–475	**Day 4** pages 476–487	**Day 5** pages 488–501
Concept Talk, 450 **Oral Vocabulary,** 451 *plumbers, painters* **Phonemic Awareness,** 452–453 ◉ Initial, Medial, and Final Sounds **Phonics,** 454–455 ◉ Decode Words **READ Kindergarten Student Reader K.6.5,** 456–457	**Concept Talk,** 476 **Oral Vocabulary,** 477 *landscapers, movers* **Review Phonemic Awareness,** 478 Isolate Sounds **Review Phonics,** 479 ◉ Decode Words **Spelling,** 480 ◉ Initial, Medial, and Final Sounds **READ Get Set, Roll! Reader 35,** 481	**Concept Wrap Up,** 488 **Oral Vocabulary,** 489 *architect, electricians, plumbers, painters, landscapers, movers* **Review Phonemic Awareness,** 490 ◉ Initial, Medial, and Final Sounds **Review Phonics,** 491 Decodable Words **Assessment,** 492–493 Monitor Progress
Comprehension, 458 ◉ Setting **READ Big Book—Second Read,** 459–469 *The House That Tony Lives In*	**Comprehension,** 482 ◉ Setting **Review Realism and Fantasy** **READ Big Book—Third Read,** 483 *The House That Tony Lives In*	**Let's Practice It!,** 494–495 Folk Tale **Assessment,** 496–497 Monitor Progress
Conventions, 470 Questions **Writing,** 471 Genre Writing: Poem **Daily Handwriting,** 471 Write Words **Listening and Speaking,** 472–473 Oral Presentation—Book Report **Wrap Up Your Day,** 474 **Extend Your Day!,** 475	**Conventions,** 484 Exclamations **Writing,** 485 Extend the Concept **Daily Handwriting,** 485 Write Words **Vocabulary,** 486 Words for Feelings **Wrap Up Your Day,** 486 **Extend Your Day!,** 487	**Review Conventions,** 498 Exclamations **Writing,** 499 This Week We… **Daily Handwriting,** 499 Write Words **Wrap Up Your Week!,** 500 Who helps to build a house? **Extend Your Day!,** 501

Week 5

Grouping Options for Differentiated Instruction
Turn the page for the small group time lesson plan.

Planning Small Group Time on Reading Street!

SMALL GROUP TIME RESOURCES

DAY 1

Look for this Small Group Time box each day to help meet the individual needs of all your children. Differentiated instruction lessons appear on the DI pages at the end of each week.

Teacher-Led

SI Strategic Intervention

Teacher-Led
- Phonemic Awareness and Phonics
- **Reread** Decodable Story

OL On-Level

Teacher-Led
- Phonemic Awareness and Phonics
- **Reread** Decodable Story

A Advanced

Teacher-Led
- Phonemic Awareness and Phonics
- **Reread** Decodable Story for Fluency

E L L Place English language learners in the groups that correspond to their reading abilities in English.

Practice Stations
- Listen Up
- Word Work

Independent Activities
- Read Independently
- *Reader's and Writer's Notebook*
- Concept Talk Video

E L L

ELL Poster 35

Day 1

SI Strategic Intervention	**Phonemic Awareness and Phonics,** DI•69	
	Reread Decodable Story 35, DI•69	
OL On-Level	**Phonemic Awareness and Phonics,** DI•74	
	Reread Decodable Story 35, DI•74	
A Advanced	**Phonemic Awareness and Phonics,** DI•77	
	Reread Decodable Story 35 for Fluency, DI•77	
E L L English Language Learners	DI•80–DI•81 Frontload Concept Phonemic Awareness and Phonics Comprehension Skill	

You Are Here!
Unit 6
Week 5

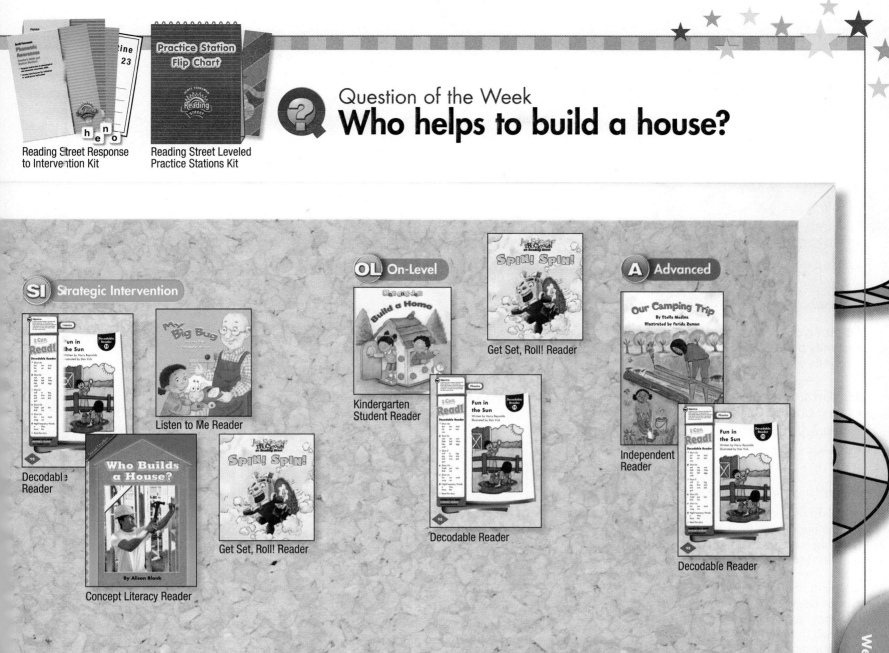

Question of the Week
Who helps to build a house?

SI Strategic Intervention

Decodable Reader

Listen to Me Reader

Who Builds a House?
By Alison Blank
Concept Literacy Reader

SPIN! SPIN!
Get Set, Roll! Reader

OL On-Level

Build a Home
Kindergarten Student Reader

SPIN! SPIN!
Get Set, Roll! Reader

Fun in the Sun
Decodable Reader

A Advanced

Our Camping Trip
By Stella Medina
Illustrated by Farida Zaman

Independent Reader

Fun in the Sun
Decodable Reader

Small Group Weekly Plan

Day 2	Day 3	Day 4	Day 5
Phonemic Awareness and Phonics, DI•70 **Reread** Decodable Reader 35, DI•70	**Phonemic Awareness and Phonics**, DI•71 **Read** Concept Literacy Reader K.6.5, DI•71	**Phonemic Awareness and Phonics**, DI•72 **Read** Get Set, Roll! Reader 35, DI•72	**Phonics Review**, DI•73 **Read** Listen to Me Reader K.6.5, DI•73
Phonemic Awareness and Phonics, DI•74 **Reread** Decodable Reader 35, DI•74	**Phonemic Awareness and Phonics**, DI•75 **Read** Kindergarten Student Reader K.6.5, DI•75	**Review Phonics and High-Frequency Words** **Read** Get Set, Roll! Reader 35, DI•76	**Phonics Review**, DI•76 **Reread** Leveled Books, DI•76
Phonics and Spelling, DI•77 **Reread** Decodable Reader 35 for Fluency, DI•77	**Read** Independent Reader K.6.5 or Kindergarten Student Reader K.6.4, DI•78	**Read** Get Set, Roll! Reader 35 or **Reread** Kindergarten Student Reader K.6.5, DI•79	**Fluency and Comprehension**, DI•79 **Reread** Independent Reader for Fluency, DI•79
DI•82 Comprehension Skill Frontload Vocabulary	DI•83 Review Phonemic Awareness and Phonics Scaffold Conventions	DI•84 Review Phonemic Awareness and Phonics Revisit Concept and Oral Language	DI•85 Language Workshop Writing

week 5

Practice Stations for Everyone on Reading Street!

Listen Up!
Beginning, middle, and ending sounds

Objectives
• Identify beginning, middle, and ending sounds of words.

Materials
• *Listen Up!* Flip Chart Activity 35
• Picture Cards
• paper, pencils

Differentiated Activities

⬤ Find two Picture Cards whose names begin with the same sound. Find two that have the same middle sound and two that end with the same sound.

▲ Find two Picture Cards whose names begin with the same sound. Find two that have the same middle sound and two that end with the same sound. On your paper, make a list of the words with the same beginning sound, the same middle sound, and the same ending sound. Use the back of the Picture Cards if you need help spelling.

◼ Find three Picture Cards whose names begin with the same sound. Find three that have the same middle sound and three that end with the same sound. Write a tongue twister sentence using your words that begin the same.

Word Work
/u/ spelled *Uu*

Objectives
• Review and build words with short *u*.

Materials
• *Word Work* Flip Chart Activity 35
• Alphabet Cards
• Picture Cards: *bus, drum, gum, jug, mug, nut, rug, sun*
• Letter Tiles
• paper, pencils

Differentiated Activities

⬤ Find the *Uu* Alphabet Card. Choose a Picture Card with short *u* in the middle. Use the Letter Tiles to build your word. Use the back of the Picture Card if you need help spelling.

▲ Find the *Uu* Alphabet Card. Look for Picture Cards with short *u* in the middle. Use the Letter Tiles to build one of your words. Change a letter to make a new word. Did you make a word you know?

◼ Find the *Uu* Alphabet Card. Look for Picture Cards with short *u* in the middle. Use the Letter Tiles to build the word on one of your cards. Take away or add letters at the beginning or the end of your word to build three new words. Write the words on your paper.

Technology
• Letter Tile Drag and Drop

Words To Know
Location words

Objectives
• Identify and use words for locations: *hospital, bank, grocery store, laundromat.*

Materials
• *Words to Know* Flip Chart Activity 35
• Find pictures (or take quick digital photos and print out) for location words: *hospital, bank, grocery store, laundromat,* and five other locations.
• Teacher-made word cards: *hospital, bank, grocery store, laundromat*
• paper, pencils, crayons

Differentiated Activities

⬤ Choose the picture cards that show a *hospital, bank, grocery store,* and *laundromat.* Say the name for each picture.

▲ Match the picture cards and word cards that show the places, *hospital, bank, grocery store,* and *laundromat.* Tell what people do at each place.

◼ Match the picture cards and word cards that show these places: *hospital, bank, grocery store,* and *laundromat.* Draw a picture or write a sentence that tells something people do at each place.

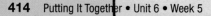

You Are Here! Unit 6 Week 5

Use this week's materials from the Reading Street Leveled Practice Stations Kit to organize this week's stations.

Practice Station Flip Chart

Let's Write!
Rhyme

Objectives
• Write a rhyme about people who build houses.

Materials
• *Let's Write!* Flip Chart Activity 35
• Picture Cards: *fan, brick, block, roof, house, clock, top, yellow, lake, woman, brown, man, rake, mop, van, hammer*
• crayons, paper, pencil

Differentiated Activities

● Look at the Picture Cards. Say the word for each card. Find two Picture Cards that rhyme. Draw a picture or write a poem that tells about people who build houses. Use some of the rhyming words.

▲ Look at the Picture Cards. Say the word for each card. Find some Picture Cards that rhyme. Write a four-line poem about people who build houses. Use some of the rhyming words.

■ Look at the Picture Cards. Say the word for each card. Find some Picture Cards that rhyme. Write an eight-line poem about people who build houses. Use some of the rhyming words.

Read For Meaning
Plot

Objectives
• Identify and describe story plot.

Materials
• *Read for Meaning* Flip Chart Activity 35
• Trade Book *Alistair and Kip's Great Adventure!*
• pencil, crayons, paper

Differentiated Activities

The **plot** is what happens in the story. A good way to understand and remember a story is to think about the plot.

● Read your book. Find a picture that shows something that happens. Tell what happened in the picture.

▲ Read your book. Draw a picture that shows what happens in the story. Write a sentence that tells what happens.

■ Read your book. Draw a picture that shows what happens in the story. Write three sentences that tell what happens.

Let's Make Art!

Objectives
• Use paint to show two friends building together.

Materials
• *Let's Make Art!* Flip Chart Activity 35
• art paper
• finger paint

Differentiated Activities

● What do you like to build with your friend? Paint a picture that shows you and your friend building together.

▲ What do you like to build with your friend? Paint a picture that shows you and your friend building together. Think about lines, shapes, and color as you paint.

■ What do you like to build with your friend? Paint a picture that shows you and your friend building together. Use lines, shapes, and color to show what you are your friend are building together.

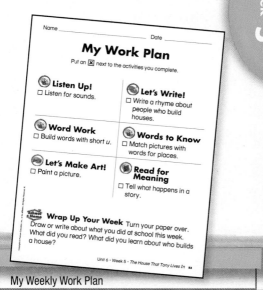

My Weekly Work Plan

Objectives

• Share information and ideas about the concept.

Today at a Glance

Oral Vocabulary
architect, electricians, plumbers, painters, landscapers, movers

Phonemic Awareness
◉ Initial, Medial, and Final Sounds

Phonics
◉ Decode Words

Handwriting
Write Words

High-Frequency Words
have, they, four, two, blue

Comprehension
◉ Setting

Conventions
Exclamations

Writing
Wonderful, Marvelous Me!

Listening and Speaking
Oral Presentation: Book Reports

TRUCKTOWN on Reading Street

Start your engines!

Display p. 18 of *Truckery Rhymes*.

• Read aloud "Rumble, Rumble, Monster Max" and track the print.

• Reread the rhyme and have children chime in as they wish.

• Ask children to identify rhyming words. (*Max, stacks; high, sky*)

Truckery Rhymes

Concept Talk

Question of the Week

Who helps to build a house?

Introduce the concept

To build concepts and to focus children's attention, tell them that this week they will talk, sing, read, and write about people who build houses. Track each word as you read the question of the week.

Play the CD that features an interview with another kind of builder. What happened to this builder? How did the builder solve the problem?

 Background Building Audio

ROUTINE Activate Prior Knowledge **Team Talk**

1. **Think** Have children think for a minute about people who build houses.

2. **Pair** Have pairs of children discuss the question of the week. Remind them to take turns speaking. Have children use complete sentences in their discussions about builders.

3. **Share** Call on a few children to share their ideas with the group. Guide discussion and encourage elaboration with prompts such as: What are some of the different jobs done by people who build houses?

Routines Flip Chart

Anchored Talk

Develop oral language

Display Talk with Me Chart 35A. This week we will be talking about people who help build a house. The chart shows some of these workers. Which worker is looking at plans or drawings of a house? Which person is working on pipes and the plumbing? Which person is working on the wires for the electricity? Continue with the other pictures.

We are going to learn six new Amazing Words. Listen as I say each word: *architect, electricians, plumbers, painters, landscapers, movers.* Say the Amazing Words with me as I point to each worker on the chart.

Display Sing with Me Chart 35B. Tell children that they are going to sing a song about building a house. Listen for the Amazing Words *architect, electricians, plumbers, painters, landscapers,* and *movers*. Read the title and have children describe the pictures. Sing the song several times to the tune of "Three Blind Mice." Have children sing with you.

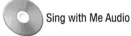 Sing with Me Audio

 **Preteach Concepts** Use the Day 1 instruction on ELL Poster 35 to assess and build background knowledge, develop concepts, and build oral vocabulary.

Talk with Me/Sing with Me Chart 35A

Let's Build a House

Let's build a house, let's build a house,
Who can help, who can help?
The architect can draw some plans,
The driver brings the supplies he can,
The construction worker
   can saw and sand,
Who else can help?

Talk with Me/Sing with Me Chart 35B

ELL Poster 35

Amazing Words

architect · electricians
plumbers · painters
landscape · movers

Writing on Demand ⏱

Develop Writing Fluency
Ask children to write about what they know about people who build houses. Have them write for two minutes. Children should write as much as they can. Tell them to try to do their best writing. You may want to discuss what children wrote during writing conferences.

ELL

English Language Learners
Build Background English learners will benefit from additional visual support to understand words in the song. As you sing, point to the words *architect, electricians, plumbers, painters, landscapers, and movers* to scaffold meaning.

ELL Support Additional ELL support and modified instruction is provided in the *ELL Handbook* and in the ELL Support lessons on pp. DI•80–85.

Objectives

⊙ Discriminate initial and final sounds.
- Identify sounds.
- Segment words.
- Blend sounds.

Check Phonemic Awareness

▌ SUCCESS PREDICTOR

Phonemic Awareness

Objectives
- Say rhymes for words that are said to you. • Blend spoken sounds to form words with one syllable. • Say the sound at the beginning of spoken one-syllable words.

Let's Listen for

Consonant and Vowel Sounds

- Point to the bat. Say the word. Say the beginning sound. Find two more things that begin with /b/.

■ Point to a cat. Say *cat*. Say the middle sound. Find two more things with /a/ in the middle.

▲ Blend /s/ /u/ /n/. What's the word? Yes, *sun*. Point to the picture.

★ What is the last sound in *sun*? Point to two more things that end with /n/, like *sun*.

♥ Say *mug*. Name two things that rhyme with *mug*.

READING STREET ONLINE
BIG QUESTION VIDEO
www.ReadingStreet.com

92   93

My Skills Buddy, pp. 92–93

Phonemic Awareness
⟳ Sounds

Teach

Today we are going to identify the sounds in a word. Display the tent Picture Card. *Tent* begins with /t/. What sound does *tent* begin with? The middle sound in *tent* is /e/. What is the middle sound in *tent*? The final sounds in *tent* are /n/ /t/. What is the last sound in *tent*?

Picture Card

Model

Have children look at the picture on pp. 92–93 of *My Skills Buddy.* Tell them that they will be listening for the beginning, middle, and last sounds in words. I see a bug on the roof. What sound do you hear at the beginning of *bug*? I hear /b/ at the beginning of *bug*. What sound do you hear in the middle of *bug*? I hear /u/ in the middle of *bug*. What is the last sound you hear in *bug*? The last sound is /g/. What other things do you see? What are the sounds in the word?

Guide practice

As children name example words from the picture, guide them in stating the beginning, middle, and ending sounds. Discuss with children some of the bulleted items on p. 92 of *My Skills Buddy.* Save the other bulleted items for discussion on Day 2.

Corrective feedback

If... children have difficulty identifying beginning, medial, and final sounds, then... say *bug* again emphasizing each sound—/b/ /u/ /g/, *bug*.

Discriminate sounds

Say *bat, cup, bed.* Do these words all begin the same? (no) *Bat* and *bed* begin with /b/ but *cup* begins with /k/. I am going to say two words. I want you to clap if the words have the same beginning sound. If the words have the same ending sound, put your hands on your head. Listen carefully. I will do the first two with you: *queen, quick* (clap); *fox, box* (put hands on head); *gum, guess; pen, pat; van, can; six, sock; will, spill.* Continue the activity having children identify which of the following pairs of words have the same middle sound: *lap, tug; cat, nap; sit, dig; frog, hop; pig, pen.*

Corrective feedback

If... children cannot discriminate beginning, middle, and final sounds in words,

then... have them say the word slowly, then say each sound in the word several times, feeling the position of their mouth and tongue.

Segment and blend

Display the *web* Picture Card. This is a *web.* What are the sounds in the word *web?* Say the sounds with me: /w/ /e/ /b/, *web.* The sounds are /w/ /e/ /b/, *web.* Have children segment the sounds in these words: *bat, jet, mug, fox, top, step, glad.*

I will say three sounds. I want you to repeat the sounds and blend them to say the word. Listen carefully: /kw/ /i/ /k/. Say the sounds with me: /kw/ /i/ /k/. Now blend the sounds together to make a word. What is the word? The word is *quick.* Repeat the blending routine with the words *hit, ten, drum, box,* and *lap.*

Differentiated Instruction

SI Strategic Intervention

Support Phonemic Awareness Tell children to listen for the sound that is the same in each set of words. Say these words and have children repeat the sound that is the same: *had, heart, hug; bed, set, pen; pad, toad, lid.*

A Advanced

Discriminate Sounds Have children identify which sound is different in each pair of words: the beginning sound, the middle sound, or the final sound. Say these words: *sat, sit; bad, bed; moat, goat; hot, hop; big, pig; tap, tan; run, sun.*

Don't Wait Until Friday

MONITOR PROGRESS ↻ **Check Phonemic Awareness/Sounds**

Say *pat.* Have children tell you all the sounds in the word. Repeat with the following words: *cob, had, ten, pod, gum, dill.*

If... children cannot identify sounds,

then... use the small-group Strategic Intervention lesson, p. DI•69, to practice segmenting and blending decodable words.

Day 1	Day 2	Day 3	Day 4	Day 5
Check Phonemic Awareness	Check Sound-Spelling/ Retelling	Check Word Reading	Check Phonemic Awareness	Check Oral Vocabulary

Success Predictor

Phonemic Awareness

Success Predictor

Objectives
◎ Decode words.

Skills Trace
◎ **Consonant Blends**
Introduce U4W3D1; U6W5D1
Practice U4W3D2; U4W3D3;
U6W5D2; U6W5D3
Reteach/Review U4W3D5;
U4W4D4; U6W5D5; U6W6D4
Assess/Test Benchmark
Assessment U4; U6

KEY:
U=Unit   W=Week   D=Day

Phonics—Teach/Model
Decode Words

Introduce
Write the word *set* on the board. Point to *s*. The name of this letter is *s*. What is the sound for *s*? (/s/) Repeat with *e* and *t*. The sounds are /s/ /e/ /t/. Point to each letter as you say the sound. I blend the sounds together to read the word: /s/ /e/ /t/, *set*. The word is *set*.

Model
Write the word *nap* on the board. Point to *n*. What is the sound for *n*? The sound is /n/. Repeat for *a* and *p*. Blend the sounds as I point to each letter and say the word: /n/ /a/ /p/, *nap*. The word is *nap*. Continue the decoding routine with the following words: *bug, log, fit, wet, not, cub, bit*.

Guide practice
Display Phonics Songs and Rhymes Chart 35. Teach children the song "Can Zelda Sip Milk from the Red Cup?" sung to the tune of "My Bonnie Lies Over the Ocean." Play the CD and sing the song several times. When children are familiar with the song, have them sing along with you. Then repeat the routine from Model, having children point to, segment, and blend the following words from the song: *can, red, sip, get*.

🔘 Phonics Songs and Rhymes Audio

Phonics Songs and Rhymes
Chart 35

On their own
Write the words below on the board. Have children read the words.

jam	jug	van	zap
quit	rag	fog	pin
mom	ran	net	not

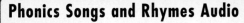

Blend Words

Review Practice the sound-spellings of previously taught letters. Display the *Aa* Alphabet Card. *This is an astronaut.* What sound does *astronaut* begin with? What letter spells that sound? Continue to review letter names and sounds with the following Alphabet Cards: *Cc, Dd, Ff, Ss, Mm, Rr.*

ROUTINE Sound-by-Sound Blending

(1) **Connect** Write the letter *u* on the board. What is the sound for this letter? The sound is /u/. Say it with me: /u/ /u/ /u/. When you see this letter in a word, what sound will you try?

(2) **Model** Write *fun* on the board.

- Touch under the letter *f.* What is the sound for this letter? Say it with me: /f/ /f/ /f/. Repeat the routine for *u* and *n.*

- Let's blend the sounds together. Listen as I blend the sounds: /f/ /u/ /n/. Say it with me: /f/ /u/ /n/. Now say it without me.

- Listen as I use *fun* in a sentence: *We had fun on the swings.* Say the sentence with me. Then have children use *fun* in their own sentences.

(3) **Guide Practice** Continue the routine established in step 2 with the words below:

Peg	dog	tug	dig	pet	pig	run	pen	mud
Hal	Tad	frog	lap	will	hop	swim	sit	nap

Children should successfully read these words before reading Decodable Story 35 on p. 451 of *Reader's and Writer's Notebook.*

Corrective Feedback If children have trouble reading a word, model blending the sounds to read the word. Then have children say it with you.

Routines Flip Chart

Objectives
- Write words.
- Learn high-frequency words.

Handwriting

Teach
Tell children the rule for writing words that begin with lowercase letters. Words that do not begin a sentence or tell someone's name do not begin with an uppercase letter.

Model writing words
Write the word *top* on the board. This word is written with lowercase letters *t, o, p.* Watch as I form each letter. The letters are written next to each other to make a word.

Guide practice
Let's write the word together. Write the word a second time on the board. Watch how I write and how I space the letters. Now you write the word on your paper. Circulate around the room, assisting children when necessary. Repeat the routine with the words *dig, jump, can,* and *pet,* and a short exclamation, such as *Oh boy!* Remind children that an exclamation is a sentence and begins with an uppercase letter.

More practice
Use *Reader's and Writer's Notebook,* pp. 449–450, for additional practice with writing words.

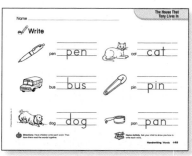

Reader's and Writer's Notebook, p. 449

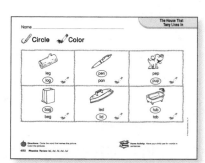

Reader's and Writer's Notebook, p. 450

High-Frequency Words

Introduce

Use the routine below to teach high-frequency words *have, they, four, two,* and *blue.*

Academic Vocabulary

Write the following on the board:

exclamation	question
setting	book report
fiction	poem
realism	fantasy
folk tale	exclamation mark

Point to the list. This week we are going to learn these important words. They are tools for learning. As we work this week, you will hear them many times. **Read the words.** Preteach the Academic Vocabulary at point-of-use by providing a child-friendly description, explanation, or example that clarifies the meaning of each term. Then ask children to restate the meaning of the Academic Vocabulary in their own words.

Differentiated Instruction

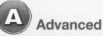 **Strategic Intervention**

Handwriting Support Have children review their writing and make sure that all the tall letters are the same height and all the short letters are the same height.

Ⓐ Advanced

Writing Words Have children review their writing to make sure that the spacing between letters is even.

English Language Learners

Reinforce High-Frequency Words Make two sets of word cards for high-frequency words *have, they, four, two* and *blue.* Have children take turns turning cards up two at a time to find matches.

Objectives
- Read high-frequency words.
- Decode and read words in context and isolation.

Decodable Story 35
🔊 Decodable Words and High-Frequency Words

Review

Review the following high-frequency words by having children read each word as you point to it on the Word Wall.

is	a	she	he	the	go

Read Decodable Story 35

Display Decodable Story 35, *What Pets Do.* Today we will read a story about some pets and what they do. **Point to the title of the story.** What is the title of the story? *What Pets Do* is the title of the story. We will read words with many different sounds in this story.

Use the routine for reading decodable books to read Decodable Story 35.

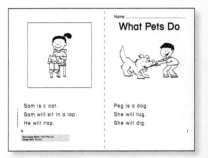

Reader's and Writer's Notebook, pp. 451–452

ROUTINE Reading Decodable Books

1. **Read Silently** Have children whisper read the story page by page as you listen in.

2. **Model Fluent Reading** Have children finger point as you read a page. Then have children reread the page without you.

3. **Read Chorally** Have children finger point as they chorally read the page. Continue reading page by page, repeating steps 1 and 2.

4. **Read Individually** Have children take turns reading aloud a page.

5. **Reread and Monitor Progress** As you listen to individual children reread, monitor progress and provide support.

6. **Reread with a Partner** Have children reread the story page by page with a partner.

Routines Flip Chart

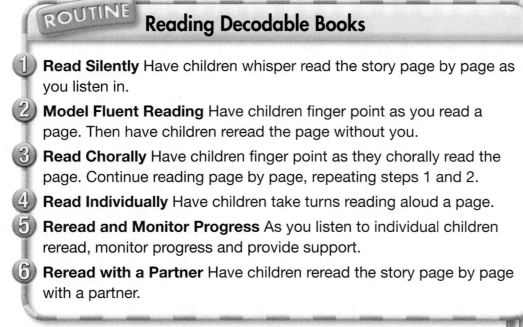

Small Group Time

DAY 1

Break into small groups after reading the Decodable Story and before the comprehension lesson.

Teacher-Led

SI Strategic Intervention	**OL** On-Level	**A** Advanced
Teacher-Led Page DI•69	**Teacher-Led** Page DI•74	**Teacher-Led** Page DI•77
• Phonemic Awareness and Phonics	• Phonemic Awareness and Phonics	• Phonemic Awareness and Phonics
• **Reread** Decodable Story 35	• **Reread** Decodable Story 35	• **Reread** Decodable Story 35 for Fluency

ELL Place English language learners in the groups that correspond to their reading abilities in English.

Practice Stations	**Independent Activities**
• Visit the Listen Up! Station	• Read independently
• Visit the Word Work Station	• Concept Talk Video
	• *Reader's and Writer's Notebook*

Differentiated Instruction

SI Strategic Intervention

Echo Reading Read each sentence in the text and have children repeat it.

ELL

English Language Learners

Access Content Have children identify the pet on each page, using first the English word and then their native language equivalent. Have children pantomime the action words associated with each pet in the story.

Objectives
◎ Identify and describe setting.

Skills Trace

◉ **Setting**

Introduce U1W2D1; U2W2D1; U4W6D1; U6W5D1

Practice U1W2D2; U1W2D3; U1W2D4; U2W2D2; U2W2D3; U2W2D4; U4W6D2; U4W6D3; U4W6D4; U6W5D2; U6W5D3; U6W5D4

Reteach/Review U1W2D5; U1W3D4; U1W4D4; U1W6D4; U2W2D5; U2W4D4; U4W4D4; U4W6D5; U6W5D5

Assess/Test Benchmark Assessment U2; U6

KEY:
U=Unit   W=Week   D=Day

My Skills Buddy, pp. 94–95

Listening Comprehension
🔁 Setting

Introduce

Envision It!

A story happens in a certain place. It also happens at a certain time. When and where a story takes place is called the **setting.** Good readers notice the setting, or time and place, of a story because it helps them understand the story.

Have children turn to pp. 94–95 in *My Skills Buddy*.

- What is the story about? (a race between a hare and a tortoise)

- Where does the story happen? Point to the Setting pullout box. (outside on a path or road in the daytime)

Model

Today I will read a story about finding the perfect place to build a home. Read **"The Perfect Place"** and model how to identify setting.

 Think Aloud

When I read, I notice where and when the story is happening. Frank begins his search in a meadow that is sunny and warm. This sounds like a good place to build, but it is not right for Frank.

Guide practice

After reading, ask children questions about the story's setting.

- Where does Frank go first? (the meadow) What does the meadow look like? (It is sunny and warm with grasses and flowers.)

- Where does Frank go next? (Next, Frank goes into the forest.) What is it like there? (quiet, dark, leafy)

- Where does Frank go last? (the pond) Why is the pond the perfect place for Frank's home? (It is wet and muddy. Frank is a frog, so he needs water and mud.)

More practice

Display the Trade Book, *Mayday! Mayday!* Recall with children that the story is about rescue at sea. The story takes place in and on the sea. Page through the story. Point out the helicopter and rescue and safety gear. Does the story happen long ago or in modern times? How do you know?

Connect to everyday life

If someone were to write a story about the house you live in, tell me what the setting of the story would be.

Academic Vocabulary

setting the place and time where a story takes place

Teacher Tip

To reinforce the concept of setting, review the setting of *Jack and the Beanstalk* with children.

English Language Learners
Oral Comprehension To prepare English learners for the Read Aloud, use the modified Read Aloud in the ELL Support lesson on p. DI•81.

The Perfect Place

Frank must build himself a new home. But he won't build his home in just any old place. No, no. It has to be the perfect place.

Frank goes to the meadow. It is sunny and warm and filled with grasses and sweet-smelling flowers. It is a lovely place. But it is not the perfect place for Frank's new home.

Frank goes to the forest. It is dark and quiet and filled with tall old trees and leafy green ferns. It is a wonderful place. But it is not the perfect place for Frank's new home.

Frank goes to the pond. It is wide and wet and filled with cool water and squishy mud. It is a lovely place. It is a wonderful place. It is the perfect place for Frank's new home—because Frank is a frog.

Objectives
- Introduce exclamations.
- Write or dictate ideas about something you learned.

Conventions
Exclamations

Teach exclamations
An exclamation is something we say to express a strong feeling or reaction to something. Exclamations burst out when we are excited.

Model
Show AlphaBuddy to the children. AlphaBuddy, did you know that we have read more than 30 books? Have the puppet say "Wow, that's terrific!" with a lot of expression and excitement. Write the exclamation on the board.

When AlphaBuddy heard that we had read more than 30 books, he exclaimed, "Wow, that's terrific!" The first word in an exclamation begins with an uppercase letter. We put an exclamation mark at the end of an exclamation. Circle the uppercase *W* and the exclamation mark in the exclamation.

Guide practice
When would you make an exclamation? If you are running to catch the school bus, you might yell to your friend, "Hurry up!" When you hear good news, you might exclaim, "That's great!" Write both phrases on the board and have children echo read them with expression and excitement. Have children point to the uppercase letter and exclamation mark in each sentence.

Hurry up!

That's great!

Team Talk Pair children and have them take turns repeating the following sentences: *Hurry up! That's great!* Remind them to raise their voice to show excitement when they see an exclamation mark at the end of the sentence.

Daily Fix-It
Use the Daily Fix-It for more conventions practice.

Writing
Wonderful, Marvelous Me!
I Just Learned...

Introduce Talk with children about learning new skills. We are always learning new things. Babies learn to walk and talk at home. Children learn to read and write at school. We learn to share our things and respect others. We learn how to tie our shoes, ride bikes, and play games. We learn from family members, teachers, and friends. Learning new things makes us feel proud. **Have children share their learning experiences and how learning makes them feel.**

Model Today we're going to write about something we learned to do. We learn by listening, watching, and doing. I learned to bake bread from my Grandpa. **As you describe the steps in the learning process, write them on the board:** *measure, mix, knead, bake.* First, I listened to Grandpa. He said we needed flour, water, yeast, salt, and sugar. Next, I watched Grandpa measure and mix the ingredients. Then I watched Grandpa knead the dough and put it in the pan. Finally, Grandpa put the bread in the oven. When it was my turn, I did everything that I watched Grandpa do. When my bread came out of the oven, I was happy! I did it myself!

Independent writing Now you're going to write about something you learned to do. Then think about how wonderful and marvelous learning something new makes you feel. When you write, use the picture dictionary on pp. 132–144 of *My Skills Buddy* to help you find what words mean and how to spell them. **Have children write or dictate their thoughts and then illustrate them.**

Daily Handwriting

Write the words *cat, fish, pup,* and *duck* on the board. Review correct letter formation of the lowercase letters and even spacing between the letters in each word.

Have children write *cat, fish, pup,* and *duck* on their Write-On Boards. Remind them to use proper left-to-right and top-to-bottom progression and proper spacing between letters in each word.

Write Guy
Jeff Anderson

Show Off—In a Good Way

Post children's successful sentences or short paragraphs! Celebrate writing as a new learning experience. Select a sentence of the week, and write it large! Display it as a poster inside or outside the classroom door.

Academic Vocabulary

exclamation a sentence that expresses strong feeling or surprise and ends with an exclamation mark

exclamation mark punctuation (!) following a word, phrase, or sentence that was exclaimed, or spoken with strong feeling

Daily Fix-It

the man had a big hat?
The man had a big hat.

This week's practice sentences appear on Teacher Resources DVD-ROM.

Writing Routine

Day 1 Wonderful, Marvelous Me!

Day 2 Respond to Literature

Day 3 Genre Writing

Day 4 Extend the Concept

Day 5 This Week We...

Objectives
- Practice book reports.
- Face the speaker when listening.
- Speak one at a time.

Listening and Speaking
Oral Presentation: Book Report

Teach
After we read a book, we can stand in front of the class and give an oral presentation about the characters, setting, and plot of the book. We also identify the title, author, and illustrator of the book.

Model
Display *Goldilocks and the Three Bears.* I am going to give a book report about *Goldilocks and the Three Bears.* Present a brief book report about setting, characters, and plot of the story. Did you remember to face me as I was speaking?

Guide practice
Help children make a brief book report about *Alistair and Kip's Great Adventure!* Have children identify the author and illustrator of the book. Then guide them to tell about the setting, characters, and plot of the story. Refer children to the Rules for Listening and Speaking on pp. 1–2 of the *Reader's and Writer's Notebook.* Remind children to speak one at a time and to face the speaker when listening.

Name _____

Speaking Rules
1. Speak clearly.
2. Tell only important ideas.
3. Choose your words carefully.
4. Take turns speaking.
5. Speak one at a time.

2 Listening and Speaking Rules

Reader's and Writer's Notebook, p. 2

Wrap Up Your Day

✔ **Oral Language** Today we learned Amazing Words for the names of workers who build houses. Let's say them together: *architect, electricians, plumbers, painters, landscapers, movers.*

✔ **Conventions** Have children practice saying exclamations with correct tone and volume of voice.

✔ **Homework Idea** Send home the Family Times Newsletter, Let's Practice It! TR•DVD 69–70.

Preview DAY 2

Tomorrow we will read about the people who help build a house.

Extend Your Day!

Science
A Plan Before Building

Materials: chart-size and regular graph paper, Talk with Me Chart 35A, pencils, marker

Investigate House Plans Point out the photo of architects looking at a house plan on Talk with Me Chart 35A. Explain how to read house plans and how a scale is used to show the relative size of the parts of a house and its contents. Show

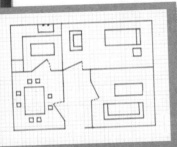

how to draw the symbols used to show the location of doors, windows, and stairs. Draw a basic floor plan on chart paper. Have children tell what they think is needed in a home.

Draw a House Plan Tell children to imagine they are architects. Distribute graph paper (half-inch squares). Have children draw a set of house plans for a house they design themselves. Have them label the rooms in the house. Remind them to include details such as doors and windows and to show where some furniture goes.

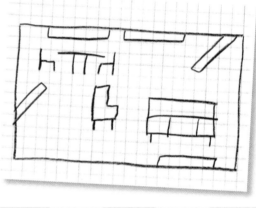

Phonics
Substitute Letters

Materials: assortment of CVC, CCVC, and CVCC Picture Cards

Make Rhyming Words Display the *cat* Picture Card. Tell children to help you write the name of the picture on the board. Identify the initial sound and letter in the word. Then have a child go to the board to make a rhyming word by substituting a new letter for the initial sound. Continue substituting initial sounds until several rhyming words are made. Begin a new activity with a different Picture Card.

cat
bat

Comprehension
Setting

Materials: previously read Trade Books and Big Books, drawing and coloring tools

Choose an Appropriate Setting Display illustrations in previously read books about animal characters to help children recall the setting in each story. Choose books whose setting reflects the natural habitat of the animal character, such as *Bear Snores On, Little Quack, The Lion and the Mouse,* and *Building Beavers.* Tell children to think of an animal they would like to write a story about and then have them draw a picture of an appropriate setting for the story, including the animal character from the story.

Objectives

- Discuss the concepts to develop oral language.
- Build oral vocabulary.

Today at a Glance

Oral Vocabulary
architect, electricians

Phonemic Awareness
◉ Initial, Medial, and Final Sounds

Phonics
◉ Decode Words

Handwriting
Write Words

Comprehension
◉ Setting

Conventions
Exclamations

Writing
Respond to Literature

Vocabulary
Words for Feelings

TRUCKTOWN on Reading Street

Start your engines! Display p. 18 of *Truckery Rhymes.* Point to "Rumble, Rumble, Monster Max." Who remembers which truck this rhyme is about? Yes, it's about Monster Max. Let's read the rhyme together. Now have a child point out the rhyming words as the class reads the rhyme again. Give additional children the opportunity to say the rhyme aloud and track the print.

Truckery Rhymes

Concept Talk

Question of the Week

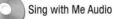 **Who helps to build a house?**

Build concepts

Write the question of the week on the board and track the print as you read it to children. Ask them to answer the question in complete sentences. Remind children to speak clearly. Display Sing with Me Chart 35B. Tell children that they are going to sing a song about who helps build a house.

💿 Sing with Me Audio

Listen for Amazing Words

Listen for the Amazing Words *architect* and *electricians.* Read the title and have children describe the picture. Sing the song several times to the tune of "Three Blind Mice." Have children sing with you and pretend to build a house when they hear the Amazing Words *architect* and *electricians.*

Talk with Me/Sing with Me Chart 35B

ELL Reinforce Vocabulary Use the Day 2 instruction on ELL Poster 35 to reinforce the meanings of high-frequency words.

ELL Poster 35

Go Digital!  Concept Talk Video | Sing with Me Animations | Sing with Me Audio

Whole Group

Oral Vocabulary
Amazing Words

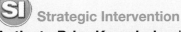

architect	electricians
plumbers	painters
landscapers	movers

Teach Amazing Words

Amazing Words — Oral Vocabulary Routine

1 **Introduce the Word** *An architect is a person who draws the plans for building a house.* What's our new Amazing Word for the person who draws the plans for a house? Say it with me: *architect.*

2 **Demonstrate** Provide examples to show meaning. *An architect draws what a building will look like when it is finished.* When do *architects* do their job, before a building is built or after?

Repeat steps 1 and 2.

Introduce the Word *Electricians install the wires in a house so it will have electricity.* What is our new Amazing Word for the people who install the electrical wires in a house? Say it with me: *electricians.*

Demonstrate *Electricians make the lights work in your house.* What other things do *electricians* make work?

3 **Apply** Have children use *architect* and *electricians* as they tell about any experiences they have had with these workers.

Routines Flip Chart

Use Amazing Words

To reinforce the concept and the Amazing Words, have children supply the appropriate Amazing Word for each sentence.

An _____ does his or her job before a building is built. (architect)

_____ know how to handle electricity safely. (Electricians)

Differentiated Instruction

 **Strategic Intervention**

Activate Prior Knowledge Have children point to or identify the parts of the school that an architect and an electrician would have helped build.

English Language Learners

Build Background Take children on a tour of the school and then help them draw a floor plan of the building to provide better understanding of an architectural drawing.

Phonemic Awareness
◉ Initial, Medial, and Final Sounds

Isolate initial, medial, and final sounds

Display the *nest* Picture Card. This is a *nest*. Listen as I say the sounds in *nest*: /n/ /e/ /st/. What is the beginning sound in *nest*? *Nest* begins with /n/. What is the middle sound in *nest*? The middle sound in *nest* is /e/. What are the last sounds in *nest*? The last sounds in *nest* are /s/ /t/. Continue the routine with the *quilt, crab,* and *flag* Picture Cards.

Picture Card

Model

Display the *ant* and *bat* Picture Cards. What is this? Point to each card and have children say the word for the picture. Which word begins with /a/: *ant* or *bat*? (*ant*) Which word has /a/ in the middle? (*bat*) Continue the routine with the following pairs of Picture Cards: *otter, fox; hen, elephant; umbrella, mug; iguana, pig.* Use these Picture Card sets to identify initial and final consonants: *dog, gum; tiger, cat.*

Picture Card

Guide practice

Have children look at the picture on *My Skills Buddy* pp. 92–93. Remember that we saw a bug in the picture. What other things do you see in the picture that begin with the same sound as *bug*? Have children identify other things in the picture and identify the beginning, middle, or ending sound. Discuss with children those bulleted items on p. 92 not discussed on Day 1.

My Skills Buddy, pp. 92–93

Corrective feedback

If... children cannot discriminate initial, medial, or final sounds, **then...** have them say each sound in the word slowly. Have them emphasize the letter in the position that is causing the most trouble.

On their own

Display Phonics Songs and Rhymes Chart 35. Remind children of the song "Can Zelda Sip Milk from the Red Cup?" sung to the tune of "My Bonnie Lies Over the Ocean." Have them sing the song with you several times. This time I want you to clap your hands when you hear /i/ in the middle of a word. Repeat the routine, having children identify medial /e/, /a/, /o/, and /u/.

Review

Segment The word *cup* is in the song. What sound does *cup* begin with? (/k/) What sound is in the middle of *cup*? (/u/) What sound does *cup* end with? (/p/) The sounds in the word *cup* are /k/ /u/ /p/. Continue having children segment the words *drink, sip,* and *quit.*

Blend

I am thinking of a word. I will give you a clue about the word, and then I will say the sounds in the word. I want you to blend the sounds together and say the word. Listen carefully. I am thinking of a word that names something to drink. The sounds are /m/ /i/ /lk/. What word am I thinking of? (*milk*) Continue the activity, giving clues and having children blend the sounds to say *red, grin, strong,* and *cup.*

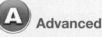

Can Zelda Sip Milk From the Red Cup?

Can Zelda sip milk from the red cup?
Can Zelda get help from Big Sis?
Can Zelda sip milk from the red cup?
Let's get her to hold on like this!

Sip it, don't quit! Yes, drink every drop
To get very strong!
Just sip it, oh, sip it; we'll grin when
You drink it all up!

Phonics Songs and Rhymes
Chart 35

Differentiated Instruction

 **Advanced**

Sound Sort Give children the *bad, bat, bed, can, cap, gum, jet,* and *mug* Picture Cards. Have them sort them according to initial sounds. Mix up the cards and have children sort them according to medial and final sounds.

English Language Learners

Support Phonemic Awareness Speakers of Hmong, Khmer, Korean, Tagalog, and Vietnamese may have difficulty distinguishing /j/ from /ch/ or /sh/. Spanish or Russian speakers may pronounce /j/ as /ch/. Provide additional practice with /j/ words.

Objectives
- ⊙ Practice decoding words.
- • Blend words.

Check Sound-Spelling
SUCCESS PREDICTOR

Phonics—Teach/Model
⊙ Decode Words

Review

Remember, we can read words by pointing to each letter in the word and saying the sound for that letter. Then we can blend those sounds together to read the word. Write *glad* on the board. Point to *gl.* The names of these letters are *g* and *l.* What is the blended sound for *g* and *l*? (/gl/) Repeat with the letters *a* and *d.* The sounds are /gl/ /a/ /d/. Point to each letter as you say the sound. Let's blend these sounds together to read this word: /gl/ /a/ /d/, *glad.*

Model

Write *crab* on the board. Point to the letters *c* and *r.* The letters *c* and *r* stand for the blended sound /kr/. Point to *a.* The letter *a* stands for the sound /a/. Point to *b.* The letter *b* stands for the sound /b/. When I blend the sounds together, I say /kr/ /a/ /b/, *crab.* Continue the decoding routine with the following words: *strong, bump, stop, gift, went, best, milk, plot, club.*

Guide practice

Envision It!

Have children open *My Skills Buddy* to p. 96. Model blending the first word. Put your finger on letter *d.* Say the sound that *d* stands for: /d/. Continue with the letters *o* and *t.* Now blend the letters quickly to read *dot.* Have children work with a partner to blend the rest of the words on the page.

Call attention to how new words are formed when letters are added. *An* plus *pl* makes *plan.* Add a *t* to the end of *plan* and the new word is *plant.*

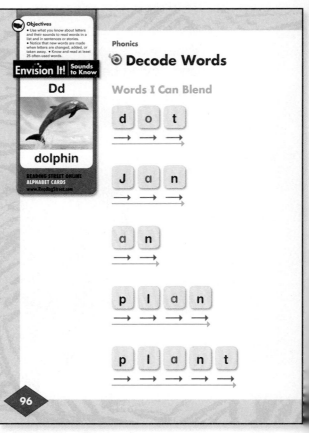

My Skills Buddy, p. 96

Blend Use the following routine to review blending words.

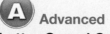 **Sound-by-Sound Blending**

1. **Connect** Write the letter *o*. What is the sound we learned for this letter? The sound is /o/. Say it with me: /o/ /o/ /o/. When you see this letter in a word, what sound will you try?

2. **Model** Write the word *dot* on the board.

   - Point to *d*. What is the sound for this letter? Say it with me: /d/ /d/ /d/. Repeat the routine for *o* and *t*.

   - Let's blend the sounds together. Listen as I blend the sounds: /d/ /o/ /t/. Say it with me: /d/ /o/ /t/. Now say it without me.

   - Listen as I use *dot* in a sentence: *The letter i has a dot.* Say it with me. Have children use *dot* in a sentence.

3. **Guide Practice** Continue the routine established in step 2 with these words:

   | Jan | fun | Todd | did | red | tan | snug | got | Kim | fell |

   Have children successfully read all of the words before reading Decodable Reader 35 on p. 98 of *My Skills Buddy*.

   Corrective Feedback Model blending the sounds to read the word. Then have children say it with you.

Routines Flip Chart

 MONITOR PROGRESS ↺ Check Sound-Spelling   Decode Words

Don't Wait Until Friday

Write *yak* on the board. Read this word. Say the sounds, and then say the whole word. Continue with *fast, lamp, fell, next, gift, zip, box, stop, club,* and *drum.*

If… children cannot read the words,

then… use the small-group Strategic Intervention lesson, p. DI•70, to practice decoding words.

Continue to monitor children's progress using other instructional opportunities during the week so that children can be successful with the Day 5 Assessment.

Day 1	Day 2	Day 3	Day 4	Day 5
Check Phonemic Awareness	Check Sound-Spelling/ Retelling	Check Word Reading	Check Phonemic Awareness	Check Oral Vocabulary

Differentiated Instruction

A **Advanced**

Letter-Sound Connection Display the Alphabet Cards on the chalkboard ledge. Show children the *red* Picture Card and have them say the word aloud. Then have them choose the Alphabet Cards that spell the sounds in *red*. Repeat the routine with the *pig, net,* and *map* Picture Cards.

SI **Strategic Intervention**

Blending Practice Write the word *sack* on the board. Erase the *s* and have children use the consonant blends *tr, sn,* and *bl* to make new words.

ELL

English Language Learners

Support Phonics After blending the words on *My Skills Buddy*, p. 96, help children employ English spelling rules for consonant blends. Remind them that some consonants blend together, such as /p/ /l/ = /pl/ and /n/ /t/ = /nt/. Then have them spell the words *plant, club,* and *plate* on their Write-On Boards.

Success Predictor

437

Sound-Spelling

Success Predictor

Objectives
- Write words with short vowels.
- Read high-frequency words.

Handwriting
Write Words

Review — Tell children the rule for writing words. Words are written with either an uppercase letter or a lowercase letter. We use an uppercase letter at the beginning of sentences or for the first letter of a person's name.

Write *Deb* on the board. This is the word *Deb.* I use an uppercase *D* at the beginning of *Deb* because it is a person's name. The letters are written next to each other to make a word. Watch how I write and how I space the letters. Write *Deb* again on the board.

Guide practice — Have children practice writing *Deb.* Now you write *Deb* on your paper. Circulate around the room, assisting children when necessary. Continue handwriting with the following words: *mud, tan, Kim, hen, snug, Rob, not, well, fat.*

High-Frequency Words

Model reading

Have children turn to p. 97 of *My Skills Buddy*. Read the high-frequency words together. Then have children point to each word and read it themselves. Read the sentences on *My Skills Buddy* page together to read the new high-frequency words in context.

Team Talk Pair children and have them take turns reading each of the sentences aloud.

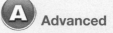

High-Frequency Words

Words I Can Read

| have |
| they |
| two |
| four |
| blue |

Sentences I Can Read

1. We have a little plan.
2. They have a big plan.
3. We will get two to help.
4. They will get four.
5. Can we fill blue cups?

97

My Skills Buddy, p. 97

On their own

Use *Reader's and Writer's Notebook*, p. 453, for additional practice with this week's high-frequency words.

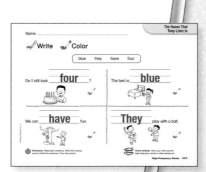

Reader's and Writer's Notebook, p. 453

Differentiated Instruction

A Advanced

High-Frequency Words Write the high-frequency words on cards and display them on the chalkboard ledge. Have children choose a card, read the word, and use it in a sentence.

English Language Learners

High-Frequency Words After the Team Talk activity, have children continue to work in pairs to check understanding. Have one child read one of the sentences aloud while another child makes a simple drawing to illustrate the sentences.

Objectives

- Make predictions based on the cover.
- Decode and read words in context and isolation.
- Read high-frequency words.

Decodable Reader 35
 Decodable Words and High-Frequency Words

Review Write the word *they* on the board. This is the word *they.* What is this word? Continue the word reading routine with *a, the,* and *have.*

Have children turn to Decodable Reader 35, *Fun in the Sun,* on p. 98 of *My Skills Buddy.* Today we will read a book about having fun in the sun. Look at the picture. What do you think this book will be about? Point to the title of the book. What is the title of the book? *Fun in the Sun* is the title of the book. We will read words with many different short vowel sounds.

Use the routine for reading decodable books to read Decodable Reader 35. Have children monitor their comprehension by asking them to think about whether they understand the story. To adjust comprehension, have them reread or read some part aloud.

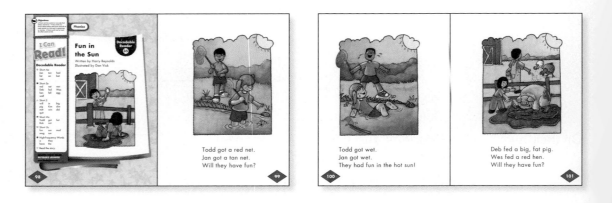

ROUTINE Reading Decodable Books

1. **Read Silently** Have children whisper read the book page by page as you listen in.

2. **Model Fluent Reading** Have children finger point as you read a page. Then have children reread the book without you.

3. **Read Chorally** Have children finger point as they chorally read the page. Continue reading page by page, repeating steps 1 and 2.

4. **Read Individually** Have children take turns reading aloud a page.

5. **Reread and Monitor Progress** As you listen to individual children reread, monitor progress and provide support.

6. **Reread with a Partner** Have children reread the book page by page with a partner.

Routines Flip Chart

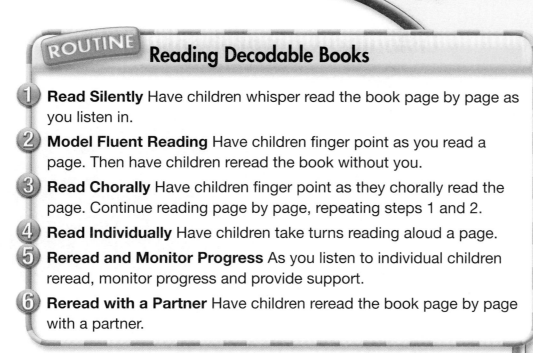

Differentiated Instruction

SI Strategic Intervention

Recognize and Read Short Vowel Words Before children read *Fun in the Sun,* review short vowel words with Picture Cards *bag, desk, pig, dog, duck, cat, egg, inch, ox,* and *sun.*

A Advanced

Sound-Letter Connection Display the *Aa* Alphabet Card. Have children name the sound and then the letter name. Repeat the routine with *Ee, Ii, Oo,* and *Uu* Alphabet Cards.

Small Group Time

DAY 2 Break into small groups after reading the Decodable Reader and before the comprehension lesson.

Teacher-Led

SI Strategic Intervention	**OL On-Level**	**A Advanced**
Teacher-Led Page DI•70	**Teacher-Led** Page DI•74	**Teacher-Led** Page DI•77
• Phonemic Awareness and Phonics	• Phonemic Awareness and Phonics	• Phonics and Spelling
• **Reread** Decodable Reader 35	• **Reread** Decodable Reader 35	• **Reread** Decodable Reader 35 for Fluency

ELL Place English language learners in the groups that correspond to their reading abilities in English.

Practice Stations	**Independent Activities**
• Visit the Word Work Station	• Read independently
• Visit the Words to Know Station	• Background Building Audio
	• *Reader's and Writer's Notebook*

 ELL

English Language Learners

Vocabulary Development Walk children through *Fun in the Sun.* Have them find the *sun, net,* and *pig* in the story. Display a word card for each of these words and have a child match each card with an appropriate picture.

Objectives
- ◎ Practice setting.
- • Preview and predict.
- • Retell a story.

Check Retelling

! **SUCCESS PREDICTOR**

Listening Comprehension
 Setting

Review

Envision It!

Where and when a story takes place is called the setting. What do we call the time and place where a story happens? **(setting)** Good readers pay attention to setting because it helps them understand what happens.

My Skills Buddy, pp. 94–95

 Triple Day Read!

First Read—Big Book
The House That Tony Lives In

Concepts of print

Display the cover of *The House That Tony Lives In*. Remind children that written words are separated by spaces. Have them count the number of words in the title.

Preview and predict

Think Aloud

Display *The House That Tony Lives In*. Look at the cover. What do you see? I see a boy in a wheelchair and his dog in front of their house. What do you think will happen in the story?

Use illustrations

Take children on a walk through the book. As we walk through the book, tell me what you see. Have children describe the illustrations.

Introduce genre

Informational fiction tells stories about imaginary people and events but also teaches us about things that happen in the real world. A fiction story may seem real. This story has make-believe characters who illustrate factual information about people who help build houses.

Set purpose

Remind children of the question of the week: *Who helps to build a house?*

Model

Read *The House That Tony Lives In* with expression for enjoyment.

DAY **2**
Read for enjoyment

DAY **3**
Reread using Develop Vocabulary notes

DAY **4**
Reread using Guide Comprehension notes

Retell

Check retelling

Envision It!

Have children turn to p. 106 of *My Skills Buddy.* Walk through the retelling boxes as children retell the story *The House That Tony Lives In.* Let's retell what happens in the first box— the beginning of the story. An architect is making a model of a house. Let's retell what happens in the next box. Continue with the rest of the boxes. After children retell the story as a group, have them draw a picture to retell a favorite part of the story. Have them write or dictate a word or sentence to go with their picture.

My Skills Buddy, p. 106

Top-Score Response A top-score response describes events in sequence with details.

Differentiated Instruction

A Advanced

Practice Retell Have children retell the story *Bear Snores On* from Unit 2, Week 4.

Academic Vocabulary

fiction stories about imaginary people and events

retell telling a story in one's own words

Retelling Plan

☑ **Week 1** Assess Advanced students.

☑ **Week 2** Assess On-Level students.

☑ **Week 3** Assess Strategic Intervention students.

☑ **Week 4** Assess Advanced students.

☑ **This week assess On-Level students.**

☐ **Week 6** Assess Strategic Intervention students.

Don't Wait Until Friday

MONITOR PROGRESS   **Check Retelling**

Grade K
Retelling Cards

If... children have difficulty retelling the story,

then... go through the story one page at a time, and ask children to tell what happens in their own words.

Day 1	Day 2	Day 3	Day 4	Day 5
Check Phonemic Awareness	Check Sound-Spelling/ Retelling	Check Word Reading	Check Phonemic Awareness	Check Oral Vocabulary

Success Predictor

Retelling

443

Success Predictor

Objectives

◎ Practice setting.
• Confirm predictions.
• Practice exclamations.

Think, Talk, and Write

Discuss concept

Imagine what it would be like to watch your house being built.

• Which would you most like to watch: the electricians or the plumbers?

• Would you rather help paint the house or landscape the garden? Why?

Confirm predictions

Have children recall their predictions before you read *The House That Tony Lives In.*

• What did you think the story would be about?

• Was your prediction correct?

Have children turn to p. 107 of *My Skills Buddy.* Read the questions and directives and have children respond.

My Skills Buddy, p. 107

Text to world

1. Look at the pictures. How does each person help to build a house? Which job would you like to do? Have you ever seen a house being built?

◉ Setting

2. Where does the story *The House That Tony Lives In* take place?

Look back and write

3. Let's look back at our story and write about it. We remember that many people help build Tony's house. Listen for what the plumbers do to help build the house. Read pp. 10–11 of *The House That Tony Lives In.* Discuss with children why plumbers are important. Record their responses on chart paper. (Possible responses: Plumbers connect pipes. Plumbers help bring water into a new house.)

Conventions
Exclamations

Review

Remind children of what they learned about exclamations. An exclamation is a special kind of sentence that expresses strong feelings about something.

Display p. 4–5 of *The House That Tony Lives In.* Before Tony's house can be built, drivers deliver supplies. When Tony sees them drive up, he might be excited and shout, "They're here!" Write this sentence on the board. This is an exclamation. It begins with an uppercase letter and ends with an exclamation mark.

Guide practice

Guide children to find other pages in the book that show work or people whom they would be excited to see. Have them pretend to be Tony and tell what they would exclaim. If necessary, ask questions. How would Tony feel to see his room being painted with stars? Write children's exclamations on the board. What kind of mark should I put at the end of the exclamations? Have children practice writing exclamations. Remind them to use an exclamation mark at the end.

On their own

Use *Reader's and Writer's Notebook*, p. 454, for more practice with exclamations.

Daily Fix-It

Use the Daily Fix-It for more conventions practice.

Reader's and Writer's
Notebook, p. 454

Writing
Respond to Literature

Discuss   Discuss *The House That Tony Lives In.* Have children tell about what each of the workers does to build a house. Suggest an exclamation that expresses feelings about each new activity. Write the exclamations below on the board, using a period at the end of each sentence instead of an exclamation point.

Model   Read the sentences aloud. Point out that the sentences express feeling.

> **Wow, those are big boards!**
>
> **Be careful with that box!**
>
> **The stars are awesome!**

Guide practice   Have children pick a page in the book. Help them write an exclamation about what the page shows.

Independent writing   Have children write or dictate their own exclamations about the workers or copy one of the exclamations from the board. Then have children illustrate their sentences. Remind them to capitalize the first word in the sentence and use an exclamation mark at the end.

Daily Handwriting

Write *happy* and *glad* on the board. Review correct letter formation of lowercase letters and even spacing between the letters in each word.

Have children write *happy* and *glad* on their Write-On Boards. Remind them to use proper left-to-right and top-to-bottom progression and proper spacing between letters in each word.

Oral Vocabulary
Amazing Words

architect   electricians
plumbers   painters
landscapers   movers

Teach Amazing Words

Amazing Words   **Oral Vocabulary Routine**

1 Introduce the Word *Plumbers are the people who connect and fix the water pipes in your house. Plumbers make sure all the water in a house flows properly.* What's our new Amazing Word for the people who connect the pipes in a house? Say it with me: *plumbers.*

2 Demonstrate *You can call a plumber when your sink is clogged. A plumber can also fix leaky faucets and pipes.* Which two rooms would a plumber do the most work in?

Repeat steps 1 and 2.

Introduce the Word *Painters are the people who paint the walls of a house.* What's our new Amazing Word for the people who paint houses? Say it with me: *painters.*

Demonstrate *A painter uses brushes, rollers, and sprayers to paint the walls in a house. Sometimes painters have to climb up tall ladders to paint the top of a house.* What else do painters paint besides the walls inside the house?

Use Amazing Words

3 Apply Have children use *plumbers* and *painters* in complete sentences. Have them act out what each person does.

Routines Flip Chart

Differentiated Instruction

SI Strategic Intervention

Access Content Tell children to act out how a *painter* paints a house. Then have them imitate a *plumber* connecting pipes with a pipe wrench.

To reinforce the concept and the Amazing Words, have children supply the appropriate Amazing Word for each sentence.

_____ **have wrenches in their toolboxes.** (Plumbers)

The _____ **quickly rolled paint on the bedroom walls.** (painters)

ELL Expand Vocabulary
Use the Day 3 instruction on ELL Poster 35 to help children expand vocabulary.

 Poster 35

ELL

English Language Learners
Visual Support Look through magazines for pictures of kitchens, bathrooms, bedrooms, and living rooms. Ask children to identify which rooms a plumber would work in and which rooms a painter would work in.

Objectives

◎ Discriminate initial, medial, and final sounds.
- Segment words.
- Blend words.

Phonemic Awareness
Initial, Medial, and Final Sounds

Isolate sounds

Say the words *pen, cab,* and *bat.* Which of these words begins with /p/? Listen as I say them again: *pen, cab, bat. Pen* begins with /p/. Which word ends with /t/: *pen, cab, bat? Bat* ends with /t/. Which of these words has /e/: *pen, cab, bat? Pen* has /e/. Have children distinguish initial, medial, and final sounds in these sets of words: *hat, big, cup; fin, cub, den; jog, mud, gas; mad, can, pet.*

Picture Card

Discriminate sounds

Display the *cat* and *red* Picture Cards. Point to each card as you say the word. Which word begins with same beginning sound as *camp?* Say the words with me: *cat* and *red.* I hear /k/ at the beginning of *cat.* Which word ends with the same sound as *head?* I hear /d/ at the end of *red.* Which word has the same middle sound as *pan?* I hear /a/ in the middle of *cat.*

On their own

Display the *duck* Picture Card. Have children fold their paper into three parts. Tell them to draw something with the same beginning, medial, and final sound as *duck* in each section of the paper. Help them identify the sounds and label their pictures.

Picture Card

Segment

I will say two words. Tell me what sound the two words share. Listen carefully: *sad, silly. Sad* and *silly* both start with /s/. They share the sound /s/. Repeat the routine for initial, medial, and final shared sounds using these word pairs: *mop, money; flag, mug; pet, hen; sun, ten; fix, sit; lamp, dump; brick, brown.*

Corrective feedback

If... children cannot segment words into initial, medial, and final sounds,

then... have them find shared initial sounds, such as *bat* and *bed*, and shared word endings in rhyming words, such as *hat* and *cat*.

Blend

Make teams of three or four children. Assign each team a sound, such as /m/. Call one member from each of three teams to the front of the room. For example, one from the /m/ group, one from the /e/ group, and one from the /t/ group. Have the three children sequence their sounds to form a word. Have them say the sounds and tell the listening children to blend the sounds to form the word. Teams can take turns answering. A team that correctly blends the sounds gets a point.

Differentiated Instruction

 **Strategic Intervention**

Support Phonemic Awareness Have children identify which of the following words does not have the same beginning sound as the others: *goose, guitar, vat, gold.* Repeat the routine for medial sounds using the words *click, milk, lost,* and *list,* and for final sounds using the words *flag, leg, dip,* and *tug.*

Teacher Tip

Use segmentation and blending activities, such as team blending, as a quick transition activity.

ELL

English Language Learners
Count the Sounds Make children more aware of number of sounds in a word by having them tap their knees for each sound they hear. Say the words *at, trap, bun, it, jam.*

Objectives
◎ Decode words.
- Substitute phonemes.
- Create new words by changing letters.
- Read high-frequency words.

Check Word Reading
SUCCESS PREDICTOR

Phonics—Teach/Model
☞ Decode Words

Practice decoding words

Write *jam* on the board. Point to the *j*. This is the letter *j*. What is the sound for *j*? (/j/) Repeat the routine for the other letters. Let's say the sounds together: /j/ /a/ /m/. Point to each letter as you say the sound. Let's blend the sounds together to read the word: /j/ /a/ /m/, *jam*. The word is *jam*.

Review

Letter Names and Sounds Use Alphabet Cards to review the following letter names and sounds: *Aa, Dd, Ee, Ff, Jj, Nn, Pp, Ss, Yy.*

Blend sounds

Let's play Word Tag. Write the word *last* on the board. What are the letters in this word? (*l, a, s, t*) What sounds do the letters stand for? Point to each letter or consonant blend as you say the sounds. /l/ /a/ /st/ are the sounds in the word. The word is *last*. What new word can I make if I change *a* to *i*? Erase *a* and write *i* in its place. Have children say the sounds in the new word and identify the word. The child who identifies the word is now "it" and replaces a letter or letters to make a new word. When children cannot think of ways to form new words, write one of the following words on the board and begin again: *trip, bet, hand, jug, risk, clap, send, plan.*

More practice

Use *Reader's and Writer's Notebook,* p. 455, for additional review of letters and sounds.

Reader's and Writer's Notebook, p. 455

Review **Sound-Spelling** Display the *Bb* Alphabet Card. What sound do you hear at the beginning of *baby*? What letter spells that sound? Yes, the letter *b* spells /b/. Review the following letters using Alphabet Cards: *Ee, Gg, Hh, Ii, Pp, Tt.*

Review **High-Frequency Words** Write the word *said* on the board. This is the word *said.* What is this word? Who can use this word in a sentence? Continue the routine with *what, you, for, like, the, a, have, look,* and *they.*

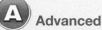

Alphabet Card

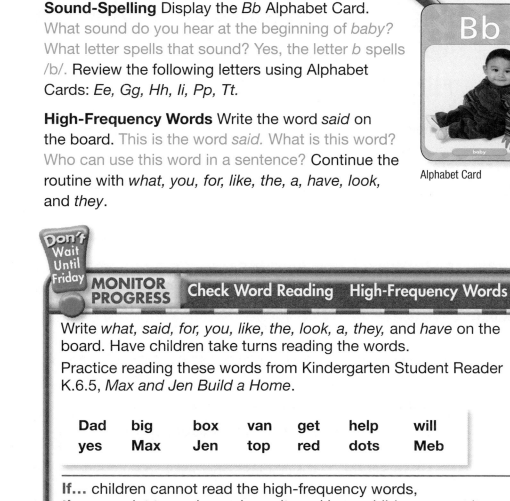

Don't Wait Until Friday

MONITOR PROGRESS **Check Word Reading** **High-Frequency Words**

Write *what, said, for, you, like, the, look, a, they,* and *have* on the board. Have children take turns reading the words.

Practice reading these words from Kindergarten Student Reader K.6.5, *Max and Jen Build a Home.*

Dad	big	box	van	get	help	will
yes	Max	Jen	top	red	dots	Meb

If... children cannot read the high-frequency words, **then...** point to each word, say it, and have children repeat it.

If... children can successfully blend sounds to read the words, **then...** have them read Kindergarten Student Reader K.6.5, *Max and Jen Build a Home.*

Day 1	Day 2	Day 3	Day 4	Day 5
Check Phonemic Awareness	Check Sound-Spelling/ Retelling	Check Word Reading	Check Phonemic Awareness	Check Oral Vocabulary

Success Predictor

Differentiated Instruction

A Advanced

High-Frequency Words Make a duplicate set of cards with the high-frequency words and have children take turns turning the cards over until they get a match.

English Language Learners
Count the Sounds Have children practice blending word families in chunks: /b/ -et, /p/ -et, /m/ -et, /l/ -et.

Word Reading

Success Predictor

Objectives
- Read decodable words.
- Read high-frequency words.

Kindergarten Student Reader K.6.5
⟳ Decodable Words and
High-Frequency Words

Review   Review the previously taught high-frequency words. Have children read each word as you point to it on the Word Wall.

a	the	what	is	for	like	from
look	said	go	have	you	they	we

Read Kindergarten Student Reader K.6.5   Display Kindergarten Student Reader K.6.5, *Max and Jen Build a Home*. Today we are going to read a new book. Point to the title of the book. The title of this book is *Max and Jen Build a Home*. The author's name is Tony Rossetti. This book was illustrated by Nan Brooks.

Use the reading decodable books routine to read the Kindergarten Student Reader.

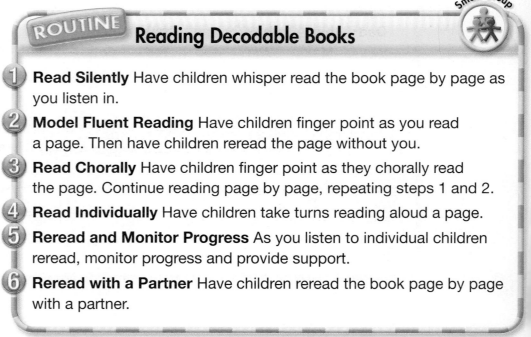

ROUTINE   **Reading Decodable Books**   *Small Group*

1. **Read Silently** Have children whisper read the book page by page as you listen in.

2. **Model Fluent Reading** Have children finger point as you read a page. Then have children reread the page without you.

3. **Read Chorally** Have children finger point as they chorally read the page. Continue reading page by page, repeating steps 1 and 2.

4. **Read Individually** Have children take turns reading aloud a page.

5. **Reread and Monitor Progress** As you listen to individual children reread, monitor progress and provide support.

6. **Reread with a Partner** Have children reread the book page by page with a partner.

Routines Flip Chart

Dad has a big box in the van.
Jen and Max help Dad
get the box.

What is in the box, Dad?
"It is for you," said Dad.
"You will like it."

Dad gets it from the box.
Jen and Max help Dad.

Kindergarten Student Reader K.6.5

Jen looks at Dad.
Dad looks at Mom.
"Yes, I will help you," Mom said.

Dad gets the top on.
Mom taps the top.
Jen and Max get the red dots on.

Jen and Max go in to look.
Look at us, Mom and Dad!
Jen and Max like it a lot.

We can get Meg and Ben.
They will like it.
We will have fun!

Differentiated Instruction

SI Strategic Intervention

Access Content Tell children to find the nouns *Jen*, *Max*, *house*, *van*, *grass*, and *box* in the story. Have them match the word in the text with its picture. Have children describe what they see.

Teacher Tip

Review the high-frequency words on each page before reading Kindergarten Student Reader K.6.5.

Small Group Time

DAY 3 Break into small groups to read the Kindergarten Student Reader before the comprehension lesson.

Teacher-Led

SI Strategic Intervention	**OL** On-Level	**A** Advanced
Teacher-Led Page DI•71	**Teacher-Led** Page DI•75	**Teacher-Led** Page DI•78
• Phonemic Awareness and Phonics	• Phonemic Awareness and Phonics	• **Read** Independent Reader K.6.5 or Kindergarten Student Reader K.6.4
• **Read** Concept Literacy Reader K.6.5 or Kindergarten Student Reader K.6.4	• **Read** Kindergarten Student Reader K.6.5	

 Place English language learners in the groups that correspond to their reading abilities in English.

Practice Stations
• Visit the Words to Know Station
• Visit the Let's Write Station

Independent Activities
• Read independently
• Audio Text of Trade Book
• *Reader's and Writer's Notebook*

English Language Learners
Peer Assisted Learning Pair children of different abilities and have them take turns reading the Kindergarten Student Reader aloud.

Objectives
- Recall and retell a story.
- Practice setting.
- Develop and use vocabulary.
- Develop and use comprehension skills.

Comprehension

Retell the story

Have children turn to p. 106 of *My Skills Buddy* and use the retelling boxes to retell the selection *The House That Tony Lives In.*

Think Aloud Direct children to the first retell box. I see a woman with a drawing and a small model. What are the drawing and model of?

Review retelling boxes, having children retell the story.

My Skills Buddy, p. 106

Review

Setting Remind children that the setting of a story is when and where the story takes place.

- Where does this story take place? (at Tony's house)

- Does Tony live in the country, the city, or a town? (town)

- When do you think this story takes place? Are the people dressed like we dress? (The things in the pictures look like they do now. There is a big truck. The story takes place in a time like today.)

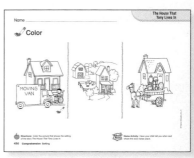

More practice

Use *Reader's and Writer's Notebook,* p. 456, for additional practice with setting.

Reader's and Writer's Notebook, p. 456

Second Read—Big Book
The House That Tony Lives In

Reread *The House That Tony Lives In.* Follow the Day 3 arrow beginning on p. 459, and use the Develop Vocabulary Notes to prompt conversations about the story.

Have children use the Amazing Words *architect, electricians, plumbers, painters, landscapers,* and *movers* to talk about the story.

DAY 2 Read for enjoyment

DAY 3 Reread using Develop Vocabulary notes

DAY 4 Reread using Guide Comprehension notes

Develop Vocabulary

DAY 3

Wh- question

What is this woman doing? (making a model)

• This woman is an architect, a person who draws plans for houses. What is she working on?

This is the architect who drew the plans for the house that Tony lives in.

Big Book, p. 3

Guide Comprehension

DAY 4

Wh- question

What is this woman's job? (She is an architect, a person who draws plans for houses.)

Where do you think she is? (She is probably in her office.)

Develop Vocabulary, continued

DAY 3

Recall

Who are these people? (truck drivers)

- These are the truck drivers who delivered the supplies to build the house that Tony lives in. What kinds of supplies did they deliver?

Develop Vocabulary truck drivers

These are the drivers who delivered the supplies to build the house that Tony lives in.

Big Book, pp. 4–5

Guide Comprehension, continued

DAY 4

Setting

Drivers have delivered supplies for building Tony's house. Where is his house being built? (The house will be in a town or subdivision close to other homes.)

Wh- question

What are these people doing? (building the house)

- People who put the house together are the construction workers. What do construction workers do?

Develop Vocabulary construction workers

Expand Vocabulary lumber

These are the construction workers who built the house that Tony lives in.

6

7

Big Book, pp. 6–7

Inferential

Why do construction workers do their job before electricians or plumbers do their jobs? (Construction workers put up the walls, floors, and roof. These things must be put up before pipes or wires can be put in.)

Develop Vocabulary, continued

DAY 3

Open-ended

These are the electricians. What are they doing? (putting in wires)

- Electricians install the wires that bring electricity into a house. What kinds of things use electricity in your house?

Expand Vocabulary installed

These are the electricians who installed the wires in the house that Tony lives in.

Big Book, pp. 8–9

Guide Comprehension, continued

DAY 4

Open-ended

Why do you think the electricians are wearing gloves? (It is not safe to touch bare electric wires. If electricity is coming through them, the electricians would get a shock.)

Open-ended

These are the plumbers. What are they doing?
(putting together pipes)

- Plumbers connect the pipes in a house that the
  water flows through. Why do you need water in
  your house?

Expand Vocabulary connected

These are the plumbers
who connected the pipes
that bring the water to
the house that Tony lives in.

Big Book, pp. 10–11

Distancing

What rooms in Tony's house will need pipes? (The
bathroom will need water pipes to the bathtub
or shower, the sink, and the toilet. The kitchen
will need water pipes to the sink and maybe a
dishwasher.)

Develop Vocabulary, continued

DAY 3

Wh- question

What are these men doing?
(painting)

- They are painting Tony's bedroom.
  What tools are the painters using?

These are the painters
who painted the walls,
in the bedroom of the
house that Tony lives in.

Big Book, pp. 12–13

Guide Comprehension, continued

DAY 4

Inferential

Why would the painter use a roller
instead of a brush to paint the wall?
(A roller applies paint more smoothly
and evenly over a bigger area than a
brush.)

Distancing

These are the landscapers. What are they doing? (planting flowers and bushes)

- Landscapers plant flowers and trees and grass in the yard. What kind of plants do you like to see around a house?

These are the landscapers who planted the garden around the house that Tony lives in.

Big Book, pp. 14–15

Wh- question

Why are grass, bushes, and flowers placed around houses? (They make the house look nicer.)

Develop Vocabulary, continued

DAY 3

Distancing

What do these people do to help? (They moved furniture into the house.)

• These are the movers who bring the furniture into Tony's house. What kind of furniture do you have in your house?

These are the movers who brought the furniture into the house that Tony lives in.

Big Book, pp. 16–17

Guide Comprehension, continued

DAY 4

Inferential

Why do movers have to be careful as they carry a family's things into a house? (They do not want to break things. They want them to be safe.)

Wh- question

Who are these people? (Tony's neighbors)

• These are the neighbors who live next door to Tony. How many of Tony's neighbors do you see here?

Develop Vocabulary neighbors

There are the neighbors who live next door to the house that Tony lives in.

Big Book, pp. 18–19

Open-ended

Will Tony and his family have fun living in this neighborhood? Why? (Yes. Their neighbors include children and pets. They have a yard so they can be outside.)

Develop Vocabulary, continued

DAY 3

Distancing

This is Tony's family. How many people are in Tony's family? **(six)**

- There are six people in Tony's family. How many people in your family live with you?

This is Tony's family who live in the house that Tony lives in.

Big Book, pp. 20–21

Guide Comprehension, continued

DAY 4

Wh- question

What is Tony's family doing? How does having a house make this possible? **(They are playing and having a cookout. Having a yard lets them spend time together outdoors.)**

Recall

Who is in this picture? (everyone who helped with Tony's house)

- Some people are still carrying their tools. Can you tell me how any of these people helped with Tony's house?

Continue with **DAY 3**

Conventions p. 470

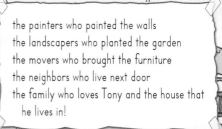

This is...
the architect who drew the plans
the drivers who delivered the supplies
the construction workers who built the house
the electricians who installed the wires
the plumbers who connected the pipes

the painters who painted the walls
the landscapers who planted the garden
the movers who brought the furniture
the neighbors who live next door
the family who loves Tony and the house that
   he lives in!

Big Book, pp. 22–23

Distancing

How is the entry to Tony's house different? Why was it made this way? (It has a ramp instead of steps so Tony's wheelchair can roll up it easily.)

Skip to **DAY 4**

Conventions p. 484

Objectives
- Review questions.
- Dictate or write a poem.

Conventions
Questions

Review

Display the *igloo* Picture Card. When I want to know about something, I ask a question: What kind of home is this? Write the question on the board. Questions begin with an uppercase letter and end with a question mark.

Guide practice

Write the sentences below on the board and read them aloud. Have children identify which sentences are questions.

> **How do you build an igloo?**
>
> **Brrr, it is freezing!**
>
> **Does an igloo have windows?**

Team Talk Pair children and have them take turns asking each other questions about their homes. Have them write one of their questions on their Write-On Boards. Remind them to begin their question with an uppercase letter and end with a question mark.

On their own

Use *Reader's and Writer's Notebook*, p. 457, for more practice with questions.

Daily Fix-It

Use the Daily Fix-It for more conventions practice.

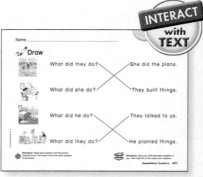

Reader's and Writer's Notebook, p. 457

Writing
Poem

Teach

I am going to write a poem about the house. A poem can tell about things around us or our feelings. A poem may or may not rhyme. A poem is written in lines. Every word in a poem is important, so I choose my words carefully. A poem has a title.

Model

Let's make a list of words we can use to tell about a house. Make a chart on the board with the headings *see, hear, smell,* and *feel*. Write the word *family* under the heading *see*. I see a family in a house. Write the word *laughing* under the heading *hear*. I hear people *laughing* in a house.

Help children brainstorm descriptive words and list them under the appropriate heading.

Guide practice

Provide the following poem for children to fill in using their own words or words from the list. Children can illustrate their poem and then share it with the class.

My House

In my house, I see a _____.

In my house, I smell _____.

In my house, I hear a _____.

In my house, I feel _____.

Independent writing

Have children turn to p. 458 of *Reader's and Writer's Notebook*. Have them copy a line from the poem about a house and then draw a picture of the house.

Reader's and Writer's Notebook, p. 458

Daily Handwriting

Write *April, rose,* and *door* on the board. Review correct letter formation of uppercase and lowercase letters and even spacing between the letters in each word.

Have children write *April, rose,* and *door* on their Write-On Boards. Remind them to use proper left-to-right and top-to-bottom progression and proper spacing between letters in each word.

Differentiated Instruction

 **Strategic Intervention**

Non-rhyming Poetry To reduce anxiety children might have about the need to rhyme, emphasize that not all poems rhyme.

A **Advanced**

Use Rhyming Words Provide more proficient writers with a list of rhyming words such as *moon/ spoon, bug/rug, pig/wig, skunk/ trunk,* and have them use the words to write a two-line poem.

Academic Vocabulary

poem an expressive imaginative piece of writing often arranged in lines having rhythm and rhyme

Daily Fix-It

you can not fix it
You can not fix it.

This week's practice sentences appear on Teacher Resources DVD-ROM.

E L L

English Language Learners

Language Prompts If children can't come up with descriptive words, ask specific questions such as *What color is a flower? What sound does a bird make? How does the wet grass feel?*

Objectives

- Practice oral presentations.
- Speak loudly and clearly.
- Face the speaker when listening.
- Speak one at a time.

Listening and Speaking
Oral Presentation—Book Report

Review

When we give a book report, we identify the title, author, and illustrator of the book. We also tell about the setting of the story, the characters in the story, and what happens in the story. We can retell what happens in the story by telling what happens in the beginning, in the middle, and at the end of the story.

My Skills Buddy, p. 109

Model

Have children turn to p. 109 of *My Skills Buddy*. Use the Listening and Speaking bullets on p. 108 to guide the discussion. Let's give a book report about the story *The House That Tony Lives In.* Point out the author, title, and illustrator on the cover. Have children tell about the setting of the story. After several children have identified and described the setting, summarize their responses: The story takes place at a house in a town. It takes place in a time like today.

Guide practice

Continue having children identify and describe the characters in the story and retell the plot. Present the entire book report for them.

Independent practice

Display the Big Book, *Bear Snores On*. Have children take turns coming to the front of the class and contributing to a class book report. Have children identify the title, author, illustrator, and setting of the story. Help them to summarize the story. The story takes place in the woods in winter. The main character is Bear, who goes to sleep in his cave for the winter. Other animals, such as Mouse, Hare, and Badger, come in the cave to get warm and eat. They wake up Bear, and the animals have a party. Then everyone but Bear goes to sleep. Speaking one at a time have children tell why they did or did not like the book. Refer children to the Rules for Listening and Speaking from pp. 1–2 of the *Reader's and Writer's Notebook*. Tell children to speak loudly and clearly. Remind listeners to face the speaker and listen politely and attentively.

Name _____

Speaking Rules

1. Speak clearly.
2. Tell only important ideas.
3. Choose your words carefully.
4. Take turns speaking.
5. Speak one at a time.

2 *Listening and Speaking Rules*

Reader's and Writer's Notebook, pp. 1–2

Get Ready For Grade 1

Be a Good Speaker

1. Speak clearly.
2. Tell only important ideas.
3. Choose your words carefully.
4. Take turns speaking.
5. Speak one at a time.

Differentiated Instruction

 **A** **Advanced**

Listening Skills Display a previously read selection and give a short book report with some incorrect information about the title, author, illustrator, setting, characters, or plot. Tell children to listen carefully and correct the mistakes.

Academic Vocabulary

book report telling important information about a book one has read

English Language Learners
Language Prompts Help children give a book report about Kindergarten Student Reader K.6.5, *Max and Jen Build a Home*. Provide sentence starters such as: *The title of the book is _____. The author is _____. The setting is _____.*

DAY 3 Language Arts

Objectives

- Review skills learned and practiced today.
- Change letters to create new words.

Wrap Up Your Day

✔ **Concept Talk** Today we read about building a playhouse. Which characters were like construction workers?

✔ **Respond to Literature** Today we read about Jen and Max building a house and the help they get from Mom and Dad. How do Mom and Dad help?

✔ **Conventions** Have children think of questions they would like to ask construction workers.

✔ **Homework Idea** Have children write three one-syllable words.

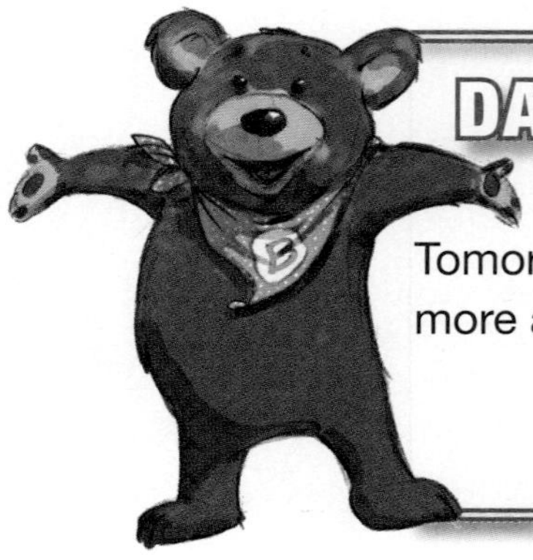

Preview DAY 4

Tomorrow we will read more about Tony's house.

Extend Your Day!

Social Studies
Tools of the Trade

Materials: paper, writing and drawing tools

Identify Tools for Tasks Make a three-column chart as shown. In the *Job* column, write the jobs of the people in *The House That Tony Lives In*. Talk about the tools used by each person. List tools in the *Tools* column. Explain the task each tool is used for and write in the third column.

Job	Tools	Task
architect	computer graph paper	draw plans
construction workers	hammers, saws, machines	build a house
plumbers	wrenches, pipe	connect pipes
electricians	wire, pliers	install wires
painters	paintbrushes, rollers, ladders	paint walls
landscapers	shovels	plant plants
movers	trucks, hand trucks	move furniture

Connect to Writing Have children use the words and phrases in the chart to write sentences about how tools are used by people to accomplish specific tasks. Then have children illustrate their sentences.

Phonics
Word Families

Materials: chart paper or Graphic Organizer 16, *Word Family Ladders;* writing tools

Put Words in Word Families Draw three word ladders or display Graphic Organizer 16, *Word Family Ladders*, with the words *cat, hen,* and *dot* written on the top rung of the ladders. Have children change the first letter of the words on the ladder and write new words on the next rung. Have them continue filling the ladders with as many new words as possible.

cat	hen	dot
hat	Ben	cot
pat	den	got
mat	men	hot
sat	pen	lot
bat	ten	not
fat		oot
rat		rot

Social Studies
Building Tony's House

Materials: Patterns on the TR•DVD, *adult female, adult male;* crayons or markers

Outfit a Worker Supply each child with a man or woman pattern to outfit as a worker from the story. Children should draw appropriate clothes and tools for the job on their person. Have them display their figure and tell about the job this person does.

Objectives

- Discuss the concept to develop oral language.
- Build oral vocabulary.

Today at a Glance

Oral Vocabulary
landscapers, movers

Phonemic Awareness
Isolate Sounds

Phonics
◉ Decode Words
Spell Words

Comprehension
◉ Setting

Conventions
Exclamations

Writing
Extend the Concept

Vocabulary
Words for Feelings

TRUCKTOWN on Reading Street

Start your engines!

- Display "Rumble, Rumble, Monster Max" and lead the group in saying the rhyme a few times.
- Have the group clap the rhythm as they recite the rhyme.
- When children master the rhythm, have them march around the room as they say the rhyme.

Truckery Rhymes

Concept Talk

Question of the Week

Who helps to build a house?

Build concepts

Write the question of the week on the board. Read the question as you track the print. Tell children to respond in complete sentences. Display Sing with Me Chart 35B.

Listen for Amazing Words

Today we are going to sing "Let's Build a House." I want you to listen for the Amazing Words *landscapers* and *movers*. Read the title and have children describe the picture. Sing the song several times to the tune of "Three Blind Mice." Tell children to sing with you. Have them clap when they hear the Amazing Word *landscapers* or *movers*.

Sing with Me Audio

Let's Build a House

Let's build a house, let's build a house,
Who can help, who can help?
The architect can draw some plans,
The driver brings the supplies he can,
The construction worker
   can saw and sand,
Who else can help?

Talk with Me/Sing with Me
Chart 35B

ELL **Produce Oral Language** Use the Day 4 instruction on ELL Poster 35 to extend and enrich language.

ELL Poster 35

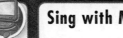
Oral Vocabulary
Amazing Words

Teach Amazing Words

Amazing Words   Oral Vocabulary Routine

1. **Introduce the Word** *Landscapers* are people who plant flowers, trees, bushes, and other plants in a yard. What is our new Amazing Word for people who plant things? Say it with me: *landscapers*.

2. **Demonstrate** *A landscaper uses a shovel to dig holes and then puts plants in the ground.* What are some plants that *landscapers* put in the ground?

   Repeat steps 1 and 2.

   Introduce the Word *Movers* are people who move furniture into a house. What is our new Amazing Word for the people who move furniture into a house? Say it with me: *movers*.

   Demonstrate *Movers must be strong so they can carry heavy furniture.* What kinds of things do *movers* bring into a house?

3. **Apply** Have children use *landscapers* and *movers* in complete sentences. Tell them to act out each job.

Routines Fl p Chart

Use Amazing Words

To reinforce the concept and the Amazing Words, have children supply the appropriate Amazing Word for each sentence.

The _____ carried boxes into the house. (movers)

_____ know a lot about growing grass, bushes, and trees. (Landscapers)

Differentiated Instruction

SI **Strategic Intervention**
Build Background Show children pictures of tools that landscapers use, such as rake, hoe, shovel, trowel, spade, lawn mower, and watering can.

English Language Learners
Access Content Explain to children that *gardener* is another word for *landscaper*. Then have them show what a *mover* does using classroom chairs.

Objectives
- Isolate sounds.
- Segment and blend words.

Check Phonemic Awareness
SUCCESS PREDICTOR

Phonemic Awareness
Isolate Sounds

Picture Card

Review

Display the *bus* Picture Card. Say the name of this picture with me: *bus*. What sound do you hear at the beginning of the word? (/b/) What sound do you hear in the middle of the word? (/u/) What sound do you hear at the end of the word? (/s/) Repeat the routine with the following Picture Cards: *jam, desk, rock, van, frog, six, pig.*

Display the *jam* Picture Card. I will say some words. Tell me which words have the same beginning sound as the name of this picture: *jelly, toast, eggs, juice.* Continue the routine for the middle and ending sounds of *jam*, using the following words: *sat, hid, bit, ran; slam, cat, ram, lid.*

Picture Card

Corrective feedback

If... children cannot discriminate initial, medial, and final sounds,
then... have them segment one-syllable words.

Draw three boxes on the board, one for each sound. Move a pointer to each box, from left to right, as you say the sounds with children.

Phonics
Decode Words

Review

Write *sun* on the board. Point to each letter. What is this letter? What is the sound for this letter? Now help me blend this word. Say the sounds as I point to each letter: /s/ /u/ /n/. What is the word? Continue the decoding routine with *Jen, kick, lug, wig, not,* and *sat.*

Don't Wait Until Friday

MONITOR PROGRESS | **Check Phonemic Awareness**

Blend Sounds to Read Words Write the words below on the board. I am going to point to a word. I want you to say the sound of each letter and then blend the sounds to read the words.

| fun | snug | hot | Deb | quit | mud | Jan | bat | slim |

If... children cannot blend the sounds to read the words,

then... use the small-group Strategic Intervention lesson, p. DI•72, to reteach blending skills.

Continue to monitor children's progress using other instructional opportunities during the week so that they can be successful with the Day 5 Assessment. See the Skills Trace on p. 420.

Day 1	Day 2	Day 3	Day 4	Day 5
Check Phonemic Awareness	Check Sound-Spelling/ Retelling	Check Word Reading	Check Phonemic Awareness	Check Oral Vocabulary

Success Predictor

Differentiated Instruction

SI **Strategic Intervention**

Support Phonemic Awareness Randomly display on the chalkboard several sets of Picture Cards with the same initial sound. Tell one child to choose a Picture Card and say the beginning sound. Then have another child pick a Picture Card with the same beginning sound. Continue the routine until all the Picture Cards have been matched.

ELL

English Language Learners
Word Families Present children with word families to practice their decoding skills. Use these words: *fan, man, tan; pig, wig, jig; hop, mop, stop; bet, met, pet; hit, fit, sit.*

Phonemic Awareness

Success Predictor

Objectives
- Spell words.
- Blend and segment words.
- Read decodable text.
- Read high-frequency words.

Spelling
↺ Initial, Medial, and Final Sounds

ROUTINE Spell Words

Spell words

1 **Review Sound-Spellings** Display the *Vv* Alphabet Card. What is the sound for this letter? (/v/) What are the names of these letters? (*Vv*) Continue the routine with the following Alphabet Cards: *Pp, Oo, Jj, Ff, Aa, Ss, Tt, Nn*.

2 **Model** Today we are going to spell some words. Listen to the three sounds in *van: /v/ /a/ /n/.*

- What is the first sound in *van*? (/v/) What is the letter for /v/? (*v*) Write *v* on the board.
- What is the middle sound in *van*? (/a/) What is the letter for /a/? (*a*) Write *a* on the board.
- What is the last sound in *van*? (/n/) What is the letter for /n/? (*n*) Write *n* on the board.
- Point to *van*. Help me blend the sound of each letter together to read this word: /v/ /a/ /n/. The word is *van*. Repeat with the word *nap*.

3 **Guide Practice** Now let's spell some words together. Listen to this word: /f/ /a/ /st/. What is the first sound in *fast*? (/f/) What is the letter for /f/? (*f*) Write *f* on the board. Now you write *f* on your paper. What is the middle sound in *fast*? (/a/) What is the letter for /a/? (*a*) Write *a* on the board. Now you write *a* on your paper. What are the last sounds in *fast*? (/s/ /t/) What letters stand for the sounds /s/ /t/? (*st*) Write *st* on the board. Now you write *st* on your paper. Now we can blend the sound of each letter together to read the word: /f/ /a/ /st/. What is the word? (*fast*) Continue spell and blend practice with the following words: *Jan, top, not, fan, snap, egg, well, bat, mud, hot.*

4 **On Your Own** This time I am going to say a word. I want you to write the word on your paper. Remember, first say the word slowly in your head and then write the letter for each sound you hear. Listen carefully. Write the word *top*. Give children time to write the word. How do you spell the word *top*? Listen to the sounds: /t/ /o/ /p/. The first sound is /t/. What is the letter for /t/? Did you write *t* on your paper? What is the letter for /o/? Did you write *o* on your paper? What is the letter for /p/? Did you write *p* on your paper? Name the letters in *top*. *Top* is spelled *t, o, p*. Continue the activity with the following words: *fan, pot, stop, vat, jot.*

Routines Flip Chart

Get Set, Roll! Reader 35
Practice Decodable Words

Review

Review the high-frequency words *they, she, go, said, he, you, of,* and *is* Have children read each word as you point to it on the Word Wall.

Read Get Set, Roll! Reader 35

Display Get Set, Roll! Reader 35, *Spin! Spin!* Today we will read a story about a race in the sand. Point to the title of the story. What is the title of the story? The title of the story is *Spin! Spin!* We will read words with many different sounds in this book.

Use the routine for reading decodable books found in the Routines Flip Chart to read Get Set, Roll! Reader 35.

Get Set, Roll! Reader 35

Small Group Time

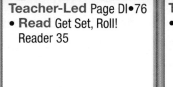

DAY 4 Break into small groups to read the Get Set, Roll! Reader before the comprehension lesson.

Teacher-Led

SI Strategic Intervention	**OL** On-Level	**A** Advanced
Teacher-Led Page DI•72 • Phonemic Awareness and Phonics • **Read** Get Set, Roll! Reader 35	**Teacher-Led** Page DI•76 • **Read** Get Set, Roll! Reader 35	**Teacher-Led** Page DI•79 • **Read** Get Set, Roll! Reader 35 or **Reread** Kindergarten Student Reader K.6.5

ELL Place English language learners in the groups that correspond to their reading abilities in English.

Practice Stations
• Visit the Let's Write! Station
• Visit the Read for Meaning Station

Independent Activities
• Read independently
• Audio Text of Big Book
• *Reader's and Writer's Notebook*

English Language Learners

Activate Prior Knowledge
Discuss a race using the words *start, go, fast, slow, winner,* and *finish line* with children before reading Get Set, Roll! Reader 35.

Comprehension
↺ Setting

Practice setting

Have children turn to the Literary Elements picture on pp. 94–95. As you look at the pictures, remind children that all stories have a setting. The setting of the story is where and when it happens.

Team Talk Pair children and have them discuss the setting of their favorite movie by identifying where and when the story takes place.

My Skills Buddy, pp. 94–95

Realism and Fantasy

Review

Direct children to the Literary Elements picture on pp. 94–95 of *My Skills Buddy.*

Remember, a story is realistic if it tells about something that could happen in real life. If the story is make-believe, it is a fantasy. Good readers notice whether a story is realistic or make-believe.

- Is this picture real or make-believe? (make-believe)
- What clues in the picture helped you know that it is make-believe? (The animals are wearing clothes. Real animals do not wear clothes. The animals are lined up for a race. Real animals do not line up for a race. Turtles do not run on their back legs like the turtle in the picture.)
- Could animals race in real life? (Yes, but not in a race like this one.)

More practice

For more practice with realism and fantasy, use *Reader's and Writer's Notebook,* p. 459.

Reader's and Writer's Notebook, p. 459

Third Read—Big Book
The House That Tony Lives In

Guide comprehension

Display *The House That Tony Lives In.* Remind children that it shows families, houses, and workers. People and things in the book are familiar. Tony and his family move into a house like many real families do.

- Are the workers who build the house make-believe? (No; construction workers, plumbers, electricians, and painters are all real workers who build houses.)

- Tony's house is in a neighborhood with lots of other houses. Is this real or make-believe? (Real; many families live in neighborhoods where many houses are next to each other.)

Reread *The House That Tony Lives In.* Return to p. 459. Follow the Day 4 arrow and use the Guide Comprehension notes to give children the opportunity to gain a more complete understanding of the story.

Differentiated Instruction

SI Strategic Intervention

Access Content Page through the Big Book *The Little School Bus* and help children identify the clues that tell this is a make-believe story.

A Advanced

Build Background Display the Big Book *Little Panda* and the Trade Book *Little Quack.* Have children identify which selection is real and which selection is make-believe and tell how they know.

DAY **2**
Read for enjoyment

DAY **3**
Reread using Develop Vocabulary notes

DAY **4**
Reread using Guide Comprehension notes

Objectives
- Identify exclamations.
- Practice exclamations.
- Write or dictate sentences about moving.
- Use a picture dictionary.

Conventions
Exclamations

Review

Remind children of what they learned about exclamations. An exclamation is something we say to express a strong feeling. If I see an amazing sight, I say, "Wow, look at that!" This is an exclamation. Exclamations begin with an uppercase letter and end with an exclamation point.

Guide practice

Write the sentences below on the board and read them with children. Point out that a good listener can hear which sentence is an exclamation by how the sentence is read with expression and excitement. A good reader knows that an exclamation mark is a signal that the writer has strong feelings.

> **That's funny!**
>
> **It is fun to play in the park.**
>
> **Oh, boy! I can't wait!**
>
> **Wait here for the bus.**

Have children describe an event when they might use each exclamation. Write children's exclamations on the board. Have children tell you which letter to make uppercase and where to put the exclamation mark.

On their own

Use *Reader's and Writer's Notebook,* p. 460, for more practice with exclamations.

Daily Fix-It

Use the Daily Fix-It for more conventions practice.

INTERAC with TEXT

Reader's and Writer's Notebook, p. 460

Writing
Extend the Concept:
Text to Self

Discuss moving to a new neighborhood

We just read a story about a boy who moved to a new home in a new neighborhood. When we move, we can have a lot of different feelings. We can be sad that we are moving away from our friends. We can be proud of our new home. We can be worried that we won't make new friends. We can be excited about going to a new school.

Ask children to think about how they felt when or would feel if they moved to a new home or went to school. Emphasize that different people can have different feelings about the same situation.

Guide practice

Use children's contribution to the discussion to write sentences.

Tom is _____ to have his own room.

Tyler is _____ about riding on the school bus.

Sara is _____ to plant flowers.

Ken is _____ to move away from his cousins.

Encourage children to help you write more sentences. Have them read the sentences with you.

Independent writing

Have children write or dictate their own sentences about moving or going to a school, or they may copy sentences from the board. Encourage children to use the picture dictionary on p. 142 for help defining and spelling words for feelings. Have children read their sentences to the class.

Daily Handwriting

Write *Iowa, Florida,* and *Texas* on the board. Review correct letter formation with children. Review correct letter formation of uppercase and lowercase letters and even spacing between the letters in each word.

Have children write *Iowa, Florida,* and *Texas* on their Write-On Boards. Remind them to use proper left-to-right and top-to-bottom progression and proper spacing between letters in each word.

Vocabulary
Words for Feelings

Teach

Write the words *frightened, worried, proud,* and *angry* on the board. Point to each word as you read it. These are words for feelings. Have children turn to p. 108 of *My Skills Buddy*. Use the last four Vocabulary bullets in the discussion. Point to the boy that shows a feeling for a situation I will tell you about. What if a boy doesn't like to walk in the dark? Is that boy frightened or proud? What if a boy can't find his dog? Is that boy worried or angry? What if a boy helps Dad rake leaves? How does that boy feel? What if a boy didn't get to go to the movies with his brother? How does that boy feel?

My Skills Buddy, p. 108

Team Talk Pair children and have them take turns using the words for feelings in complete sentences.

Wrap Up Your Day

✔ **Concept Talk** Revisit the question of the day: *How does a plumber help build a house?* Review children's responses from the beginning of the lesson. Should we change any of our information? What information can we add?

✔ **Oral Language** Sing "Let's Build a House." Have children tap with their "hammers" when they hear an Amazing Word—*architect, electricians, plumbers, painters, landscapers, movers.*

✔ **Phonemic Awareness** I will read some words. Clap when you hear words with the same middle sound as *fun: box, brush, shrub, deck, dig, cut, dust.*

✔ **Homework Idea** Have children write an exclamation they might say at home.

Preview DAY 5

Tell children that tomorrow they will review some of the books and stories they have read this week.

Extend Your Day!

Social Studies
Under Construction

Materials: glue; craft sticks; construction paper; supplies such as chenille sticks, buttons, uncooked pasta, cereal boxes, cartons, cardboard

Identify Things People Build Discuss things that architects, plumbers, electricians, construction workers, and painters build. Write children's responses on the board. Talk about the materials, tools, and machines used to build the items, as well as the workers who help build them.

> houses, office buildings, bridges, roads, tunnels, stores, schools

Build Something Provide children with a collection of materials that can be glued together. Tell children to use their imaginations and the materials to build one of the items listed on the board. Display children's models. Have each child tell about what he or she built.

Reading
Word Search

Complete a Word Search Puzzle Write one CVC word in each row of a four-square-by-six-square grid. Write random letters in the remaining boxes in each row. Challenge children to find and circle the word hidden in each row. Have children read the words they find.

c	a	t	r
e	p	i	g
h	e	n	t
x	t	o	p
t	j	a	m
w	a	x	o

Phonics
Three of a Kind

Materials: short vowel words written on index cards

Collect Short Vowel Words Give each group of four to six children a stack of decodable word cards. Each player starts with three cards. In turn each player asks another for an /a/, /e/, /i/, /o/, or /u/ card. If that child has a word with that sound, he or she gives it to the asker. If not, the asker draws a card from the pile. When one player gets three cards with one vowel sound, he or she shows the cards and reads the words.

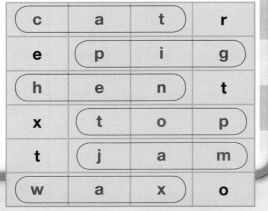

Objectives
- Review the concepts.
- Build oral vocabulary.

Today at a Glance

Oral Vocabulary
architect, electricians, plumbers, painters, landscapers, movers

Phonemic Awareness
◎ Initial, Medial, and Final Sounds

Phonics
◎ Decode Words

Comprehension
◎ Setting

Conventions
Exclamations

Writing
This Week We…

Check Oral Vocabulary
SUCCESS PREDICTOR

TRUCKTOWN on Reading Street

Start your engines!

- Display "Rumble, Rumble, Monster Max" and lead the group in saying the rhyme a few times.
- Have half the group recite the rhyme while the other half acts it out.
- Then have the groups change roles.

Truckery Rhymes

Concept Wrap Up

Question of the Week
Who helps to build a house?

Listen for Amazing Words

Write the question of the week on the board. Track the print as you read it to children. Have them answer the question in complete sentences. Remind children to speak one at a time. Display Sing with Me Chart 35B. Let's sing "Let's Build a House." Listen for the Amazing Words we learned this week. Say them with me: *architect, electricians, plumbers, painters, landscapers, movers.* Sing the song several times to the tune of "Three Blind Mice." Have children sing with you. Tell children to act out each of the Amazing Words when they sing them.

💿 Sing with Me Audio

Let's Build a House

Let's build a house, let's build a house,
Who can help, who can help?
The architect can draw some plans,
The driver brings the supplies he can,
The construction worker
    can saw and sand,
Who else can help?

Talk with Me/Sing with Me Chart 35B

ⒺⓁⓁ Check Concepts and Language Use the Day 5 instruction on ELL Poster 35 to monitor children's understanding of the lesson concept.

ⒺⓁⓁ Poster 35

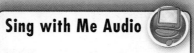

Oral Vocabulary
Amazing Words

architect	electricians
plumbers	painters
landscapers	movers

Review

Let's Talk Display Talk with Me Chart 35A. We learned six new Amazing Words this week. Let's say the Amazing Word as I point to the pictures on the chart. Point to each picture and give children the chance to say the appropriate Amazing Word before offering it.

The _____ put flowers in the ground. (landscapers)

_____ fit the water pipes together. (Plumbers)

The plan for the house is made by an _____. (architect)

_____ put in wires that bring electricity into the house. (Electricians)

The _____ had new brushes and green paint. (painters)

The _____ carried boxes into the house. (movers)

Talk with Me/Sing with Me Chart 35A

It's Friday

MONITOR PROGRESS | Check Oral Vocabulary

Demonstrate Word Knowledge Monitor the Amazing Words by asking the following questions. Have children use the Amazing Word in their answer.

- **Who draws the plans for a house?** (architect)
- **Who uses a roller and a paintbrush?** (painters)
- **Who puts pipes together with a wrench?** (plumbers)
- **Who puts in wires for the TV and refrigerator?** (electricians)
- **Who carries furniture and boxes into the house?** (movers)
- **Who plants things to make the yard look nice?** (landscapers)

If... children have difficulty using the Amazing Words,

then... reteach unknown words using the Oral Vocabulary Routine on the Routines Flip Chart.

Day 1	Day 2	Day 3	Day 4	Day 5
Check Phonemic Awareness	Check Sound-Spelling/ Retelling	Check Word Reading	Check Phonemic Awareness	Check Oral Vocabulary

Success Predictor

Oral Vocabulary

Success Predictor

Phonemic Awareness Review

Initial, Medial, and Final Sounds

Isolate sounds

Display the *fox* and *pan* Picture Cards. Say these words with me: *fox, pan.* Which word ends with /n/, *fox* or *pan*? (*pan*) Which word begins with /p/, *fox* or *pan*? (*pan*) Which word has /o/ in the middle, *fox* or *pan*? (*fox*) Repeat the routine with the following pairs of Picture Cards: *mug, bat; jet, hen; net, six; yak, bed.*

Display the *quilt* Picture Card. What is the first sound in *quilt*? Say the word with me: /kw/ /kw/ /kw/, *quilt.* Review /kw/ with *quarter* and *queen* Picture Cards.

Picture Card

Discriminate sounds

I am going to say some words. When you hear the same beginning sound in all three words, I want you to clap your hands. Listen carefully: *July, jig, join; cape, club, lock.* Now listen for the same ending sound and clap your hands: *can, pin, pig; net, hit, pot.* Now listen for the same middle sound and clap your hands: *brush, truck, club; get, hot, web.*

Picture Card

Phonics Review
🎯 Decode Words

Read words

Write this sentence on the board: *Pets can not jump on beds.* Let's read this sentence together. Have children say the sound of each letter in *pets* as you point to it. Now let's blend the sounds: /p/ /e/ /t/ /s/, *pets.* Repeat the decoding routine with each word in the sentence. Continue with *Red cats can jump up* and *Jen and Max can fit it.*

High-frequency words

Write *have* on the board. This is the word *have.* What is this word? Continue the routine with *they, look, from, go,* and *said.*

Apply phonics in familiar text

Let's Reread Have children reread one of the books used this week to review sounds and letters. Review the decodable words and the high-frequency words that appear in each book prior to rereading.

My Skills Buddy, p. 98

Kindergarten Student Reader K.6.5

Get Set, Roll! Reader 35

Differentiated Instruction

SI Strategic Intervention

Sound-Letter Connection Display the Alphabet Cards *Jj, Mm, Tt,* and *Ww.* Have children say a word that begins with each sound and identify the letter that makes the sound.

A Advanced

Sound Discrimination Say the following words and have children identify the word that doesn't belong in each group: *sad, sip, got; fish, lid, tap; mud, hop, Dad.*

Small Group Time

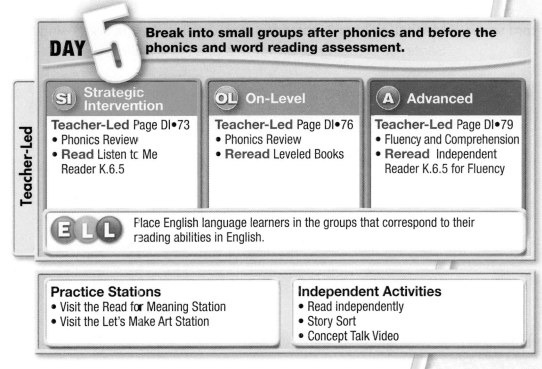

DAY 5 Break into small groups after phonics and before the phonics and word reading assessment.

Teacher-Led

SI Strategic Intervention

Teacher-Led Page DI•73
• Phonics Review
• **Read** Listen to Me Reader K.6.5

OL On-Level

Teacher-Led Page DI•76
• Phonics Review
• **Reread** Leveled Books

A Advanced

Teacher-Led Page DI•79
• Fluency and Comprehension
• **Reread** Independent Reader K.6.5 for Fluency

ELL Place English language learners in the groups that correspond to their reading abilities in English.

Practice Stations
• Visit the Read for Meaning Station
• Visit the Let's Make Art Station

Independent Activities
• Read independently
• Story Sort
• Concept Talk Video

Assessment
Monitor Progress

Decode words

Whole Class Divide a paper into four equal sections for each child. Display Picture Cards *bus, crab, flag,* and *ten.* Have children write the letters for the sounds in each word in a box.

MONITOR PROGRESS | **Check Word and Sentence Reading**

If... children cannot complete the whole-class assessment,
then... use the Reteach lesson in *First Stop.*

If... you are unsure of a child's grasp of this week's skills,
then... use the assessment below to obtain a clearer evaluation of the child's progress.

Decode words and high-frequency words

One-on-One To facilitate individual progress monitoring, assess some children on Day 4 and the rest on Day 5. While individual children are being assessed, the rest of the class can reread this week's books and look for words with short vowels.

Word reading

Use the word lists on reproducible p. 493 to assess a child's ability to read words with short vowels and high-frequency words. We're going to read some words. I'll read the first word, and you read the rest. The first word is *bug, /b/ /u/ /g/.* Have children read the words aloud to you.

Sentence reading

Use the sentences on reproducible p. 493 to assess a child's ability to read words in sentences. Have the child read two sentences aloud. Have each child read different sentences. Start over with sentence one if necessary.

Record scores

Monitor children's accuracy by recording their scores using the Word and Sentence Reading Chart for this unit in *First Stop.*

Name _____

Read the Words

bug	☐	went	☐
here	☐	trip	☐
log	☐	last	☐
zip	☐	four	☐
she	☐	jug	☐
end	☐	they	☐

Read the Sentences

1. Here is a red bug.

2. They see the ant hop.

3. Come to where Meg skips.

4. The little mug is hot.

5. I hid my box here.

Note to Teacher: Children read each word. Children read two sentences.

Scoring for Read the Words: Score 1 point for each correct word.

Short Vowels *a, e, i, o, u* (*bug, log, zip, end, went, trip, last, jug*) _____ /__8__
High-Frequency Words (*here, she, four, they*) _____ /__4__

MONITOR PROGRESS

- Review short vowels
- Review high-frequency words

Objectives
- Recognize a folk tale.
- Identify the theme of a folk tale.

My Skills Buddy, pp. 110–111

Let's Practice It!
Folk Tale

Teach

Remind children what they know about a folk tale. A folk tale is a story that is handed down and retold from generation to generation. Review the features of a folk tale with children.

- A folk tale tells a story.
- Folk tales often begin the same way.
- The characters in folk tales can be people or animals.
- A folk tale teaches a lesson.

Have children turn to pp. 110–111 of *My Skills Buddy.* I am going to read a folk tale called "Juan Bobo." Have children make inferences based on the title and the illustrations. For example, children should infer that the story is going to be about a man named Juan Bobo and two women.

Guide practice

Discuss the features of a folk tale and the bulleted text on p. 110 of *My Skills Buddy*.

- A folk tale tells a story. What happens at the beginning, in the middle, and at the end of "Juan Bobo"? (beginning— Juan carries water in a bag; middle—Juan cuts the hoe into small pieces; end—Juan carries a burro on his shoulders and the merchant's daughter laughs for the first time in years.)
- The characters in folk tales can be people or animals. Who are the characters in the story? (Juan, Juan's mother, the merchant's daughter)
- Folk tales often begin the same way. How does this folk tale begin? (There once was a…)
- What is the setting of the story? (Juan Bobo's village)
- Folk tales teach a lesson. What lesson does this folk tale teach? (Don't be quick to call someone foolish.)

Differentiated Instruction

 **Strategic Intervention**

Folk Tale Have children review the Big Book *Jack and the Beanstalk* and identify the literary elements.

Academic Vocabulary

folk tale story that is handed down and retold from generation to generation

ELL

English Language Learners
Build Background Have children retell a folk tale from their culture and explain its meaning.

 Read Aloud

Juan Bobo

There once was a boy called Juan Bobo, or Foolish Juan. He was called this because he could never seem to do the right thing at the right time. When his mother sent him to the river to get water, Juan Bobo put the water in a bag. By the time he got home, all the water had leaked out.

"Juan," sighed his mother, "you should have put the water in a bucket. Remember that."

So when his mother sent him to Tía Maria's house to borrow a hoe, Juan Bobo remembered, and he cut the hoe into small pieces so that it would fit in a bucket.

"Juan," groaned his mother, "you should have carried the hoe on your shoulder. Remember that."

So when his mother sent him to Tío Pedro's house to fetch their burro, Juan Bobo remembered, and he crouched under the burro so that he could lift it onto his shoulder.

As he was walking, or rather staggering, home, Juan Bobo passed the house of a wealthy merchant. Sitting at the window was the merchant's daughter, who was always sad. When she saw Juan Bobo carrying a burro on his shoulder, she laughed for the first time in years.

(continued on p. 502a)

Comprehension Assessment
Monitor Progress

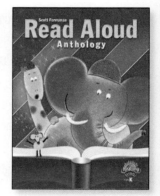

Read Aloud Anthology

Review **Setting** A story happens in a certain time and place. Where and when a story takes place is called its setting. What do we call the time and place of a story? (setting)

Good readers picture the setting of a story so they can understand what the time and place are like.

Read "A House by the Sea" Today we will read a poem about someone who wants to live in a house by the sea. As you listen to the poem, listen to the details that help us identify when and where the story takes place. When I finish, I will ask you to tell me about the setting. Read "A House by the Sea" on p. 83 of *Read Aloud Anthology*.

Check setting After you read the poem, tell children to identify the setting. Remind children that setting is the time and place of the story.

- Where does the poem take place? (beside the sea, on a beach, or in the water, or in a little house)
- What details in the poem help you identify where it takes place? (the seals, a whale, an octopus, sand, seaweed, water, and the crab games)
- What is the weather like in the beginning of the poem? (It is raining.)
- What happens at night? (The person sees stars in the sky, sings to the moon, and rides on a whale.)
- Who would live by the person in the house by the sea? (an octopus)

Corrective feedback If... children cannot identify and describe the setting, then... reteach setting using the Reteach lesson in *First Stop*.

Assess setting Use the blackline master on p. 497. Copy one page for each child. Have children look at the three pictures and color the one that shows the setting for the story.

Name _____

Setting

Color the picture that shows "A House by the Sea."

Note to Teacher: Have children color the picture that is an appropriate setting for the story.

Objectives

- Practice exclamations.
- Write or dictate words for a song.

Conventions
Exclamations

Review   When we feel strongly about something or have a strong reaction to something, we use an exclamation. Exclamations begin with an uppercase letter. An exclamation mark at the end shows excitement.

Model   Write *Watch out!* on the board. This is an exclamation you might yell if you saw something about to fall on your friend's head.

Guide practice   Read the following scenarios to children. Have them say what they might exclaim in that situation. Instruct children to use a lot of expression and emotion in their exclamations.

- You see a really, really big bear.
- You eat something yummy.
- You hear great news.
- Somebody tells you a very funny joke.

On their own   Have children illustrate an exclamation they made for one of the situations above. Have them write their exclamation below their picture using proper capitalization and punctuation.

Daily Fix-It   Use the Daily Fix-It for more conventions practice.

Writing
This Week We…

Review Display *The House That Tony Lives In,* Phonics Songs and Rhymes Chart 35, Sing with Me Chart 35B, Decodable Reader 35 from *My Skills Buddy,* Kindergarten Student Reader K.6.5, and Get Set, Roll! Reader 35. This week we read about people who build things. Which book or song was your favorite?

Team Talk Pair children and have take turns discussing their favorite book or song.

Let's sing a song about the people who help build a house. Teach children the song below to the tune of "Here We Go 'Round the Mulberry Bush."

> **This is the way we build a house,**
> **build a house, build a house.**
> **This is the way we build a house.**
> **Lots of people help.**

Model I am going to write a verse about how an architect helps build a house. Write the new verse on the board and sing it with children.

> **This is the way we draw the plans,**
> **draw the plans, draw the plans.**
> **This is the way we draw the plans.**
> **That's what architects do.**

Guide practice Have children write or dictate a verse about how people help build a house. Sing each verse together.

On their own Have children illustrate a verse of the song and label it with the name of the worker.

Daily Handwriting

Write the words *plan, city, build,* and *house* on the board. Review correct letter formation of the lowercase letters and even spacing between the letters in each word.

Have children write *plan, city, build,* and *house* on their Write-On Boards. Remind them to use proper left-to-right and top-to-bottom progression and proper spacing between letters in each word.

Differentiated Instruction

 **SI** **Strategic Intervention**

Use Conventions Help children prepare a list of exclamations they can use to write about their illustrations, such as *Oh no!; Look out!; Step back!; Stay away!;* and *Danger!*

A **Advanced**

Support Writing As children write or dictate, supply words if needed to express their ideas.

Daily Fix-It

did you pet the cat
<u>D</u>id you pet the cat<u>?</u>

This week's practice sentences appear on Teacher Resources DVD-ROM.

 **ELL**

English Language Learners
Poster Preview Prepare children for next week by using Week 6 ELL Poster number 36. Read the Poster Talk-Through to introduce the concept and vocabulary. Ask children to identify and describe objects and actions in the art.

Objectives
• Review weekly concept.

Wrap Up Your Week!

 ## Question of the Week
Who helps to build a house?

This week we talked about workers who help build a house. Some workers put things together. Some workers carry or deliver. Some workers make things look pretty and neat.

- Make a three-column chart like the one pictured or use Graphic Organizer 5. Name the workers discussed this week: *delivery truck drivers, construction workers, architects, electricians, plumbers, painters, landscapers, movers.*

- Discuss what each worker does. Remind children to speak one at a time. Then have children direct you in which column to write the worker's title.

- When the entire chart has been completed, have the children echo read it with you.

Review Concept

Amazing Words

You've learned **0 0 6** words this week!

You've learned **2 1 0** words this year!

Carry Things	Put Things Together	Make Things Look Nice
delivery truck drivers	construction workers	painters
movers	electricians	landscapers
	plumbers	

Next Week's Question
How do ants build their homes?

Discuss next week's question. Guide children in making connections between the ways people and animals build homes.

Preview NEXT WEEK

Tell children that next week they will read about ants and the nests they live in.

Extend Your Day!

Science
Learning to Be a Landscaper

Materials: photographs of landscaped yards; diagrams of parts of a flower and grass plant; small, rooted plants; potting soil, plastic cups, water

Discuss Planting and Care of Plants Display photographs of yards with grass, flowers, and shrubs. Talk with children about the steps it took to plant the plants. Display diagrams showing the roots, stems, and leaves of several kinds of plants. Have children identify the parts. Then model how to plant a young plant, such as a bean seedling, in a plastic cup with potting soil. Add water and explain why the plant needs water.

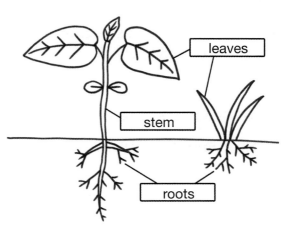

Plant a Seedling Supervise as each child plants his or her own seedling in a cup with potting soil. Measure a small amount of water into separate cups so each child can water his or her plant. Observe the plants for several days before children take them home.

Math
Addresses

Materials: envelopes, four strips of poster board, marker

Read the Numbers Write one street name, such as *Red Street,* on each of four sheets of poster board. Display the street signs around the room. Address envelopes with different numbers for each of the street names, one per child. Give each child an envelope. Have children take turns reading the addresses and standing in numerical order near the appropriate street sign.

6 Red Street   15 Red Street   9 Red Street

Social Studies
Buildings Bingo

Materials: game cards, counters

Community Places Make one game card for each child by writing place names in random order in each square of a 3 x 3 square grid. Talk about the places on the card and where these places are in the community. Provide each child with a card and several counters. Read one of the place names and have children cover that square. Continue until a child has covered a row across or down.

library	school	house
fire station	police station	store
bank	gas station	post office

Weekly Assessment

Use the whole-class assessment on pages 492–493 and 496–497 in this Teacher's Edition to check:

✔ ◉ **Short Vowels**

✔ ◉ **Comprehension Skill** *Setting*

✔ **High-Frequency Words**

Teacher's Edition, Day 5

Managing Assessment

Use the Assessment Handbook for:

✔ **Observation Checklists**

✔ **Record-Keeping Forms**

✔ **Portfolio Assessment**

Assessment Handbook

continued from p. 495

The merchant and his wife were very happy that their daughter was laughing again. To show their appreciation, they gave Juan Bobo a bag of gold coins and their daughter's hand in marriage. After that, no one called him Juan Bobo ever again.

Small Group Time

Pacing Small Group Instruction

20–30 mins.

5 Day Plan

DAY 1	• Phonemic Awareness/ Phonics • Decodable Story 35
DAY 2	• Phonemic Awareness/ Phonics • Decodable Reader 35
DAY 3	• Phonemic Awareness/ Phonics • Concept Literacy Reader K.6.5 or Kindergarten Student Reader K.6.5
DAY 4	• Phonemic Awareness/ Phonics • Get Set, Roll! Reader 35
DAY 5	• Phonics Review • Listen to Me Reader K.6.5

3 or 4 Day Plan

DAY 1	• Phonemic Awareness/ Phonics • Decodable Story 35
DAY 2	• Phonemic Awareness/ Phonics • Decodable Reader 35
DAY 3	• Phonemic Awareness/ Phonics • Concept Literacy Reader K.6.5 or Kindergarten Student Reader K.6.5
DAY 4	• Phonemic Awareness/ Phonics • Get Set, Roll! Reader 35

3 Day Plan: Eliminate the shaded box.

 **SI** Strategic Intervention **DAY 1**

Phonemic Awareness•Phonics

■ **Isolate Sounds** Display the *web, waffle,* and *tent* Picture Cards. Which two words begin with the same sound? (*web* and *waffle*) What is the beginning sound in *web* and *waffle*? (/w/) Repeat with *cap, bat, carrot; desk, duck, fan;* and *house, mitten, moon.*

■ **Segmenting** Say *run.* I hear three sounds in *run, /r/ /u/ /n/, run.* How many sounds do you hear in *drum*? What are they? (four, /d/ /r/ /u/ /m/) Continue with *silk, tent, tap, fast,* and *flip.*

■ **Connect Sound to Letter** Write the word *map* on the board. What is the sound for *m*? (/m/) What is the sound we learned for *a*? (/a/) What is the sound for *p*? (/p/) Say the sound for each letter as I point to it: /m/ /a/ /p/. Now blend the sounds together to read the word: *map.* What is the word? The word is *map.* Continue with the following words: *pet, mud, big, not, van, jam, zip.*

Decodable Story 35

■ **Review** Review the previously taught high-frequency words by writing each word on the board and having children read the word with you.

is	a	she	he	the

> **If...** children have difficulty reading the words,
> **then...** say a word and have children point to the word. Repeat several times, giving assistance as needed.

■ **Read** Have children read *What Pets Do* aloud. Then have them reread the story several times individually.

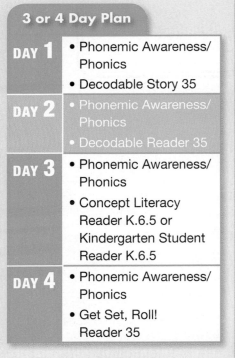

Reader's and Writer's Notebook, pp. 451–452

Objectives

• Identify the common sounds that letters represent.
• Read at least 25 high-frequency words from a commonly used list.

 Strategic Intervention   **DAY 2**

Phonemic Awareness•Phonics

■ **Blending** Write *flat* on the board. Help me blend this word. Listen as I say each sound: /f/ /l/ /a/ /t/. Now let's blend the sound together to read the word /f/ /l/ /a/ /t/, *flat.* Continue with *rap, ramp, flip, snap,* and *lid.*

■ **Discriminate Blends** Display Phonics Songs and Rhymes Chart 35. Sing "Can Zelda Sip Milk From the Red Cup?" to the tune of "My Bonnie Lies Over the Ocean" several times with children. Have children clap when they hear blends in the song.

■ **Recognize Blends** Ask children to name words that begin with the following blends: *dr, gr, st.* List the words on the board as children say them. Have children echo read the list of words. Then ask them to take turns circling the initial blends *dr, gr,* and *st* in the words on the board.

Decodable Reader 35

■ **Review** Review the high-frequency words by writing *they* on the board. This is the word *they.* What word is this? Continue with the following words: *a, have, the.*

> **If…** children have difficulty reading the words,
> **then…** say a word and have children point to the word. Repeat several times, giving assistance as needed.

■ **Read** Display the cover of *Fun in the Sun* on p. 98 of *My Skills Buddy.* Ask a volunteer to read the first page of the story. Have children tell what the children in the story do in the sun. Continue through the story in this manner.

My Skills Buddy

Objectives
- Identify the common sounds that letters represent.
- Read at least 25 high-frequency words from a commonly used list.
- Retell a main event from a story read aloud.

More Reading

Use Leveled Readers or other text at children's instructional level.

Small Group Time

Phonemic Awareness•Phonics

- **Isolate Blends** Say the word *trip.* This word is *trip.* What sounds do you hear? Say it with me: /tr/ /i/ /p/, *trip.* *Trip* begins with /tr/, then has /i/, and ends with /p/. Repeat with *ant, flag,* and *vest.*

- **Connect Sound to Letter** Show the *duck* Picture Card. This is a *duck. Duck* begins with /d/. Write the letters *Dd* on the board. The letter *d* stands for /d/. Say it with me: /d/ /d/ /d/, *duck.* What noise does a *duck* make? When you hear a word that begins or ends with /d/, quack like a duck. Use the following words: *bubble, desk, bed, pig, dark, can, den.*

- **Blend Sounds** Write *big* on the board. Have children blend the sound of each letter to read the word. Repeat the routine with the words *tug, pen, slip,* and *lap.*

- **Review High-Frequency Words** Write *have* on the board. Have volunteers say the word and use it in a sentence. Continue with the word *they, for, two,* and *blue.*

- **Read** To practice phonics and high-frequency words, have children read Kindergarten Student Reader K.6.5. Use the instruction on pp. 456–457.

For a complete lesson plan and additional practice, see the **Leveled Reader Teaching Guide**.

Concept Literacy Reader K.6.5

- **Preview and Predict** Display the cover of the Concept Literacy Reader K.6.5. Point to the title of the book. The title of the book is *Who Builds a House?* What do you think the book is about? Have children tell about the cover and what they think the book might be about.

- **Set a Purpose** We talked about the title of the book. Let's read the book to learn about what workers do to help build a house. Have children read the Concept Literacy Reader.

- **Read** Provide corrective feedback as children read the book orally. During reading, ask them if they are able to confirm any of the predictions they made prior to reading.

If... children have difficulty reading the book individually,
then... read a sentence aloud as children point to each word. Then have the group reread the sentences as they continue pointing to the words.

- **Retell** Have children retell the content as you page through the book. Help them identify what the book is about. Also call attention to the tools the workers use to build a house.

Concept Literacy Reader K.6.5

Objectives

- Identify the common sounds that letters represent. • Predict what might happen next based on the cover.
- Predict what might happen next based on the title. • Retell important facts in a text, heard or read.

SI Strategic Intervention

DAY **4**

Phonemic Awareness•Phonics

■ **Isolate Sounds** Display the *doll* Picture Card. This is a doll. Write *doll* on the board. *Doll* begins with /d/. The letter *d* makes the sound /d/. Say it with me: /d/ /d/ /d/, *doll*. What is the middle sound in *doll*? /o/ is the middle sound in *doll*. The sound we learned for the letter *o* is /o/. What is the final sound in *doll*? /l/ is the final sound in *doll*. The letter *l* or the letters *ll* make the sound /l/. Say the three sounds together: /d/ /o/ /l/, *doll*. **Repeat with** *fan, gum,* and *map.*

■ **Discriminate Blends** Display the *flag* Picture Card. This is a *flag. Flag* begins with /fl/. Say it with me: /fl/ /a/ /g/, *flag*. Does *frog* begin with the same sound as *flag*? No, *frog* does not begin with /fl/. **Repeat with** *flower, trip, fling, flash, train,* and *flight.*

Get Set, Roll! Reader 35

■ **Review** Review the following high-frequency words with children prior to reading the story: *they, she, go, said, a, you, of, is, the.*

■ **Read** Display Get Set, Roll! Reader 35, *Spin! Spin!* Today we will read a new story about a race in the sand. Point to the title of the story. The title of the story is *Spin! Spin!* Look at the cover and think about the title. What do you think this story will be about?

> **If...** children have difficulty reading the story individually, **then...** read a sentence aloud as children point to each word. Then have the group reread the sentences as they continue pointing to the words.

Get Set, Roll! Reader 35

■ **Reread** Use echo reading of Get Set, Roll! Reader 35 to model fluent reading. Use your oral reading to model for children where to pause, when to change pitch, and which words to stress. Then have children reread orally three to four times, or until they can read with few or no mistakes.

Objectives
• Identify the common sounds that letters represent.
• Read at least 25 high-frequency words from a commonly used list.
• Predict what might happen next based on the cover.

More Reading
Use Leveled Readers or other text at children's instructional level.

Small Group Time

More Reading

Use Leveled Readers or other text at children's instructional level.

SI *Strategic Intervention*

DAY 5

Phonics Review

■ **Pin the Letter** Play a variation of "Pin the Tail on the Donkey." Write the letters of the alphabet in random order on the board. Have a volunteer close his or her eyes. Turn the child around two times and position him or her in front of the board. Give the child a self-stick note to stick on the board. Then have the child open his or her eyes, identify the letter the note is covering, say the sound the class learned for that letter, and name a word that begins with that letter. Repeat until many children get a turn to identify a letter and sound and name a word.

Listen to Me Reader K.6.5

■ **Preview and Predict** Display the cover of the book. The title of this story is *My Big Bug.* It is written by Larry Kelly. It is illustrated by Ann Iosa. Look at the picture. What do you think this story will be about?

Listen to Me Reader K.6.5

■ **Set a Purpose** Review children's ideas. Point out that after they read, they will know more about how the man fixes the big bug. Tell children that you will read the story with them. Follow along with your finger as I read. Then we will take turns reading this page. Repeat this routine through all of the pages. Guide children to decode words.

■ **Reread for Fluency** Use echo reading of Listen to Me Reader K.6.5 to model reading fluently. Use your oral reading to model for children when to pause, when to change pitch, and which words to stress. Then have children reread orally three to four times, or until they can read with few or no mistakes.

Objectives

• Isolate the initial sound in spoken one-syllable words.
• Identify the common sounds that letters represent.
• Predict what might happen next based on the cover.

OL On-Level **DAY 1**

Phonemic Awareness•Phonics

■ **Listen for Initial Blends** Tell children you will tell them a story and they should listen for initial blends. When you say a word that begins with an initial blend, such as *pl, sl, fl, cl,* or *gl,* children should clap and repeat the word. Tell a simple story, emphasizing the initial blend words and pausing to give children a chance to clap and repeat the word. *Glen* and *Flora play* at the *playground. Glen climbs* to the top of the *slide. Glen* goes down the *slippery slide.* Now it is *Flora's* turn. Stay *clear* for *Flora!* Then write several story sentences on the board. Have volunteers circle the letters that make initial blends.

Objectives
• Isolate the initial sound in spoken one-syllable words.

Pacing Small Group Instruction

20–30 mins.

5 Day Plan

DAY 1	• Phonemic Awareness/ Phonics
	• Decodable Story 35
DAY 2	• Phonemic Awareness/ Phonics
	• High-Frequency Words
	• Decodable Reader 35
DAY 3	• Phonemic Awareness/ Phonics
	• Kindergarten Student Reader K.6.5
DAY 4	• Get Set, Roll! Reader 35
DAY 5	• Phonics Review

OL On-Level **DAY 2**

Phonemic Awareness•Phonics

■ **Recognize Blends** Write uppercase *C* on the board. Name the letter as you write it several times. Have children trace the letter in the air. Then write a lowercase *r* on the board. Blend the sounds together. What sound do these letters stand for? Yes, they stand for the blend /kr/. Name the sound and ask a volunteer to name a word that begins with /kr/. Continue the routine with *br, dr, fr, gr, st,* and *tr.*

■ **High-Frequency Words** Display the following word cards: *have, they, four, two, blue.* Say the word *blue* and select a child to point to the word. Have children say the word and use it in a sentence. Continue with the other words.

Objectives
• Identify the common sounds that letters represent.
• Read at least 25 high-frequency words from a commonly used list.

3 or 4 Day Plan

DAY 1	• Phonemic Awareness/ Phonics
	• Decodable Story 35
DAY 2	• Phonemic Awareness/ Phonics
	• High-Frequency Words
	• Decodable Reader 35
DAY 3	• Phonemic Awareness/ Phonics
	• Kindergarten Student Reader K.6.5
DAY 4	• Get Set, Roll! Reader 35

3 Day Plan: Eliminate the shaded box.

More Practice

For additional practice with this week's phonics skills, have children reread the Decodable Story (Day 1) and the Decodable Reader (Day 2).

Phonemic Awareness•Phonics

■ **Rhyme Time** Rhyming words are words with the same ending sounds, such as *hat* and *cat* or *top* and *hop*. **Say the following words:** *vest, nest.* Do these words rhyme? Yes, *vest* and *nest* rhyme. Does *desk* rhyme with *vest* and *nest?* No, it does not. Does *rest* rhyme with *vest* and *nest?* Yes, *rest* rhymes with *vest* and *nest.* Tell children you will say three words. Have them identify the word that does not rhyme. Use the following sets of words: *frog, flop, log; plan, flip, slip; twig, big, mop; fist, play, list; flap, rock, lock.*

Kindergarten Student Reader K.6.5

Kindergarten Student
Reader K.6.5

■ **Preview and Predict** Display the cover of the book. The title of this story is *Max and Jen Build a Home.* What do you think this story will be about?

■ **Set a Purpose** Review the list of things children think might happen in the story. Remind children they will read to find out how Max and Jen build a home.

■ **Read** Have children follow along as they read the story with you. After reading p. 2, ask children to tell how Max and Jen help Dad. Continue with each page. Ask the following questions:

• Who helps Max and Jen build a home?
• What does Mom do?
• What do Max and Jen do?
• Do Max and Jen like the home?

■ **Summarize** Have children retell the story to a partner and tell how Max and Jen play with the house at the end.

■ **Text to Self** Help children make personal connections to the story as they tell their experiences with building things.

Objectives

• Distinguish orally presented rhyming pairs of words from non-rhyming pairs.
• Predict what might happen next based on the title.
• Respond to questions about text.

OL On-Level   DAY **4**

Get Set, Roll! Reader 35

■ **Review** Review the words *they, she, go, said, a, you, of, is,* and *the* by writing each word on the board and saying the word with children. Then give clues to a word and have children tell which word it is.

■ **Read** Display Get Set, Roll! Reader 35, *Spin! Spin!* Today we will read a story about Max and Jack. Point to the title of the story. *Spin! Spin!* is the title of the story. We can read all the words in this story. Look at the cover of the story. What do you think this story is about? Let's read to find out.

Objectives
- Read at least 25 high-frequency words from a commonly used list.
- Predict what might happen next based on the cover.

OL On-Level   DAY **5**

Phonics Review

■ **Blend the Words** Write the following words on index cards so that two letters are on each half of the card: *flag, drum, crab, sled, milk, gift, desk, nest, fist.* Then cut the cards to form puzzle-like pieces. Give each child a puzzle piece and have children fit the pieces back together to form words. When all of the cards are matched up, have children read the words. Remind them to say the sound for each letter and then blend the sounds to read the words. Explain to children that these words have initial or final two-letter blends.

Objectives
- Blend spoken phonemes to form one-syllable words.
- Identify the common sounds that letters represent.

More Reading

Use Leveled Readers or other text at children's instructional level to develop fluency.

Small **Group Time**

Pacing Small Group Instruction

5 Day Plan

DAY 1	• Phonemic Awareness/ Phonics • Decodable Story 35
DAY 2	• Phonics • Spelling • Decodable Reader 35
DAY 3	• Independent Reader K.6.5 or Kindergarten Student Reader 35
DAY 4	• Get Set, Roll! Reader 35 or Kindergarten Student Reader K.6.5
DAY 5	• Fluency • Comprehension

3 or 4 Day Plan

DAY 1	• Phonemic Awareness/ Phonics • Decodable Story 35
DAY 2	• Phonics • Spelling • Decodable Reader 35
DAY 3	• Independent Reader K.6.5 or Kindergarten Student Reader 35
DAY 4	• Get Set, Roll! Reader 35 or Kindergarten Student Reader K.6.5

3 Day Plan: Eliminate the shaded box.

More Practice

For additional practice with this week's phonics skills and to develop fluency, have children reread the Decodable Story (Day 1) and the Decodable Reader (Day 2).

A — Advanced — **DAY 1**

Phonemic Awareness•Phonics

■ **Add a Letter** Give children Letter Tiles and have them make the word *sip*. Listen to the sounds and repeat them with me: /s/ /i/ /p/. Tell children to add a letter to the word *sip* to make another word with an initial blend. If children are unable to think of a word, say: Try the letters *l, r, k,* or *m.* Which of these letters can be added to *sip* to make a new word? (*l* and *k* make *slip* and *skip.*) Continue with the words *cap, lap, rib,* and *lip.*

Objectives
• Identify the common sounds that letters represent.
• Recognize that new words are created when letters are added.

A — Advanced — **DAY 2**

Phonics•Spelling

■ **Discriminate Initial Blends** Draw eight triangles on the board. Collect twelve Picture Cards, including the following initial blend cards: *block, brown, cloud, dress, flag, slide, starfish, train.* Mix the cards and display them one at a time. Have a child name the picture. If the name has an initial blend, have the child write the blend in one of the triangles.

■ **Spell Sounds** Give each child the following letter tiles: *a, b, c, d, i, k, l, m, o, p, r, s, t.* Listen to the sounds in the word *slim:* /s/ /l/ /i/ /m/, *slim.* What are the letters for /s/ /l/? They are *s* and *l.* Place your *s* and *l* tiles in front of you. Continue with the remaining sounds. Then have children blend the sounds to read the word. Then have children spell *drop, crab, spot,* and *milk.*

Objectives
• Identify the common sounds that letters represent.
• Use letter-sound correspondences to spell consonant-vowel-consonant (CVC) words.

A Advanced

DAY 3

For a complete lesson plan and additional practice, see the **Leveled Reader Teaching Guide**.

Independent Reader K.6.5

■ **Practice High-Frequency Words** Write the previously taught high-frequency words on the board. Have volunteers say each word and use it in a sentence.

we	for	one	here	said	like

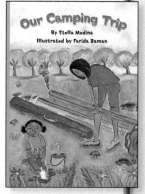

Independent Reader K.6.5

■ **Activate Prior Knowledge** Remind children that many people enjoy camping at a campground. Encourage children to share what they know about camping. Have you ever gone camping? Did you help put up the tent? Did you go on a nature walk?

■ **Setting** Display the cover of *Our Camping Trip.* Have children tell about the place the family sets up their tent. Is the place real or make-believe?

■ **Reread for Fluency** After rereading with children, model reading fluently for them. I am going to read this book aloud. I will read the words with no mistakes. I want you to read it aloud with me. Try to read the words just as I do.

• Use echo reading of Independent Reader K.6.5 to model reading fluently. Use your oral reading to model for children where to pause, when to change pitch, and which words to stress. Then have children reread orally three to four times, or until they can read with few or no mistakes.

■ For more practice with phonics and high-frequency words and to develop fluency, have children read Kinderegarten Student Reader K.6.5. Use the instruction on pp. 456–457.

More Reading

Use Leveled Readers or other text at children's instructional level.

Objectives
• Read at least 25 high-frequency words from a commonly used list.
• Identify elements of a story including setting.

Small Group Time

More Reading
Use Leveled Readers or other text at children's instructional level.

Kindergarten Student Reader K.6.5

- **Activate Prior Knowledge** In this story Max and Jen are going to help build a home. What do you know about building a home? Remind them they learned about workers who help build a home in *The House That Tony Lives In.*

- **Reread** Use Kindergarten Student Reader K.6.5 to practice reading fluently.

- **Text to Self** Ask children to think about how to build a home. What would you like to do to help build a home?

- **Read** Have children read Get Set, Roll! Reader 35, *Spin! Spin!* Use the instruction on p. 481.

Kindergarten Student Reader K.6.5

Objectives
- Read at least 25 high-frequency words from a commonly used list.

Fluency•Comprehension

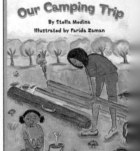

- **Reread for Fluency** Use the Independent Reader K.6.5 to model reading fluently for children. I am going to read this selection aloud. I will read the words with no mistakes. I want you to read it aloud with me. Try to read the words just as I do.

- **Comprehension** After children have finished reading, have them retell what happens in the selection. Then have children write or draw a picture that shows a good setting for a campsite.

Independent Reader K.6.5

Objectives
- Read at least 25 high-frequency words from a commonly used list.
- Identify elements of a story including setting.

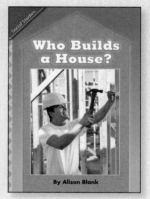

Concept Development

■ **Read the Concept Literacy Reader** To build background and vocabulary, read *Who Builds a House?* pausing to discuss each page. Model sentence patterns and vocabulary that describe the pictures. This woman draws pictures. She is an architect. Her pictures show what a house will look like. Other people will use the pictures. On a second reading, have children talk about the different ways people help to build a house. It takes many people to build a house. People have different jobs. Why would you dig a hole to build a house?

■ **Develop Oral Language** Revisit *Who Builds a House?*, pointing out the different ways people help build a house. Then have children recite the following chant with you based on ways people help build a house:

> Draw the plans and break the ground,
> This is how we build our house.
> Stand the walls and raise the roof,
> Miles of wires, paint on the walls,
> This is how we build our house.

Phonemic Awareness/Phonics

■ **Frontload Consonant and Vowel Sounds** Have children look at the picture on pp. 92–93 of *My Skills Buddy*. This picture shows a house. A house has rooms. This house has bedrooms and a kitchen. Listen to the word *house*. What sound does *house* begin with? *House* begins with /h/. Then use this routine to introduce picture words that have the same initial, medial, or final sound: I'm in the house and so are you. Who can find a *bed* in the house? (Pause for an answer.) (Child's name) can find a *bed* in the house. How many *beds* are in the house? Have children point to the two beds in the picture. Which word begins the same as *bed, flower* or *balloons*? (Pause for an answer.) *Bed* and *balloon* both begin with /b/. Point to the balloons on the page. Repeat the routine with other words in the picture that share initial, medial, or final sounds, such as *bug/mug* (medial), *bag/cat* (medial), and *clock/cook* (final).

■ **Letter-Sound Correspondence** Use letter tiles to display the words *fun* and *stilt* or write them on the board. This word is *fun: /f/ /u/ /n/, fun.* Say the word with me. Have children write the word *fun* and circle the letter that makes /f/. Have them underline the letter that makes /u/. Repeat with the word *stilt*.

Content Objective
• Develop content knowledge related to who helps to build a house.

Language Objectives
• Understand and use grade-level content area vocabulary.

• Recognize the sounds of English.

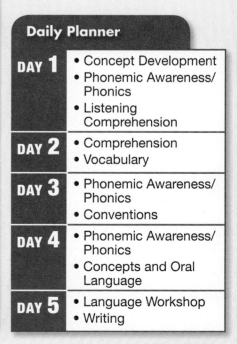

Concept Literacy Reader K.6.5

Daily Planner

DAY 1	• Concept Development • Phonemic Awareness/ Phonics • Listening Comprehension
DAY 2	• Comprehension • Vocabulary
DAY 3	• Phonemic Awareness/ Phonics • Conventions
DAY 4	• Phonemic Awareness/ Phonics • Concepts and Oral Language
DAY 5	• Language Workshop • Writing

Support for English Language Learners

Content Objective
• Understand setting.

Language Objective
• Learn and use academic vocabulary.

My Skills Buddy, pp. 94–95

Listening Comprehension: Setting

■ **Provide Scaffolding** Discuss the pictures on pp. 94–95 in *My Skills Buddy* to frontload vocabulary. Point out the Characters box. This tells you who is in the story. Point to the Plot box. This tells you what happens in the story. Point to the Setting box. This shows where the story happens. The place where the story happens is called the setting. What is in the setting box? **(a path)** The setting of this story is a path. The tortoise and the hare race on the path.

■ **Prepare for the Read Aloud** The modified Read Aloud below prepares children for listening to the oral reading "The Perfect Place" on p. 427.

Read Aloud

The Perfect Place

Frank must build a new home. He must find the perfect place.

Frank goes to the meadow. It is sunny and warm. It has grasses and flowers. It is a lovely place. But it is not the perfect place for Frank's new home.

Frank goes to the forest. It is dark and quiet. It has tall old trees and leafy green ferns. It is a wonderful place. But it is not the perfect place for Frank's new home.

Frank goes to the pond. It is wide and wet. It has cool water and squishy mud. It is a lovely place. It is a wonderful place. It is the perfect place for Frank's new home—because Frank is a frog.

■ **First Listening** Write the title of the Read Aloud on the board. This story is about Frank. Frank must build a new home. Listen to find out how Frank finds the perfect place for his new home. After reading, ask children to recall the places Frank goes. What does Frank see in the meadow? Where is the perfect place for Frank's home? Why is the pond a perfect place for Frank?

■ **Second Listening** Make a T-chart on the board and label it with the words *Setting* and *Frank sees*. As you listen to the story, think about where Frank goes. What does Frank see in each place? After reading, point to the word *Setting* and have children tell the places Frank goes in the story.

Objectives
• Understand the main points of spoken language ranging from situations in which contexts are familiar to unfamiliar. • Understand implicit ideas in increasingly complex spoken language commensurate with grade-level learning expectations.

Comprehension

■ **Provide Scaffolding** Display *The House That Tony Lives In.* Lead a detailed picture walk through the story, naming what you see in the illustrations and describing what is happening. Use gestures and facial expressions to convey meaning. Focus on the following:

• **Set the Scene** Prepare children for the concepts in the Big Book by asking questions about who builds a house. People work together to build a house. These people have different jobs. I know someone has to put up walls. What else do people need to build for a house? Allow children to use their prior knowledge to discuss parts of a house that need to be built. Use the cover of the Big Book to help children understand that this story takes place where Tony's house is being built.

• **Frontload Vocabulary** As you lead the picture walk, use the illustrations to introduce unfamiliar words in the text. Look at the illustrations on pp. 4–5. These drivers deliver supplies. Supplies are things we need to do work. These trucks are the supplies that will help do the work to build Tony's house. Include the following words: *deliver* (p. 5), *wires* (p. 8), *pipes* (p. 10), *garden* (p. 14), *furniture* (p. 17), *neighbors* (p. 18).

Vocabulary: Words for Feelings

■ **Frontload Vocabulary** Have children turn to pp. 108–109 of *My Skills Buddy.* Talk about each illustration, using the words *frightened, worried, proud,* and *angry.* For example, point to the first illustration. This boy is *frightened. Something scared the boy.* Have children talk about the illustrations using the words for feelings.

■ **Provide Scaffolding** Write the words *frightened, worried, proud,* and *angry* on the board. Read the words aloud with children. These words tell us about feelings. Point to the word *frightened. Who can tell what *frightened* means? How might you look if you were frightened?* Then say a sentence using the word and have children repeat the sentence: The thunder frightened the boy. Repeat with the other words for feelings.

■ **Practice** Arrange children into four small groups. Assign one of the words for feelings to each group. Have groups draw pictures about when they experienced the feeling. Then ask them to share their drawings by telling about the experience and stating the feeling word: *I was proud when our team won the game.*

Content Objective
• Develop background knowledge.

Language Objective
• Learn and use words for feelings.

Use Learning Strategies
Remind children that if they have trouble naming an item in their pictures, they can ask their group members for help.

Big Book

Objectives
• Speak using learning strategies. • Use accessible language and learn new language in the process.
• Demonstrate listening comprehension of increasingly complex spoken English by collaborating with peers commensurate with content and grade-level needs.

The House That Tony Lives In **DI•82**

Support for English Language Learners

Content Objective
- Use learning strategies.

Language Objectives
- Isolate initial, medial, and final sounds.
- Create exclamations.

Transfer Skills

Identifying Sounds Children's ability to listen for and identify initial, middle, and final sounds will help them identify sounds in other languages they study or know. Even if the sounds in another language are different, their practice with the skill of selective listening will help them hear and repeat the sounds.

Use Learning Strategies

Help children understand that some words can be used differently. Write *frightened* and *worried* on the board. Remind children that words ending in /d/ are often past-tense verbs. Explain that in the case of *frightened* and *worried,* the two words can name actions that happened in the past or they can tell about how a person feels, or describe a person. Tell children that words that describe are called *adjectives.* Make sentences to show how the two words are used differently.

Phonemic Awareness/Phonics

- **Review Initial, Medial, and Final Sounds** To review sounds in words, first write and say short words, such as *at, is, it, on,* and *up.* Which word has /a/? Repeat the words, having children identify which words have /i/, /u/, and /o/. Then ask children to identify the end sound of each word. Then say pairs of words, including: *sun, fun; lot, cot; pet, let; nap, gap.* After you say a pair of words, ask children to identify which has a specific initial consonant sound. For example, say *fun* and *sun.* Which word starts with /f/?

- **Spell Words with Initial, Medial, and Final Sounds** Say the word *cat.* Segment the word into sounds and write each letter on the board. I just spelled the word *cat.* Let's spell more words. Remember, say each sound in the word and write the letter for each sound. Use these words: *mop, rat, sun, pig, pen, fan, bat, slip, drum.*

Conventions: Exclamations

- **Provide Scaffolding** On the board, write the exclamation *Look out!* Say the exclamation and have children say it with you. This is an exclamation. We say exclamations when we are excited or have a strong feeling. Why might you shout *Look out!?* Remember, we use an uppercase letter for the first letter in a exclamation. Point to the exclamation mark. An exclamation uses an exclamation mark at the end. Repeat the routine with these exclamations: *Oh, boy!, Ouch!, Thank you!, Slow down!*

- **Practice** Page through the Big Book *The House That Tony Lives In.* Have children use the illustrations to create dialog. Help children use the illustrations to imagine a scenario where an exclamation might be used. For example, on pp. 6–7, a construction worker might say, *Watch out!* Write children's exclamations on the board.

Beginning/Intermediate Have children repeat exclamations that other children make up. Then have them tell what kind of punctuation mark belongs at the end of an exclamation.

Advanced/Advanced-High Have pairs of children create a short dialog about building a house. Encourage children to use one or two exclamations in their dialogs.

Objectives
- Internalize new academic language by using and reusing it in meaningful ways in speaking activities that build concept and language attainment. • Learn new expressions heard during classroom instruction and interactions.

 ELL English Language Learners DAY 4

Phonemic Awareness/Phonics

■ **Review Identifying Sounds in Words** Have children listen as you say these sentences: The ducks quack and swim for fun. The hill in back has a lot of sand. Say the sentences once more, and ask children to repeat after you. Then pick words from the sentences and have children identify the initial, medial, or final sound, as well as other words that contain the sound. What is the beginning sound of quack? Confirm that the answer is /kw/. What is another word that begins with /kw/? (quarter, question, quick, quiet)

■ **Connect to Spelling** Write the words flip, trap, pen, desk, hand, and leg on the board. Have children read each word as you run your hand under it. Have children identify the initial, medial, and final sounds. Check each child's progress. Monitor pronunciation for clarity but not for perfection.

Concepts and Oral Language

■ **Revisit Talk with Me Chart 35A** Display the chart. Have children describe each image on the page. Help them by describing different ways people help build a house.

■ **Develop Oral Language** Introduce language patterns that help describe the pictures on Talk with Me Chart 35A. Write this sentence frame on the board: The architect _____. Let's use this sentence pattern to talk about the architect: The architect draws. The architect plans. Have children suggest other sentences using the frame. Then add this sentence frame: The electricians _____. Now let's use this sentence pattern to talk about the electricians: The electricians work together. The electricians connect wires. Have children suggest other sentences using the sentence frame. Then continue the exercise to describe the other pictures on the chart.

 Leveled Support

Beginning Have children repeat the sentences that other children make up. Let them take a turn pointing to a picture on the chart.

Intermediate Ask questions to help children notice more details by asking questions, such as What tools are the architects using? What are the movers moving?

Advanced/Advanced-High Encourage children to use their prior knowledge about building a house to think of other action words for what the people are doing.

Content Objectives
- Develop oral language.
- Use learning strategies.

Language Objectives
- Connect sounds to letters.
- Learn English language patterns.

Use Learning Strategies
With children, brainstorm some Wh- questions about the pictures in the Talk with Me Chart. On the board, write Who, What, Why, and Where. Point to each word and help children ask questions using the Amazing Words.

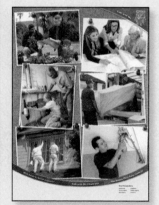

Talk with Me Chart 35A

Objectives
• Use strategic learning techniques to acquire basic vocabulary. • Speak using a variety of grammatical structures with increasing accuracy and ease as more English is acquired. • Speak using grade-level content area vocabulary in context to internalize new English words.

Support for English Language Learners

Content Objectives

- Understand *The House That Tony Lives In.*
- Practice setting.

Language Objectives

- Respond to the book through speaking and writing.
- Write using grade-level vocabulary.

Monitor and Self-Correct

Remind children that if they don't know which words to write in their poem, they can say the words aloud to see if they rhyme.

Home Language Support

Invite children to share ideas in their home languages before creating their poems.

Language Workshop: Talk About Poems

- **Introduce and Model** How would you feel if the workers were building your new house? New things are very exciting. Let's write a poem about it.

- **Practice** A poem sounds like a song. It has rhythm, like clapping to a beat. The words often rhyme. Explain that you will be writing a poem together about building a house. Write the poem below on the board:

    The workers gather in the sun,

    Many jobs have to be done.

Read the poem, stressing the rhythm. Then have children say the poem with you. Encourage them to march to the beat. Then ask them which words rhyme. (*sun* and *done*) Guide children in making a list of other rhyming words that tell about events in *The House That Tony Lives In,* such as *man/plan; planned/land; big/dig;* and *wires/tires.* Record the rhyming words on the board.

Writing: Write a Poem

- **Prepare for Writing** We read a poem about *The House That Tony Lives In.* Now let's write our own poem.

- **Create Poems About Building a House** Write the following poem frame on a sheet of paper and make a copy for each child.

    Building houses can be _____!
    Many jobs have to be _____.
    Working hard in the hot _____,
    Building houses one by _____!

Then write the following list of words on the board: *fun, hard, one, moon, sun, house, done, run,* and *day.* Have children complete the poem by choosing rhyming words from the list and dictating or writing them in the blanks. Then have children illustrate their poems. When children are finished, have them share their poem with the class. Have the class march to the beat of the poem to help them recognize the rhythm.

Beginning/Intermediate Write the words *fun, done, sun,* and *one,* and have children choose the correct word to put in each blank.

Advanced/Advanced-High Encourage children to copy the poem frame on their own.

Objectives

• Monitor written language production and employ self-corrective techniques or other resources. • Distinguish intonation patterns of English with increasing ease. • Learn new expressions heard during classroom instruction and interactions. • Write using content-based grade-level vocabulary.

This Week's ELL Overview

ELL Handbook

English Language Learners HANDBOOK

SCOTT FORESMAN
READING STREET K

- Maximize Literacy and Cognitive Engagement
- Research Into Practice
- Full Weekly Support for Every Selection

Ants and Their Nest

- Routines to Support Instruction

- Transfer Activities
- Professional Development

Daily Leveled ELL Notes

ELL notes appear throughout this week's instruction and ELL Support is on the DI pages of your Teacher's Edition. The following is a sample of an ELL note from this week.

English Language Learners

Beginning Build Background English learners will benefit from additional visual support to understand words in the song. Point to the *colony, twigs,* and *pebbles* in the art to scaffold meaning.

Intermediate Identify High-Frequency Words Write the high-frequency words *you, see, said, look,* and *three* on cards and give each child a card. Read the following sentences and have children hold up their card when they hear their word in these sentences: *Will you play a game with me? Do you see the rainbow? Tom said he will help Dad wash the car. Look at that pretty red flower! Pam has three brothers.*

Advanced Composing Sentences Write the nouns *dogs, girls, babies,* and *friends* on one set of cards and the verbs *run, play, bark,* and *giggle* on another set of cards. Display the cards and have children choose a card from each set to make a complete sentence.

Advanced High Make a Word Write the letters for the words *sun* and *fan* on cards. Distribute cards to children. Ask the children who have the letters that form the word *sun* to come to the front of the class and stand in a sequence to form the word *sun.* Have children blend the sounds and then read the word aloud. Continue with *fan.*

ELL by Strand

The ELL lessons on this week's Support for English Language Learners pages are organized by strand. They offer additional scaffolding for the core curriculum. Leveled support notes on these pages address the different proficiency levels in your class. See pages DI•97–DI•102.

ELL Guy
Dr. Jim Cummins

——— The Three Pillars of ELL Instruction ———

ELL Strands	Activate Prior Knowledge	Access Content	Extend Language
Vocabulary p. DI•99	Frontload Vocabulary	Provide Scaffolding	Practice
Reading Comprehension p. DI•99	Provide Scaffolding	Set the Scene	Frontload Vocabulary
Phonics, Spelling, and Word Analysis pp. DI•97, DI•100–DI•101	Frontload Words with Initial, Medial, and Final Sounds	Isolate Initial, Medial, and Final Sounds	Review Initial, Medial, and Final Sounds
Listening Comprehension p. DI•98	Prepare for the Read Aloud	First Listening	Second Listening
Conventions and Writing pp. DI•100, DI•102	Provide Scaffolding/ Introduce and Model	Practice	Leveled Practice Activities/ Leveled Writing Activities
Concept Development p. DI•97	Read the Concept Literacy Reader	Read the Concept Literacy Reader	Develop Oral Language

This Week's Practice Stations Overview

Six Weekly Practice Stations with Leveled Activities can be found at the beginning of each week of instruction. For this week's Practice Stations, see pp. 510–511.

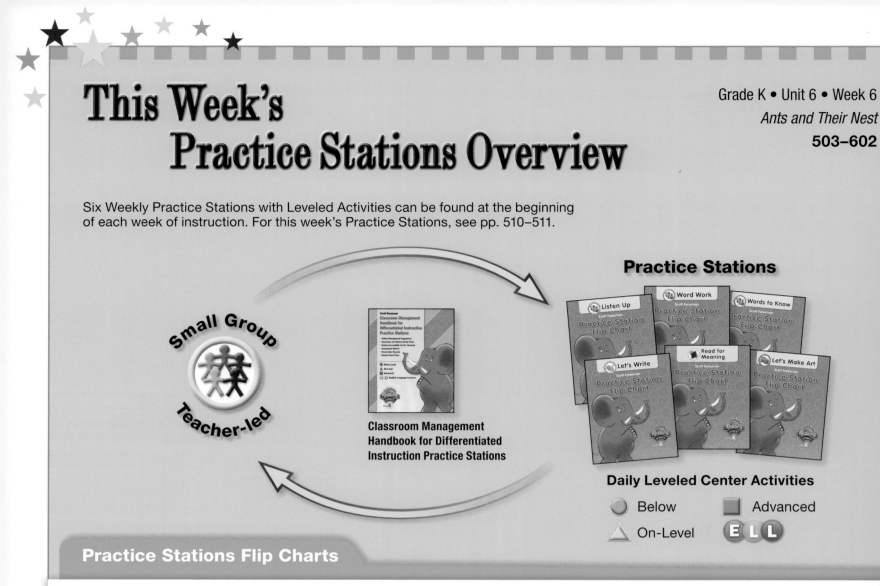

Small Group Teacher-led

Classroom Management Handbook for Differentiated Instruction Practice Stations

Practice Stations

Daily Leveled Center Activities

◯ Below   ▢ Advanced

△ On-Level   **E L L**

Practice Stations Flip Charts

	Listen Up	Word Work	Words to Know	Let's Write	Read for Meaning	Let's Make Art
Objectives	• Identify and use short vowels and consonants.	• Review and build words with short vowel sounds.	• Identify and use words for feelings.	• Write a poem that tells who helps to build a house.	• Identify and describe story setting.	• Draw pictures to show what people do to help build a house.
Materials	• *Listen Up* Flip Chart Activity 36 • Picture Cards: *bat, bed, box, bus, cap, cat, doll, fan, fox, gun, hat, hen, jet, jug, man, map, mop, mug, net, nut, pen, pig, red, rug, six, sock, sun, ten, top, tub, van, web, wig, yak* • paper, pencils	• *Word Work* Flip Chart Activity 36 • Alphabet Cards • Letter Tiles • paper, pencils	• *Words to Know* Flip Chart Activity 36 • Find pictures for feeling words: *frightened, worried, proud, angry* • Teacher-made Word Cards: *frightened, worried, proud, angry* • small mirror • paper, pencils, crayons	• *Let's Write* Flip Chart Activity 36 • Find pictures (or take quick digital photos and print out) for words: *hammering, painting, digging, measuring, sawing* • crayons, paper, pencil	• *Read for Meaning* Flip Chart Activity 36 • Little Book *The House That Tony Lives In* • pencil, crayons, paper	• *Let's Make Art* Flip Chart Activity 36 • index cards • crayons

This Week on Reading Street!

Question of the Week
How do ants build their nests?

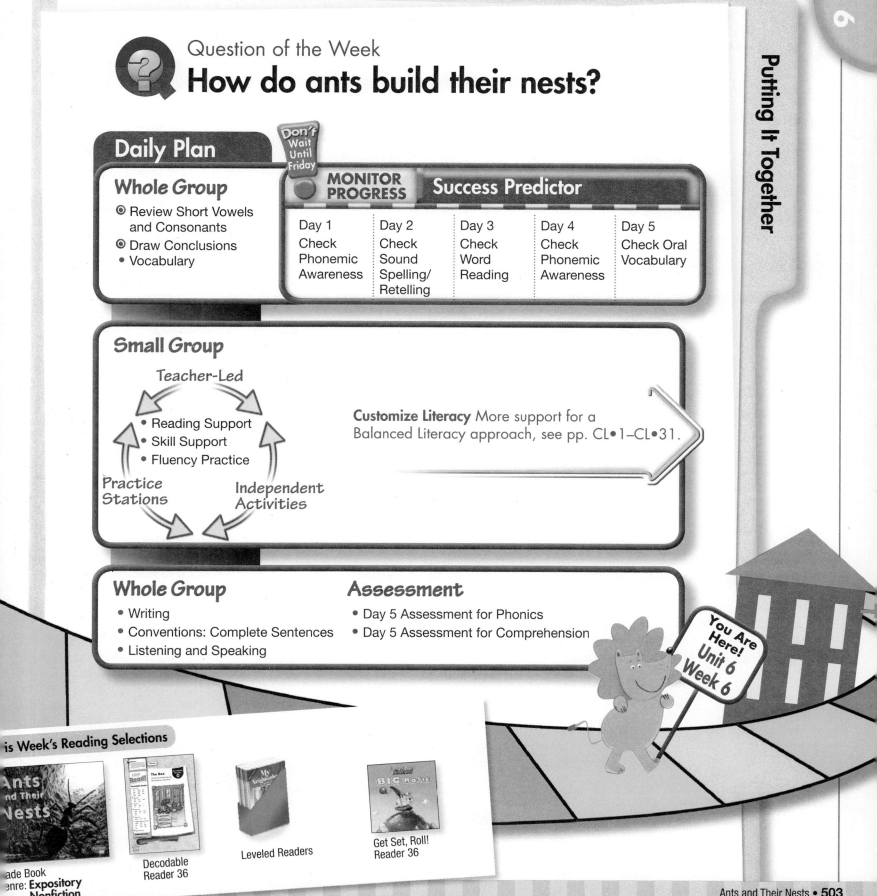

Daily Plan

Don't Wait Until Friday

Whole Group

- ◉ Review Short Vowels and Consonants
- ◉ Draw Conclusions
- • Vocabulary

MONITOR PROGRESS | **Success Predictor**

Day 1	Day 2	Day 3	Day 4	Day 5
Check Phonemic Awareness	Check Sound Spelling/ Retelling	Check Word Reading	Check Phonemic Awareness	Check Oral Vocabulary

Small Group

Teacher-Led

- • Reading Support
- • Skill Support
- • Fluency Practice

Practice Stations

Independent Activities

Customize Literacy More support for a Balanced Literacy approach, see pp. CL•1–CL•31.

Whole Group

- • Writing
- • Conventions: Complete Sentences
- • Listening and Speaking

Assessment

- • Day 5 Assessment for Phonics
- • Day 5 Assessment for Comprehension

You Are Here! Unit 6 Week 6

is Week's Reading Selections

Ants and Their Nests
ade Book
enre: Expository Nonfiction

Decodable Reader 36

Leveled Readers

Get Set, Roll! Reader 36

Resources on Reading Street!

	Build Concepts	Phonemic Awareness and Phonics	Vocabulary
Whole Group	Talk With Me/ Sing With Me	Student Edition pp. 112–113 • Student Edition p. 116	Student Edition p. 117 • Student Edition p. 128
Go Digital	• Concept Talk Video • Sing with Me Animations	• eReaders	
Small Group and Independent Practice	Practice Station Flip Chart • Leveled Readers	Practice Station Flip Chart • Decodable Reader 36 • Leveled Readers • Get Set, Roll! Reader 36	Practice Station Flip Chart • Student Edition p. 117
Go Digital	• eReaders	• eReaders • Letter Tile Drag and Drop	
Customize Literacy	• Leveled Readers	• Decodable Reader	• High-Frequency Words Cards
Go Digital	• Concept Talk Video • Big Question Video • eReaders	• eReaders	• Sing with Me Animations

Question of the Week
How do ants build their nests?

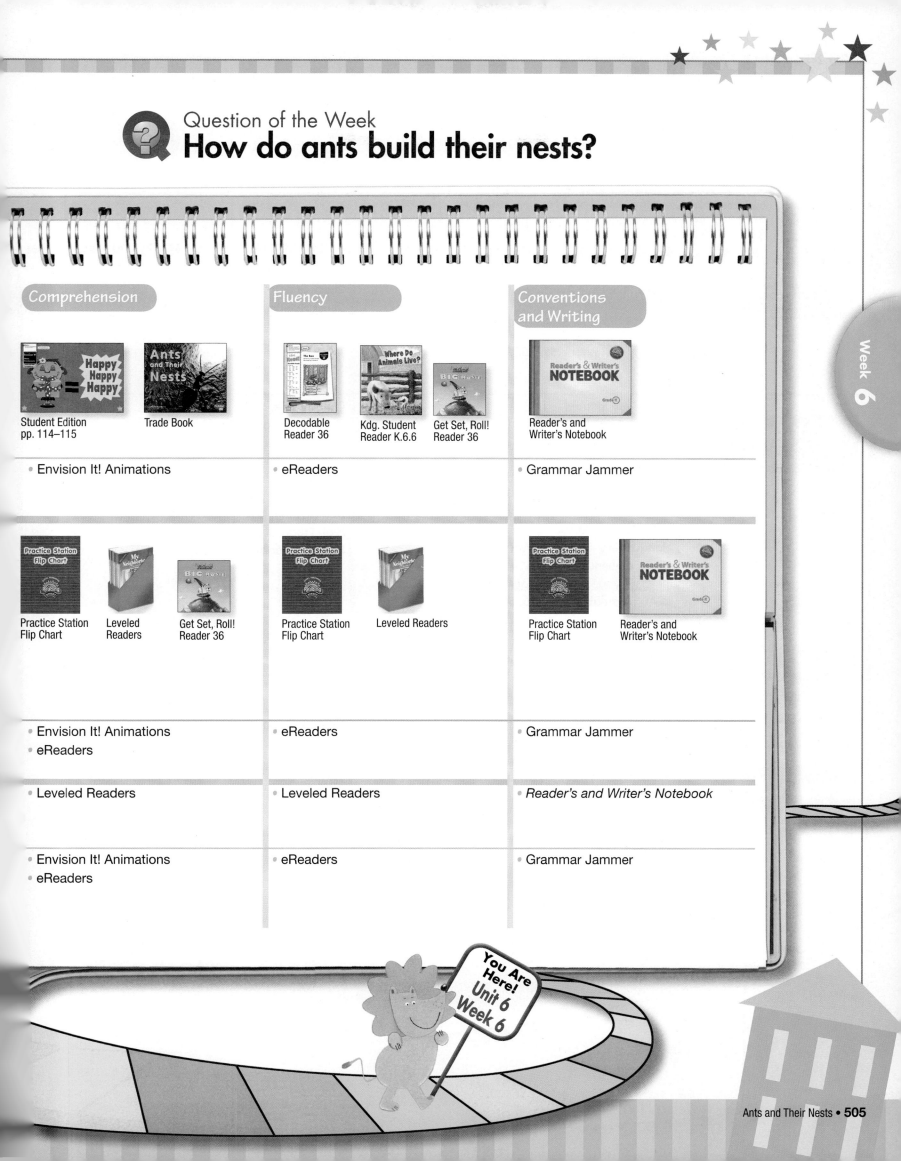

Comprehension	Fluency	Conventions and Writing
Student Edition pp. 114–115 / Trade Book	Decodable Reader 36 / Kdg. Student Reader K.6.6 / Get Set, Roll! Reader 36	Reader's and Writer's Notebook
• Envision It! Animations	• eReaders	• Grammar Jammer
Practice Station Flip Chart / Leveled Readers / Get Set, Roll! Reader 36	Practice Station Flip Chart / Leveled Readers	Practice Station Flip Chart / Reader's and Writer's Notebook
• Envision It! Animations • eReaders	• eReaders	• Grammar Jammer
• Leveled Readers	• Leveled Readers	• *Reader's and Writer's Notebook*
• Envision It! Animations • eReaders	• eReaders	• Grammar Jammer

Week 6

You Are Here!
Unit 6
Week 6

My 5-Day Planner for Reading Street!

Don't Wait Until Friday

MONITOR PROGRESS

	Check Phonemic Awareness **Day 1** pages 512–527	**Check Sound-Spelling** **Check Retelling** **Day 2** pages 528–545
Get Ready to Read	**Get Ready to Read** **Concept Talk,** 512 **Oral Vocabulary,** 513 *colony, underground, chambers, silk, twigs, pebbles* **Phonemic Awareness,** 514–515 ◉ Initial, Medial, and Final Sounds **Phonics,** 516–517 ◉ Decode Words **Handwriting,** 518 Write Words **High-Frequency Words,** 519 Review *you, see, said, look, three* **READ Decodable Story 36,** 520–521	**Concept Talk,** 528 **Oral Vocabulary,** 529 *colony, underground* **Phonemic Awareness,** 530–531 ◉ Initial, Medial, and Final Sounds **Phonics,** 532–533 ◉ Decode Words **Handwriting,** 534 Write Words **High-Frequency Words,** 535 *you, see, said, look, three* **READ Decodable Reader 36,** 536–537
Read and Comprehend	**Listening Comprehension,** 522–523 ◉ Draw Conclusions	**Listening Comprehension,** 538 ◉ Draw Conclusions **READ Trade Book—First Read,** 538 *Ants and Their Nests* **Retell,** 539 **Think, Talk, and Write,** 540
Language Arts	**Conventions,** 524 Complete Sentences **Writing,** 525 Writing Process: Plan a Report **Listening and Speaking,** 526 Discuss Literary Elements—Setting **Wrap Up Your Day,** 526 **Extend Your Day!,** 527	**Conventions,** 541 Complete Sentences **Writing,** 542 Writing Process: Plan a Report **Vocabulary,** 543 Words for Bugs **Wrap Up Your Day,** 544 **Extend Your Day!,** 545

You Are Here! Unit 6 Week 6

Question of the Week

How do ants build their nests?

Check Word Reading	Check Phonemic Awareness	Check Oral Vocabulary
Day 3 pages 546–573	**Day 4** pages 574–585	**Day 5** pages 586–599

Concept Talk, 546
Oral Vocabulary, 547 *chambers, silk*
Phonemic Awareness, 548–549
  ◉ Initial, Medial, and Final Sounds
Phonics, 550–551
  ◉ Decode Words
READ Kindergarten Student Reader K.6.6, 552–553
	Concept Talk, 574
	Oral Vocabulary, 575 *twigs, pebbles*
	`Review` **Phonemic Awareness,** 576
	  ◉ Initial, Medial, and Final Sounds
	`Review` **Phonics,** 577
	  ◉ Decode Words
	Spelling, 578 Initial, Medial, and Final Sounds
	READ Get Set, Roll! Reader 36, 579
		Concept Wrap Up, 586
		Oral Vocabulary, 587 *colony, underground, chambers, silk, twigs, pebbles*
		`Review` **Phonemic Awareness,** 588
		  ◉ Initial, Medial, and Final Sounds
		`Review` **Phonics,** 589
		  ◉ Decode Words
		Assessment, 590–591
		Monitor Progress

Comprehension, 554–555
  ◉ Draw Conclusions
READ Trade Book—Second Read, 556–567 *Ants and Their Nests*
	Comprehension, 580
	  ◉ Draw Conclusions
	  `Review` Compare and Contrast
	READ Trade Book—Third Read, 581 *Ants and Their Nests*
		Let's Practice It!, 592–593
		Poem
		Assessment, 584–595
		Monitor Progress

Conventions, 568 Exclamations **Writing,** 569 Writing Process: Draft a Report **Listening and Speaking,** 570–571 Discuss Literary Elements—Setting **Wrap Up Your Day,** 572 **Extend Your Day!,** 573	**Conventions,** 582 Complete Sentences **Writing,** 583 Writing Process: Revise a Report **Vocabulary,** 584 Words for Bugs **Wrap Up Your Day,** 584 **Extend Your Day!,** 585	`Review` **Conventions,** 596 Complete Sentences **Writing,** 597 Writing Process: Edit and Share a Report **Wrap Up Your Week!,** 598 ❓ How do ants build their nests? **Extend Your Day!,** 599

Week 6

Grouping Options for Differentiated Instruction
Turn the page for the small group time lesson plan.

Planning Small Group Time on Reading Street!

SMALL GROUP TIME RESOURCES

DAY 1

Look for this Small Group Time box each day to help meet the individual needs of all your children. Differentiated instruction lessons appear on the DI pages at the end of each week.

Teacher-Led

SI Strategic Intervention	**OL** On-Level	**A** Advanced
Teacher-Led	**Teacher-Led**	**Teacher-Led**
• Phonemic Awareness and Phonics	• Phonemic Awareness and Phonics	• Phonemic Awareness and Phonics
Reread Decodable Story	**Reread** Decodable Story	**Reread** Decodable Story for Fluency

ELL Place English language learners in the groups that correspond to their reading abilities in English.

Practice Stations
• Listen Up
• Word Work

Independent Activities
• Read Independently
• *Reader's and Writer's Notebook*
• Concept Talk Video

ELL

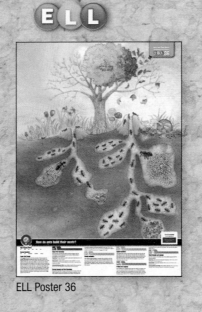

ELL Poster 36

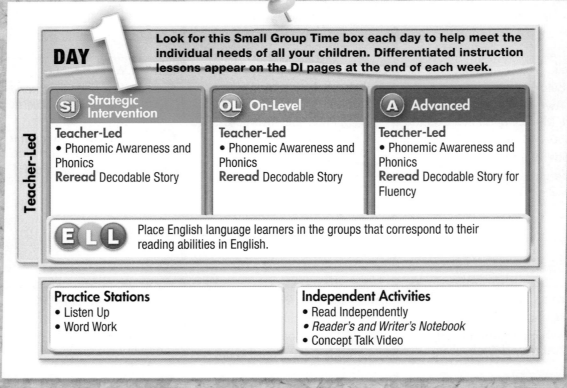

Day 1

SI Strategic Intervention	**Phonemic Awareness and Phonics**, DI•86 **Reread** Decodable Story 36, DI•86
OL On-Level	**Phonemic Awareness and Phonics**, DI•91 **Reread** Decodable Story 36, DI•91
A Advanced	**Phonemic Awareness and Phonics**, DI•94 **Reread** Decodable Story 36 for Fluency, DI•94
ELL English Language Learners	DI•97–DI•98 Frontload Concept Phonemic Awareness and Phonics Comprehension Skill

You Are Here!
Unit 6
Week 6

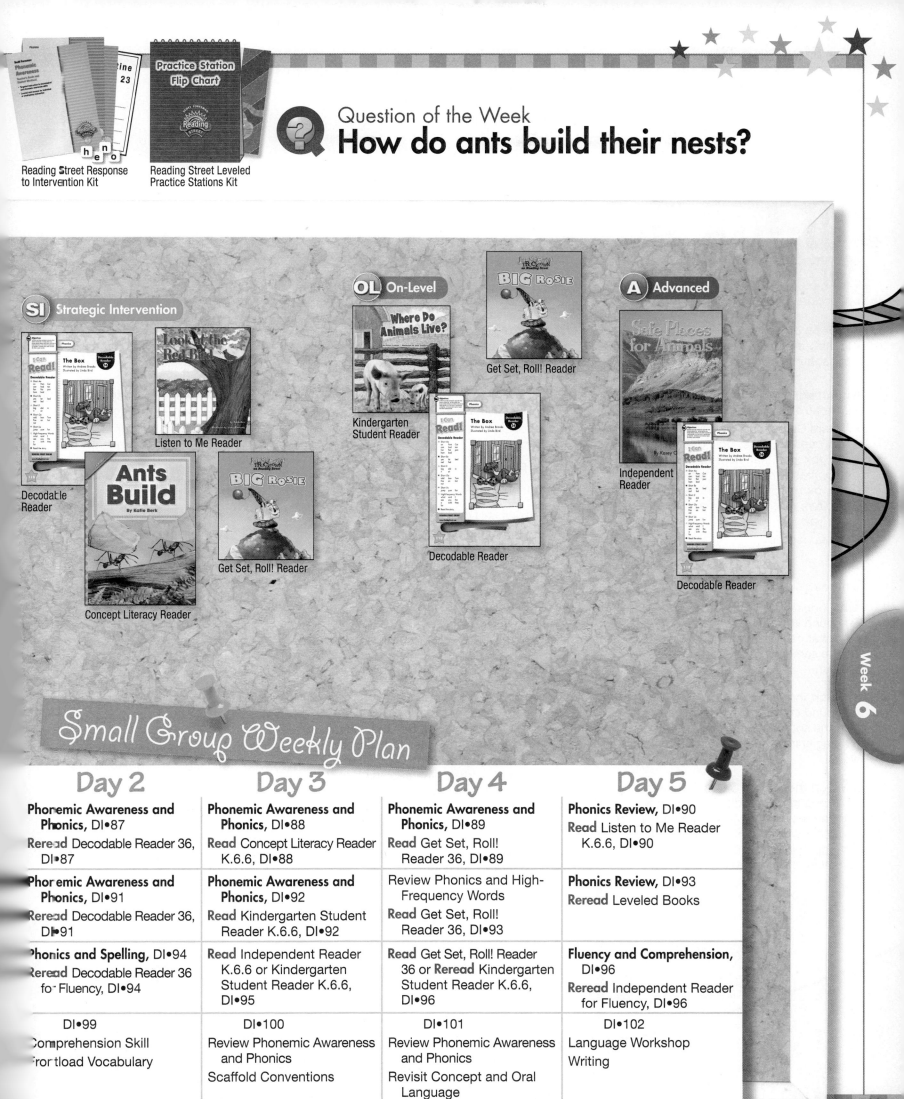

Question of the Week
How do ants build their nests?

SI Strategic Intervention

The Box — Decodable Reader

Look at the Red Bird — Listen to Me Reader

Ants Build — By Katie Berk — Concept Literacy Reader

BIG ROSIE — Get Set, Roll! Reader

OL On-Level

Where Do Animals Live? — Kindergarten Student Reader

BIG ROSIE — Get Set, Roll! Reader

The Box — Decodable Reader

A Advanced

Safe Places for Animals — Independent Reader

The Box — Decodable Reader

Small Group Weekly Plan

Day 2	Day 3	Day 4	Day 5
Phonemic Awareness and Phonics, DI•87 **Reread** Decodable Reader 36, DI•87	**Phonemic Awareness and Phonics,** DI•88 **Read** Concept Literacy Reader K.6.6, DI•88	**Phonemic Awareness and Phonics,** DI•89 **Read** Get Set, Roll! Reader 36, DI•89	**Phonics Review,** DI•90 **Read** Listen to Me Reader K.6.6, DI•90
Phonemic Awareness and Phonics, DI•91 **Reread** Decodable Reader 36, DI•91	**Phonemic Awareness and Phonics,** DI•92 **Read** Kindergarten Student Reader K.6.6, DI•92	Review Phonics and High-Frequency Words **Read** Get Set, Roll! Reader 36, DI•93	**Phonics Review,** DI•93 **Reread** Leveled Books
Phonics and Spelling, DI•94 **Reread** Decodable Reader 36 for Fluency, DI•94	**Read** Independent Reader K.6.6 or Kindergarten Student Reader K.6.6, DI•95	**Read** Get Set, Roll! Reader 36 or **Reread** Kindergarten Student Reader K.6.6, DI•96	**Fluency and Comprehension,** DI•96 **Reread** Independent Reader for Fluency, DI•96
DI•99 Comprehension Skill Frontload Vocabulary	DI•100 Review Phonemic Awareness and Phonics Scaffold Conventions	DI•101 Review Phonemic Awareness and Phonics Revisit Concept and Oral Language	DI•102 Language Workshop Writing

Practice Stations for Everyone on Reading Street!

Listen Up!
Short vowels and consonants

Objectives
• Identify and use short vowels and consonants.

Materials
• *Listen Up!* Flip Chart Activity 36
• Picture Cards: *bag, bat, bed, box, bus, can, cap, cat, crab, doll, drum, fan, flag, fox, gun, hat, hen, jam, jet, jug, map, mask, mop, mug, nest, net, nut, pan, pen, pig, red, rug, six, sled, sock, sun, ten, tent, top, tub, van, vest, web, wig, yak*
• paper, pencils

Differentiated Activities

⬤ Choose a Picture Card that has the /a/ sound in the middle. Find another card that has the same middle sound. Do the same with the sounds /e/, /i/, /o/, and /u/.

▲ Sort the Picture Cards that have the /a/ sound in the middle. Do the same with the sounds /e/, /i/, /o/, and /u/. Say the beginning and ending sound of each word.

⬛ Sort the Picture Cards that have the /a/ sound in the middle. Do the same with the sounds /e/, /i/, /o/, and /u/. Write two other words for each middle sound. Change the beginning and ending consonant sounds to make new words.

Word Work
Consonants short vowels

Objectives
• Review and build words with short vowel sounds.

Materials
• *Word Work* Flip Chart Activity 36
• Alphabet Cards
• Letter Tiles
• paper, pencils

Differentiated Activities

⬤ Find the Alphabet Cards for the letters *Aa, Ee, Ii, Oo,* and *Uu.* Say the sound for each. Use the Letter Tiles to build the words *cat, hen, pig, fox,* and *cub.*

▲ Find the Alphabet Cards for the letters *Aa, Ee, Ii, Oo,* and *Uu.* Say the sound for each. Use the Letter Tiles to build the words *cat, hen, pig, fox,* and *cub.* Take away the beginning letter of each and build a new word.

⬛ Find the Alphabet Cards for the letters *Aa, Ee, Ii, Oo,* and *Uu.* Say the sound for each. Use the Letter Tiles to build the words *cat, hen, pig, fox,* and *cub.* Take away and add letters at the beginning or end to build two new words. Write the words on your paper.

Technology
• Letter Tile Drag and Drop

Words To Know
Words for feelings

Objectives
• Identify and use words for feelings.

Materials
• *Words to Know* Flip Chart Activity 36
• Find pictures (or take quick digital photos and print out) for feelings words: *frightened, worried, proud, angry*
• Teacher-made word cards: *frightened, worried, proud, angry*
• small mirror
• paper, pencils, crayons

Differentiated Activities

⬤ Choose the picture card that shows frightened. Say the name for the picture. Look in the mirror and make a face to match the word. Continue with *worried, proud,* and *angry.*

▲ Choose the picture card that shows frightened. Say the name for the picture. Look in the mirror and make a face to match the word. Tell what might make you feel that way. Continue with *worried, proud,* and *angry.*

⬛ Match the picture cards and word cards that show *frightened, worried, proud,* and *angry.* Draw a picture that shows what you look like when you are *frightened, worried, proud,* or *angry.*

You Are Here!
Unit 6
Week 6

Use this week's materials from the Reading Street Leveled Practice Stations Kit to organize this week's stations.

Key
○ Below-Level Activities
△ On-Level Activities
▢ Advanced Activities

Practice Station Flip Chart

Let's Write!
Poem

Objectives
• Write a poem that tells who helps to build a house.

Materials
• *Let's Write!* Flip Chart Activity 36
• Find pictures (or take quick digital photos and print out) for words: *hammering, painting, digging, measuring, sawing*
• crayons, paper, pencil

Differentiated Activities

○ Look at the picture cards. Think about what people do to help build a house. Write a four-line poem about it. Draw a picture to go with your poem.

△ Write an eight-line poem about what people do to help build a house. Draw pictures to go with your poem.

▢ Write an ten-line poem about what people do to help build a house. Use action words to tell what people do. Draw pictures to go with your poem.

Read For Meaning
Setting

Objectives
• Identify and describe story setting.

Materials
• *Read for Meaning* Flip Chart Activity 36
• Little Book *The House That Tony Lives In*
• pencil, crayons, paper

Differentiated Activities

The story **setting** is where the story takes place. A good way to understand a story is to think about the setting.

○ Read your book. Find a picture that shows where the story takes place. Tell what you see.

△ Read your book. Draw a picture that shows where the story takes place. Write a sentence to go with your picture.

▢ Read your book. Find pictures and words that give information about the setting. Write a sentence that tells about the setting of the story.

Let's Make Art!

Objectives
• Draw pictures to show what people do to help build a house.

Materials
• *Let's Make Art!* Flip Chart Activity 36
• index cards
• crayons

Differentiated Activities

○ What do people do to help build a house? What tools do they use? Use three cards to draw three pictures of people helping to build a house. Use three more cards to draw three pictures of the tools they use. Match the cards to show the people and the tools they use.

△ What do people do to help build a house? What tools do they use? Use five cards to draw pictures of people helping to build a house. Use five more cards to draw pictures of the tools they use. Match the cards to show the people and the tools they use.

▢ What do people do to help build a house? What tools do they use? Use eight cards to draw pictures of people helping to build a house. Use eight more cards to draw pictures of the tools they use. Match the cards to show the people and the tools they use.

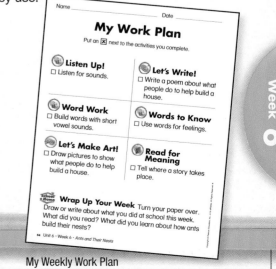

My Work Plan
Put an ☒ next to the activities you complete.

Listen Up!
☐ Listen for sounds.

Let's Write!
☐ Write a poem about what people do to help build a house.

Word Work
☐ Build words with short vowel sounds.

Words to Know
☐ Use words for feelings.

Let's Make Art!
☐ Draw pictures to show what people do to help build a house.

Read for Meaning
☐ Tell where a story takes place.

Wrap Up Your Week Turn your paper over. Draw or write about what you did at school this week. What did you read? What did you learn about how ants build their nests?

My Weekly Work Plan

Week 6

Objectives
• Share information and ideas about the concept.

Today at a Glance

Oral Vocabulary
colony, underground, chambers, silk, twigs, pebbles

Phonemic Awareness
◉ Initial, Medial, and Final Sounds

Phonics
◉ Decode Words

Handwriting
Write Names and Words

High-Frequency Words
you, said, see, look, three

Comprehension
◉ Draw Conclusions

Conventions
Complete Sentences

Writing
Writing Process: Plan a Report

Listening and Speaking
Discuss Literary Elements: Setting

TRUCKTOWN on Reading Street

Start your engines!

Display p. 19 of *Truckery Rhymes*.

• Read aloud "Pop! Blows the Diesel" and track the print.

• Reread the rhyme and have children chime in as they wish.

• Tell children to identify the rhyming words. (*hose, goes*)

Truckery Rhymes

Concept Talk

Question of the Week

How do ants build their nests?

Introduce the concept

To build concepts and to focus their attention, tell children that this week they will talk, sing, read, and write about ants and their homes. Write the question of the week and track the print as you read it.

Play the CD that features a game show about animal homes. Where do birds build their homes? Why do many animals build their homes in the ground?

🔘 Background Building Audio

ROUTINE — **Activate Prior Knowledge** — **Team Talk**

1. **Think** Have children think for a minute about ants.

2. **Pair** Have pairs of children discuss the question of the week. Remind them to take turns speaking. Have children use complete sentences in their discussions about how ants build their nests.

3. **Share** Call on a few children to share their ideas with the group. Guide discussion and encourage elaboration with prompts such as: Where is a good place for ants to build their nests?

Routines Flip Chart

Anchored Talk

Develop oral language

Display Talk with Me Chart 36A. This week we will talk about ants and their homes, which are called nests. The chart shows some of the features of ants' nests. What do you see in this picture? Do ants build their nests above ground or underground? Continue with the other pictures.

We are going to learn six new Amazing Words. Listen as I say the words. You may know some of them: *colony, underground, chambers, silk, twigs, pebbles.* Say the Amazing Words with me as I point to the pictures.

Display Sing with Me Chart 36B. Today we are going to sing a song about ants building a nest. Listen for the Amazing Words *colony, underground, chambers, silk, twigs,* and *pebbles.* Read the title and have children tell what is happening in the picture. Sing the song several times to the tune of "The Itsy-Bitsy Spider." Then ask children to sing along with you.

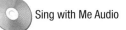 Sing with Me Audio

ELL Preteach Concepts Use the Day 1 instruction on ELL Poster 36 to assess and build background knowledge, develop concepts, and build oral vocabulary.

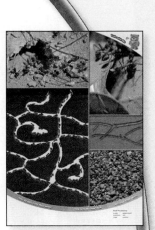

Talk with Me/Sing with Me Chart 36A

Talk with Me/Sing with Me Chart 36B

ELL Poster 36

Amazing Words

colony	underground
chambers	silk
twigs	pebbles

 **Writing on Demand**

Develop Writing Fluency

Ask children to write about what they know about how ants build nests. Have them write for two minutes. Children should write as much as they can. Tell them to try to do their best writing. You may want to discuss what children wrote during writing conferences.

English Language Learners

Build Background English learners will benefit from additional visual support to understand words in the song. Point to the *colony, twigs,* and *pebbles* in the art to scaffold meaning.

Media To have children derive meaning from a variety of media find an appropriate Web site, CD ROM, or DVD that provides an audio and video account of ants. Have children listen to and derive meaning to build and reinforce concept and language attainment. To assess their concept and language attainment have them create a class book on ants.

Objectives
- ⊙ Identify initial, medial, and final sounds.

Check Phonemic Awareness
SUCCESS PREDICTOR

Objectives
- Point out groups of spoken words that begin with the same sound.
- Say the sound at the beginning of spoken one-syllable words.

Phonemic Awareness

Let's Listen for

Blends

- ● Point to the broom. Say the word. Say the beginning blend. Find two more things that begin with /br/.

- ■ Point to the limb. Say *limb*. Say the middle sound. Find two more things with /i/ in the middle.

- ▲ Point to a plant. Say the word. Say the blend you hear at the end. Find two more things that end with /nt/.

- ★ Point to these pictures and say the words: *brown, bricks, brush.* Do they begin the same? What about *drink, sticks, broom?*

READING STREET ONLINE
BIG QUESTION VIDEO
www.ReadingStreet.com

My Skills Buddy, pp. 112–113

Phonemic Awareness
Initial, Medial, and Final Sounds

Teach

Today we will use what we learned about consonant and short vowel sounds to identify beginning, middle, and ending sounds in words.

Display the *gum* Picture Card. This is gum. What is the beginning sound in *gum?* (/g/) What is the middle sound in *gum?* (/u/) What is the ending sound in *gum?* (/m/) The word *gum* has three sounds: /g/ /u/ /m/. Continue with the *fan, bed, six, top,* and *yak* Picture Cards.

Model

Have children look at the picture on pp. 112–113 of *My Skills Buddy.* Tell them that they will be listening for the beginning, middle, and ending sounds in words. I see a building made of brick. I hear the blend /br/ at the beginning of *brick.* What sound do you hear in the middle of *brick?* I hear /i/ in the middle of *brick.* What is the last sound you hear in *brick?* The last sound is /k/. What other things do you see that begin with a blend?

Guide practice

As children name example words from the picture, guide them in stating the beginning, middle, and ending sound. Discuss with children some of the bulleted items on p. 112 of *My Skills Buddy.* Save the other bulleted items for discussion on Day 2.

Corrective feedback

If... children have difficulty identifying beginning, medial, and final sounds **then...** say *brick* again, emphasizing each sound—/br/, /i/, /k/, *brick.*

Discriminate sounds

Hold up the *drum* Picture Card. I am going to say two words. One word will begin with /dr/, like *drum*. I want you to tell me which word begins like *drum*. I will do the first one: *down, drip.* Which word begins like *drum?* *Drip* begins with /dr/, like *drum*. Continue with the following pairs of words: *dry, broom; wagon, dragon; run, drag*. Repeat the routine holding up the *jet* Picture Card and asking children to identify the word in each pair that has the middle sound /e/, like *jet: bed, bag; mess, dish; flag, wet*. Display the *green* Picture Card and ask children to identify the word in each pair that has the ending sound /n/, like *green: run, net; pillow, balloon; rain, map*.

Corrective feedback

If... children cannot identify the sounds in the picture names, **then...** continue to model identifying the sounds and have children repeat the sounds after you several times.

Segment and blend

Display the *tent* Picture Card. What is this? (tent) What are the sounds in the word *tent?* (/t/ /e/ /nt/) Have children continue segmenting the sounds in words using the *sled, crab, drum, flag, sock,* and *mask* Picture Cards.

I am going to say some sounds. I want you to repeat the sounds and then blend them together to say the word. Listen carefully: /l/ /a/ /nd/. Repeat the sounds: /l/ /a/ /nd/. Now blend the sounds together. What is this word? (*land*) Continue the routine with the words *fast, tan, hot, cats, him,* and *pest*.

Don't Wait Until Friday

MONITOR PROGRESS ⟳ Check Phonemic Awareness Phoneme Segmentation

Say *lap.* Have children tell you the sounds in the word. Repeat with the following words: *hop, sit, grab, sent, dug, web, just.*

If... children cannot identify sounds in words,

then... use the small-group Strategic Intervention lesson, p. DI•86, to reteach identifying sounds.

Day 1	**Day 2**	**Day 3**	**Day 4**	**Day 5**
Check Phonemic Awareness	Check Sound-Spelling/ Retelling	Check Word Reading	Check Phonemic Awareness	Check Oral Vocabulary

Success Predictor

Differentiated Instruction

SI Strategic Intervention

Support Phonemic Awareness
Tell children to listen for the sound that is the same in each set of words. Say these words: *brush, broom, brother; clean, club, clue; glad, glue, globe*. Have children repeat the beginning consonant blend in each group of words.

English Language Learners
Since Spanish generally does not allow /m/ at the end of a word, Spanish speakers may substitute /n/ for final /m/ in words such as *drum* and *him*.

Objectives
◎ Decode words.
• Blend and read words.

Skills Trace

◎ **Consonants and Short Vowels**

Introduce U1W5-6 D1-2;
U2W1-6 D1; U3W1-6 D1-2;
U4W1-W6 D1; U5W1-6 D1-2;
U6W6D1

Practice U1W5-6 D2-3;
U2W1-6 D2-3; U3W1-6 D2-3;
U4W1-W6 D2-3; U5W1-6 D2-3;
U6W6D2; U6W6D3

Reteach/Review U1W5-6
D5; U2W1-6 D5; U3W1-6 D5;
U4W1-W6 D5; U5W1-6 D5;
U6W6D5

Assess/Test Benchmark
Assessment U1; U2; U3; U4;
U5; U6

KEY:
U=Unit   W=Week   D=Day

Phonics—Teach/Model
Decode Words

Review

Sound-Spellings Practice the sound-spellings of all previously taught letters. Display all of the Alphabet Cards in order on the chalk ledge. Point to the uppercase *A* on the *Aa* Alphabet Card. What is the sound we learned for this letter? What is the name of this letter? Repeat for lowercase *a*. Continue to review sounds and letter names with children.

Now we will use what we have learned about sounds and the letters for the sounds to read words.

Alphabet Card

Model

Write the word *pot* on the board. What is this word? I will say the sound for each letter as I point to it: /p/ /o/ /t/. Now I will blend the sounds together to read the word: /p/ /o/ /t/, *pot*. What is the word? The word is *pot*.

Guide practice

Display Phonics Songs and Rhymes Chart 36. Teach children the song "Quickly, Thump on the Mud" sung to the tune of "Billy Boy (Oh, Where Have You Been)." Play the CD or sing the song several times. When children are familiar with the song, have them sing along with you. Then repeat the routine from Model, having children point to, segment, and blend the following words from the song: *dam, fix, ten, log, tuck.*

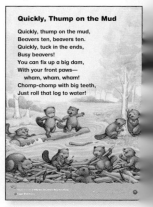

Quickly, Thump on the Mud

Quickly, thump on the mud,
Beavers ten, beavers ten.
Quickly, tuck in the ends,
Busy beavers!
You can fix up a big dam,
With your front paws—
    wham, wham, wham!
Chomp-chomp with big teeth,
Just roll that log to water!

Phonics Songs and Rhymes Audio

Phonics Songs and Rhymes
Chart 36

On their own

Write the words below on the board. Pair children and have them take turns reading the words aloud.

mug	zap	fox	quack	eggs
wet	rag	drum	lips	clock
job	win	bell	bun	quit

Blend Words

Review

To review previously taught sound-spellings, use the Alphabet Cards *Aa, Cc, Nn, Rr,* and *Tt* and the *ant, crab, tent,* and *nest* Picture Cards. Then use this routine for sound-by-sound blending to have children blend new words.

ROUTINE **Sound-by-Sound Blending**

① **Connect** Write the letter *a* on the board. What is the sound for this letter? The sound is /a/. Say it with me: /a/ /a/ /a/. When you see this letter in a word, what sound will you say?

② **Model** Write *fast* on the board.

- Touch under the letter *f*. What is the sound for this letter? Say it with me: /f/ /f/ /f/. Repeat the routine touching under *a, s,* and *t.*

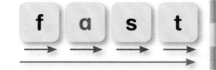

- Let's blend the sounds together. Listen as I blend the sounds: /f/ /a/ /st/. Say it with me: /f/ /a/ /st/. Now say it without me.

- Listen as I use *fast* in a sentence: *That car is fast.* Say it with me. Then have children use *fast* in their own sentences.

③ **Guide Practice** Continue the routine established in step 2 with the words below:

and	fed	dogs	jump	legs

Children should successfully read these words before reading Decodable Story 36 on p. 463 of *Reader's and Writer's Notebook.*

Corrective Feedback If children have trouble reading a word, model blending the sounds to read the word. Then have children say it with you.

Routines Flip Chart

Differentiated Instruction

A **Advanced**

Sound Scavenger Hunt Give each child an Alphabet Card. Have children search for things in the classroom whose names contain the sound represented by the letter. Have children say the name of the object and the sound represented by their Alphabet Card.

English Language Learners

Sound-Spelling Transfer In Spanish the letters *b, c, d, f, l, m, n, p, q, s,* and *t* represent sounds that transfer readily to English. English learners need minimal phonics instruction for these consonants. However, vowel letters look the same in Spanish and English but are named differently and represent very different sounds. The one-to-one correspondence between vowel letters and vowel sounds in Spanish does not hold true in English. This may present a challenge to children whose family members are literate in Spanish.

Handwriting

Teach	Remind children that words are written with either an uppercase letter or a lowercase letter at the beginning. We use an uppercase letter as the first letter of the first word in a sentence or as the first letter of a person's name.
Model writing names	Write *Ann* and *Al* on the board. These are the names *Ann* and *Al*. I use an uppercase *A* at the beginning of *Ann* and *Al* because they are people's names. Watch how I write the names. Write *Ann* and *Al* on the board again.
Guide practice	Have children practice writing *Ann* and *Al* on their Write-On Boards. Circulate around the room, assisting them when necessary.
Model writing words	Write *can* and *bed* on the board. These are the words *can* and *bed*. I use a lowercase *a* and *e* because they are in the middle of the word. Watch how I write the words. Write *can* and *bed* on the board again.
Guide practice	Have children practice writing *can* and *bed*. Now you write *can* and *bed*. Then have them write the words to make a complete sentence.
More practice	Use *Reader's and Writer's Notebook,* p. 461, for additional practice with writing words.

Reader's and Writer's Notebook, p. 461

High-Frequency Words

Teach

Use the routine below to teach high-frequency words *you, see, said, look,* and *three.*

> ### ROUTINE — Nondecodable Words
>
> **1 Say and Spell** Some words we have learned by remembering the letters rather than saying the sounds. We say and spell the words to help learn them. Write *you* on the board. This is the word *you*. It has three letters. The letters in *you* are *y, o, u.* Have children say and spell the word, first with you and then without you.
>
> **2 Demonstrate Meaning** I can use the word *you* in lots of sentences. Here is one sentence: *I will go to the park with you.* Now you use the word in a sentence.
>
> Repeat the routine with the words *see, said, look,* and *three.*

Routines Flip Chart

Academic Vocabulary

Write the following on the board:

draw conclusions	expository nonfiction
retell	exclamation
setting	prediction
draft	revise
edit	limerick
rhythm	

Point to the list. Boys and girls, this week we are going to learn these important words. They are tools for learning. As we work this week, you will hear them many times. Read the words. Preteach the Academic Vocabulary at point-of-use by providing a child-friendly description, explanation, or example that clarifies the meaning of each term. Then ask children to restate the meaning of the Academic Vocabulary in their own words.

Decodable Story 36
Decodable Words and High-Frequency Words

Review

Review the previously taught high-frequency words *here, is, look, he, the, little, see, she, go, from, me, to, you, I, my, what,* and *do*. Have children read each word as you point to it on the Word Wall.

here	look	little	see	she	from	you	what	do

Read Decodable Story 36

Display Decodable Story 36, *What Can You Do?* Today we will read a story about the things that several children can do. **Point to the title of the story.** What is the title of this story? *What Can You Do?* is the title of the story. We can read all the words in this story. Have children read Decodable Story 36 on pp. 463–464 in *Reader's and Writer's Notebook.*

Reader's and Writer's Notebook, pp. 463–464

Use the routine for reading decodable books to read Decodable Story 36.

 **Reading Decodable Books**

1. **Read Silently** Have children whisper read the story page by page as you listen in.

2. **Model Fluent Reading** Have children finger point as you read a page. Then have children reread the page without you.

3. **Read Chorally** Have children finger point as they chorally read the page. Continue reading page by page, repeating steps 1 and 2.

4. **Read Individually** Have children take turns reading aloud a page.

5. **Reread and Monitor Progress** As you listen to individual children reread, monitor progress and provide support.

6. **Reread with a Partner** Have children reread the story page by page with a partner.

Routines Flip Chart

Differentiated Instruction

SI Strategic Intervention

Access Content Have children use letter-sound relationships to decode the words in Decodable Story 36 before reading the story.

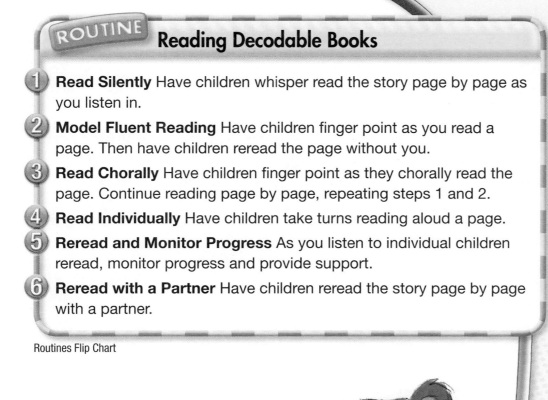

Small Group Time

DAY 1

Break into small groups after reading the Decodable Story and before the comprehension lesson.

Teacher-Led

SI Strategic Intervention	**OL** On-Level	**A** Advanced
Teacher-Led Page DI•86	**Teacher-Led** Page DI•91	**Teacher-Led** Page DI•94
• Phonemic Awareness and Phonics	• Phonemic Awareness and Phonics	• Phonemic Awareness and Phonics
• **Reread** Decodable Story 36	• **Reread** Decodable Story 36, DI•91	• **Reread** Decodable Story 36 for Fluency, DI•94

ELL Place English language learners in the groups that correspond to their reading abilities in English.

Practice Stations	**Independent Activities**
• Visit the Listen Up! Station	• Read independently
• Visit the Word Work Station	• Concept Talk Video
	• *Reader's and Writer's Notebook*

English Language Learners

Fluency Many language learners will read and speak English with an accent. Children can read fluently in English with a native language accent.

Skills Trace

◉ **Draw Conclusions**

Introduce U3W5D1; U5W6D1; U6W6D1

Practice U3W5D2; U3W5D3; U3W5D4; U5W6D2; U5W6D3; U5W6D4; U6W6D2; U6W6D3; U6W6D4

Reteach/Review U3W5D5; U4W3D4; U5W3D4; U5W6D5; U6W1D4; U6W4D4; U6W6D5

KEY:
U=Unit   W=Week   D=Day

My Skills Buddy, pp. 114–115

Listening Comprehension
🎯 Draw Conclusions

Introduce

When you listen to a selection and look at the pictures, think about what you hear and see. Use what you know to make up your mind about things in the selection. This is called **drawing conclusions.** Good readers draw conclusions as they read because it helps them better understand the ideas in what they are reading. What do good readers do?

Have children turn to pp. 114–115 in *My Skills Buddy* and look at the pictures. These pictures tell a story.

- What is the girl holding? (a present)

- How does the girl feel about the present? (She is happy about it.)

- How did you draw that conclusion? (The girl is smiling. People smile when they are happy. I can conclude that the girl is happy.)

Model

Today I will read a selection that describes the home of an animal called a prairie dog. Read **"A Prairie Dog Home"** and model how to draw conclusions.

> **Think Aloud**
>
> As I read, I draw conclusions. I connect the ideas in what I am reading to what I already know. "A Prairie Dog Home" says that a prairie dog is a rodent. I know that rodents' teeth are good for gnawing, so I can conclude that a prairie dog has teeth that are good for gnawing.

Guide practice

Reread the second paragraph of the selection. Have children recall what a beaver dam does. What conclusion can you draw about how a prairie dog's mound of dirt and a beaver's dam are alike? (Both hold back water.)

More practice

Display *The House That Tony Lives In.* Page through the selection. What conclusion can you draw about where Tony's new house is? (Tony's house is in a small town or the suburbs because the houses have yards and trees around them.)

Connect to everyday life

Every day we use what we know to help us make up our minds about things. If you go to the library and you can't find the book you want, what can you conclude about where the book might be?

Academic Vocabulary

draw conclusions make a reasonable guess based on what is known

Teacher Tip

Show children pictures from magazines and have them use prior knowledge and picture clues to draw conclusions.

Read Aloud

A Prairie Dog Home

A prairie dog is not a dog but a rodent, much like a squirrel. The prairie dog is also a fine builder.

The prairie dog's home is underground. With its long, curved claws, it digs a deep tunnel. The mound of dirt from digging helps keep water out of its home and makes a good lookout tower. A prairie dog often sits up on top of this mound, watching for enemies.

The burrow home is surprisingly large. A room close to the entrance is a safe place to listen for enemies. Nesting and sleeping rooms are farther down. Some tunnels lead to back doors. These are important. If a hungry snake, ferret, or badger crawls into the burrow, the prairie dog must have ways to escape.

English Language Learners
Oral Comprehension To prepare English learners for the Read Aloud, use the modified Read Aloud in the ELL Support lesson on p. DI•98.

Objectives
- Introduce complete sentences.
- Generate ideas for a class report.
- Choose an idea for a class report.

Conventions
Complete Sentences

Teach sentences

Hold up AlphaBuddy. AlphaBuddy, what did you eat for lunch? Have AlphaBuddy say, "I ate a ham sandwich." AlphaBuddy answered my question using a complete sentence. When I asked him what he ate for lunch, he said, "I ate a sandwich," not "a sandwich."

Model

Write *a sandwich* on the board. This is not a complete sentence. A complete sentence has a subject and a predicate. Change the sentence to read: *AlphaBuddy ate a sandwich.* This is a complete sentence. It has a subject (underline *AlphaBuddy*) that tells who or what the sentence is about. It has a predicate (circle *ate a sandwich*) that tells what the person or thing does.

Guide practice

Write the following groups of words on the board and read them.

> **oatmeal and juice**
>
> **I had oatmeal and juice.**

If you asked me what I had for breakfast, and I answered you using a complete sentence, which of these groups of words did I use?

Team Talk Pair children and have them take turns telling what they had for breakfast this morning. Remind them to use complete sentences.

Daily Fix-It

Use the Daily Fix-It for more conventions practice.

Writing
Writing Process: Plan a Report

Teach: Generate ideas

Talk with children about informational or expository writing. Some writing gives us information about something. Display *Ants and Their Nests.* This book tells us interesting information about how ants build their nests. Read aloud sentences from the book that tell how ants build their nests.

This week we are going to write a report about how another kind of animal builds its home. A report gives readers information about something. It includes important facts.

Model: Generate ideas

When we write a report, the first thing we do is choose a topic or subject that we will write about. I am going to think of an animal I would like to learn more about. I know that a fox can be red and has a bushy tail, but I don't know where a fox lives or how it builds its home. I will ask myself, *How does a fox build its home?* Write *fox* in a list titled *How does this animal build its home?*

Guide practice: Generate ideas and choose a topic

Encourage children to generate topic ideas for the list. Think about animals you would like to learn more about. Ask yourself a question you want to answer. Then we will choose one animal to write about.

Have children turn to p. 465 in *Reader's and Writer's Notebook* and draw pictures of animals as topic ideas. Then continue the topics list you began, adding children's ideas. As a class, select one animal as the report topic (for example, how a bird builds its nest). Write the question *How does a bird build its nest?* on the board.

Independent writing

Have children illustrate or copy the question on p. 466 in *Reader's and Writer's Notebook*.

Reader's and Writer's Notebook, pp. 465–466

Daily Fix-It

sit on the top step
Sit on the top step.

This week's practice sentences appear on Teacher Resources DVD-ROM.

Writing Routine

Day 1 Plan a Report
Day 2 Plan a Report
Day 3 Draft a Report
Day 4 Revise a Report
Day 5 Edit and Share a Report

English Language Learners
Composing Sentences Write the nouns *dogs, girls, babies,* and *friends* on one set of cards and the verbs *run, play, bark,* and *giggle* on another set of cards. Display the cards and have children choose a card from each set to make a complete sentence.

Listening and Speaking
Discuss Literary Elements: Setting

Teach   All stories happen in a certain place and at a certain time. This is the setting of the story. We can use what happens in the story and the pictures to help us understand where and when the story takes place.

Model   Display pp. 4–5 of the Trade Book *Old MacDonald had a Woodshop.* Where does this story take place? It takes place in a woodshop on a farm. What do I see in the picture that helps me know when the story takes place? The pigs are riding on a tractor. Farms long ago did not have tractors, so I know the story takes place in modern times.

Guide practice   Display the cover of the Big Book *A Bed for Winter.* Have children discuss the setting. What details in the pictures help you know that? Refer children to the Rules for Speaking and Listening on pp. 1–2 of *Reader's and Writer's Notebook.* Tell children to speak one at a time.

Name _____

Speaking Rules

1. Speak clearly.
2. Tell only important ideas.
3. Choose your words carefully.
4. Take turns speaking.
5. Speak one at a time.

2 Listening and Speaking Rules

Reader's and Writer's Notebook, p. 2

Wrap Up Your Day

✔ **Oral Language** Today we sang a song about ants building a nest. Say the Amazing Words with me again: *colony, underground, chambers, silk, twigs, pebbles.*

✔ **Phonemic Awareness** What is the beginning (middle, ending) sound in *lamp? desk? flag?*

✔ **Conventions** Today we learned about complete sentences. What makes a sentence complete?

✔ **Homework Idea** Send home the Family Times Newsletter on Let's Practice It!, TR DVD•71–72.

Preview DAY 2

Tomorrow we will read a selection about ants and their nests.

Extend Your Day!

Science
Favorite Animals

Materials: chart paper, markers, pencils, four-column graphs

Name Kinds of Animals Have children think of and name different kinds of animals. Remind them to include insects, fish, reptiles, and mammals. Write their responses in a list on chart paper. Have children share what they know about each animal's appearance and behavior. Remind them to speak one at a time.

Take a Survey Choose four animals from the list for children to vote on as their favorite animal. Conduct a survey and write the number of votes for each animal next to its name.

Make a Graph Provide each child with a four-column graph. Have children display the results of the survey on the graph by writing the animals' names in the boxes at the bottom of the graph and coloring one box above an animal's name for each vote the animal received. Then have children write or dictate sentences summarizing the data on the graph.

Conventions
Word Substitution

Materials: nouns and verbs written on index cards

Change Nouns and Verbs in the Subject and Predicate Provide each child with an index card that has a noun or a verb written on it. Write a sentence on the board. Read the sentence with children. Have a child come to the board to replace either the noun in the subject or the verb in the predicate of the sentence with the word on his or her card. Read each new sentence together. Continue until all children have had a chance to use their word.

Phonemic Awareness
What Do I Spy?

Materials: Picture Cards

Play an Initial Sound I will give you a clue about something I see in the room. I will tell the beginning sound in its name. I may say, "I spy something whose name begins with /b/." You would look around the room and guess things you see whose names begin with /b/. When you guess that I am thinking of a book, then it is your turn to give the class a clue about an object in the room. The child who identifies the correct object gets to give the initial sound clue for the next object.

Objectives

- Discuss the concepts to develop oral language.
- Build oral vocabulary.

Today at a Glance

Oral Vocabulary
colony, underground

Phonemic Awareness
⊚ Initial, Medial, and Final Sounds

Phonics
⊚ Decode Words

Handwriting
Write Words

Comprehension
⊚ Draw Conclusions

Conventions
Complete Sentences

Writing
Writing Process: Plan A Report

Vocabulary
Words for Bugs

TRUCKTOWN on Reading Street

Start your engines! Display p. 19 of *Truckery Rhymes*. Point to "Pop! Blows the Diesel." Who remembers which trucks this rhyme is about? Yes, it's about Pumper Pat and Hook and Ladder Lucy. Let's read the rhyme together. Point out the rhyming words as the class reads the rhyme again. Give children the opportunity to say the rhyme aloud and track the print.

Truckery Rhymes

Concept Talk

Question of the Week
 How do ants build their nests?

Build concepts

Write the question of the week on the board and track the print as you read it aloud. Have children answer the question in complete sentences. To reinforce the concept and focus children's attention, display Sing with Me Chart 36B. Tell children that they are going to sing a song about ants building a house.

🔘 Sing with Me Audio

Listen for Amazing Words

The Amazing Words *colony* and *underground* are in the song we are going to sing. Read the title and have children tell what is happening in the picture. Sing the song several times to the tune of "The Itsy-Bitsy Spider" until children become familiar with words and can sing along. Have them clap when they say the Amazing Word *colony* or *underground*.

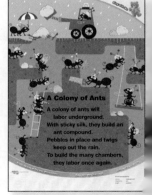

Talk with Me/Sing with Me Chart 36B

ELL Reinforce Vocabulary Use the Day 2 instruction on ELL Poster 36 to reinforce the meanings of high-frequency words.

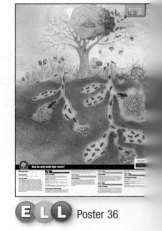

ELL Poster 36

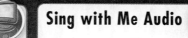

Oral Vocabulary
Amazing Words

Amazing Words

Amazing Words

colony	underground
chambers	silk
twigs	pebbles

Teach Amazing Words

Amazing Words Oral Vocabulary Routine

1 **Introduce the Word** A *colony* is a group of animals that live together. The animals in a *colony* work together to build a nest. What's our new Amazing Word for a group of animals that live together? Say it with me: *colony*.

2 **Demonstrate** Provide examples to show meaning. *Most ants live in a colony.* What other kinds of animals live in a colony?

Repeat steps 1 and 2.

Introduce the Word Something that is *underground* is below the surface of the ground. Many animals build their homes *underground*. What's our new Amazing Word for below the surface of the ground? Say it with me: *underground*.

Demonstrate *Many ants build their nests underground.* What other kinds of animals live underground?

3 **Apply** Have children use *colony* and *underground* in complete sentences to describe how and where ants live.

Routines Flip Chart

Use Amazing Words

To reinforce the concept and the Amazing Words, have children supply the appropriate Amazing Word for each sentence.

A _____ is a large group of ants living together. (colony)

Ants build their nests _____. (underground)

Differentiated Instruction

SI Strategic Intervention

Use Vocabulary Words If children have difficulty completing the sentences, say the sentence with the correct Amazing Word. Have children repeat the sentence and identify the Amazing Word.

English Language Learners
Build Background Provide examples of other things found underground, such as carrots, a basement, a coal mine, and a subway, to help children understand the word.

Objectives
- Practice initial, medial, and final sounds.
- Blend sounds.

Phonemic Awareness
⟲ Initial, Medial, and Final Sounds

Picture Card

Isolate initial, medial, and final sounds

Display the *desk* Picture Card. This is a *desk*. The beginning sound is /d/. What is the middle sound in *desk?* The middle sound is /e/. What are the ending sounds in *desk?* The ending sounds are /s/ /k/. The word *desk* has these sounds: /d/ /e/ /s/ /k/.

Model

Display the *sled* Picture Cards. This is a *sled*. Listen carefully to the sounds: /s/ /l/ /e/ /d/. I hear /s/ /l/ at the beginning of *sled*. What are the beginning sounds you hear in *sled?* I hear /e/ in the middle of *sled*. What is the middle sound you hear in *sled?* I hear /d/ at the end of *sled*. What is the ending sound you hear in *sled?* **Continue the routine with the *brick, frog,* and *truck* Picture Cards.**

Picture Card

Guide practice

Have children look at the picture on *My Skills Buddy* pp. 112–113. Remember that we saw a *brick* in the picture. *Brick* begins with /br/. What other things that begin with /br/ did we find in the picture? Name other things that begin with /br/. **Repeat the routine with the following words and sounds:** *drink*, medial /i/; *tent*, final /nt/. Discuss with children those bulleted items on p. 112 not discussed on Day 1.

My Skills Buddy, pp. 112–113

Corrective feedback

If... children cannot identify the sounds in the picture names, **then...** continue to model identifying the sounds and have children repeat the sounds after you several times.

On their own

Display Phonics Songs and Rhymes Chart 36. Remind children of the song "Quickly, Thump on the Mud" sung to the tune of "Billy Boy (Oh, Where Have You Been)." Have them sing the song with you once. This time when we sing the song, I want you to clap when you hear a word with /u/ in the middle. Children should clap for the words *thump, mud, tuck, up,* and *just.* When we sing the song again, I want you to clap when you hear a word with /b/ at the beginning. Children should clap for the words *beavers, busy,* and *big.* Now when we sing the song, I want you to clap when you hear a word with /n/ at the end. Children should clap for the words *on, ten, in,* and *can.*

Quickly, Thump on the Mud

Quickly, thump on the mud,
Beavers ten, beavers ten.
Quickly, tuck in the ends,
Busy beavers!
You can fix up a big dam,
With your front paws—
   wham, wham, wham!
Chomp-chomp with big teeth,
Just roll that log to water!

Phonics Songs and Rhymes Chart 36

Review

Display the *black* Picture Card. What is this? (the color black) Say the word *black* slowly. What are the sounds in the word *black?* (/b/ /l/ /a/ /k/) Have children continue counting and segmenting the sounds in words using the *lamp, tent, quilt, doll,* and *tub* Picture Cards.

Listen to the sounds in this word: /f/ /l/ /a/ /p/. Say them with me: /f/ /l/ /a/ /p/. Now I want you to blend the sounds together to say the word: /f/ /l/ /a/ /p/, *flap.* Let's try some more. Listen carefully: /s/ /e/ /n/ /d/. Repeat the sounds, /s/ /e/ /n/ /d/. Now blend the sounds together. What is this word? (*send*) Continue the routine with the words *kick, plot, hunt, slam, west,* and *crisp.*

Differentiated Instruction

 **Strategic Intervention**

Match Sounds Mix up the *ant, cap, dog, gum, hat, jet, lake, net, six,* and *top* Picture Cards. Choose a card and tell all the children whose names begin with that sound to stand up. Continue the activity using Picture Cards that have the same sound as names of children in the class.

English Language Learners

English Sounds Approximations of the English /t/ exist in many languages. Since pronunciation varies, work with children to help them produce the sharp /t/ that is heard when the letter *t* is in the initial position. Demonstrate how air comes out of the mouth when we say /t/.

Phonics—Review/Model
◎ Decode Words

Review

Display the *Mm, Uu, Ss,* and *Tt* Alphabet Cards. Point to each lowercase letter in turn. What is the sound for this letter? What are the names of these letters? We can use what we have learned about sounds and the letters for the sounds to read words.

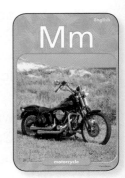

Alphabet Card

Model

Write the word *must* on the board. Point to the *m*. The sound for this letter is /m/. The name of this letter is *m*. Repeat with the other letters. Now I will blend these sounds together to read the word. Have children blend the sounds with you as you point to the letters. What is this word? This word is *must*. Continue the routine with these words: *cuts, limp, sips, wet, box, fan, legs, hand.*

Guide practice

Have children open *My Skills Buddy* to p. 116. Model blending the first word. Put your finger on the red arrow below the *y*. Say the sound that we learned *y* stands for: /y/. Continue with the letters *e* and *s*. Now I run my finger along the blue arrow as I blend the letters quickly to read it. Repeat with the word *spit*. Have children work with a partner to blend the rest of the words on the page.

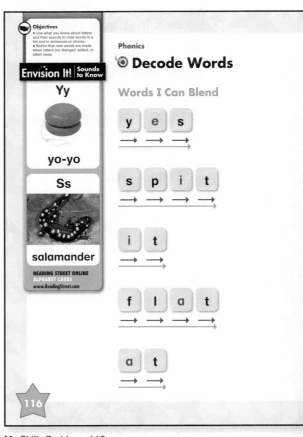

My Skills Buddy, p. 116

Blend   Use the following routine to review blending words.

ROUTINE — Sound-by-Sound Blending

(1) Connect Write the letter *e*. What is the sound we learned for this letter? The sound is /e/. Say it with me: /e/ /e/ /e/. When you see this letter in a word, what sound will you try?

(2) Model Write the word *pet* on the board.

- Point to *p*. What is the sound for this letter? Say it with me: /p/ /p/ /p/. Repeat the routine for *e* and *t*.
- Let's blend the sounds together. Listen as I blend the sounds: /p/ /e/ /t/, *pet*. Say it with me: /p/ /e/ /t/, *pet*. Now say it without me.
- Listen as I use *pet* in a sentence: *I feed my pet every day*. Say it with me. Have children use *pet* in a sentence.

(3) Guide Practice Continue the routine in step 2 with these words:

red	sit	flat	hot	yum	fun

Have children successfully read all of the words before reading Decodable Reader 36 on p. 118 of *My Skills Buddy*.

Corrective Feedback If children have difficulty blending the words, model blending the sounds to read the word. Then have children say it with you.

Routines Flip Chart

A Advanced

Blend Words Make cards with the letters *c, fl, m,* and *r* and give to children who will be the beginning sounds in a word. Make a card with the letter *a* and give to one child who will be the middle sound and a card with the letter *p* to one child who will be the ending sound. Tell children to hold up their cards to form the words *cap, flap, map,* and *rap*. Tell the rest of the class to blend the sounds and say the words.

ELL

English Language Learners
Make a Word Write the letters for the words *sun* and *fan* on cards. Distribute cards to children. Ask the children who have the letters that form the word *sun* to come to the front of the class and stand in a sequence to form the word *sun*. Have children blend the sounds and then read the word aloud. Continue with *fun*.

Don't Wait Until Friday

MONITOR PROGRESS — ↻ Check Sound-Spelling   Decode Words

Write *belt* on the board. Read this word the best you can. You may say the sounds or you may say the whole word. Continue the routine with *land, mug, fix,* and *got*.

If... children cannot read the words,

then... use the small-group Strategic Intervention lesson, p. DI•87, to reteach decoding words.

Continue to monitor children's progress using other instructional opportunities during the week so that children can be successful with the Day 5 Assessment.

Day 1	Day 2	Day 3	Day 4	Day 5
Check Phonemic Awareness	**Check Sound-Spelling/ Retelling**	Check Word Reading	Check Phonemic Awareness	Check Oral Vocabulary

533

Success Predictor

Objectives
- Write words.
- Read high-frequency words.

Handwriting
Write Words

Review

Remind children that words are written with either an uppercase letter or a lowercase letter at the beginning. We use an uppercase letter as the first letter of the first word in a sentence or as the first letter of a person's name.

Write *Ben* and *bats* on the board. I use an uppercase *B* at the beginning of *Ben* because *Ben* is a person's name. I use a lowercase *b* at the beginning of the word *bats* because *bats* is not a person's name and it is not at the beginning of a sentence. Watch how I write *Ben* and *bats*. Write *Ben* and *bats* on the board again.

Guide practice

Have children practice writing *Ben* and *bats* on their Write-On Boards. Now you write *Ben* and *bats*. Circulate around the room, assisting children when necessary. Continue handwriting with these words: *big, bags*. Then have children write all four words to make the complete sentence *Ben bats big bags*.

High-Frequency Words

Model reading

Have children turn to p. 117 of *My Skills Buddy*. Read the high-frequency words together. Then have children point to each word and read it themselves. Read the sentences on the *My Skills Buddy* page together to read the new high-frequency words in context.

Team Talk Have children in groups chorally read the sentences.

High-Frequency Words

Words I Can Read

you
see
said
look
three

Sentences I Can Read

1. Do you see that?
2. "They are fast," said Dad.
3. "Look at the pups!" I said.
4. "I see three," Dad said.
5. Can I have a pup, Dad?

117

My Skills Buddy, p. 117

On their own

Use *Reader's and Writer's Notebook*, p. 467, for additional practice with this week's high-frequency words.

Reader's and Writer's Notebook, p. 467

Differentiated Instruction

 **Strategic Intervention**

Recognize High-Frequency Words Write the high-frequency words *you, see, said, look,* and *three* on cards and display them on the chalkboard ledge. Have children read the sentences on p. 117 of *My Skills Buddy* and find a word card for the high-frequency word in the sentence.

ELL

English Language Learners

High-Frequency Words After the Team Talk activity, have children continue to work in pairs to check understanding. Have one child read one of the sentences aloud while another child makes a simple drawing to illustrate the sentences.

Objectives
- Read high-frequency words.
- Decode and read words in context and isolation.

Decodable Reader 36
↻ Decodable Words and High-Frequency Words

Review Review the previously taught high-frequency words. Have children read each word as you point to it on the Word Wall.

what	said	I	see	you	the	a	with	they	for

Have children turn to Decodable Reader 36, *The Box,* on p. 118 of *My Skills Buddy.* Today we will read a story about a cat named Pam and a big box. **Point to the title.** What is the title of this story? The title of the story is *The Box.* What do you see in the picture on the cover? What do you think this story will be about? **Point to the name of the author.** The author's name is Andrea Brooks. What does the author of a book do? The illustrator's name is Linda Bird. What does the illustrator of a book do? We can read all the words in this story.

Use the routine for reading decodable books to read Decodable Reader 36.

My Skills Buddy, pp. 118–125

Reading Decodable Books

1. **Read Silently** Have children whisper read the book page by page as you listen in.

2. **Model Fluent Reading** Have children finger point as you read a page. Then have children reread the book without you.

3. **Read Chorally** Have children finger point as they chorally read the page. Continue reading page by page, repeating steps 1 and 2.

4. **Read Individually** Have children take turns reading aloud a page.

5. **Reread and Monitor Progress** As you listen to individual children reread, monitor progress and provide support.

6. **Reread with a Partner** Have children reread the book page by page with a partner.

Routines Flip Chart

Differentiated Instruction

SI Strategic Intervention

Recognize Sound-Spellings
Before children read *The Box,* review all sound-spellings using one Picture Card for each consonant and short vowel sound.

A Advanced

Sound-Spelling Connection
Display the Alphabet Cards on the chalk ledge. Point to letters in random order. Have children name the sound for the letter and then the letter name.

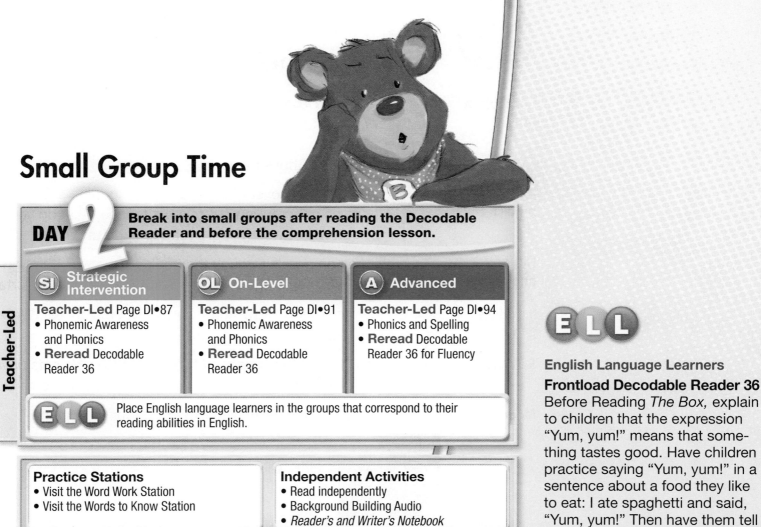

Small Group Time

DAY 2

Break into small groups after reading the Decodable Reader and before the comprehension lesson.

Teacher-Led	**SI** Strategic Intervention	**OL** On-Level	**A** Advanced
	Teacher-Led Page DI•87	**Teacher-Led** Page DI•91	**Teacher-Led** Page DI•94
	• Phonemic Awareness and Phonics	• Phonemic Awareness and Phonics	• Phonics and Spelling
	• **Reread** Decodable Reader 36	• **Reread** Decodable Reader 36	• **Reread** Decodable Reader 36 for Fluency

ELL Place English language learners in the groups that correspond to their reading abilities in English.

Practice Stations	**Independent Activities**
• Visit the Word Work Station	• Read independently
• Visit the Words to Know Station	• Background Building Audio
	• *Reader's and Writer's Notebook*

ELL

English Language Learners

Frontload Decodable Reader 36
Before Reading *The Box,* explain to children that the expression "Yum, yum!" means that something tastes good. Have children practice saying "Yum, yum!" in a sentence about a food they like to eat: I ate spaghetti and said, "Yum, yum!" Then have them tell a similar expression from their home languages.

Objectives
- ◎ Practice draw conclusions.
- • Preview and predict.
- • Retell a selection.

Check Retelling
SUCCESS PREDICTOR

Listening Comprehension
◎ Draw Conclusions

Review

Envision It!

When we draw conclusions, we use what we know to make up our mind about things we read and see. What do we do when we draw conclusions? (make a reasonable guess based on what is known) Good readers draw conclusions as they read because it helps them better understand the ideas in what they are reading.

My Skills Buddy, pp. 114–115

Triple Day Read!

First Read—Trade Book
Ants and Their Nests

Concepts of print

Display *Ants and Their Nests.* Turn to the title page of the book. The title page tells us that the title of this book is *Ants and Their Nests.* It also tells us that the author of the book is Linda Tagliaferro. Tell children to point to the title and the author's name.

Preview and predict

Think Aloud

Display the cover of the book. What do you see on the cover? I see an ant crawling out of a dirt tunnel. What do you think this book will be about? Let's read to find out.

Use photographs

Take children on a walk through the book. As we walk through the book, tell me what you see in the photographs. Why are they important?

Introduce genre

Expository nonfiction gives information about real things. We will read this selection to learn about ants and their nests.

Set purpose

Remind children of the question of the week: *How do ants build their nests?* Have children listen as you read to find out how ants build nests.

Model

Read *Ants and Their Nests* with expression for enjoyment.

DAY 2 Read for enjoyment

DAY 3 Reread using Develop Vocabulary notes

DAY 4 Reread using Guide Comprehension notes

Retell

Check retelling

Have children turn to p. 126 of *My Skills Buddy*. Walk through the retelling boxes as children retell the selection *Ants and Their Nests.* Let's retell what happens in the first box—the beginning of the story. Ants build a hill around the opening to their underground nests. Let's retell what happens in the next box. Continue with the rest of the boxes. After children retell the selection as a group, have them draw a picture to retell a favorite part of the selection. Have them write or dictate a word or sentence to go with their picture.

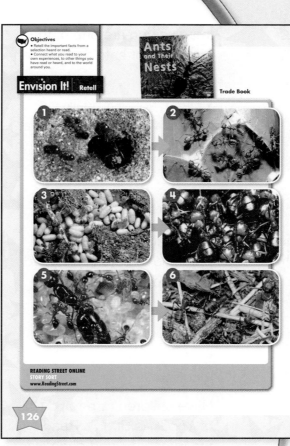

My Skills Buddy, p. 126

Top-Score Response A top-score response identifies the topic and details.

MONITOR PROGRESS Check Retelling

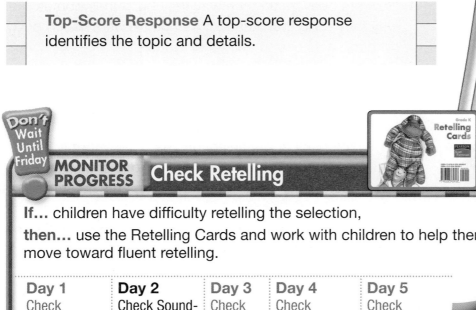

If... children have difficulty retelling the selection,

then... use the Retelling Cards and work with children to help them move toward fluent retelling.

Day 1	Day 2	Day 3	Day 4	Day 5
Check Phonemic Awareness	Check Sound-Spelling/ Retelling	Check Word Reading	Check Phonemic Awareness	Check Oral Vocabulary

Success Predictor

Differentiated Instruction

A Advanced

Access Content Have children retell the selection *Flowers* from Unit 2, Week 1.

Academic Vocabulary

expository nonfiction text that gives information about real things

retell retelling a selection in one's own words

prediction a statement that tells what will happen next based on known information

Retelling Plan

☑ **Week 1** Assess Advanced students.

☑ **Week 2** Assess On-Level students.

☑ **Week 3** Assess Strategic Intervention students.

☑ **Week 4** Assess Advanced students.

☑ **Week 5** Assess On-Level students.

☑ **This week assess Strategic Intervention students.**

Objectives
◎ Practice draw conclusions.
• Confirm predictions.
• Practice complete sentences.

Think, Talk, and Write

Discuss concept

Imagine you are one of the hundreds of ants that live in a colony.

• What would it be like to live with hundreds of other ants? Why?

• Would you rather be a queen ant or a worker ant? Why?

Confirm predictions

Have children recall their predictions before you read *Ants and Their Nests.*

• What did you think the selection would be about?

• Was your prediction correct?

Have children turn to p. 127 of *My Skills Buddy.* Read the questions and directives and have children respond.

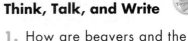

Think, Talk, and Write

1. How are beavers and the way they build their homes like ants and the way they build their nests? Text to Text

2. Think about what **sticky** means. Why do you think ants use sticky silk to build their nests?  Draw Conclusions

3. Look back and write.

My Skills Buddy, p. 127

Text to text

1. How are beavers and the way they build their homes like ants and the way they build their nests? What do beavers use to build their homes? What do ants use to build their homes?

◎ **Draw conclusions**

2. Think about what *sticky* means. Why do you think ants use sticky silk to build their nests? How did you draw that conclusion? Did you use the pictures and the words?

Look back and write

3. Let's look back at our selection and write about it. Think about what you have learned about how ants build nests. Read p. 16 of *Ants and Their Nests.* Why is it important for the ants' nest to be safe? Now let's write our ideas. Record children's responses on chart paper. (Possible responses: The queen lays her eggs in the nest. Other animals might e̶ the ants. People might step on the ants.)

Conventions
Complete Sentences

Review

Remind children of what they learned about complete sentences. A complete sentence has a subject and a predicate. A subject is who or what the sentence is about, and a predicate is the action part.

Read the first sentence on p. 4 of *Ants and Their Nests* to children. This is a complete sentence. How do I know that? The sentence has a subject, *Ants,* that tells what the sentence is about, and it has a predicate, *live in nests,* that tells what the ants do. Point out that the sentence begins with an uppercase letter and ends with a period.

Guide practice

Let's make up sentences that tell about ants. As children suggest sentences, write them on the board.

> **Ants look for food.**
>
> **Ants live in underground nests.**

Read each sentence aloud. Is this a complete sentence? How do we know this is a complete sentence? What is at the beginning of this sentence? What is at the end of this sentence?

On their own

Use *Reader's and Writer's Notebook,* p. 468, for more practice with complete sentences.

Daily Fix-It

Use the Daily Fix-It for more conventions practice.

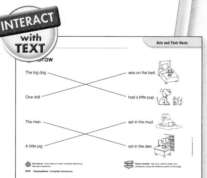

Reader's and Writer's
Notebook, p. 468

Written Responses Let children write their own responses to the questions.

Daily Fix-It

the dog jump on the bed
The dog jumps on the bed.

This week's practice sentences appear on Teacher Resources DVD-ROM.

English Language Learners
Model Show children how you would answer one or more of the questions. Be sure to explain your feelings in each situation.

Objectives
- Discuss different media and their techniques.
- Choose and evaluate sources of information.
- Identify and use words for bugs.

Writing
Writing Process: Plan a Report

Teach: Choose sources

Review with children what you discussed yesterday about reports. When we write a report, we must find facts, or information, to put in our report. How do we do that? We can go to the library and look for books and magazines. We can get information from people, such as a librarian, a teacher, our parents, or experts on a subject. We can get information from a TV show. We can also look on the Internet. These are all sources we can use. A source can be anything that gives us correct information about our topic.

Model: Choose and evaluate sources

We are going to write a report about how a bird builds its home, so we need to think about sources we can use to gather information. The sources we use must have facts about birds, so a book about birds from the library could be a good source. What other sources could we use? Discuss with children other possible sources in the classroom, the school, the library, and the home, and their credibility (for example, an encyclopedia, a nature magazine, a newspaper article, a TV show about animals, an Internet Web site, a science teacher, a family member or neighbor who knows about birds, or an expert at a nature museum).

Guide practice: Choose and evaluate sources

Explain to children why one source might be better than another. For example, ask: If you can't read or write very well, what source might be a good one to use? Yes, a TV or radio show would be helpful. Why? Discuss with children that TV and radio use pictures and sound to give information. People don't need to read; they can listen and watch. Then talk about sources to use to get specific information. Have children suggest a source that would be helpful if they wanted to find out about animal homes. (book, computer, encyclopedia).

Independent writing

Have children complete pp. 469–470 in *Reader's and Writer's Notebook* to review sources and media used in research.

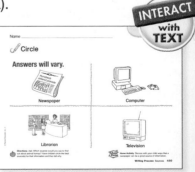

Reader's and Writer's Notebook, pp. 469–470

Vocabulary
Words for Bugs

Model

Have children turn to p. 128 of *My Skills Buddy.* Use the first Vocabulary bullet on the page to guide the discussion. These pictures show different kinds of bugs. Direct them to the picture of the ant. This small bug is an ant. An ant has two feelers on top of its head and six legs. Direct them to the picture of a bee. A bee is yellow and black with a striped body. Direct them to the picture of a fly. A fly has six legs and two wings. Direct them to the picture of the spider. The spider has two body parts and eight legs. If children are confused because they count 10 "legs," point out the two short antennae coming from the spider's front body.

My Skills Buddy, p. 128

Guide Practice

Write the words *ant, bee, fly,* and *spider* on the board. Point to each word as you read it.

ant	bee	fly	spider

Let's practice our new words. Have children look at the pictures on p. 128 of *My Skills Buddy.* I will give you clues about each bug. Listen carefully and then point to the bug I am talking about. This is the biggest bug. **(spider)** This is a yellow and black bug that buzzes. **(bee)** This black bug has six legs and two wings. **(fly)** This bug has six legs that help it run fast. **(ant)**

On their own

Have children draw a picture of a bug and write a telling sentence about their picture. Sort the pictures according to the type of bug and display in the classroom.

Objectives
- Review skills learned and practiced today.

Wrap Up Your Day

✔ **Concept Talk** Today we read a selection about ants and their nests. Where do ants build their nests? What do they use to build their nests?

✔ **Phonemic Awareness** What are the sounds in *plant? crust? spot? milk?*

✔ **Vocabulary Skill** Show the pictures of a bee, ant, fly, and spider and have children identify each kind of insect.

✔ **Homework Idea** Have children write a complete sentence about an insect they have encountered in their home or yard. Remind them to begin their sentence with an uppercase letter and end it with a period.

Preview DAY 3

Tomorrow we will reread the selection about ants and how they build their nests.

Extend Your Day!

Science
Ants and Their Parts

Materials: Trade Book *Ants and Their Nests*, modeling clay, chenille sticks

Discuss Ants and Their Body Parts Display the cover of *Ants and Their Nests*. How many legs does the ant have? (6) How many feelers, or antennae, does the ant have? (2) The ant's body has three parts: the head, thorax, and abdomen. Its antennae are attached to its head. Its legs are attached to its thorax, the middle part. The bottom part, or abdomen, is much bigger than the other two parts. **Point to each body part and have children name it.** Then explain that ants are a kind of insect, and insects have six legs, two antennae, and three body parts.

Make Ant Models Give modeling clay and eight pipe cleaners to each child. Tell children they are going to make a model of an ant. Have them use clay to make a head, thorax, and abdomen. Have them use pipe cleaners to make antennae and legs. Have children show their ant model to a partner, pointing to and naming its parts.

Comprehension
What Can You Conclude?

Use Clues to Draw Conclusions Tell children that you are going to give them two clues. One clue will tell something they know. The other clue will tell something they see. They are to use the two clues to make up their mind about things, or to draw a conclusion. (There may be more than one possible conclusion.)

• You know…Tim plays soccer on Thursdays.
  You see…Tim carrying a soccer ball.
  You conclude…today must be Thursday.

Phonemic Awareness
Sound Matching

Materials: Picture Cards—(initial) *bat, bed, fan, fox, map, mug, pen, pig, six, sun;* (medial) *bat, map, bed, web, pig, six, fox, dog, sun, rug;* (final) *web, crab, dog, pig, sun, pen, bat, nut, fox, six*

Match by Sounds Randomly distribute one Picture Card from the first set to each child. Have children identify the picture on their card and the beginning sound in the picture name. Have each child find the other child whose picture name has the same initial sound. Have pairs name the pictures on their cards and identify the shared initial sound. Repeat with middle and final sounds.

Objectives

- Share information and ideas about the concept.
- Build oral vocabulary.

Today at a Glance

Oral Vocabulary
chambers, silk

Phonemic Awareness
◉ Initial, Medial and Final Sounds

Phonics
◉ Decode words

Comprehension
◉ Draw Conclusions

Conventions
Exclamations

Writing
Writing Process: Draft a Report

Listening and Speaking
Discuss Literary Elements—Setting

TRUCKTOWN on Reading Street

Start your engines! Display p. 19 of *Truckery Rhymes.* "Pop! Blows the Diesel" is like another rhyme that I know. Do you know the rhyme "Pop! Goes the Weasel"? Recite it first, and then have children repeat it with you:

All around the mulberry bush,
The monkey chased the weasel.
The monkey thought it was
all in fun.
Pop! goes the weasel.

Truckery Rhymes

Concept Talk

? Question of the Week
How do ants build their nests?

Write the question of the week on the board. Read the question as you track the print. Talk with children about how ants work together to build a nest. Have children respond in complete sentences. Remind children to speak clearly and to take turns speaking.

Listen for Amazing Words

Let's Sing Display Sing with Me Chart 36B. Tell children they are going to sing a song about ants building a nest. Today we are going to listen for the Amazing Words *chambers* and *silk*. Read the title and have children tell what is happening in the picture. Sing the song several times to the tune of "The Itsy-Bitsy Spider." Have children sing along with you, clapping their hands when they say the Amazing Word *chambers* or *silk*.

🔘 Sing with Me Audio

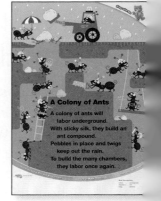

Talk with Me/Sing with Me Chart 36B

Oral Vocabulary
Amazing Words

Amazing Words

colony	underground
chambers	silk
twigs	pebbles

Amazing Words Oral Vocabulary Routine

Teach Amazing Words

1 **Introduce the Word** *Chambers* is another word for rooms. Ants dig tunnels and *chambers* underground. What's our new Amazing Word for rooms? Say it with me: *chambers*.

2 **Demonstrate** Provide examples to show meaning. *Ants have rooms, or chambers, in their homes.* What *chambers* do you have in your home?

Repeat steps 1 and 2.

Introduce the Word *Silk* is a thin, sticky fiber some animals can make. Some ants use *silk* in their nests. What's our new Amazing Word for a thin, sticky fiber some animals can make? Say it with me: *silk*.

Demonstrate *Some ants can make silk.* What other animals do you know that can make *silk*?

3 **Apply** Have children use *chambers* and *silk* to describe ants' nests.

Routines Flip Chart

Use Amazing Words

To reinforce the concept and the Amazing Words, have children supply the appropriate Amazing Word for each sentence.

Spiders make _____ to weave into webs. (silk)

An ant nest may have dozens of _____. (chambers)

ELL Expand Vocabulary
Use the Day 3 instruction on ELL Poster 36 to help children expand vocabulary.

Differentiated Instruction

A Advanced

Build Background Explain to children that caterpillars use silk to bind leaves and twigs to build a shelter and spiders use silk to spin a web. If possible, show pictures of a caterpillar larva and spider web.

ELL Poster 36

English Language Learners
Point to the pictures on the Talk with Me Chart 36A and have children name them several times before they try to complete the sentences.

Objectives

◎ Identify initial, medial, and final sounds in words.

• Segment and blend sounds in words.

Phonemic Awareness

Initial, Medial, and Final Sounds

Review

I am going to say two words. I want you to listen to the beginning sounds in the words: *mug, bat.* Which word begins with /b/? (*bat*) *Bat* begins with /b/. Now I want you to listen to the middle sounds: *mug, bat.* Which word has /a/ in the middle? (*bat*) *Bat* has /a/ in the middle. Now I want you to listen to the ending sounds: *mug, bat.* Which word ends with /g/? (*mug*) *Mug* ends with /g/. Continue asking children to identify initial, medial, and final sounds using these word pairs: *cut, web; pin, dog; men, cab; pet, sun.*

Teach initial, medial, and final sounds

Use the *duck* Picture Card to isolate beginning, medial, and final sounds. This is a duck. I hear /d/ at the beginning of *duck*. I hear /u/ in the middle of *duck*. I hear /k/ at the end of *duck*. Practice initial, medial, and final sounds with the Picture Cards *frog* and *mask*.

Discriminate sounds

Display the *bed* and *jam* Picture Cards. Point to each card as you say the word. Which of these words begins with the same sound as *bird*? Say the words with me: *bed, bird.* I hear /b/ at the beginning of *bed* and *bird*. Which word has the same middle sound as *pan*? I hear /a/ in the middle of *jam* and *pan*. Say the words with me: *jam, pan.* Which word has the same ending sound as *mud*? I hear /d/ at the end of *bed* and *mud*.

Picture Card

On their own

Display the *hen, jug,* and *pan* Picture Cards. Have children choose one of the pictures to draw and label. Tell children to circle the beginning sound, underline the middle sound, and color the ending sound in their picture labels.

Picture Card

Picture Card

Segment and blend

Gather the *fan, nest, wig, sock, bus, lamp,* and *dress* Picture Cards. I am going to hold a picture behind my back. I want you to figure out what the picture name is by the sounds I give you. Hold the *fan* Picture Card behind your back. Give clues until a child correctly identifies the picture. The name of this object has three sounds. The first sound is /f/. The second sound is /a/. The third sound is /n/. Let's blend the sounds together: /f/ /a/ /n/, *fan.* Display the *fan* Picture Card for children to see. Continue the routine with the other Picture Cards.

Corrective feedback

If... children cannot blend phonemes to make words, **then...** give the beginning sound and word chunk as clues.

Substitute sounds

Listen to this word: *slip.* Say the sounds in the word with me: /sl/ /i/ /p/, *slip.* I can make a new word by changing the middle sound from /i/ to /a/. Say the sounds with me: /sl/ /a/ /p/. What is the new word? The new word is *slap.* I can make another new word by changing the ending sound from /p/ to /m/. Say the sounds with me: /sl/ /a/ /m/. What is the new word? (*slam*) Continue dropping, adding, or substituting sounds to make the following words: *ham, hum, hunt, grunt.*

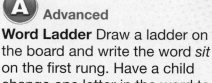

Differentiated Instruction

(A) **Advanced**

Word Ladder Draw a ladder on the board and write the word *sit* on the first rung. Have a child change one letter in the word to form a new word and write the word on the second rung. Tell children to continue changing letters to make new words and climb up the ladder.

Teacher Tip

Use sound substitution activities to show children how they can build vocabulary quickly.

English Language Learners

If children have difficulty discriminating medial or final sounds, have them practice saying sets of words in which the sounds are the same except for the medial or final sound: *pat, pet, pit, pot; hat, hit, hot, hut; cab, can, cap, cat; rib, rig, rim, rip.*

Objectives
- ◎ Decode words.
- • Read words fluently.

Check Word Reading
SUCCESS PREDICTOR

Phonics—Teach/Model
⊙ Decode Words

Practice decoding words

Write *wig* on the board. Point to the *w*. This is the letter *w*. What is the sound for *w*? (/w/) Repeat the routine for the other letters. Let's say the sounds together: /w/ /i/ /g/. Point to each letter as you say the sound. Let's blend the sounds together to read the word: /w/ /i/ /g/, *wig*. The word is *wig*.

Review

Letter Names and Sounds Use Alphabet Cards to review the following letter names and sounds: *Cc, Gg, Kk, Ll, Oo, Rr, Uu, Ww*.

Blend sounds

Write *web* on the board. Point to the *w*. What is the sound for this letter? (/w/) What is the name of this letter? (*w*) Repeat for the letters *e* and *b*. Let's say the sounds together: /w/ /e/ /b/. What is the word? The word is *web*. Continue the routine with the words *grass, swim, sun,* and *egg*.

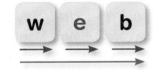

More practice

Use *Reader's and Writer's Notebook,* p. 471, for additional practice with decoding words.

Reader's and Writer's Notebook, p. 471

Review **Sound-Spelling** Display the *Ss* Alphabet Card. *This is a salamander. What sound does salamander begin with? What letter spells that sound?* Continue to display Alphabet Cards and review sound-spellings.

Review **High-Frequency Words** Write *little* on the board. *This is the word little. What is this word?* Continue the routine with *where, blue, what, here,* and *from*.

Alphabet Card

Don't Wait Until Friday

MONITOR PROGRESS   Check Word Reading   High-Frequency Words

Write these high-frequency words on the board. Have individuals take turns reading the words.

the	is	to	see	from
where	blue	a	what	here

If... children cannot read the high-frequency words,
then... write the words on cards for them to practice at home.

If... children can successfully read the high-frequency words,
then... have them read Kindergarten Student Reader K.6.6, *Where Do Animals Live?*

Day 1	**Day 2**	**Day 3**	**Day 4**	**Day 5**
Check Phonemic Awareness	Check Sound-Spelling/ Retelling	Check Word Reading	Check Phonemic Awareness	Check Oral Vocabulary

Differentiated Instruction

A **Advanced**

High-Frequency Words Write the high-frequency words *the, is, to, see, from,* and *blue* on cards. Have one child read the word, use the word in a sentence, and pass the card to another child who repeats the routine.

ELL

English Language Learners
Decoding Support Have children page through Kindergarten Student Reader K.6.6. and use picture clues to help decode words.

Success Predictor

Objectives
- Read decodable words.
- Read high-frequency words.

Kindergarten Student Reader K.6.6
 Decodable Words and High-Frequency Words

Review

Review the previously taught high-frequency words. Have children read each word as you point to it on the Word Wall.

is	a	you	the	what	little
see	here	from	blue	one	to

Teach rebus words

Write the word *fish* on the board. This is the word *fish*. Name the letters with me: *f, i, s, h*. Look for the word *fish* in the book we read today. There will be a picture above the word to help you read it.

Read Kindergarten Student Reader K.6.6

Display Kindergarten Student Reader K.6.6. Today we are going to read a new book. Point to the title of the book. The title of this book is *Where Do Animals Live?* What do you think the book will be about? What animals do you see on the cover? Where are they?

Use the reading decodable books routine to read the Kindergarten Student Reader.

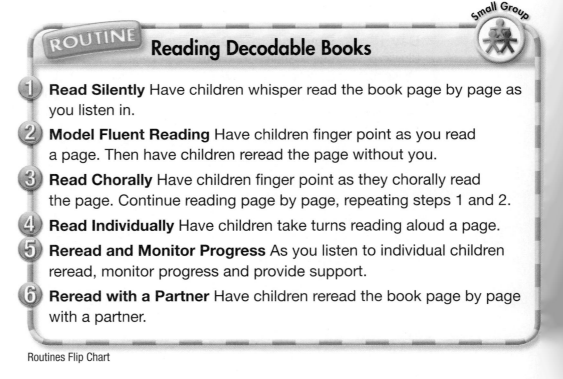

ROUTINE   **Reading Decodable Books**   *Small Group*

1. **Read Silently** Have children whisper read the book page by page as you listen in.

2. **Model Fluent Reading** Have children finger point as you read a page. Then have children reread the page without you.

3. **Read Chorally** Have children finger point as they chorally read the page. Continue reading page by page, repeating steps 1 and 2.

4. **Read Individually** Have children take turns reading aloud a page.

5. **Reread and Monitor Progress** As you listen to individual children reread, monitor progress and provide support.

6. **Reread with a Partner** Have children reread the book page by page with a partner.

Routines Flip Chart

Where Do Animals Live?
By Donna Latham • Illustrated by John Sandford

It is a big nest.
Can you spot the egg in it?
What can rest in the nest? A hen!
2

Kindergarten Student Reader K.6.6

It is a pen.
What can get fed in the pen?
A big pig and a little pig!
3

It is a big den.
What will stop in the den to rest?
Can you tell what it is?
4

See the big web in the hot sun.
What can sit in the web?
Can you tell what it is?
5

Here is a bat.
The bat can drop from the top.
Can you tell where the bat is?
6

Here is a blue fish.
It can swim and swim.
Can you tell where the fish is?
7

It can set up a nest in the grass.
A little one set up a hill here.
What is it? An ant!
8

Differentiated Instruction

SI Strategic Intervention

Access Content Tell children to find the nouns *hen, pig, bat,* and *fish* in the story. Have them match the word in the text with its picture. Have children describe what they see.

Teacher Tip

Review the high-frequency words on each page before reading Kindergarten Student Reader K.6.6.

Small Group Time

DAY 3 Break into small groups to read the Kindergarten Student Reader before the comprehension lesson.

Teacher-Led

SI Strategic Intervention

Teacher-Led Page DI•88
- Phonemic Awareness and Phonics
- **Read** Concept Literacy Reader K.6.6 or Kindergarten Student Reader K.6.6

OL On-Level

Teacher-Led Page DI•92
- Phonemic Awareness and Phonics
- **Read** Kindergarten Student Reader K.6.6

A Advanced

Teacher-Led Page DI•95
- **Read** Independent Reader K.6.6 or Kindergarten Student Reader K.6.6

ELL Place English language learners in the groups that correspond to their reading abilities in English.

Practice Stations
- Visit the Words to Know Station
- Visit the Let's Write! Station

Independent Activities
- Read independently
- Audio Text of Trade Book
- *Reader's and Writer's Notebook*

ELL

English Language Learners
Peer Support Have children reread a Kindergarten Student Reader from a previous week with a partner to practice reading high-frequency words.

Objectives
- Recall and retell a selection.
- ◎ Practice drawing conclusions.
- Develop and use vocabulary.
- Develop and use comprehension skills.

Comprehension

Retell the story

Have children turn to p. 126 of *My Skills Buddy* and use the retelling boxes to retell the selection *Ants and Their Nests*.

Envision It!

Think Aloud Direct children to the first retell box. Ants build their nests underground. Tell me how the ants build their nests.

Continue reviewing the retelling boxes and having children retell the selection.

My Skills Buddy, p. 126

Review

Draw Conclusions Remind children that when they draw a conclusion, they use what they know to make up their mind about things.

- Think about what you know about summer and winter. Why don't ants build their nests in summer or winter? (Summer is probably too hot, and winter is probably too cold.)

- Think about what you know about soil and wood. Where do ants that build nests in soil live? (underground) Where do ants that build nests in wood live? (inside trees)

- Think about what you know about tunnels and chambers. Why do ants need both tunnels and chambers in their nests? (Tunnels are like halls, and chambers are like rooms. Ants need tunnels to get from one place to another. They need the chambers to store food and raise their young in.)

More practice

Use *Reader's and Writer's Notebook,* p. 472, for additional practice with draw conclusions.

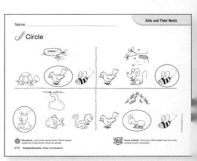

Reader's and Writer's Notebook, p. 472

Gc Digital! Story Sort

Second Read—Trade Book

Ants and Their Nests

Develop vocabulary

Reread *Ants and Their Nests.* Follow the Day 3 arrow beginning on p. 556, and use the Develop Vocabulary notes to prompt conversations about the selection.

Have children use the Amazing Words *colony, underground, chambers, silk, twigs,* and *pebbles* to talk about the selection.

DAY 2
Read for enjoyment

DAY 3
Reread using Develop Vocabulary notes

DAY 4
Reread using Guide Comprehension notes

Develop Vocabulary

DAY 3

Wh- question

This page is called the table of contents. What can we find out from the table of contents? **(what is in the book)**

- The table of contents tells us what each part of the book is about and where each part begins. What part would we go to if we wanted to know about ants' eggs?

Pebble Plus is published by Capstone Press,
151 Good Counsel Drive, P.O. Box 669, Mankato, Minnesota 56002.

Copyright © 2004 by Capstone Press. All rights reserved.
No part of this publication may be reproduced in whole or in part, or stored in a retrieval system, or transmitted in any form or by any means, electronic, mechanical, photocopying , recording, or otherwise, without written permission of the publisher. For information regarding permission, write to Capstone Press, 151 Good Counsel Drive, P.O. Box 669, Dept. R, Mankato, Minnesota 56002.
Printed in the United States of America

1 2 3 4 5 6 09 08 07 06 05 04

Library of Congress Cataloging-in-Publication Data
Tagliaferro, Linda.
  Ants and their nests / by Linda Tagliaferro.
  p. cm.—(Pebble Plus, Animal homes)
  Summary: Simple text and photographs describe ants and the nests in which they live.
  Includes bibliographical references (p. 23) and index.
  ISBN 0-7368-2380-8 (hardcover)
  ISBN 0-7368-5120-8 (paperback)
  1. Ants—Nests—Juvenile literature. [1. Ants—Nests. 2. Ants—Habits and behavior.]
I. Title. II. Series.
QL568.F7T24 2004
595.79'6—dc22   2003013421

Editorial Credits
Martha E. H. Rustad, editor; Linda Clavel, series designer; Deirdre Barton and Wanda Winch, photo researchers; Karen Risch, product planning editor

Photographs
Every effort has been made to secure permission and provide appropriate credit for photographic material. The publisher deeply regrets any omission and pledges to correct errors called to its attention in subsequent editions.

Unless otherwise acknowledged, all photographs are the property of Scott Foresman, a division of Pearson Education.

Photo locators denoted as follow: Top (T), Center (C), Bottom (B), Left (L), Right (R), Background (Bkgd).

Cover: ©George B. Diebold/Corbis; 1 ©Joe McDonald; 5 ©John Mitchell/Bruce Colman Inc.; 7 ©Frans Lanting/Minden Pictures; 9 ©Gerry Ellis/Minden Pictures; 11©Konrad Wothe/Minden Pictures; 13 ©Milton Rand; 15 ©Mark Moffett/Minden Pictures; 17©Anthony Bannister/Gallo Images/Corbis; 19©Biophoto/Van Baelinghem Thierry/Peter Arnold, Inc.; 21 ©Michael Rose/Frank Lane Pictures Agency/Corbis

Table of Contents

Trade Book, pp. 2–3

Guide Comprehension

DAY 4

Wh- question

How does the table of contents help readers? (It tells them more about what is in the book. It lets them go right to the part they are most interested in, if they wish.)

Wh- question

What do ants live in? (nests)

- Ants live in nests. When do ants build their nests?

Develop Vocabulary ant, spring, fall

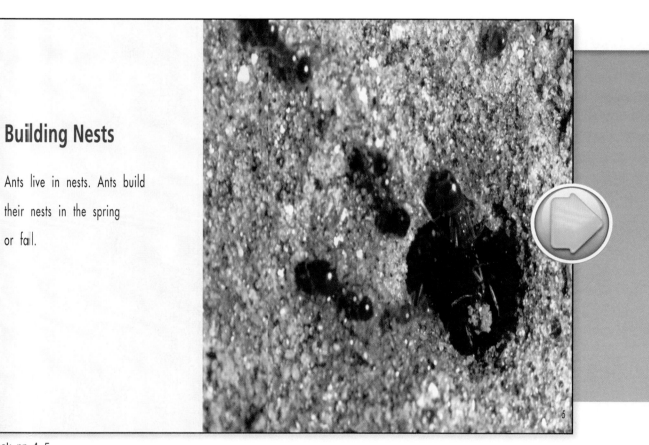

Building Nests

Ants live in nests. Ants build their nests in the spring or fall.

4

5

Trade Book, pp. 4–5

Recall

What are ants' homes called? (They are called nests.)

Develop Vocabulary, continued

DAY 3

Recall

What do you see in the photograph? (the hill around the opening into an ant nest)

- Some ants build a hill around the opening to their nest. How long do you think it took the ants to build this hill?

Develop Vocabulary months

Some ants build nests in five days. Other ants take months to build their nests.

6

Trade Book, pp. 6–7

Guide Comprehension, continued

DAY 4

Draw Conclusions • Inferential

Why do you think these ants built a hill around the opening to their nest? (They dig out a lot of dirt when they dig tunnels and chambers. They have to put the dirt somewhere. Also, the hill would help keep other animals out of the nest.)

Wh- question

What materials do ants use to build their nests? (leaves, sticky silk, soil, wood)

- Some ants use leaves and sticky silk to build their nests. Some ants use soil or wood. What are the ants in this photograph using?

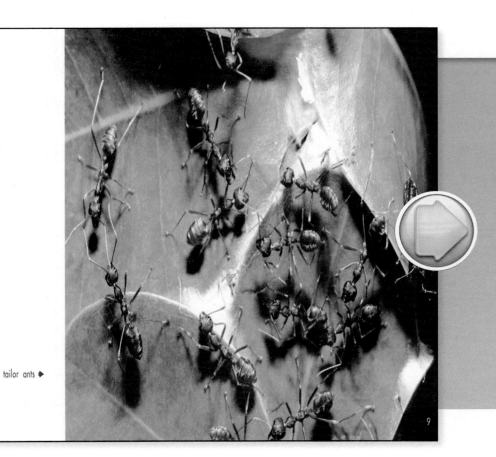

Some ants build nests
with leaves and sticky silk.
Other ants build nests
in soil or wood.

tailor ants ▶

8   9

Trade Book, pp. 8–9

Draw Conclusions • Inferential

A tailor sews together pieces of cloth with thread to make clothes. Why are these ants called tailor ants? (The ants use sticky silk to glue leaves together to make their nest, like a tailor uses thread to sew pieces of cloth together to make clothes.)

Develop Vocabulary, continued

DAY 3

Recall

What do ants build in their tunnels?
(chambers)

- Ants build chambers in their tunnels. What do they use the chambers for?

Ants dig tunnels underground or inside trees. They build chambers in the tunnels. Ants store food and raise their young in the chambers.

yellow ants ▶

10

Trade Book, pp. 10–11

Guide Comprehension, continued

DAY 4

Draw Conclusions • Inferential

Look at the photograph. What can you conclude about what the yellow ants have put in the chamber?
(Ants raise their young in chambers. I know ants begin as eggs. I can conclude that these are yellow ant eggs.)

Distancing

How many ants live in a colony? (hundreds and thousands)

- Hundreds and thousands of ants live in a colony. What do you think it would be like to live in an ant colony?

Develop Vocabulary hundreds

Colonies and Eggs

A colony is a group of ants living together in a nest. Hundreds and thousands of ants live in a colony.

red ants ▶

12

13

Trade Book, pp. 12–13

Distancing

Ants live in a colony. What other kinds of animals do you know that live in a colony? (termites, bees, bats, coral, sponges, penguins)

Develop Vocabulary, continued

DAY 3

Open-ended
What does the queen ant do in the nest? (lays her eggs)

- The queen ant lays her eggs in the nest. Which ant in the photograph do you think is the queen ant? Why?

The queen ant lays her eggs in the nest. Worker ants take care of young ants.

fire ants ▶

14

Trade Book, pp. 14–15

Guide Comprehension, continued

DAY 4

Compare and Contrast • Recall
How are the queen ant and the worker ants alike? (They are ants. They live and work in the same colony.) How are they different? (The queen ant lays eggs. She is much bigger. The worker ants take care of her and the young. They are much smaller.)

Recall

What do these ants use to close the opening to their nest? **(pebbles)**

- These ants use pebbles to close the opening to their nest. Why do they do that?

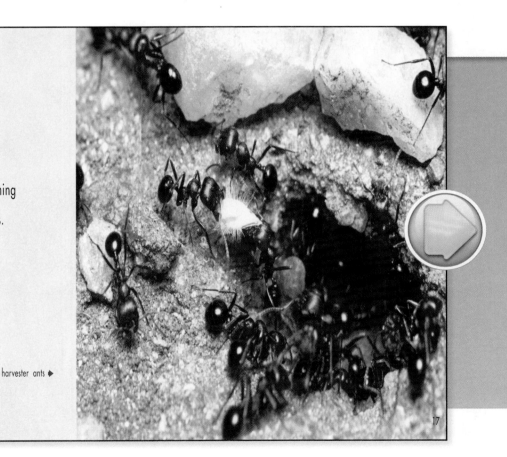

Staying Safe

Some ants close the opening to their nest with pebbles. The pebbles keep out other animals.

harvester ants ▶

16　　17

Trade Book, pp. 16–17

Draw Conclusions • Inferential

Look at the sizes of the pebbles and the ants. What can you conclude about how the ants move the pebbles? **(Either ants are much stronger than their size would indicate or it takes many ants working together to move each pebble—or both.)**

Develop Vocabulary, continued

DAY 3

Recall

What have these ants put on top of their nest? (twigs)

- These ants have put twigs on top of their nest. Why did they do that?

Some ants put twigs on top of their nests. The twigs keep out rain.

18

Trade Book, pp. 18–19

Guide Comprehension, continued

DAY 4

Compare and Contrast • Inferential

How are the twigs on top of an ant nest and the roof on a house alike? (They both keep rain out of the homes. They both protect the homes.)

Distancing

What are good homes for ants? (nests)

- Nests are good homes for ants. What other kinds of animals have nests as their homes?

A Good Home

Different kinds of ants build different kinds of nests. Nests are good homes for ants.

fire ant nest ▶

20

Trade Book, pp. 20–21

Draw Conclusions • Inferential

Read the first sentence. Look at the photographs on pp. 9, 11, 16, 19, and 21. Do you agree with the author's conclusion? Why or why not? (I agree with her conclusion because the photographs show that each kind of ant builds a different kind of nest.)

Develop Vocabulary, continued

DAY 3

Wh- question

Page 22 is called a glossary.
What do you see on that page?
(words and their meanings)

- A glossary lists words used in a
  book and gives the meanings of
  those words. What is the meaning
  of *tunnel*?

Glossary

chamber—a room in an ant nest

colony—a large group of animals that live together; thousands of ants live together in some colonies.

queen ant—an adult female ant that lays eggs; most colonies have only one queen ant.

silk—a sticky fiber made by some ants

tunnel—a passage under the ground

twig—a small stick or branch

worker ant—an adult female ant that does not lay eggs; worker ants build nests and take care of young ants.

22

Read More

Frost, Helen. *Leaf-Cutting Ants.* Rain Forest Animals. Mankato, Minn.: Pebble Books, 2003.

Loewen, Nancy. *Tiny Workers: Ants in Your Backyard.* Backyard Bugs. Minnneapolis: Picture Window Books, 2003.

Robinson, W. Wright. *How Insects Build Their Amazing Homes.* Animal Architects. Woodbridge, Conn.: Blackbirch Press, 1999.

23

Trade Book, pp. 22–23

Guide Comprehension, continued

DAY 4

Distancing

The Read More section on p. 23
lists three other books about ants
and how they build their homes.
Where would you go to find these
books? (I would go to the library or
a bookstore to find them.)

Wh- question

This page is called the Index/Word List.
What do you see at the ends of the lines?
(numbers)

- The numbers at the ends of the lines tell us on which pages we will find information about those topics. On what page can we find out about chambers? about worker ants?

Continue with **DAY 3**
Conventions p. 568

Index/Word List

animals, 16	queen ant, 14
build, 4, 6, 8, 10, 20	raise, 10
chambers, 10	silk, 8
colony, 12	soil, 8
dig, 10	sticky, 8
eggs, 14	store, 10
food, 10	trees, 10
homes, 20	tunnels, 10
lays, 14	twigs, 18
leaves, 8	underground, 10
opening, 16	wood, 8
pebbles, 16	worker ants, 14
	young, 10, 14

24

Trade Book, p. 24

Inferential

How does the Index/Word List help readers?
(They can use it to find the meanings of the words listed. They can use it to find the pages that have information on the topics they are interested in.)

Skip to **DAY 4**
Conventions p. 582

Conventions

Exclamations

Review   Remind children of what they know about exclamations. An exclamation is something we say to express a strong feeling or reaction to something. It starts with an uppercase letter and ends with an exclamation mark.

If I saw a tiny ant carrying a huge leaf, I might say, "That ant is strong!" Write the exclamation on the board. This is an exclamation. I was surprised by what I saw, so I said this with a lot of feeling. I put an uppercase letter at the beginning and an exclamation mark at the end.

Guide practice   Write the following sentences on the board: *Look out! Ned is six. I am so happy! Pam got a gift.* Have children identify the exclamations and explain how they recognized them. Then read the exclamations together with appropriate expression and excitement.

Team Talk Pair children and have them take turns telling about an exciting thing that happened at school. Remind them to use appropriate expression and excitement when using an exclamation.

On their own   Use *Reader's and Writer's Notebook*, p. 473, for more practice with exclamations.

Daily Fix-It   Use the Daily Fix-It for more conventions practice.

INTERACT with TEXT

Reader's and Writer's Notebook, p. 473

Writing
Writing Process: Draft a Report

**Teach:
Gather
evidence**

Today we will gather the information for our report on how a bird builds its nest. Then we will start writing a draft of our report. A draft is a first try at writing. We'll come back to our draft later and make it better. Right now we just want to get the main words down on the paper in the right order.

**Model:
Gather
evidence**

Display the library book about birds that you discussed yesterday. Here's the book we thought would be a good one for gathering facts about birds and their nests.

Read aloud information about how birds choose locations for their nests. In this book, we learn that the first thing a bird does when it builds a nest is look for the right place, often in a tree. Record this information using words and an illustration. Write the number *1* next to them. (Possible sentence: First, the bird finds a place in a tree.)

**Guide
practice:
Gather
evidence**

Listen for the next thing a bird does when it builds a nest. Read aloud information from the book about how birds collect materials for their nests. What should we write next? Write and illustrate children's suggestions. Write the number *2* next to them. (Possible sentence: Next, the bird gathers materials.)

Listen for the last thing a bird does when it builds a nest. Read aloud information about how birds use the materials they have gathered to make nests. Again, write and illustrate children's suggestions about what you just read. Write the number *3* next to them. (Possible sentence: Last, the bird uses these materials to make a nest.)

**Independent
practice**

Reread and discuss what you wrote, underlining key words in your draft. Have children write or dictate the group draft or copy the underlined key words on p. 474 in *Reader's and Writer's Notebook*.

Reader's and Writer's Notebook,
p. 474

Objectives
- Discuss setting.
- Speak one at a time.
- Take turns speaking.

Listening and Speaking
Discuss Literary Elements: Setting

Review   Remind children that when they have a discussion, they need to take turns and speak one at a time. Point out that good listeners listen attentively and wait for their turn to contribute to the discussion.

Model   As you listen to a story, think about where and when the story takes place. Display Trade Book *Mayday! Mayday!* Where and when does this story take place? I see a boat on the water and a helicopter in the sky. It looks dark out. This story takes place on the water at night.

Guide practice   Have children turn to p. 129 of *My Skills Buddy.* Use the Listening and Speaking bullets on p. 128 in the discussion. I see a picture of a mother duck and her ducklings. Discuss with children what this picture tells about the setting of a story.

- Where does the story take place? (in a pond)

- Think about when baby animals are born. When do you think this story takes place, spring or fall? (spring)

Help children understand that a pond is the setting because that is where ducks live and build their nests.

My Skills Buddy, p. 129

Independent practice

Remind children that an author has to think about where and when a story takes place. Tell them to imagine they are an author who is writing a story. Group children and have them discuss where and when the story would happen if they were writing about:

- a beaver that doesn't know how to build a lodge.
- a whale that helps save a fishing boat.
- a bear that forgets to wake up in the spring.
- a bat that doesn't like to hang upside down.

Refer children to their Rules for Listening and Speaking from pp. 1–2 of the *Reader's and Writer's Notebook.* Remind them to take turns speaking and to speak one at a time.

Reader's and Writer's Notebook, pp. 1–2

Be a Good Listener

1. Face the person who is speaking.
2. Be quiet while someone is speaking.
3. Pay attention to the speaker.
4. Ask questions if you don't understand.

Differentiated Instruction

SI Strategic Intervention

Access Content Understanding the connections among the setting, characters, and plot of a story helps improve children's overall understanding of the story. Use the illustrations in *Where Do Animals Live?* to help children see the connection between the setting and the characters.

Academic Vocabulary

setting the place and time where a story takes place

English Language Learners

Access Content Have children page through *Little Quack* and point out clues to the setting.

Objectives
- Review skills learned and practiced today.

Wrap Up Your Day

✔ **Concept Talk** Today we reread the selection about ants and their nests. What does the queen ant do? What do the worker ants do?

✔ **Respond to Literature** Today we read about some animals and their homes. What kind of animal lives in a web? What kind of animal lives in a den?

✔ **Conventions** Have children give examples of times when they would use an exclamation.

✔ **Homework Idea** Have children write as many words as they can that begin with *c*.

Preview DAY 4

Tell children that tomorrow the class will reread the selection about ants and their nests.

Extend Your Day!

Science
Where Do Animals Live?

Materials: index cards, markers, Kindergarten Student Reader K.6.6

Discuss Animals' Homes Write the following animal names on index cards: *hen, pig, bear, spider, bat, fish, ant*. Show children each card and have them read the animal name. If necessary, show them a picture of the animal. Tell me about this animal's home. What kind of home does it live in? Save the cards to use in the next activity.

Match Animals and Homes Write the following names of animal homes on index cards: *nest, pen, den, web, cave, pond, nest*. On a bulletin board, set up a T-chart with the headings *Animal* and *Home.* Lay the index cards of animal homes and the index cards of animal names out on a tabletop. First, have children pick out the animal names and attach them to the bulletin board under *Animal.* Then have children identify the name of each animal's home and attach the word next to the animal's name under *Home.* Have children draw a picture of an animal and its home from the chart.

Conventions
Make Up Sentences

Materials: nouns and verbs written on index cards

Use Nouns and Verbs to Make Complete Sentences Write verbs on one set of index cards and nouns on another set. Put each set of cards in a separate stack. Have a child take a card from each stack and make a complete sentence, using the noun in the naming part and the verb in the action part. Continue until all children have had a turn. Let them have fun and make up silly sentences if they wish.

Phonemic Awareness
Do What Simon Says

Blend Sounds to Make Words in Directions Play "Simon Says" using sounds in place of one direction word. For example, say: Simon says, "Raise your /h/ /a/ /n/ /d/." Use these commands:

- /k/ /l/ /a/ /p/ your hands.
- Lift your left /l/ /e/ /g/.
- /s/ /n/ /a/ /p/ your fingers.
- /g/ /r/ /a/ /b/ your hair.
- /s/ /i/ /t/ down.
- /s/ /t/ /a/ /n/ /d/ up.
- /k/ /i/ /k/ your right foot.
- /t/ /u/ /g/ your left ear.

Objectives
- Discuss the concept to develop oral language.
- Build oral vocabulary.

Today at a Glance

Oral Vocabulary
twigs, pebbles

Phonemic Awareness
Initial, Medial, and Final Sounds

Phonics
Decode Words
Spell Words

Comprehension
◉ Draw Conclusions

Conventions
Complete Sentences

Writing
Writing Process: Revise a Report

Vocabulary
Words for Bugs

TRUCKTOWN on Reading Street

Start your engines!

- Display "Pop! Blows the Diesel" and lead the group in saying the rhyme a few times.
- Next, have the group clap the rhythm as they recite the rhyme.
- When children master the rhythm, have them march around the room to the rhythm as they say the rhyme.

Truckery Rhymes

Concept Talk

Question of the Week

? How do ants build their nests?

Build concepts

Write the question of the week on the board. Read the question as you track the print. Tell children to respond in complete sentences. Display Sing with Me Chart 36B.

Listen for Amazing Words

Today we are going to sing about ants building a nest. I want you to listen for the Amazing Words *twigs* and *pebbles.* Read the title and have children tell what is happening in the picture. Sing the song several times to the tune of "The Itsy-Bitsy Spider." Tell children to sing along with you. Have them stand up when they hear the Amazing Word *twigs* or *pebbles.*

Sing with Me Audio

Talk with Me/Sing with Me Chart 36B

ELL Produce Oral Language Use the Day 4 instruction on ELL Poster 36 to extend and enrich language.

ELL Poster 36

Oral Vocabulary
Amazing Words

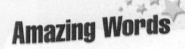
Amazing Words

colony	underground
chambers	silk
twigs	pebbles

Teach Amazing Words

Amazing Words — Oral Vocabulary Routine

1 Introduce the Word Twigs are small sticks or branches. Twigs keep rain out of the ants' nest. What is our new Amazing Word for small sticks or branches? Say it with me: *twigs.*

2 Demonstrate Provide examples to show meaning. *Ants use twigs when they build their homes.* Why do you think ants use twigs rather than branches?

Repeat steps 1 and 2.

Introduce the Word Pebbles are small stones that are usually smooth and round. Pebbles keep other animals out of the ants' nest. What is our new Amazing Word for small stones? Say it with me: *pebbles.*

Demonstrate *Ants use pebbles when they build their homes.* Why do you think ants use *pebbles* rather than stones or rocks?

3 Apply Have children use *twigs* and *pebbles* to explain what ants do to keep their homes safe.

Routines Flip Chart

Use Amazing Words

To reinforce the concept and the Amazing Words, have children supply the appropriate Amazing Word for each sentence.

The robin made a nest out of dried grass and _____. (twigs)

The beach was made of smooth, round _____, not sand. (pebbles)

Differentiated Instruction

SI Strategic Intervention

Access Content If children need help completing the sentences, say a sentence using several of the Amazing Words, one at a time, and ask children to choose the sentence that makes sense.

English Language Learners

Build Background Pass a small bowl of pebbles around and have children describe the color and texture.

Phonemic Awareness
Review Initial, Medial, and Final Sounds

Picture Card

Review

Display the *cat, hen, pig, fox,* and *duck* Picture Cards. Have children identify the name of a picture based on clues you give.

- Which picture name has /f/ at the beginning? (*fox*)
- Which picture name has /e/ in the middle? (*hen*)
- Which picture name has /k/ at the end? (*duck*)
- Which picture name has /p/ at the beginning? (*pig*)
- Which picture name has /a/ in the middle? (*cat*)

Segment and blend sounds

I am going to say a word. I want you to tell me the sounds in the word. Listen carefully: *back*. What are the sounds in the word *back*? (/b/ /a/ /k/) Have children segment the sounds in *mend, zip, flop, plum, drag, step.*

Picture Card

Now I am going to say some sounds. I want you to repeat the sounds and then blend them together to say the word. Listen carefully: /pl/ /o/ /t/. Repeat the sounds: /pl/ /o/ /t/. Now blend the sounds together. What is this word? (*plot*) Have children blend the sounds in the words *stuck, band, fell, skin, trot,* and *bump.*

Picture Card

Corrective feedback

If... children have difficulty with segmenting or blending sounds, **then...** model how to segment or blend sounds several times.

Phonics
Decode Words

Review

Use the Alphabet Cards to review the sounds for the letters and the letter names. Say a sound and have children point to and name the correct letter.

Write *fix* on the board. Point to each letter. What is the sound for this letter? What is the name of this letter? Say the sounds with me: /f/ /i/ /ks/. Blend the sounds as I point to the letters: /f/ /i/ /ks/. What is the word? The word is *fix*. Continue the routine with the following words: *crust, clam, spell, list, block, cup, jam, ten, dip, pond, hug.*

Don't Wait Until Friday

MONITOR PROGRESS | Check Phonemic Awareness

Blend and Read Words Write these words on the board. Have children blend the sound of the letters to read the words.

hot	fun	did	bed	tan	red	sit
box	yum	Pam	let	big	in	fan

If... children cannot blend the sounds to read the words, **then...** use the small-group Strategic Intervention lesson, p. DI•89, to reteach blending skills.

Continue to monitor children's progress using other instructional opportunities during the week so that they can be successful with the Day 5 Assessment. See the Skills Trace on p. 516.

Day 1	Day 2	Day 3	**Day 4**	Day 5
Check Phonemic Awareness	Check Sound-Spelling/ Retelling	Check Word Reading	Check Phonemic Awareness	Check Oral Vocabulary

Success Predictor

Phonemic Awareness

Success Predictor

Objectives
- Spell words.
- Blend and segment words.
- Read decodable text.
- Read high-frequency words.

Spelling
Initial, Medial, and Final Sounds

ROUTINE **Spell Words**

Spell words

1 **Review Sound-Spellings** Display the *Ww* Alphabet Card. This is a *watermelon*. *Watermelon* begins with /w/. What is the letter for /w/? (*w*) Continue the routine with the following Alphabet Cards: *Aa, Bb, Dd, Ee, Ff, Gg, Hh, Ii, Ll, Mm, Nn, Oo, Pp, Ss, Tt, Uu, Vv, Xx.*

2 **Model** Today we are going to spell some words. Listen to the three sounds in *wag*: /w/ /a/ /g/.

- What is the first sound in *wag*? (/w/) What is the letter for /w/? (*w*) Write *w* on the board.
- What is the middle sound in *wag*? (/a/) What is the letter for /a/? (*a*) Write *a* on the board.
- What is the last sound in *wag*? (/g/) What is the letter for /g/? (*g*) Write *g* on the board.
- Point to *wag.* Help me blend the sound of each letter together to read this word: /w/ /a/ /g/. The word is *wag.* Repeat the modeling with the word *vet.*

3 **Guide Practice** Now let's spell some words together. Listen to this word: /b/ /u/ /s/. What is the first sound in *bus*? (/b/) What is the letter for /b/? (*b*) Write *b* on the board. Now you write *b* on your paper. What is the middle sound in *bus*? (/u/) What is the letter for /u/? (*u*) Write *u* on the board. Now you write *u* on your paper. What is the last sound in *bus*? (/s/) What is the letter for /s/? (*s*) Write *s* on the board. Now you write *s* on your paper. Now we can blend the sound of each letter together to read the word: /b/ /u/ /s/. What is the word? (*bus*) Continue spell and blend practice with *hid, leg, gas,* and *pod.*

4 **On Your Own** This time I will say a word and I want you to write the word on your paper. Remember, first, say the word slowly in your head and then write the letter for each sound. Listen carefully. Write the word *fin*. Give children time to write the word. How do you spell the word *fin*? Listen to the sounds: /f/ /i/ /n/. The first sound is /f/. Did you write *f* on your paper? What is the letter for /i/? Did you write *i* on your paper? What is the letter for /n/? Did you write *n* on your paper? Name the letters in *fin*. *Fin* is spelled *f, i, n.* Continue the activity with *tab, hop, mix,* and *sub.*

Routines Flip Chart

Get Set, Roll! Reader 36
🔊 Practice Decodable Words

Review

Review the previously taught high-frequency words *where, come, yellow,* and *have.* Have children read each word as you point to it on the Word Wall.

Teach rebus words

Write the word *trucks* on the board. This is the word *trucks.* Name the letters with me: *t, r, u, c, k, s.* Look for the word *trucks* in the story we read today. A picture above the word will help you read it.

Read Get Set, Roll! Reader 36

Display Get Set, Roll! Reader 36, *Big Rosie.* Today we will read a story about a truck named Rosie. Point to the title of the story. What is the title of the story? *Big Rosie* is the title of the story.

Use the routine for reading decodable books found in the Routines Flip Chart to read Get Set, Roll! Reader 36.

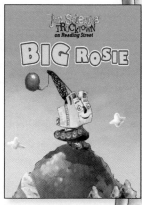

Get Set, Roll! Reader 36

Small Group Time

DAY 4 Break into small groups to read the Get Set, Roll! Reader before the comprehension lesson.

Teacher-Led

(SI) Strategic Intervention	(OL) On-Level	(A) Advanced
Teacher-Led Page DI•89 • Phonemic Awareness and Phonics • **Read** Get Set, Roll! Reader 36	**Teacher-Led** Page DI•93 • **Read** Get Set, Roll! Reader 36	**Teacher-Led** Page DI•96 • **Read** Get Set, Roll! Reader 36 or **Reread** Kindergarten Student Reader K.6.6

ELL Place English language learners in the groups that correspond to their reading abilities in English.

Practice Stations
• Visit the Let's Write! Station
• Visit the Read for Meaning Station

Independent Activities
• Read independently
• Audio Text of the Trade Book
• *Reader's and Writer's Notebook*

English Language Learners

Frontload Reader Do a picture walk to preview the reader before starting the routine.

Objectives

- ◎ Practice draw conclusions.
- • Review compare and contrast.

Comprehension
Draw Conclusions

Practice draw conclusions

Have children turn to the Draw Conclusions picture on pp. 114–115 of *My Skills Buddy*. As you look at the picture, remind children that when we draw conclusions, we use what we know to make up our minds about things we read and see.

My Skills Buddy, pp. 114–115

Team Talk Give children the following clues and have them draw a conclusion about the thing you are describing: *I have four legs. I play in the yard. I bark when I want to come inside.* (dog) Pair children and have them take turns giving clues and drawing conclusions about animals.

Compare and Contrast

Review

Direct children to the Compare and Contrast picture on pp. 14–15 of *My Skills Buddy*. When we compare, we tell how things are alike. Alike means how things are the same. When we contrast, we tell how things are different. Different means how things are not the same. Good readers compare and contrast things as they read. They look for how things are alike and different.

- Compare the skies. Are they alike or different? (The skies are different. There is a rain cloud in one sky and a sun in the other.)
- Compare the bikes. How are they alike, or the same? (They are the same size. They have two big wheels.)
- Contrast the bikes. How are they different, or not the same? (One bike has training wheels. One bike does not.)

More practice

For more practice with compare and contrast, use *Reader's and Writer's Notebook,* p. 475.

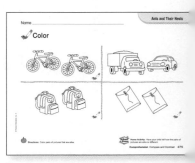

Reader's and Writer's Notebook, p. 475

Third Read—Trade Book
Ants and Their Nests

Guide comprehension

This selection is about how ants build a nest.

- How is an ant's nest like your house?
- How is an ant's nest different from your house?

Reread *Ants and Their Nests.* Return to p. 556. Follow the Day 4 arrow and use the Guide Comprehension notes to give children the opportunity to gain a more complete understanding of the selection.

DAY **2**
Read for enjoyment

DAY **3**
Reread using Develop Vocabulary notes

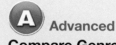

DAY **4**
Reread using Guide Comprehension notes

Differentiated Instruction

SI Strategic Intervention

Access Content Page through the Trade Book *The Lion and the Mouse* and have children compare and contrast the characters.

A Advanced

Compare Genres Have children list the ways the classic fable *The Lion and the Mouse* and the informational text *One Little Mouse* are alike and different.

Objectives
• Use complete sentences.
• Revise a class report by adding details and sentences.

Conventions
Complete Sentences

Review   Remind children what they learned about complete sentences. A complete sentence has a subject and a predicate. The subject tells who or what the sentence is about. The predicate tells what a person or thing does.

AlphaBuddy is going to ask me a question, and I will answer him with a complete sentence. *What day is today? Today is Thursday.* My sentence has a naming part and an action part, so it is a complete sentence.

Guide practice   Have AlphaBuddy ask children questions such as these: *What is your name? How old are you? Where do you live? What is your favorite color?* Have children answer using complete sentences.

On their own   Use *Reader's and Writer's Notebook,* p. 476, for more practice with complete sentences.

Daily Fix-It   Use the Daily Fix-It for more conventions practice.

Reader's and Writer's Notebook, p. 476

Writing
Writing Process: Revise a Report

Teach

Yesterday we wrote a draft of our report on how a bird builds a nest. We put the events in order. Today we're going to revise our report. When we revise our writing, we make it better. One way to make our writing better is to add more information. How can adding information make writing better? **Encourage children to share their thoughts and ideas. (Adding more information can make the report more interesting.)**

Model

Let's look at the writing we did yesterday. We learned three things a bird does to build its nest. **Review with children the information you documented.** Yesterday we learned where a bird builds its nest, but we didn't learn *why* the bird builds a nest. I think we should add that information to our report. Let's look at our source again and ask ourselves, *Why does a bird build a nest?* **Read aloud text from the book you used yesterday that explains why birds build nests.** Now we know that a bird builds a nest as a place to lay its eggs and to raise its babies. Let's add that information to the beginning of our report. **(Possible sentences: A bird needs a nest. It lays its eggs and raises its babies in a nest.)**

Guide practice

We also learned that a bird collects materials to build its nest. Do you think readers would be interested to know *what kinds* of materials the bird uses for its nest? Let's go back to our source—the book about birds—and find that information. **Read aloud text that tells what kinds of materials birds use to build their nests.** What information should we add to our report? Where should we add it? Good job! **(Possible addition: such as grass, twigs, and leaves) Together review the report. (A bird needs a nest. It lays its eggs and raises its babies in a nest. First, the bird finds a place in a tree. Next, the bird gathers materials, such as grass, twigs, and leaves. Last, the bird uses these materials to make a nest.)**

Independent practice

On p. 477 in *Reader's and Writer's Notebook,* have children draw pictures of and write or dictate additional information that could be included in the research report. Then children can write or dictate the entire report on p. 478 in *Reader's and Writer's Notebook.*

Reader's and Writer's Notebook, p. 477

Vocabulary
Words for Bugs

Teach

Write the words *ant, bee, fly,* and *spider* on the board. Point to each word as you read it. These are words for bugs. Have children turn to p. 128 of *My Skills Buddy.* Listen to my clues and point to the picture. This bug had eight legs and spins a web. (spider) This bug builds nests underground. (ant) This striped bug flies from flower to flower in the garden. (bee) This small bug has wings. (fly) Discuss the last two vocabulary bullets with children.

Team Talk Pair children and have them take turns using the words for bugs in complete sentences.

My Skills Buddy, p. 128

Wrap Up Your Day

✔ **Concept Talk** How do ants keep their nests safe? Let's look at how we answered this question at the beginning of the lesson. Do we want to change or add to our answers?

✔ **Oral Language** Sing "A Colony of Ants" with me. Tap your desk when you hear an Amazing Word—*colony, underground, chambers, silk, twigs, pebbles.*

✔ **Phonemic Awareness** Have children identify the sounds in the words *ramp, dress, pick,* and *club.*

✔ **Homework Idea** Have children copy a complete sentence from a book or magazine and explain how they know it is a complete sentence.

Preview DAY 5

Tell children that tomorrow they will review some of the books and stories they have read this week.

Extend Your Day!

Science
Make More Insects

Materials: modeling clay; chenille sticks; construction paper; pictures of a bee, wasp, cricket, and beetle

Discuss Insects' Body Parts Display the pictures of a bee, wasp, cricket, and beetle. Have children identify the four insects and their body parts: legs, wings, head, antennae. Remind children that bees, wasps, crickets, and beetles are insects, so they have bodies that are divided into three parts—head, thorax, abdomen—just as ants' bodies are.

Make Insect Models Give modeling clay, pipe cleaners, and construction paper to each child. Tell children they are going to make models of a bee, wasp, cricket, and beetle to go with their ant model. (You may wish to assign one of the four insects to each child so that the child makes only one model.) Remind children they can use the pictures as their guides. When they are finished, have them use their models to discuss how these insects are alike and different.

Spell Words
Name That Animal

Materials: pencils, paper

Guess and Write Animal Names Tell children you are going to give them clues about a particular animal. As soon as they are able to guess the animal, they are to write its name or draw its picture on their paper and then raise their hand. For each animal, give one or more clues, such as the following:

- *dog:* It wags its tail. It barks.
- *cat:* It licks its paws. It meows.
- *pig:* It has a curly tail. It grunts and oinks.
- *hen:* It has feathers. It lays eggs. It clucks.

Phonics
Word Change Game

Materials: letter tiles

Change Sound-Spellings to Make New Words Have children sit on the floor in a circle. Provide each child with three letter tiles. Make the word *fan* with letter tiles in the middle of the circle. Have one child begin the game by replacing one of the letters in *fan* with one of his or her letters to make a new word, such as *pan, fin,* or *fat.* If a child cannot use any of his or her letters, that child passes, and the next child takes a turn. Continue until each child has used all three of his or her letter tiles.

Objectives
- Review the concepts.
- Build oral vocabulary.

Today at a Glance

Oral Vocabulary
colony, underground, chambers, silk, twigs, pebbles

Phonemic Awareness
◉ Initial, Medial, and Final Sounds

Phonics
◉ Decode Words

Comprehension
◉ Draw Conclusions

Conventions
Complete Sentences

Writing
Writing Process: Edit and Share a Report

Check Oral Vocabulary
SUCCESS PREDICTOR

TRUCKTOWN on Reading Street

Start your engines!

- Display "Pop! Blows the Diesel" and lead the group in saying the rhyme a few times.

- Have half the group recite the first stanza and the other half recite the second stanza.

- Then have the boys recite the first stanza and the girls recite the second stanza.

Truckery Rhymes

Concept Wrap Up

Question of the Week
❓ How do ants build their nests?

Listen for Amazing Words

Write the question of the week on the board. Track the print as you read it to children. Have them use Amazing Words in their responses (*colony, underground, chambers, silk, twigs, pebbles*). Remind children to speak one at a time. Display Sing with Me Chart 36B. Let's sing "A Colony of Ants." I want you to listen for the Amazing Words we learned this week. Have children listen and say "Amazing!" each time they hear an Amazing Word. Then have them sing the song with you, clapping each time they say an Amazing Word. Sing the song several times.

A Colony of Ants

A colony of ants will labor underground.
With sticky silk, they build an ant compound.
Pebbles in place and twigs keep out the rain.
To build the many chambers, they labor once again.

Talk with Me/Sing with Me Chart 36B

 Sing with Me Audio

ⒺⓁⓁ Check Concepts and Language Use the Day 5 instruction on ELL Poster 36 to monitor children's understanding of the lesson concept.

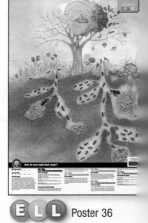

ⒺⓁⓁ Poster 36

Oral Vocabulary
Amazing Words

Review

Let's Talk Display Talk with Me Chart 36A. We learned six new Amazing Words this week. Let's say the Amazing Words as I point to the pictures on the chart. Point to each picture and give children the chance to say the appropriate Amazing Word before offering it.

Have children supply the appropriate Amazing Word to complete each sentence.

> **A prairie dog's burrow has tunnels and _____.** (chambers)
>
> **Ants live in a large group called a _____.** (colony)
>
> **Water had made the _____ smooth and round.** (pebbles)
>
> **Like some ants, some spiders can make _____.** (silk)
>
> **Like many ants, earthworms live _____.** (underground)
>
> **After the storm, the ground was covered with _____ and branches.** (twigs)

Amazing Words

colony	underground
chambers	silk
twigs	pebbles

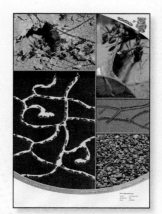

Talk with Me/Sing with Me Chart 36A

It's Friday

MONITOR PROGRESS | **Check Oral Vocabulary**

Demonstrate Word Knowledge Monitor the Amazing Words by asking the following questions. Have children use the Amazing Word in their answer.

- **What do some ants use to hold leaves together for a nest?** (silk)
- **Where do some ants build their homes?** (underground)
- **What do some ants use to keep other animals out of their nest?** (pebbles)
- **Where do ants store food in their nest?** (chambers)
- **What do you call a large group of ants living together?** (colony)
- **What do some ants use to keep rain out of their nest?** (twigs)

If... children have difficulty using the Amazing Words,

then... reteach the words using the Oral Vocabulary Routine on the Routines Flip Chart.

Day 1	Day 2	Day 3	Day 4	Day 5
Check Phonemic Awareness	Check Sound-Spelling/ Retelling	Check Word Reading	Check Phonemic Awareness	Check Oral Vocabulary

Success Predictor

587 | *Oral Vocabulary* **Success Predictor**

Objectives
- ◎ Discriminate sounds in words.
- ◎ Decode words.
- • Review short vowels and consonants.

Phonemic Awareness Review
Initial, Medial, and Final Sounds

Discriminate sounds

Display the *red, van, wig, mop,* and *tub* Picture Cards. Have children say the picture name for each card. Which picture name has /r/ at the beginning? (*red*) Which picture name has /a/ in the middle? (*van*) Which picture name has /b/ at the end? (*tub*) Continue until children have identified all the initial, medial, and final sounds in the words.

Segment and blend sounds

Say the word *cut.* What are the sounds in *cut*? (/k/ /u/ /t/) Have children segment the sounds in the words *sack, peg, slid, not,* and *grub.* Say these sounds: /tr/ /i/ /p/. Blend the sounds together to say the word. What is the word? (*trip*) Continue the routine with the sounds for the words *pond, rust, bend, snap,* and *pick.*

Picture Card

Picture Card

Picture Card

Phonics Review
 Decode Words

Decode words

Write this sentence on the board: *Cats jump in black hats.* Let's read this sentence together. Point to the first word. Have children say the sound for each letter as you point to the letter. Let's blend the sounds together to read the word: /k/ /a/ /t/ /s/, *cats.* Continue to decode the other words in the sentence.

High-frequency words

Write the word *was* on the board. This is the word *was.* What is this word? Continue the routine with *go, five, are, you, she, like,* and *the.*

Apply phonics in familiar text

Let's Reread Have children reread one of the readers specific to the target sound-spelling. Review the decodable words, rebus words, and high-frequency words in the readers prior to rereading.

Decodable Reader 36
My Skills Buddy, p. 118

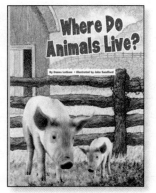

Kindergarten Student
Reader K.6.6

Get Set, Roll!
Reader 36

Small Group Time

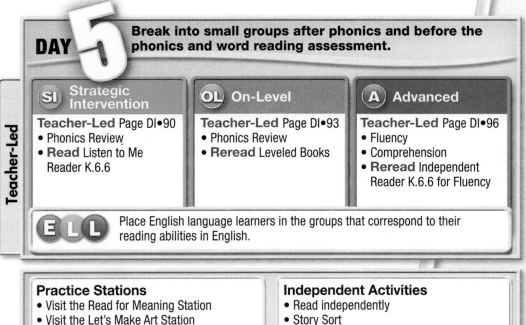

DAY 5 Break into small groups after phonics and before the phonics and word reading assessment.

Teacher-Led

SI Strategic Intervention	**OL On-Level**	**A Advanced**
Teacher-Led Page DI•90	**Teacher-Led** Page DI•93	**Teacher-Led** Page DI•96
• Phonics Review	• Phonics Review	• Fluency
• **Read** Listen to Me Reader K.6.6	• **Reread** Leveled Books	• Comprehension
		• **Reread** Independent Reader K.6.6 for Fluency

ELL Place English language learners in the groups that correspond to their reading abilities in English.

Practice Stations
• Visit the Read for Meaning Station
• Visit the Let's Make Art Station

Independent Activities
• Read independently
• Story Sort
• Concept Talk Video

Assessment
Monitor Progress

Decode words

Whole Class Write the following sets of words on a sheet of paper. Provide each child with a copy.

1.	jet	pot	box
2.	tops	quit	tent
3.	cast	desk	fat
4.	win	gas	lap
5.	hug	rub	yam

Read one word from each row. Have children circle the word you say.

> **MONITOR PROGRESS** **Check Word and Sentence Reading**
>
> **If...** children cannot complete the whole-class assessment, **then...** use the Reteach lesson in *First Stop*.
>
> **If...** you are unsure of a child's grasp of this week's skills, **then...** use the assessment below to obtain a clearer evaluation of the child's progress.

Decode words and high-frequency words

One-on-One To facilitate individual progress monitoring, assess some children on Day 4 and the rest on Day 5. While individual children are being assessed, the rest of the class can reread this week's books.

Word reading

Use the reproducible word lists on p. 591 to assess a child's ability to read words. We're going to read some words. I'll read the first word, and you read the rest. The first word is *wax: /w/ /a/ /ks/.* The first word is *wax.* For each child, record any decoding problems.

Sentence reading

Use the reproducible sentences on p. 591 to assess a child's ability to read words in sentences. Have each child read two sentences aloud. Have each child read different sentences. Start over with sentence one if necessary.

Record scores

Monitor children's accuracy by recording their scores using the Word and Sentence Reading Chart for this unit in *First Stop*.

Name ________________________________

Read the Words

wax	☐	bug	☐
six	☐	pens	☐
jog	☐	was	☐
what	☐	stop	☐
met	☐	glad	☐
blue	☐	where	☐

Read the Sentences

1. We see six bugs here.
2. The nuts are from Pat.
3. Is that mask from Tom?
4. We jog to that end.
5. She said Fred looks fit.

Note to Teacher: Children read each word. Children read two sentences.

Scoring for Read the Words: Score 1 point for each correct word.

Short Vowels *a, e, i, o, u* (*wax, six, jog, met, bug, pens, stop, glad*) ______ / 8
High-Frequency Words (*what, blue, was, where*) ______ / 4

MONITOR PROGRESS
- Review short vowels
- Review high-frequency words

Objectives
- Recognize a limerick.
- Identify rhythm and rhyme.

My Skills Buddy, pp. 130–131

Let's Practice It!
Poem—Limerick

Teach

Tell children that today they will listen to a limerick. A limerick is a funny poem. Review the features of a limerick with children.

- A limerick tells a funny story.
- A limerick has five lines.
- A limerick has rhyming words.
- A limerick has a special rhythm or beat.

Have children turn to pp. 130–131 of *My Skills Buddy*. I am going to read a limerick called "A Man at a Restaurant in Crewe." Look at the pictures as I read. Read the text of "A Man at a Restaurant in Crewe." As you read, direct children to look at the appropriate picture.

Guide practice

Discuss the features of a limerick and the bulleted text on p. 130 of *My Skills Buddy*.

- A limerick tells a funny story in five lines. What is "A Man at a Restaurant in Crewe" about? (a man who found a bug in his stew)
- A limerick has rhyming words. What are the rhyming words in "A Man at a Restaurant in Crewe?" (*Crewe, stew, too; shout, about*)
- A limerick has a special rhythm. What lines have the same rhythm? (The first, second, and fifth lines have the same rhythm. The third and fourth lines have a different rhythm.)
- Listen to the rhythm of "A Man at a Restaurant in Crewe" as I read and clap my hands to the beat. Reread the limerick, clapping to the beat. Then read the limerick again and have children clap with you to the rhythm.

Differentiated Instruction

 **Advanced**

Limerick Adaptations Write the limerick "A Man at a Restaurant in Crewe" on the board and underline the rhyming words *Crewe, stew,* and *too*. Have children make a list of rhyming words they could substitute for the words at the end of lines 1, 2, and 5. Write the new words and have the class read the limerick aloud.

Academic Vocabulary

limerick funny poem with five lines

rhythm strong beat found in songs and poems

ELL

English Language Learners
Build Background Some children might not understand the subtle humor of the limerick. Discuss the scenario before reading the limerick. Ask children to tell what they would do if they found a bug in their food.

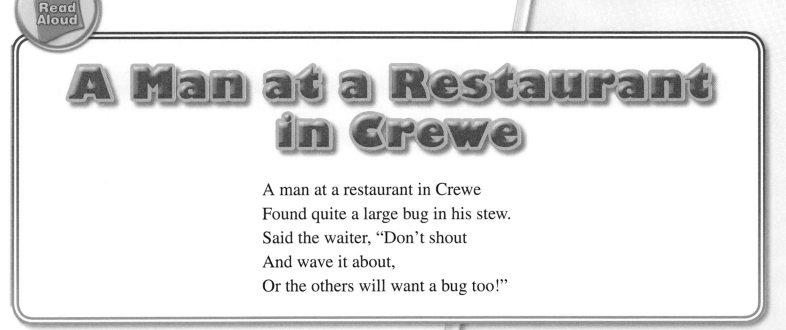

A Man at a Restaurant in Crewe

A man at a restaurant in Crewe
Found quite a large bug in his stew.
Said the waiter, "Don't shout
And wave it about,
Or the others will want a bug too!"

Assess
◉ Draw conclusions in a text.

Comprehension Assessment
Monitor Progress

Review

◉ **Draw Conclusions** When we draw conclusions, we use what we know to make up our minds about things we read and see. What do we do when we draw conclusions? Good readers draw conclusions as they read because it helps them better understand the ideas in what they are reading.

Read "Animals' Houses"

Tell children that you are going to read them a poem about animals' houses. As you listen to the poem, think about what you hear. Use what you already know to make up your mind about things in the poem. When I finish, I will ask you to connect the ideas in what I am reading to what you already know. Read "Animals' Houses" on p. 87 of the *Read Aloud Anthology.*

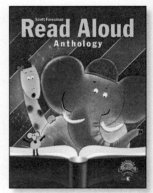

Read Aloud Anthology

Check draw conclusions

After you read the poem, have children draw conclusions.

• In which category—square or round—does the author put people's houses? How do you know? (square; He says "Cows have square houses/And so do I," referring to himself, a person.)

• Why does the author put a snail's shell and a rabbit's burrow in the round category? (They are not square; one curls around, and the other twists and turns.)

• In which category—square or round—does the author put the sea? Why? (round; He thinks of the sea as being like a huge round fishbowl.)

Corrective feedback

If... children cannot draw conclusions,
then... reteach draw conclusions using the Reteach lesson in *First Stop.*

Assess draw conclusions

Use the blackline master on page 595. Make one copy for each child. Have children use the information in the text and what they already know to color the correct building that is made using the items shown.

Name _____

Draw Conclusions

Look at the machines, tools, and parts. What is made using all of these items? Color the picture.

Note to Teacher: Have children use the information in the text to color the correct building that was made using the items shown.

Objectives

- Review complete sentences.
- Edit a class report by checking letter and word spacing, initial capitalization, and end punctuation.
- Prepare a final copy of a class report to share with others.

Conventions
Complete Sentences

Review   Remind children of what they learned about complete sentences. A complete sentence has a subject and a predicate. A sentence tells a complete idea.

Model   Write these words on the board: *my family*. Read the words aloud. This is not a complete sentence. It does not tell a complete idea. It does not have a subject and a predicate. Change the words to this sentence: *My family went to the library*. This is a complete sentence. It tells a complete idea. It has a subject, *My family,* and a predicate, *went to the library*.

Guide practice   Write the following groups of words on the board. Have children come to the board, add words to each group of words to make it a complete sentence, and write the sentence correctly.

got in bed	**had a box**
a big dog	**the red van**

Have children check to see that their sentence has a subject, a predicate, an uppercase letter at the beginning, and a period at the end.

Daily Fix-It   Use the Daily Fix-It for more conventions practice.

Writing
Writing Process:
Edit and Share a Report

Teach: Edit

Remind children of the work they have done on their reports so far. What steps in the writing process have we done so far in writing our report? (We chose a topic; we decided which sources to use; we wrote down and/or drew the information in order; we added information, or revised, our report.) Today we will edit our report or check to make sure we've written it correctly. Did we use correct spacing between words and letters? Did we use uppercase letters and periods correctly? Remind children that we leave small spaces between letters in a word and bigger spaces between words in a sentence. Point out that we also begin each sentence with an uppercase letter and end it with a period, question mark, or exclamation mark.

Model: Edit

Reread the report you wrote. Point out the correct spacing between letters and words and the correct use of uppercase letters and end punctuation. Have children point out other things that need to be fixed. Show them how to mark the corrections.

Guide practice: Edit

Work with children to complete the editing activity on p. 479 in *Reader's and Writer's Notebook.*

Teach: Share

Display the report you have written together. Now it's time to share our work with others. First, we will rewrite our report using our best handwriting. We will correct any mistakes we found during editing. We can add pictures if we choose, and we can make a cover. Then our report will be ready to share with others.

Reader's and Writer's
Notebook, pp. 479–480

Model: Share

Now I will rewrite our report using my best handwriting. Check letter and word spacing, capitalization, and end punctuation.

Guide practice: Share

Work with children to write their reports on a separate sheet of paper. Encourage them to draw pictures and add a cover with a title and their name. Make each child's report into a booklet.

After they have completed their report and shared it with others, have children complete p. 480 in *Reader's and Writer's Notebook.* As a group, discuss reviewers' reactions to the reports. Have children save their reports to add to the classroom library.

Differentiated Instruction

SI Strategic Intervention
Writing Rubric Provide a checklist for children to use as an editing guide to review their writing. The list should remind children to check for letter and word spacing, correct spelling, complete sentences, capitalization, and end punctuation.

A Advanced
Writing Evaluation After children have completed and shared their reports, have them discuss the writing process. Use these prompts: *What part of report writing did you like best? What can readers learn from our report? What will you do differently the next time you write a report?*

Academic Vocabulary

edit correct errors

Daily Fix-It

stop the bus?
Stop the bus!

This week's practice sentences appear on Teacher Resources DVD-ROM.

ELL

English Language Learners
Support Writing As children write or dictate, provide English words if needed to help them express their ideas.

Objectives
• Review weekly concept.

Wrap Up Your Week!

 Question of the Week

How do ants build their nests?

Illustrate draw conclusions

This week we talked about ants and their nests. We learned many interesting facts about ants' nests.

• Make a concept web like the one shown.

• Have children share what they learned about where ants build their nests, what materials ants use, and what the nests look like. Write children's responses on the lines of the web.

• When the web is finished, have children echo read it with you.

• Give each child a sheet of paper. Have them draw an ant's nest and write or dictate labels for the parts of the nest.

• Display all of the drawings.

Amazing Words

You've learned
| 0 | 0 | 6 |
words this week!

You've learned
| 2 | 1 | 6 |
words this year!

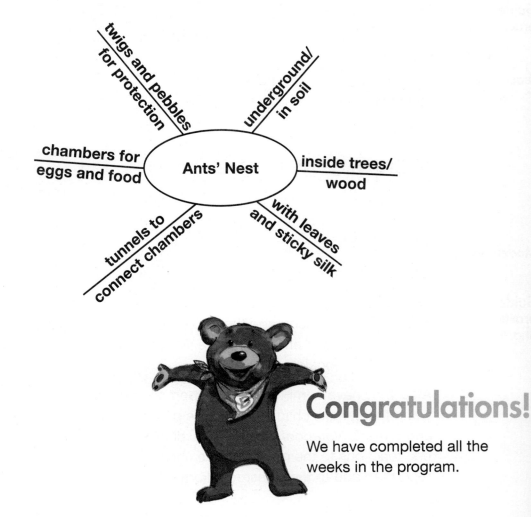

twigs and pebbles for protection
underground/ in soil
chambers for eggs and food
Ants' Nest
inside trees/ wood
tunnels to connect chambers
with leaves and sticky silk

Congratulations!

We have completed all the weeks in the program.

Extend Your Day!

Science
Different Animals

Materials: chart paper, markers

Compare and Contrast Animals Remind children they have learned about many different kinds of animals. What are some of the animals we have read and learned about? Group the animals according to whether they are mammals, reptiles, fish, birds, amphibians, or insects. Then read each list and discuss with children how the animals are alike and different.

Make a Comparison Chart Draw a five-column chart as shown. Read the animal names and the categories to children. Together fill in the boxes under *Ant*. How many legs does an ant have? unusual body parts? How does it move? live? Continue with the rest of the chart. Have children echo read the chart with you. Then ask them questions using information from the chart: Which animal has the most legs? fewest legs? has wings? walks or runs? lives in nests?

	Ant	Prairie Dog	Robin	Goldfish
Legs	6	4	2	0
Body Parts	feelers	long claws	wings	fins
Moves	walks/ runs	walks/ runs	flies	swims
Lives	nest	burrow	nest	water

Comprehension
What Can You Conclude? Round 2

Use Clues to Draw Conclusions Give children two clues: One clue tells something they know; the other clue tells something they see. Have them use the clues to draw a conclusion.

- **You know. . .** the school playground is muddy.
  You see. . . Teresa has mud on her shoes.
  You conclude. . . Teresa was out on the playground.

- **You know. . .** lightning comes before thunder.
  You see. . . a streak of lightning.
  You conclude. . . you will hear thunder.

Phonics
Word Spell

Materials: letters written on index cards

Spell Words with Letter Cards Divide the class into groups. Give each child five or six letter cards, making sure that one letter is a vowel. Players try to make three- or four-letter words with their cards. Then have them change or delete a letter to make a new word. Continue until one player has used all of his or her letter cards.

Unit Wrap-Up

 Question of the Week
How is a school built?

Concept Knowledge

Children understand that big machines:

- are used to build a school
- each has a special job to do

Question of the Week
What tools do you need to build things?

Concept Knowledge

Children understand that different tools:

- are used to do special jobs
- can help build things

 The Big Question

What are different ways of building?

Understanding By Design

Grant Wiggins, Ed. D. Reading Street Author

"A big idea may be thought of as a *linchpin*. The *linchpin* is the device that keeps the wheel in place on an axle. Thus, a linchpin is one that is essential for understanding. Without grasping the idea and using it to 'hold together' related content knowledge, we are left with bits and pieces of inert facts that cannot take us anywhere."

Discuss the Big Question

Help children relate the theme question for this unit to the selections and their own experiences. Write the big question and prompt discussion with questions such as the following:

What different ways of building did we learn about in the stories we read? Possible responses:

- Dad takes his son to work to learn how a new school is built.
- The animals use many different small tools to make a farm.
- Beavers use their teeth to cut down trees and carry the wood to streams to build lodges and dams to live in.
- Alistair and Kip build a boat together and use it to have an adventure.

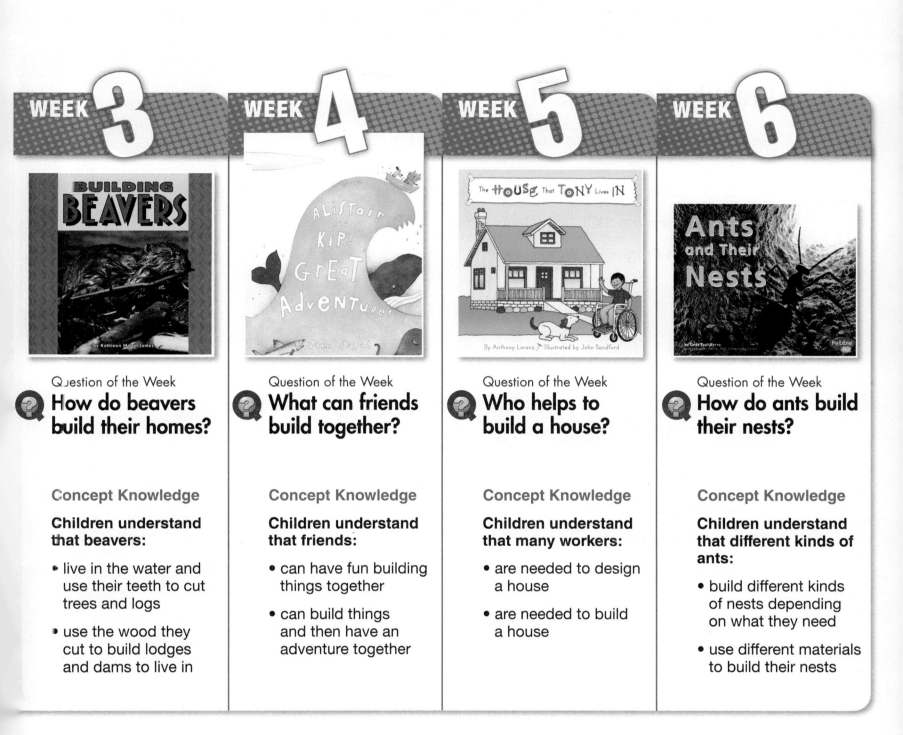

BUILDING **BEAVERS**
by Kathleen Martin James

ALiSTair and KiPS GreaT Adventure!
John Segal

The HOUSE That TONY Lives IN
By Anthony Lorenz · Illustrated by John Sandford

Ants and Their Nests
by Linda Tagliaferro
Pebble

Question of the Week

How do beavers build their homes?

Question of the Week

What can friends build together?

Question of the Week

Who helps to build a house?

Question of the Week

How do ants build their nests?

Concept Knowledge

Children understand that beavers:

• live in the water and use their teeth to cut trees and logs

• use the wood they cut to build lodges and dams to live in

Concept Knowledge

Children understand that friends:

• can have fun building things together

• can build things and then have an adventure together

Concept Knowledge

Children understand that many workers:

• are needed to design a house

• are needed to build a house

Concept Knowledge

Children understand that different kinds of ants:

• build different kinds of nests depending on what they need

• use different materials to build their nests

• We learned about the many people it takes to build a new house.

• Ants build different kinds of nests depending on what they need.

What kind of building have you done? Responses will vary but might include:

• building with blocks or other toys

• building many different things in a sandbox

What do you see being built in your city or town? Possible responses:

• new homes or office buildings being constructed

• new roads, highways, or bridges

• new schools, libraries, or stores

Weekly Assessment

Use the whole-class assessment on pages 590–591 and 594–595 in this Teacher's Edition to check:

✔ ⦿ **Short Vowels**

✔ ⦿ **Comprehension Skill** *Draw Conclusions*

✔ **Review High-Frequency Words**

Teacher's Edition, Day 5

Managing Assessment

Use the Assessment Handbook for:

✔ **Observation Checklists**

✔ **Record-Keeping Forms**

✔ **Portfolio Assessment**

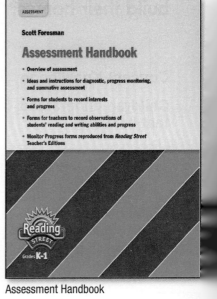

Assessment Handbook

Unit Assessment

Use the Unit 6 Assessment to check progress in:

✔ **Phonemic Awareness**

✔ **Phonics**

✔ **High-Frequency Words**

✔ **Comprehension** *Character, Setting, Plot*

✔ **Conventions in Writing**

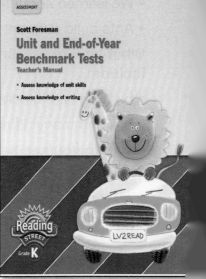

Unit Assessment

Teacher Notes

Small **Group Time**

Pacing Small Group Instruction

20-30 mins.

5 Day Plan

DAY 1
- Phonemic Awareness/ Phonics
- Decodable Story 36

DAY 2
- Phonemic Awareness/ Phonics
- Decodable Reader 36

DAY 3
- Phonemic Awareness/ Phonics
- Concept Literacy Reader K.6.6 or Kindergarten Student Reader K.6.6

DAY 4
- Phonemic Awareness/ Phonics
- Get Set, Roll! Reader 36

DAY 5
- Phonics Review
- Listen to Me Reader K.6.6

3 or 4 Day Plan

DAY 1
- Phonemic Awareness/ Phonics
- Decodable Story 36

DAY 2
- Phonemic Awareness/ Phonics
- Decodable Reader 36

DAY 3
- Phonemic Awareness/ Phonics
- Concept Literacy Reader K.6.6 or Kindergarten Student Reader K.6.6

DAY 4
- Phonemic Awareness/ Phonics
- Get Set, Roll! Reader 36

3 Day Plan: Eliminate the shaded box.

 **SI** Strategic Intervention

Phonemic Awareness•Phonics

■ **Isolate Sounds** Display the *jug* Picture Card. What is this? (a *jug*) What sound does *jug* begin with? (/j/) Yes, *jug* begins with /j/. What is the middle sound in *jug?* (/u/) What is the final sound in *jug?* (/g/) Have children continue to identify initial, medial, and final sounds using the following Picture Cards: *top, red, six, wig, can, bat, tub.*

■ **Connect Sound to Letter** Say the word *ten.* Listen to the sounds in the word *ten: /t/ /e/ /n/.* What is the letter for /t/? Have a volunteer write the letter on the board. Continue with /e/ and /n/. The letters for *ten* are *t, e, n.* Let's read the word together and then spell it: *ten, t, e, n.* Continue with the words *wet, bug, mud, vet, pig, sat,* and *lot.*

Decodable Story 36

■ **Review** Review the previously taught high-frequency words by writing each word on the board and having children read the word with you.

| is | look | he | fed | little | see | she | go | me | you |

> **If…** children have difficulty reading the words,
> **then…** say a word and have children point to the word. Repeat several times, giving assistance as needed.

■ **Read** Have children read *What Can You Do?* orally. Then have them reread the story several times individually.

Reader's and Writer's Notebook, pp. 463–464

Objectives
- Identify the common sounds that letters represent.
- Read at least 25 high-frequency words from a commonly used list.

Phonemic Awareness•Phonics

■ **Blending** Write *clip* on the board. Help me blend this word. Listen as I say each sound: /k/ /l/ /i/ /p/. Now let's blend the sounds together to read the word: /k/ /l/ /i/ /p/, *clip.* Continue with *let, mug, hot, drip,* and *stop.*

■ **Discriminate Blends** Display Phonics Songs and Rhymes Chart 36. Sing "Quickly, Thump on the Mud" to the tune of "Billy Boy (Oh, Where Have You Been)" several times with children. Have children clap their hands when they hear blends.

■ **Recognize Blends** Ask children to name words that begin with the blend /fr/. List the words on the board as they say them. Have children echo read the list of words. Then ask children to circle the letters *f* and *r* in the words on the board.

Decodable Reader 36

■ **Review** Review the high-frequency words by writing *you* on the board. This is the word *you.* What word is this? Continue with the following words: *what, see, a, for, said, with, I, the, they.*

> **If...** children have difficulty reading the words,
> **then...** say a word and have children point to the word. Repeat several times, giving assistance as needed.

My Skills Buddy p.118

■ **Read** Display the cover of *The Box* on p. 118 of *My Skills Buddy.* Ask a volunteer to read the first page of the story. After children finish reading the story, have children tell about the big box.

Objectives
- Identify the common sounds that letters represent.
- Read at least 25 high-frequency words from a commonly used list.
- Retell a main event from a story read aloud.

Phonemic Awareness•Phonics

■ **Isolate Sounds** Say the word *top.* Do you hear /o/ in *top?* Say it with me: /t/ /o/ /p/, *top. Top* has /o/ in the middle. What sound does *top* begin with? (/t/) What sound does *top* end with? (/p/) Repeat with *bed, cat,* and *lap.*

■ **Connect Sound to Letter** Display the *fox* Picture Card. This is a *fox. Fox* begins with /f/. Say it with me: /f/ /f/ /f/. What is the letter for this sound? (*f*) What is the middle sound in *fox?* (/o/) What is the letter for /o/? (*o*) What is the final sound in *fox?* (/ks/) What is the letter for /ks/? (*x*) Which word begins the same as *fox, fun* or *pen?* (fun) Which word ends the same as *fox, house* or *box?* (box)

■ **Blend Sounds** Write *nest* on the board. Have children blend the sound of each letter to read the word. Repeat the routine with the words *sit, sun, spot,* and *stop.*

■ **Review High-Frequency Words** Write *you* on the board. Have volunteers say the word and use it in a sentence. Continue with the word *said, see, look,* and *three.*

■ **Read** To practice phonics and high-frequency words, have children read Kindergarten Student Reader K.6.6. Use the instruction on pp. 552–553.

For a complete lesson plan and additional practice, see the **Leveled Reader Teaching Guide**.

Concept Literacy Reader K.6.6

■ **Preview and Predict** Display the cover of the Concept Literacy Reader K.6.6. Point to the title of the book. The title of the book is *Ants Build.* What do you think the book is about? Have children tell about the cover and what they think the book might be about.

■ **Set a Purpose** We talked about the title of the book. Let's read the book to learn about what ants use to build. Have children read the Concept Literacy Reader.

■ **Read** Provide corrective feedback as children read the book orally. During reading, ask them if they are able to confirm any of the predictions they made prior to reading.

If... children have difficulty reading the book individually,

then... read a sentence aloud as children point to each word. Then have the group reread the sentences as they continue pointing to the words.

■ **Retell** Have children retell the content as you page through the book. Help them identify what the book is about. Also call attention to how ants carry the things they use to build.

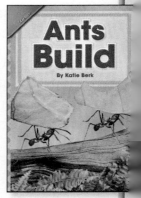

Concept Literacy Reader K.6.6

Objectives

• Identify the common sounds that letters represent. • Predict what might happen next based on the cover.
• Predict what might happen next based on the title. • Retell important facts in a text, heard or read.

SI Strategic Intervention

DAY **4**

More Reading

Use Leveled Readers or other text at children's instructional level.

Phonemic Awareness•Phonics

■ **Isolate Sound** Display the *yak* Picture Card. This is a *yak. Yak* begins with /y/. Say it with me: /y/ /y/ /y/, *yak.* What is the middle sound in *yak?* /a/ is the middle sound in *yak.* What is the final sound in *yak?* /k/ is the final sound in *yak.* Say the three sounds together: /y/ /a/ /k/, *yak.* Repeat with *yam, yell,* and *yes.* Then write *Yy* on the board. The sound for *Yy* is /y/.

■ **Blending** Write *mix* on the board. Help me blend this word. Listen as I say each sound: /m/ /i/ /ks/. Now let's blend the sounds together to read the word: /m/ /i/ /ks/, *mix.* Continue with *sad, glad, him, bunt,* and *sent.*

■ **Discriminate Blends** Write *left* on the board. This is the word *left. Left* ends with the blend /ft/. Say it with me: /l/ /e/ /ft/, *left.* Does *past* end with the same sound as *left?* No, *past* does not end with /ft/. Repeat with *raft, mask, loft, camp, land, lift,* and *sift.*

Get Set, Roll! Reader 36

■ **Review** Review the following high-frequency words prior to reading the story: *a, she, with, they, look, is, was.*

■ **Review Rebus Word** Write *trucks* on the board. This is the word *trucks.* Name the letters with me: *t, r, u, c, k, s, trucks.* This word is in the story we will read today. There will be a picture above the word to help use read it.

Get Set, Roll! Reader 36

■ **Read** Display Get Set, Roll! Reader 36, *Big Rosie.* Today we will read a new story that has a lot of trucks. Point to the title of the story. The title of the story is *Big Rosie.*

> **If…** children have difficulty reading the story individually, **then…** read a sentence aloud as children point to each word. Then have the group reread the sentences as they continue pointing to the words.

■ **Reread** Use echo reading of Get Set, Roll! Reader 36 to model fluent reading. Use your oral reading to model for children where to pause, when to change pitch, and which words to stress. Then have children reread orally three to four times, or until they can read with few or no mistakes.

Objectives
• Identify the common sounds that letters represent.
• Read at least 25 high-frequency words from a commonly used list.

Small Group Time

More Reading

Use Leveled Readers or other text at children's instructional level.

Phonics Review

■ **Place the Sticky!** Gather the following objects and display them in front of the class: *pen, crayon, calculator, book, clock, tape, stapler, glue, marker.* Write each of the following letters on a self-stick note: *b, c, cl, cr, gl, m, p, st, t.* Give each note to a child. Have children read the letter or letters and identify the sound. Then have them stick the note to the object that begins with that letter or blend.

Listen to Me Reader K.6.6

■ **Preview and Predict** Display the cover of the book. The title of this story is *Look at the Red Bird.* It is written by Jim Lobes. It is illustrated by Nancy Harrison. Look at the cover. What do you think this story will be about?

■ **Teach Rebus Word** Write the word *bird* on the board. This is the word *bird.* Name the letters with me: *b, i, r, d, bird.* How does a bird move? What kind of home does a bird have? We will see the word *bird* in the story we read today. There will be a picture above the word to help us read it.

Listen to Me Reader K.6.6

■ **Set a Purpose** Review children's ideas. Point out that after they read, they will know more about the red bird. Tell children that you will read the story with them. Follow along with your finger as I read. Then we will take turns reading this page. Repeat this routine through all of the pages. Guide children to decode words.

■ **Reread for Fluency** Use echo reading of Listen to Me Reader K.6.6 to model reading fluently. Use your oral reading to model for children when to pause, when to change pitch, and which words to stress. Then have children reread orally three to four times, or until they can read with few or no mistakes.

Objectives
- Isolate the initial sound in spoken one-syllable words.
- Identify the common sounds that letters represent.
- Predict what might happen next based on the cover.

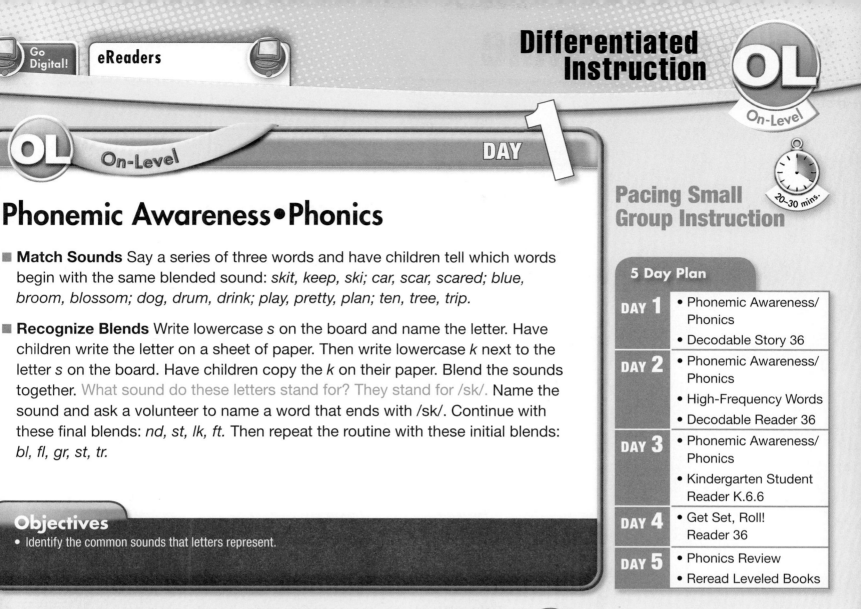
OL On-Level — DAY 1

Phonemic Awareness•Phonics

■ **Match Sounds** Say a series of three words and have children tell which words begin with the same blended sound: *skit, keep, ski; car, scar, scared; blue, broom, blossom; dog, drum, drink; play, pretty, plan; ten, tree, trip.*

■ **Recognize Blends** Write lowercase *s* on the board and name the letter. Have children write the letter on a sheet of paper. Then write lowercase *k* next to the letter *s* on the board. Have children copy the *k* on their paper. Blend the sounds together. What sound do these letters stand for? They stand for /sk/. Name the sound and ask a volunteer to name a word that ends with /sk/. Continue with these final blends: *nd, st, lk, ft.* Then repeat the routine with these initial blends: *bl, fl, gr, st, tr.*

Objectives
• Identify the common sounds that letters represent.

5 Day Plan

DAY 1	• Phonemic Awareness/ Phonics • Decodable Story 36
DAY 2	• Phonemic Awareness/ Phonics • High-Frequency Words • Decodable Reader 36
DAY 3	• Phonemic Awareness/ Phonics • Kindergarten Student Reader K.6.6
DAY 4	• Get Set, Roll! Reader 36
DAY 5	• Phonics Review • Reread Leveled Books

OL On-Level — DAY 2

Phonemic Awareness•Phonics

■ **Discriminate Final Blends** Draw seven diamond shapes on the board. Collect twelve Picture Cards, including: *lamp, desk, mask, nest, stamp, tent, vest.* Mix the cards and display them one at a time. Have a child name the picture. If the name has a final blend, have the child write the blend in one of the diamonds.

■ **High-Frequency Words** Display the following word cards: *you, said, see, look, three.* Say the word *you* and select a child to point to the word. Have children say the word and use it in a sentence. Continue with the other words.

Objectives
• Identify the common sounds that letters represent.
• Identify at least 25 high-frequency words from a commonly used list.

3 or 4 Day Plan

DAY 1	• Phonemic Awareness/ Phonics • Decodable Story 36
DAY 2	• Phonemic Awareness/ Phonics • High-Frequency Words • Decodable Reader 36
DAY 3	• Phonemic Awareness/ Phonics • Kindergarten Student Reader K.6.6
DAY 4	• Get Set, Roll! Reader 36

3 Day Plan: Eliminate the shaded box.

More Practice

For additional practice with this week's phonics skills, have children reread the Decodable Story (Day 1) and the Decodable Reader (Day 2).

OL On-Level

DAY 3

Phonemic Awareness•Phonics

■ **Go to the Square** Write *beginning*, *middle*, and *end* on sheets of construction paper and place them in three separate areas around the room. Gather the following Picture Cards: *apple, box, crab, doll, flag, gum, lemon, mask, pig, rock, six, tent.* Display one card at a time and say: The word is *apple.* Where is /a/ in *apple?* Children should answer the question by going to the area labeled *beginning.* Repeat with other words, having children move to the different areas around the room.

■ **Decode the Words** Write *box* on the board. Point to the *b.* This is the letter *b.* What is the sound for *b?* (/b/) Repeat the routine for the other letters. Let's blend the sounds together to read the word: /b/ /o/ /ks/, *box.* The word is *box.* Repeat with *gum, mask, pig, six,* and *tent.*

Kindergarten Student Reader K.6.6

■ **Preview and Predict** Display the cover of the book. The title of this story is *Where Do Animals Live?* What do you think this story will be about?

■ **Review Rebus Word** Write the word *fish* on the board. This is the word fish. Name the letters with me: *f, i, s, h, fish.* What do you know about fish? Look for the word *fish* in the story we will read today. There will be a picture above it to help us read the word.

■ **Set a Purpose** Review the list of things children think might happen in the story. Remind children they will read to find out where some animals live.

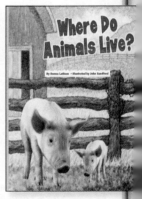

Kindergarten Student Reader K.6.6

■ **Read** Have children follow along as they read the story with you. After reading p. 2, ask children to tell about the hen and where it rests. Continue with each page. Ask the following questions:

• What animal lives in a pen?
• What animal rests in a den?
• What does a spider sit in?
• Where does the bat live?

■ **Summarize** Have children retell the story to a partner.

■ **Text to Self** Help children make personal connections to the story as they tell about the place they live.

Objectives
• Predict what might happen next based on the title.
• Respond to questions about text.

OL On-Level

DAY **4**

Get Set, Roll! Reader 36

■ **Review** Review the words *a, she, with, they, look, is,* and *was* by writing each word on the board and saying the word with children. Then give clues to a word and have children tell which word it is.

■ **Review Rebus Words** Write the word *trucks* on the board. This is the word *trucks.* Name the letters with me: *t, r, u, c, k, s, trucks.* What can you can tell me about *trucks*? Remember, there will be a picture above the word *trucks* to help you read it.

■ **Read** Display Get Set, Roll! Reader 36, *Big Rosie.* Today we will read a story about the Trucktown trucks. Point to the title of the story. *Big Rosie* is the title of the story. Look at the cover of the book. Let's read to find out.

Objectives
• Read at least 25 high-frequency words from a commonly used list.
• Predict what might happen next based on the cover.

More Reading

Use Leveled Readers or other text at children's instructional level to develop fluency.

OL On-Level

DAY **5**

Phonics Review

■ **Play Phonics Bingo!** Give each child a piece of paper. Help children make three rows of three boxes. Write the following words on the board and have them copy one of words into each box: *cat, slip, pig, ox, hen, stop, yak, crab, bat, duck, spot, fox, plum.* Give children six markers. Choose one of the words and sound it out for children. This word has /k/ /a/ /t/. Have children place a marker over the word *cat* if they find it on their card. Continue until a child places three markers in a row—vertically, horizontally, or diagonally. That child then names the words and the sounds.

Objectives
• Blend spoken phonemes to form one-syllable words.
• Identify the common sounds that letters represent.

Small Group Time

5 Day Plan

DAY 1	• Phonemic Awareness/ Phonics • Decodable Story 36
DAY 2	• Phonics • Spelling • Decodable Reader 36
DAY 3	• Independent Reader K.6.6 or Kindergarten Student Reader K.6.6
DAY 4	• Get Set, Roll! Reader 36 or Kindergarten Student Reader K.6.6
DAY 5	• Fluency/Comprehension • Independent Reader K.6.6

3 or 4 Day Plan

DAY 1	• Phonemic Awareness/ Phonics • Decodable Story 36
DAY 2	• Phonics • Spelling • Decodable Reader 36
DAY 3	• Independent Reader K.6.6 or Kindergarten Student Reader K.6.6
DAY 4	• Get Set, Roll! Reader 36 or Kindergarten Student Reader K.6.6

3 Day Plan: Eliminate the shaded box.

More Practice

For additional practice with this week's phonics skills and to develop fluency, have children reread the Decodable Story (Day 1) and the Decodable Reader (Day 2).

A Advanced **DAY 1**

Phonemic Awareness•Phonics

■ **Beginning, Middle, End** Listen to these word pairs and tell me whether the beginning, middle, or end of each word sounds the same: *mass, man; hat, can; pot, let; baby, boy; big, dog; top, cup.*

■ **Make a Blend** Write each of the following words and letters on index cards: *lip, rip, led, lap, lot, rag, c, f, s, d.* Give the four letter cards to volunteers. Hold up the word index cards one at a time. Have children decide whether they can add their letter to the start of the word to make a new word. If their letter forms an initial blend, have them hold up their letter card. For example, if you show the word *lip,* children with *c, f,* and *s* should hold up their cards because they can form the words *clip, flip,* and *slip.* Continue the routine with the rest of the words.

Objectives
• Identify the common sounds that letters represent.
• Recognize that new words are created when letters are added.

A Advanced **DAY 2**

Phonics•Spelling

■ **Write Words with Blends** Say *slip.* Have children say the sounds /sl/ /i/ /p/. Ask children to write letters for the sounds. Then write *slip* on the board and have children check that they wrote the correct letters. Continue with *plan, skip,* and *flop.*

■ **Spell Sounds** Give each child the following letter tiles: *a, b, c, d, g, i, l, n, o, p, r, s, t.* Listen to the sounds in *spot:* /sp/ /o/ /t/, *spot.* What are the letters for /sp/?  They are *s* and *p.* Place your *s* and *p* tiles in front of you. Continue with the remaining sounds. Then have children blend the sounds to read the word. Have children take away the *s* tile. What new word did we make? Blend the sounds to read the new word: /p/ /o/ /t/, *pot.* Then have children spell *drip, crib, glad,* and *slab* and take away the first letter tile to make new words.

Objectives
• Identify the common sounds that letters represent.
• Recognize that new words are created when letters are deleted.
• Use letter-sound correspondences to spell consonant-vowel-consonant (CVC) words.

 eReaders

A Advanced

DAY **3**

For a complete lesson plan and additional practice, see the **Leveled Reader Teaching Guide**.

Independent Reader K.6.6

Independent Reader K.6.6

- **Practice High-Frequency Words** Write the previously taught high-frequency words on the board. Have volunteers say the word and use it in a sentence.

the	was	for	them	they	are

- **Activate Prior Knowledge** Remind children that animals need homes to live in. When people build their homes too close to where wild animals live, the animals need to move away. Help children understand that these animals need to be protected.

- **Draw Conclusions** Display the cover of *Safe Places for Animals.* Have children tell why animals need special places to be safe in the wild.

- **Reread for Fluency** After rereading with children, model reading fluently for them. I am going to read this book aloud. I will read the words with no mistakes. I want you to read it aloud with me. Try to read the words just as I do.

  • Use echo reading of Independent Reader K.6.6 to model reading fluently. Use your oral reading to model for children where to pause, when to change pitch, and which words to stress. Then have children reread orally three to four times, or until they can read with few or no mistakes.

- For more practice with phonics and high-frequency words and to develop fluency, have children read Kindergarten Student Reader K.6.6. Use the instruction on pp. 552–553.

Objectives
• Read at least 25 high-frequency words from a commonly used list.
• Make inferences based on the plot.

More Reading
Use Leveled Readers or other text at children's instructional level.

Small Group Time

More Reading

Use Leveled Readers or other text at children's instructional level.

A Advanced   DAY **4**

Kindergarten Student Reader K.6.6

- **Revisit Rebus Word** Write the word *fish* on the board. This is the word *fish.* Name the letters with me: *f, i, s, h, fish.* How do fish move? Look for the word *fish* in the story. There will be a picture above the word to help you read it.

- **Reread** Use Kindergarten Student Reader K.6.6 to practice reading fluently.

- **Text to World** Ask children to think about animals they know. Have them name an animal and tell about its home.

- **Read** Have children read Get Set, Roll! Reader 36, *Big Rosie.* Use the instruction on p. 579.

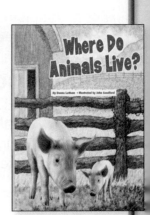

Kindergarten Student
Reader K.6.6

Objectives
- Read at least 25 high-frequency words from a commonly used list.

A Advanced   DAY **5**

Fluency•Comprehension

- **Reread for Fluency** Use the Independent Reader K.6.6 to model reading fluently for children. I am going to read this selection aloud. I will read the words with no mistakes. I want you to read it aloud with me. Try to read the words just as I do.

- **Comprehension** After children have finished reading, have them retell what happens in the selection. Then have children write or draw a picture that tells why people had fun making safe places for animals.

Independent
Reader K.6.6

Objectives
- Read at least 25 high-frequency words from a commonly used list.

Concept Development

■ **Read the Concept Literacy Reader** To build background and vocabulary, read *Ants Build* with children, pausing to discuss each page. Model sentence patterns and vocabulary that describe the pictures. On a second reading, invite children to talk about how the ants build their nests.

■ **Develop Oral Language** Revisit *Ants Build*, pointing out ways that ants build a nest. Then have children sing this song with you to the tune of "Billy Boy":

How do you build, Little ant, little ant? How do you build, tiny builder?	I carry heavy loads, And I tunnel through the soil, And I sing a song about a tiny builder.

Phonemic Awareness/Phonics

■ **Frontload Words with Initial, Medial, and Final Sounds** Have children look at the illustration on pp. 112–113 of *My Skills Buddy*. This picture shows people working outside. What work does your family do outside? Listen to the word *broom*. What blend does *broom* begin with? *Broom* begins with /br/, *broom*. Then use the chant to introduce picture words with blends:

Come on over and work with me.
Tell me, tell me, what do you see?

Ask children to find something that begins with /br/. Have children point to the branch in the picture. *Branch* begins with /br/.

Repeat the chant with other words in the picture that have initial and final consonant blends, such as *limb, broken, dirt, brick, grass, first aid, tree, grow, trim, ant, plant, paint, tent,* and *drink.* Then use the chant to help children identify the medial vowel sounds in these words.

■ **Letter-Sound Correspondence** Use letter tiles to display the words *Brit, tent,* and *grass* or write them on the board. This word is *Brit:* /br/ /i/ /t/, *Brit.* Say the word with me. Have children write the word *Brit* and circle the letters that make /br/. Have them underline the letter that makes /i/. Repeat with the other words. Continue with *tent* and *grass.*

Content Objective
• Develop content knowledge related to how ants build their nests.

Language Objectives
• Understand and use grade-level content area vocabulary.

• Recognize the sounds of English.

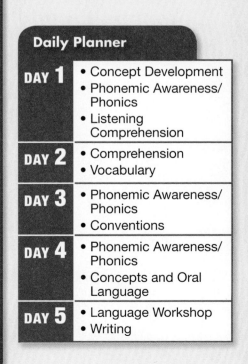

Concept Literacy Reader K.6.6

Support for English Language Learners

Content Objective
- Understand drawing conclusions.

Language Objective
- Learn and use academic vocabulary.

My Skills Buddy, pp. 114–115

Listening Comprehension: Draw Conclusions

- **Frontload Vocabulary** Discuss the illustration on pp. 114–115 in *My Skills Buddy* to frontload vocabulary. Cover p. 115 so that only p. 114 is showing. What do you see in the picture? (a girl) What is the girl holding? (a present) Look at the girl's face. What is she doing? (smiling) How do you think she feels? (happy) Now uncover p. 115 and discuss the illustration. This page has the words *Happy Happy Happy*. The equal sign tells us that the first picture "equals" the second picture. So, the smiling girl with present equals *Happy Happy Happy*.

- **Provide Scaffolding** Look at the illustrations on pp. 114–115. Explain what is happening in the spread. Explain to children that, when they looked at the smiling girl and guessed that she felt happy, they were drawing a conclusion about the girl. Help them understand that drawing conclusions means using what you already know to make a statement about something. When we see a girl smiling, we can conclude that she is happy.

- **Prepare for the Read Aloud** The modified Read Aloud below prepares children for listening to the oral reading "A Prairie Dog Home" on p. 523.

A Prairie Dog Home

A prairie dog is not a dog. It is a rodent. Prairie dogs are builders.

Prairie dogs live underground. They have long, curved claws. They dig tunnels. The dirt they dig out is in a mound. It keeps water out of the tunnel. Prairie dogs sit on the mound. They watch for enemies.

The home is called a burrow. It is large. There is a room near the entrance. Prairie dogs listen for enemies there. Prairie dogs nest and sleep farther down.

Some tunnels lead to back doors. These help the prairie dog escape.

- **First Listening** Write the title of the Read Aloud on the board. This story tells about a prairie dog's home. Listen to find out about a prairie dog's home. After reading, ask children to recall details about a prairie dog's home. Where does the prairie dog live? How does a prairie dog dig?

- **Second Listening** Write the words *Draw Conclusions* on the board. As you listen to the story, think about why prairie dogs build their homes the way they do. After reading, help children draw a conclusion about how prairie dogs build and behave.

Objectives
- Understand the main points of spoken language ranging from situations in which contexts are familiar to unfamiliar. • Expand reading skills by employing inferential skills commensurate with content area needs.

ELL English Language Learners

DAY 2

Comprehension

■ **Provide Scaffolding** Display *Ants and Their Nests.* Lead a detailed picture walk through the story, naming what you see in the illustrations and describing what is happening. Use gestures and facial expressions to convey meaning.

• **Set the Scene** Use the cover of the Trade Book to help children understand that this story is about how different ants build their nests. Describe different places where ants build. Ants live in nests. They build the nests. Ants use different things to build their nests. What do you think an ant might use to make a nest where you live?

• **Frontload Vocabulary** As you lead the picture walk, use the illustrations to introduce unfamiliar words in the text. Include some words for bugs. Look at the picture on pages 6–7. This anthill is in the desert. The ants dig tunnels in the ground. Why do you think the ants make a hill around the hole? Point out any difficult words in the text and use them in sentences. Include *thousands* (p. 12); *worker ant, queen ant* (p. 14); and *twigs* (p. 18).

Vocabulary: Words for Bugs

■ **Frontload Vocabulary** Have children turn to p. 128 of *My Skills Buddy.* Talk about each picture and illustration, using the words *ant, bee, fly,* and *spider.* For example, point to the picture of the ant. This is an ant. How many legs does the ant have? (six) What color is the ant? (red) Then invite children to talk about the pictures using the words for bugs.

■ **Provide Scaffolding** Write the words *ant, bee, fly,* and *spider* on the board and on large cards. Read the words aloud with children. These words name bugs, or insects. They are nouns. Hold up the card with the word *bee. Bee* names a thing. *Bee* is a noun. It names a kind of bug. Say a sentence using the word and have children repeat the sentence: The bee helped make honey. Repeat with the other words for bugs.

■ **Practice** What are some other words related to bugs? Help children identify and use words that are related to insects. Begin by saying a sentence about a fly, such as *The fly buzzed around the room.* Ask children to identify what the fly did. Make a list of these words on the board. Have children say their own sentences and add words to the list.

Content Objective

• Develop background knowledge.

Language Objective

• Learn and use words for bugs.

Use Learning Strategies

Remind children that if they have trouble using bug words in sentences, they can ask for help.

Trade Book

Support for English Language Learners

Content Objective
- Use learning strategies.

Language Objectives
- Practice letter-sound correspondences.
- Use complete sentences.

Transfer Skills

Have children discuss different insects in their native country and share words for these insects.

Use Learning Strategies

Help children understand that nouns name a person, place, or thing. On the board, write a list of nouns and verbs. Point to a word and ask children whether the word names a person, a place, or a thing. If the word names none of these, help children see that the word names an action and is a verb.

Phonemic Awareness/Phonics

- **Isolate Initial, Medial, and Final Sounds** On the board, write *tent, plant, twig, spider, grass, nest,* and *silk.* Point to and say *tent.* Help children isolate /t/, /e/, and the blend /nt/. Have them underline the letter that makes /e/ and circle the letters that make /nt/. Continue the exercise using the other words.

- **Practice Initial, Medial, and Final Sounds in Words** Write these words for insects on the board or display them with letter tiles: *bee, wasp, ant, fly.* Have children read each word as you run your hand under it. Have children identify the sounds and say them aloud. Check each child's progress. Monitor pronunciation for clarity but not for perfection.

Conventions: Complete Sentences

- **Provide Scaffolding** Direct children to pp. 4–5 of *Ants and Their Nests* and read the page aloud. Ants build nests. Write this sentence on the board and repeat the sentence. This is a sentence. What does the sentence tell us? (Ants build nests.) A sentence has a noun and a verb. *Ants* names a thing. It is a noun. *Build* is an action word, or verb. It tells what ants do. *Ants* is the first word in the sentence. We use a capital *A.* We put a period at the end of the sentence.

- **Practice** Have children look at pp. 10–11. Read the passage aloud. On the board, write *Ants dig tunnels.* Invite children to tell which word is the noun and which is the verb. Ask questions about what each word does. Remind children that the first letter in a complete sentence is capitalized and that the sentence is followed by a period. Continue with other sentences from the story.

Leveled Support **Beginning/Intermediate** For each sentence, have a child demonstrate the action. While the child is acting out the sentence, explain what is happening: (Child's name) digs. Have children repeat the sentence after you and then identify the noun and verb.

Advanced/Advanced-High Write each sentence on the board, including improper capitalization and missing periods. Have children identify the errors and tell how to correct them.

Objectives
- Expand repertoire of learning strategies commensurate with grade-level learning expectations. • Use visual and contextual support to develop grasp of language structures needed to comprehend increasingly challenging language.

 **English Language Learners**

DAY 4

Phonemic Awareness/Phonics

■ **Review Initial, Medial, and Final Sounds** Help children review sounds in words by saying the following sentence:

Fred went up the great tree.

Repeat the sentence in parts (such as *Fred went*) so children can repeat the words. Then have them blend sounds, such as /F/ /r/ /e/ /d/ = *Fred*.

■ **Letter-Sound Correspondence** Show words from sentences such as *Fred went up the great tree.* Model reading the words, isolating beginning and final blends and medial vowel sounds. Show all the sound-letter correspondences (for example, /w/ /e/ /n/ /t/ = *went*). Repeat the modeling using other words and sentences.

Concepts and Oral Language

■ **Revisit Talk with Me Chart 36A** Display the chart. Have children describe each image on the page. Help them by describing ways ants build nests and dig tunnels.

■ **Develop Oral Language** Introduce language patterns that help describe the pictures on Talk with Me Chart 36A. Write this sentence frame on the board: *The ants _____.* Now let's use this sentence pattern to talk about what the ants do: *The ants dig tunnels. The ants work together.* Have children suggest other sentences using the sentence frame. Repeat the exercise using all pictures on the chart. Then play a game with children in which you ask a question about the pictures, such as: Which picture shows ants carrying things? Have children point to the correct picture and then answer your question with a sentence, such as *This picture shows ants carrying twigs.*

 Beginning Have children repeat the question you ask. Let them take a turn pointing to a picture on the chart.

Intermediate Ask questions to help children notice more details about the pictures, such as *Do you think it is crowded in the nest?*

Advanced/Advanced-High Encourage children to use their prior knowledge about ants to use the Amazing Words in sentences.

Content Objectives
- Develop oral language.
- Use learning strategies.

Language Objectives
- Practice initial, medial, and final sounds.
- Learn English language patterns.

Use Learning Strategies
With children, brainstorm some sentences using words from the pictures in the Talk with Me Chart. Work with children to create complete sentences describing the pictures in the chart.

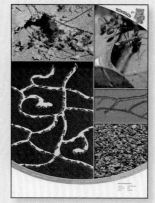
Talk with Me Chart 36A

Objectives
• Use strategic learning techniques to acquire basic vocabulary. • Speak using a variety of grammatical structures with increasing accuracy and ease as more English is acquired. • Speak using grade-level content area vocabulary in context to internalize new English words.

Support for English Language Learners

Content Objectives

- Understand *Ants and Their Nests.*
- Make a chart.

Language Objectives

- Make comparisons through speaking and writing.
- Write using grade-level vocabulary.

Monitor and Self-Correct

Remind children that if they don't know how to write the words, they can see if the words in the class chart will help them.

Home Language Support

Invite children to share ideas in their home languages before creating their sentences.

Language Workshop: Make Comparisons

■ **Introduce and Model** Turn to pp. 8–9 of *Ants and Their Nests*. These ants build nests with leaves and silk. Why do you think they use the sticky silk? Ask children what kinds of things they build. What materials do you use? What do you like most to build? What materials are best? When we talk about how things are the same and different, we compare and contrast. When we compare things, we talk about how they are alike. When we contrast things, we talk about how they are different.

■ **Practice** Think about ways different ants build nests. How are ants similar? What are some ways they are different? How are the queen ant and the worker ants different? Create a T-chart titled *Queen Ant and Worker Ants.* Label the columns *Alike* and *Different.* After adding each similarity or difference, have volunteers share their opinions about which nests are better. Restate that there is no right or wrong answer.

Writing: Make Comparisons

■ **Prepare for Writing** We talked about how ants build nests. Now let's write about working in a nest. Have each child fold a piece of paper in half to create two sections.

■ **Create Sentences About Building a Nest** Have children title their papers *Working In the Nest.* Then have them copy this sentence frame at the bottom of the first section: *It is good to be a queen ant because _____.* Have them copy this sentence frame at the bottom of the second section: *It is good to be a worker ant because _____.* In the first section, have children draw something that shows why it is good to be the queen ant. Have them make a drawing that shows why it is good to be a worker ant in the second section. Have them complete the sentence frames. Have children refer to the chart of differences and similarities that was created for the Language Workshop. When children finish their sentences, have them read their sentences to a partner several times. Display the books for the class to see.

Leveled LS Support

Beginning Provide the sentence frame in each section, and have children dictate or write words to complete the sentences.

Intermediate Guide children in writing words to complete the sentences.

Advanced/Advanced-High Encourage children to write their sentences on their own. You might also have children help less-proficient partners complete their sentences.

Objectives

• Expand and internalize initial English vocabulary by learning and using high-frequency English words necessary for identifying and describing people, places, and objects. • Write using content-based grade-level vocabulary.

Customize Literacy in Your Classroom

Table of Contents
for Customize Literacy

Customize Literacy is organized into different sections, each one designed to help you organize and carry out an effective literacy program. Each section contains strategies and support for teaching comprehension skills and strategies. Customize Literacy also shows how to use weekly text sets of readers in your literacy program.

Weekly Text Sets
to Customize Literacy

The following readers can be used to enhance your literacy instruction.

	Decodable Reader	Concept Literacy Reader	Below-Level Reader	On-Level Reader	Advanced Reader
Unit 6 WEEK 4	Fun with Spot	What Can We Make Together?	We Get Up!	Max and Jen: A Busy Day	The Box
Unit 6 WEEK 5	Fun in the Sun	Who Builds a House?	My Big Bug	Max and Jen Build a Home	Our Camping Trip
Unit 6 WEEK 6	The Box	Ants Build	Look at the Red Bird	Where Do Animals Live?	Safe Places for Animals

Customize Literacy
in Your Classroom

Instruction in comprehension skills and strategies provides readers with avenues to understanding a text. Through teacher modeling and guided, collaborative, and independent practice, children become independent thinkers who employ a variety of skills and strategies to help them make meaning as they read.

Envision It!
A Comprehension Handbook

Mini-Lessons for Comprehension Skills and Strategies

Unit 1	Character, Setting, Sequence, Classify and Categorize, Predict and Set Purpose, Recall and Retell
Unit 2	Compare and Contrast, Setting, Main Idea, Realism and Fantasy, Sequence, Predict and Set Purpose, Recall and Retell
Unit 3	Compare and Contrast, Plot, Cause and Effect, Draw Conclusions, Main Idea, Predict and Set Purpose, Recall and Retell
Unit 4	Sequence, Cause and Effect, Character, Classify and Categorize, Setting, Predict and Set Purpose, Recall and Retell
Unit 5	Realism and Fantasy, Cause and Effect, Compare and Contrast, Plot, Main Idea, Draw Conclusions, Predict and Set Purpose, Recall and Retell
Unit 6	Compare and Contrast, Character, Main Idea, Plot, Setting, Draw Conclusions, Predict and Set Purpose, Recall and Retell

Envision It! | Visual Skills Handbook

Author's Purpose
Categorize and Classify
Cause and Effect
Compare and Contrast
Draw Conclusions
Fact and Opinion
Generalize
Graphic Sources
Literary Elements
Main Idea and Details
Sequence

Envision It! | Visual Strategies Handbook

Background Knowledge
Important Ideas
Inferring
Monitor and Clarify
Predict and Set Purpose
Questioning
Story Structure
Summarize
Text Structure
Visualize

Anchor Chart Anchor charts are provided with each strategy lesson. These charts incorporate the language of strategic thinkers. They help students make their thinking visible and permanent and provide students with a means to clarify their thinking about how and when to use each strategy. As children gain more experience with a strategy, the chart may undergo revision.

See pages 97–113 in the *First Stop on Reading Street* Teacher's Edition for additional support as you customize literacy in your classroom.

Good Readers DRA2 users will find additional resources in the *First Stop on Reading Street* Teacher's Edition on pages 100–102.

Contents

Section 1 **Planning**

Pacing Guide

This chart shows the instructional sequence from *Scott Foresman Reading Street* for Grade K. You can use this pacing guide as is to ensure you are following a comprehensive scope and sequence. Or, you can adjust the sequence to match your calendar, curriculum map, or testing schedule.

Grade K — LANGUAGE ARTS

UNIT 1

	Week 1	Week 2	Week 3	Week 4	Week 5	Week 6
Phonological/ Phonemic Awareness	Rhyming Words	Syllables Sound Discrimination	Discriminate Sounds Segment Syllables	Discriminate Sounds	Isolate /m/ Discriminate Sounds	Isolate /t/ Discriminate Sounds Rhyme
Phonics	Letter Recognition: *Aa, Bb, Cc, Dd, Ee*	Letter Recognition: *Ff, Gg, Hh, Ii, Jj, Kk, Ll, Mm, Nn*	Letter Recognition: *Oo, Pp, Qq, Rr, Ss*	Letter Recognition: *Tt, Uu, Vv, Ww, Xx, Yy, Zz*	/m/ Spelled *Mm*	/t/ Spelled *Tt*
High-Frequency Words	*I, am*	*I, am*	*the, little*	*the, little*	*a, to*	*a, to*
Listening Comprehension	Character	Setting	Sequence	Classify and Categorize	Character	Classify and Categorize
Comprehension Strategies	Preview and Predict, Retell					

UNIT 2

	Week 1	Week 2
Phonological/ Phonemic Awareness	Isolate /a/ Oral Blending	Isolate /s/ Oral Blending
Phonics	/a/ Spelled *Aa*	/s/ Spelled *Ss*
High-Frequency Words	*have, is*	*have, is*
Listening Comprehension	Compare and Contrast	Setting

UNIT 4

	Week 1	Week 2	Week 3	Week 4	Week 5	Week 6
Phonemic Awareness	Isolate /h/ Oral Blending Segment Phonemes	Isolate /l/ Oral Blending Segment Phonemes	Isolate Blends Discriminate Phonemes Segment Phonemes	Isolate /g/ Segment Phonemes	Isolate /e/ Segment Phonemes Discriminate Phonemes	Isolate /e/ Segment Phonemes Discriminate Phonemes
Phonics	/h/ Spelled *Hh*	/l/ Spelled *Ll*	Consonant Blends	/g/ Spelled *Gg*	/e/ Spelled *Ee*	/e/ Spelled *Ee*
High-Frequency Words	*are, that, do*	*are, that, do*	*one, two, three, four, five*	*one, two, three, four, five*	*here, go, from*	*here, go, from*
Listening Comprehension	Sequence	Cause and Effect	Sequence	Character	Classify and Categorize	Setting
Comprehension Strategies	Preview and Predict, Retell					

UNIT 5

	Week 1	Week 2
Phonemic Awareness	Isolate /j/, /w/ Oral Blending Segment Phonemes	Isolate /ks/ Oral Blending Segment Phonemes
Phonics	/j/ Spelled *Jj* and /w/ Spelled *Ww*	/ks/ Spelled *Xx*
High-Frequency Words	*yellow, blue, green*	*yellow, blue, green*
Listening Comprehension	Realism and Fantasy	Cause and Effect

> Are you the adventurous type? Want to use some of your own ideas and materials in your teaching? But you worry you might be leaving out some critical instruction kids need? **Customize Literacy** can help.

Week 3	Week 4	Week 5	Week 6
Isolate /p/ Oral Blending	Isolate /k/ Oral Blending	Isolate /i/ Discriminate Sounds Oral Blending	Isolate /i/ Discriminate Sounds Oral Blending
/p/ Spelled *Pp*	/k/ Spelled *Cc*	/i/ Spelled *Ii*	/i/ Spelled *Ii*
we, my, like	*we, my, like*	*he, for*	*he, for*
Main Idea	Realism and Fantasy	Sequence	Realism and Fantasy
Preview and Predict, Retell			

UNIT 3

Week 1	Week 2	Week 3	Week 4	Week 5	Week 6
Isolate /n/, /b/ Oral Blending Segment Phonemes	Isolate /r/ Oral Blending Segment Phonemes	Isolate /d/, /k/ Oral Blending Segment Phonemes	Isolate /f/ Oral Blending Segment Phonemes	Isolate /o/ Oral Blending Segment Phonemes	Isolate /o/ Oral Blending Segment Phonemes
/n/ Spelled *Nn* and /b/ Spelled *Bb*	/r/ Spelled *Rr*	/d/ Spelled *Dd* and /k/ Spelled *Kk*	/f/ Spelled *Ff*	/o/ Spelled *Oo*	/o/ Spelled *Oo*
me, with, she	*me, with, she*	*see, look*	*see, look*	*they, you, of*	*they, you, of*
Compare and Contrast	Plot	Cause and Effect	Plot	Draw Conclusions	Main Idea
Preview and Predict, Retell					

Week 3	Week 4	Week 5	Week 6
Isolate /u/ Oral Blending Segment Phonemes	Isolate /u/ Oral Blending Segment Phonemes	Isolate /v/, /z/ Oral Blending Segment Phonemes	Isolate /y/, /kw/ Oral Blending Segment Phonemes
/u/ Spelled *Uu*	/u/ Spelled *Uu*	/v/ Spelled *Vv* and /z/ Spelled *Zz*	/y/ Spelled *Yy* and /kw/ Spelled *qu*
what, said, was	*what, said, was*	*where, come*	*where, come*
Compare and Contrast	Plot	Main Idea	Draw Conclusions
Preview and Predict, Retell			

UNIT 6

Week 1	Week 2	Week 3	Week 4	Week 5	Week 6
Isolate /a/ and /i/ Blend Phonemes Segment Phonemes	Isolate /o/ Blend Phonemes Segment Phonemes	Isolate /e/ Blend Phonemes Segment Phonemes	Isolate /u/ Blend Phonemes Segment Phonemes	Consonant and Vowel Sounds	Consonant and Vowel Sounds
/a/ Spelled *Aa* and /i/ Spelled *Ii*	/o/ Spelled *Oo*	/e/ Spelled *Ee*	/u/ Spelled *Uu*	Consonants and Short Vowels	Consonants and Short Vowels
here, do, little, with, what	*where, is, go, that, come*	*the, was, to, like, from*	*for, of, my, we, yellow*	*have, they, four, two, blue*	*you, said, see, look, three*
Compare and Contrast	Character	Main Idea	Plot	Setting	Draw Conclusions
Preview and Predict, Retell					

Pacing Guide

Grade K — LANGUAGE ARTS

UNIT 1

	Week 1	Week 2	Week 3	Week 4	Week 5	Week 6
Speaking and Listening	Follow Directions	Drama—Respond to Literature	Listen for Rhyme and Rhythm	Talk About Me	Announcements and Messages	Drama—Respond to Literature
Grammar/ Conventions	Say Our Names	Write Our Names	What We Look Like	What We Can Do	Nouns for People and Animals	Nouns for Places and Things
Writing	Song	Invitation	Poem	Instructions	Caption	Personal Narrative

UNIT 2

	Week 1	Week 2
Speaking and Listening	Listen for Sequence	Listen for Directions
Grammar/ Conventions	Nouns for More Than One	Proper Nouns
Writing	Label	List

UNIT 4

	Week 1	Week 2	Week 3	Week 4	Week 5	Week 6
Speaking and Listening	Give Directions	Compare and Contrast	Listen for Sequence	Discuss Authors and Illustrators	Listen for Story Elements: Character	Listen to Poems
Grammar/ Conventions	Subjects (Naming Parts)	Predicates (Action Parts)	Complete Sentences	Telling Sentences	Capital Letters and Periods	Pronouns *I* and *me*
Writing	Directions	Poem	Description	List	Informal Letter	List

UNIT 5

	Week 1	Week 2
Speaking and Listening	Ask and Answer Questions	Drama—Respond to Literature
Grammar/ Conventions	Questions	Question Marks and Capital Letters
Writing	Caption	Rhyme

Week 3	Week 4	Week 5	Week 6
Discussions	Listen for Setting	Give a Description	Listen for Plot
Adjectives: Colors and Shapes	Adjectives: Sizes and Numbers	Adjectives: Opposites	Adjectives
Notes	Poem	Caption	Story

UNIT 3

Week 1	Week 2	Week 3	Week 4	Week 5	Week 6
Respond to Literature	Sequence	Recite Rhymes	Oral Presentation	Messages and Letters	Ask and Answer Questions
Verbs	Verbs for Now and the Past	Verbs That Add -s	Verbs for Now and the Future	Meaningful Word Groups	Sentences
Summary	Invitation	Persuasive Statement	Caption	List	Poem

Week 3	Week 4	Week 5	Week 6
Discuss Literature	Sequence	Oral Presentation—Description	Discuss Literary Elements: Plot
Prepositions	Nouns	Nouns in Sentences	Verbs
Poem	Formal Letter	Invitation	How-to Report

UNIT 6

Week 1	Week 2	Week 3	Week 4	Week 5	Week 6
Recite Language	Discuss Fact and Opinion	Interpret Information	Discuss Literary Elements: Character	Oral Presentation—Book Report	Discuss Literary Elements: Setting
Pronouns I and me	Prepositional Phrases	Telling Sentences	Questions	Exclamations	Complete Sentences
List	Song	Rhyme	Rhyme	Poem	Report

Teaching Record Chart

This chart shows the critical comprehension skills and strategies you need to cover. Check off each one as you provide instruction.

Reading/Comprehension	DATES OF INSTRUCTION		
Predict what might happen next in text based on the cover, title, and illustrations.			
Ask and respond to questions about texts read aloud.			
Identify elements of a story including setting, character, and key events.			
Discuss the big idea (theme) of a well-known folk tale or fable and connect it to personal experience.			
Recognize sensory details.			
Recognize recurring phrases and characters in traditional fairy tales, lullabies, and folk tales from various cultures.			
Respond to rhythm and rhyme in poetry through identifying a regular beat and similarities in word sounds.			
Retell a main event from a story read aloud.			
Describe characters in a story and the reasons for their actions.			
Identify the topic of an informational text heard.			

> **Tired of using slips of paper or stickies to make sure you teach everything you need to? Need an easier way to keep track of what you have taught, and what you still need to cover? Customize Literacy can help.**

Reading/Comprehension	DATES OF INSTRUCTION		
Identify the topic and details in expository text heard or read, referring to the words and/or illustrations.			
Retell important facts in a text, heard or read.			
Discuss the ways authors group information in text.			
Use titles and illustrations to make predictions about text.			
Follow pictorial directions (e.g., recipes, science experiments).			
Identify the meaning of specific signs (e.g., traffic signs, warning signs).			
Discuss the purposes for reading and listening to various texts (e.g., to become involved in real and imagined events, settings, actions, and to enjoy language).			
Ask and respond to questions about text.			
Monitor and adjust comprehension (e.g., using background knowledge, creating sensory images, re-reading a portion aloud).			
Make inferences based on the cover, title, illustrations, and plot.			
Retell or act out important events in stories.			
Make connections to own experiences, to ideas in other texts, and to the larger community and discuss textual evidence.			

Section 2 Instruction

Plot

Mini-Lesson

Objectives:
- Children know that a story is made up of events that happen one after another.
- Children know that a story has a beginning, middle, and end.

Texts for Teaching
- *Little Quack*
- *Farfallina and Marcel*
- *The Little Engine That Could*
- *Alistair and Kip's Great Adventure!*

Leveled Readers
- See pages CL16–CL17 for a list of Leveled Readers.

Understand the Skill

Student Edition K.6, pp. 74–75

The **plot** is the series of events in a story. Children learn that the events happen in a certain order. They talk about what happens in the beginning, middle, and end of a story.

Teach

Use the **Envision It!** lesson on K.6, pages 74–75 to visually teach plot.

Remind children that stories have a beginning, middle, and end. Ask: What is the first thing that happens in this story about the tortoise and the hare? What happens next? What happens at the end of the story? Use a story chart to record children's responses.

Practice

Tell children that stories happen in order. Retell a familiar story, such as "The Three Little Pigs" or "Goldilocks and the Three Bears." Show children picture cards of story events and have them put the cards in story order. Retell the story using the picture cards and the words *beginning, middle,* and *end*.

If... children have difficulty describing the order of story events,

then... give children two events from the story and ask: *Did the pig build the brick house before the pig built the house of straw?* Use pictures to help children as necessary.

Apply

Tell children to listen carefully as you read to know what happens in the beginning, middle, and end of a story. They can use the pictures to help them. Have children retell the story using *beginning, middle,* and *end*. You may wish to use a story chart to help children retell the story.

Writing

Children can write and/or draw what happens in the beginning, middle, and end of a story.

Objectives:
- Children identify where a story takes place.
- Children tell when a story takes place.

Texts for Teaching
- *We Are So Proud!*
- *Nature Spy*
- *Abuela*
- *The House That Tony Lives In*

Leveled Readers
- See pages CL16–CL17 for a list of Leveled Readers.

Setting

Mini-Lesson

Understand the Skill

The **setting** is the time and place in which a story occurs. Illustrations and text clues help children understand setting. Sensory details like smells, sights, and tastes can help children think about where a story takes place.

Student Edition K.6, pp. 94–95

Teach

Use the **Envision It!** lesson on K.6, pages 94–95 to visually teach setting. Have children point out the details that tell where and when the story takes place.

Remind children that the setting is when and where the story happens. Show children a familiar story. Ask: What do you see on the cover? Do you think the story happens in a swamp/house/playground? How do you know? Do you think the story happens in the morning? at night? How do you know?

Practice

Explain that books can happen in the same places. Show children a selection of fiction and nonfiction books. Ask: Where does this story happen? How do you know? Have children put books about the same place together.

If... children have difficulty describing the setting in the story,
then... point to a picture, have children name the things they see in the picture, and give choices about where they might see those things (inside/outside, forest/playground).

Apply

Tell children to listen carefully as you read to find out where the story happens. They can use the pictures to help them. Have them talk about where and when the story happens. Children can name the clues in the pictures that helped them know when and where the story took place.

Writing

Children can write and illustrate a sentence about their favorite place.

Draw Conclusions

Mini-Lesson

Student Edition K.6, pp. 114–115

Objectives:
- Children use what they already know to make decisions about what happens in pictures and books.
- Children make decisions about characters based on text and pictures.
- Children support their decisions.

Texts for Teaching
- *Then and Now*
- *This Is the Way We Go to School*
- *Ants and Their Nests*

Leveled Readers
- See pages CL16–CL17 for a list of Leveled Readers.

Understand the Skill

Drawing conclusions means taking what you already know and what you see in the world, see in a picture, or hear from a story to make a decision about something. Children learn that they have many experiences that can help them make decisions about characters or books.

Teach

Use the Envision It! lesson on K.6, pages 114–115 to visually teach draw conclusions. Help children use clues to conclude the girl is happy.

Tell children that they can use clues from the pictures to figure out what is happening in a story. Think aloud as you model drawing conclusions from pictures. Show children a familiar book.

This book is about a girl who makes a present for her mom. I can use the pictures to figure out how the girl feels about making the present. In this picture she is smiling. know that I smile when I am happy. The girl must be happy.

Talk about other emotions that children know, such as sadness or anger. Ask: How do you know when someone is sad or angry?

Practice

Tell children that they can use what they know to figure out how a character feels. Show children a familiar book and use clues from the pictures to make decisions about characters. Ask: What do you think the character feels in this story? What is the character doing in this picture? Why? Have children tell you why they think as they do.

If... children have difficulty drawing conclusions,

then... talk about what they do when they feel sad, happy, or excited, and help children connect what they do to what the character is doing in the pictures.

Apply

Tell children to listen carefully to the story and look at the pictures as you read so they can make decisions about the characters. Ask questions about the characters such as What did the characters do that was kind? mean? Do you think this character is strong? brave? friendly? Have children tell you why they think as they do.

Writing

Children can complete sentences: *When I am _____, I _____.*

Objectives:

- Children identify important ideas in a story.
- Children recall facts and details in a book.
- Children retell story events in their own words.

Texts for Teaching

- *Recall/Retell is a strategy that can be applied to any selection. Encourage children to recall and retell after they read.*

Recall/Retell

Mini-Lesson

Understand the Strategy

Recall/Retell is related to summarizing, which children begin in Grade 1. This strategy means picking out the important ideas in a story or an article and restating them in one's own words. Being able to recall/retell enables readers to organize information and evaluate the importance of what they read.

Teach

Tell children that they can retell what happens in a book. They should not tell everything that happened. They should think about the important ideas. They should put the important ideas in their own words. Using a familiar fiction or nonfiction book, model asking questions to help determine the important ideas. (Use a fiction book one day, and a nonfiction book another.) Then summarize in a sentence or two.

This book is about winter and how animals get ready for it. Some animals hibernate during winter and some go where it's warmer.

The main character wants to earn money to buy his Mom a gift. Instead of buying something, he ends up baking cookies for her with his Dad.

Questions for Fiction
• What happened first in this book?
• What did the main character want to do?
• Did he or she do it? How?
• What happened at the end of this book?

Questions for Nonfiction
• What is this book mostly about?
• What is one thing you learned in this book?

Practice and Apply

Read a story together and use the questions to talk about the story. Then use pictures and have children retell the story.

If... children have difficulty retelling,

then... talk about what happened first, next, and last.

Anchor Chart

Anchor charts help children make their thinking visible and permanent. With an anchor chart, the group can clarify their thinking about how to use a strategy. You might make a chart of the questions to help children recall and retell and hang it in the classroom.

Glossary of Literacy Terms

This glossary lists academic language terms that are related to literacy.
They are provided for your information and professional use.

A

alliteration	the repetition of a consonant sound in a group of words, especially in poetry
animal fantasy	a story about animals that talk and act like people
antonym	a word that means the opposite of another word
author's purpose	the reason the author wrote the text
autobiography	the story of a real person's life written by that person

B

background knowledge	the information and experience that a reader brings to a text
biography	the story of a real person's life written by another person

C

cause	why something happens
character	a person, an animal, or a personified object in a story
classify and categorize	put things, such as pictures or words, into groups
compare and contrast	tell how things are the same and different
comprehension	understanding of text being read—the ultimate goal of reading
comprehension strategy	a conscious plan used by a reader to gain understanding of text. Comprehension strategies may be used before, during, or after reading.
context clue	the words, phrases, or sentences near an unknown word that give the reader clues to the word's meaning

D

details	small pieces of information
dialogue	written conversation
draw conclusions	arrive at decisions or opinions after thinking about facts and details and using prior knowledge

E

effect	what happens as the result of a cause
expository text	text that contains facts and information. Also called *informational text.*

F

fable	a story, usually with animal characters, that is written to teach a moral, or lesson
fact	piece of information that can be proved to be true
fairy tale	a folk story with magical characters and events
fantasy	a story that could not really happen
fiction	writing that tells about imaginary people, things, and events
folk tale	a story that has been passed down by word of mouth
foreshadowing	the use of hints or clues about what will happen later in a story

generalize   make a broad statement or rule after examining particular facts

graphic organizer   a drawing, chart, or web that illustrates concepts or shows how ideas relate to each other. Readers use graphic organizers to help them keep track of and understand important information and ideas as they read. Story maps, word webs, Venn diagrams, and KWL charts are graphic organizers.

graphic source   a chart, diagram, or map within a text that adds to readers' understanding of the text

G

historical fiction   realistic fiction that takes place in the past. It is an imaginary story based on historical events and characters.

humor   writing or speech that has a funny or amusing quality

H

idiom   a phrase whose meaning differs from the ordinary meaning of the words. *A stone's throw* is an idiom meaning "a short distance."

imagery   the use of language to create beautiful or forceful pictures in the reader's mind

inference   conclusion reached on the basis of evidence and reasoning

inform   give knowledge, facts, or news to someone

informational text   writing that contains facts and information. Also called *expository text*.

interview   a face-to-face conversation in which someone responds to questions

I

legend   a story coming down from the past about the great deeds of a hero. Although a legend may be based on historical people and events, it is not regarded as historically true.

literary elements   the characters, setting, plot, and theme of a narrative text

L

main idea   the big idea that tells what a paragraph or a selection is mainly about; the most important idea of a text

metacognition   an awareness of one's own thinking processes and the ability to monitor and direct them to a desired goal. Good readers use metacognition to monitor their reading and adjust their reading strategies.

monitor and clarify   a comprehension strategy by which readers actively think about understanding their reading and know when they understand and when they do not. Readers use appropriate strategies to make sense of difficult words, ideas, or passages.

M

Instruction

M

moral	the lesson or teaching of a fable or story
mystery	a story about mysterious events that are not explained until the end, so as to keep the reader in suspense
myth	a story that attempts to explain something in nature

N

narrative	a story, made up or true, that someone tells or narrates
narrator	the character in a selection who tells the story
nonfiction	writing that tells about real things, real people, and real events

O

onomatopoeia	the use of words that sound like their meanings, such as *buzz* and *hum*
opinion	someone's judgment, belief, or way of thinking
oral vocabulary	the words needed for speaking and listening

P

personification	a figure of speech in which human traits or actions are given to animals or inanimate objects, as in *The sunbeam danced on the waves.*
persuade	convince someone to do or to believe something
play	a story that is written to be acted out for an audience
plot	a series of related events at the beginning, middle, and end of a story; the action of a story
poem	an expressive, imaginative piece of writing often arranged in lines having rhythm and rhyme. In a poem, the patterns made by the sounds of the words have special importance.
pourquoi tale	a type of folk story that explains why things in nature came to be. *Pourquoi* is a French word meaning "why."
predict	tell what a selection might be about or what might happen in a text. Readers use text features and information to predict. They confirm or revise their predictions as they read.
preview	look over a text before reading it

Q

questioning	a reading strategy in which readers ask and answer questions to help make sense of what they read

R

reading vocabulary	the words we recognize or use in print
realistic fiction	a story about imaginary people and events that could happen in real life

repetition	the repeated use of some aspect of language
rhyme	to end in the same sound(s)
rhythm	a pattern of strong beats in speech or writing, especially poetry

R

science fiction	a story based on science that often tells what life in the future might be like
semantic map	a graphic organizer, often a web, used to display words or concepts that are meaningfully related
sequence	the order of events in a selection or the order of the steps in which something is completed
sequence words	clue words such as *first*, *next*, *then*, and *finally* that signal the order of events in a selection
setting	where and when a story takes place
stanza	a group of lines in a poem
steps in a process	the order of the steps in which something is completed
story map	a graphic organizer used to record the literary elements and the sequence of events in a narrative text
story structure	how the characters, setting, and events of a story are organized into a plot
summarize	give the most important ideas of what was read. Readers summarize important information in the selection to keep track of what they are reading.
supporting detail	piece of information that tells about the main idea

S

tall tale	a humorous story that uses exaggeration to describe impossible happenings
text structure	the organization of a piece of nonfiction writing. Text structures of informational text include cause/effect, chronological, compare/contrast, description, problem/solution, proposition/support, and ask/answer questions.
theme	the big idea or author's message in a story
think aloud	an instructional strategy in which a teacher verbalizes his or her thinking to model the process of comprehension or the application of a skill
topic	the subject of a discussion, conversation, or piece of text

T

visualize	picture in one's mind what is happening in the text. Visualizing helps readers imagine the things they read about.

V

Instruction

Leveled Readers Skills Chart

Scott Foresman Reading Street provides more than six hundred leveled readers. Each one is designed to:

- Practice critical skills and strategies
- Build vocabulary and concepts
- Build fluency
- Develop a lifelong love of reading

Grade K

Title	Level*	DRA Level	Genre
Max the Duck	A	1	Fantasy
Fun for Us	B	2	Informational Text
Nick the Fix-It Man	B	2	Informational Text
Red and Blue	B	2	Realistic Fiction
We Have Fun Together	B	2	Fantasy
Two or Three?	B	2	Realistic Fiction
Buds for Mom	B	2	Realistic Fiction
A Walk in the Forest	B	2	Realistic Fiction
Looking for Animals	B	2	Realistic Fiction
Skip and Run	C	3	Fantasy
A Winter Home	C	3	Informational Text
A Yard for All	C	3	Fantasy
The Fawn	C	3	Realistic Fiction
We Can Do It!	C	3	Realistic Fiction
Fun with Gram	C	3	Realistic Fiction
They Will Grow	C	3	Realistic Fiction
What Can You Do?	C	3	Informational Text
Sad and Glad	C	3	Realistic Fiction
The Trip	C	3	Informational Text
Pigs	C	3	Informational Text
Frog's New Home	C	3	Informational Text
Five Bears	C	3	Fantasy
My Walk in Antarctica	C	3	Realistic Fiction
A Trip to Washington, D.C.	C	3	Informational Text
The Bus Ride	C	3	Realistic Fiction
The Boat Ride	C	3	Realistic Fiction
Ming on the Job	C	3	Realistic Fiction
The Big Train	D	4	Realistic Fiction
Get On the Bus!	D	4	Realistic Fiction
Catch the Ball!	D	4	Realistic Fiction
Homes	D	4	Informational Text
The Best Club Hut	D	4	Realistic Fiction
A Small Trip	D	4	Informational Text
The Box	D	4	Informational Text
Our Camping Trip	D	4	Realistic Fiction
Safe Places for Animals	D	4	Informational Text

* Suggested Guided Reading Level. Use your knowledge of children's abilities to adjust levels as needed.

This chart lists titles of leveled readers appropriate for children in Kindergarten. Use the chart to find titles that meet your children's interest and instructional needs. The books in this list were leveled using the criteria suggested in *Matching Books to Readers: Using Leveled Books in Guided Reading, Grades K–3* by Irene C. Fountas and Gay Su Pinnell. For more on leveling, see the *Reading Street Leveled Readers Leveling Guide.*

Comprehension Strategy	Target Comprehension Skill	Additional Comprehension Instruction	Vocabulary
Recall/Retell	Character	N/A	N/A
Recall/Retell	Setting	N/A	N/A
Recall/Retell	Sequence	N/A	N/A
Recall/Retell	Classify and Categorize	N/A	N/A
Recall/Retell	Character	N/A	N/A
Recall/Retell	Classify and Categorize	N/A	N/A
Recall/Retell	Compare and Contrast	N/A	N/A
Recall/Retell	Setting	N/A	N/A
Recall/Retell	Main Idea	N/A	N/A
Recall/Retell	Realism and Fantasy	N/A	N/A
Recall/Retell	Sequence	N/A	N/A
Recall/Retell	Realism and Fantasy	N/A	N/A
Recall/Retell	Compare and Contrast	N/A	N/A
Recall/Retell	Plot	N/A	N/A
Recall/Retell	Cause and Effect	N/A	N/A
Recall/Retell	Plot	N/A	N/A
Recall/Retell	Draw Conclusions	N/A	N/A
Recall/Retell	Main Idea	N/A	N/A
Recall/Retell	Sequence	N/A	N/A
Recall/Retell	Cause and Effect	N/A	N/A
Recall/Retell	Sequence	N/A	N/A
Recall/Retell	Character	N/A	N/A
Recall/Retell	Classify and Categorize	N/A	N/A
Recall/Retell	Setting	N/A	N/A
Recall/Retell	Realism and Fantasy	N/A	N/A
Recall/Retell	Cause and Effect	N/A	N/A
Recall/Retell	Compare and Contrast	N/A	N/A
Recall/Retell	Plot	N/A	N/A
Recall/Retell	Main Idea	N/A	N/A
Recall/Retell	Draw Conclusions	N/A	N/A
Recall/Retell	Compare and Contrast	N/A	N/A
Recall/Retell	Character	N/A	N/A
Recall/Retell	Main Idea	N/A	N/A
Recall/Retell	Plot	N/A	N/A
Recall/Retell	Setting	N/A	N/A
Recall/Retell	Draw Conclusions	N/A	N/A

What Good Readers Do

You can use the characteristics and behaviors of good readers to help all your children read better. But what are these characteristics and behaviors? And how can you use them to foster good reading behaviors for all your children? Here are some helpful tips.

Good Readers enjoy reading! They have favorite books, authors, and genres. Good readers often have a preference about where and when they read. They talk about books and recommend their favorites.

Develop this behavior by giving children opportunities to respond in different ways to what they read. Get them talking about what they read, and why they like or dislike it.

This behavior is important because book sharing alerts you to children who are somewhat passive about reading or have limited literacy experiences. Book sharing also helps you when you select books for the class.

Good Readers select books they can read.

Develop this behavior by providing a range of three or four texts appropriate for the child and then letting the child choose.

This behavior is important because children gain control over reading when they can choose from books they can read. This helps them become more independent in the classroom.

Good Readers use text features to help them preview and set purposes.

Develop this behavior by having children use the title and illustrations in fiction texts or the title, contents, headings, and other graphic features in nonfiction texts to make predictions about what they will be reading.

This behavior is important because previewing actually makes reading easier! Looking at features and sampling the text enables readers to predict and set expectations for reading.

Good Readers predict and ask questions before and while they read.

Develop this behavior by asking questions. After reading a passage, ask children what they think will happen next in a fiction text. Have them ask a question they think will be answered in a nonfiction text and read on to see if it is.

This behavior is important because when children predict and ask questions as they read, they are engaged. They have a purpose for reading and a basis for monitoring their comprehension.

66 **Want to improve your children's performance by fostering good reading behaviors? Customize Literacy can help.** 99

Good Readers use effective strategies and sources of information to figure out unknown words.

Develop this behavior by teaching specific strategies for figuring out unknown words, such as sounding out clusters of letters, using context, reading on, and using references.

This behavior is important because when readers have a variety of strategies to use, they are more able to decode and self-correct quickly. Readers who do these things view themselves as good readers.

Good Readers construct meaning as they read and then share or demonstrate their understanding.

Develop this behavior by having children retell what they read or write a summary of what they read in their own words.

This behavior is important because the ability to retell or write a summary is essential for success in reading. It shows how well a child has constructed meaning.

Good Readers make connections.

Develop this behavior by asking questions to help children make connections: *What does this remind you of? Have you ever read or experienced anything like this?*

This behavior is important because making connections helps readers understand and appreciate a text. Making connections to self, the world, and other texts supports high-level thinking.

Matching Books & Readers

Conversation Starters

Asking Good Questions Children want to read and listen to interesting and thought-provoking books! You can help them talk about these books. Use questions such as the following to assess listening comprehension and help children think about books. As you read longer books, pause often to ask questions about past and future events.

Cause and Effect

- What happens in this story?
- Why does it happen?

Classify and Categorize

- How are these things alike?
- Do these things belong in the same group?
- Is this thing like the others? Does it belong in the group?
- How do you know that it is like/not like the others?
- How would you group these things?

Character

- Who is in this story?
- What does this character like to do?
- How did the character feel in this part of the book?
- What does this character think about what happens in the book?
- Does this character seem real or made-up? What makes you think so?
- What character would you like to be? Why?

Compare and Contrast

- How are these things/characters/stories alike?
- How are these things/characters/stories different?

Draw Conclusions

- What happens in the story?
- What did the characters do to show you that they are kind/mean/strong?
- Which character do you like best? Why?
- Do you like this story? What makes you like it or dislike it?

Main Idea

- What is this story all about?

- What is the big idea of this story?

- What clues help you know what the story is about?

Plot

- In the story, what happens at the beginning? in the middle? at the end?

- What are other important things that happen in the story?

- What do you think is the most exciting/ important thing that happens?

- What is the problem that the character must solve/fix?

- How is that problem solved or fixed?

Realism and Fantasy

- Could this story happen in real life? Why do you think as you do?

- What things in the story could happen in real life?

- Do the people in this story act like people you know?

- How do you know if a story is make-believe or could really happen?

Sequence

- In this story, what happened first? next? last?

Setting

- What do the pictures tell you about when and where this story happened?

- What is this place like? What do you think it would be like?

- Does the place seem real or made-up? How can you tell?

- Do you want to visit this place? Why?

Connecting Science and Social Studies

Scott Foresman Reading Street Leveled Readers are perfect for covering, supporting, or enriching science and social studies content. Using these books ensures that all children can access important concepts.

Grade K Leveled Readers

Science

Earth and Space Science

Fiction Books
- *We Can Do It!*

Life Science

Nonfiction Books
- *A Winter Home*
- *What Can You Do?*
- *The Trip*
- *Pigs*
- *Frog's New Home*
- *A Small Trip*
- *Safe Places for Animals*

Fiction Books
- *A Walk in the Forest*
- *Looking for Animals*
- *Skip and Run*
- *A Yard for All*
- *The Fawn*
- *Fun with Gram*
- *They Will Grow*
- *Sad and Glad*

Physical Science

Fiction Books
- *Catch the Ball!*
- *The Best Club Hut*

Grade K Leveled Readers

Social Studies

Citizenship

Nonfiction Books
- Fun for Us
- Nick the Fix-It Man
- The Box

Fiction Books
- Red and Blue
- We Have Fun Together
- Two or Three?
- Buds for Mom
- Ming on the Job

Culture

Nonfiction Books
- Homes

Fiction Books
- Max the Duck
- Five Bears
- My Walk in Antarctica
- The Bus Ride
- The Boat Ride
- Get On the Bus!
- Our Camping Trip

History

Fiction Books
- The Big Train

Geography

Nonfiction Books
- A Trip to Washington, D.C.

Connecting Science and Social Studies

Grade 1 Leveled Readers

Science

Earth and Space Science

Nonfiction Books

- All About the Weather
- The Communication Story
- Over the Years
- Ready for Winter?
- Using the Telephone

Fiction Books

- Cody's Adventure
- Marla's Good Idea
- What a Detective Does

Life Science

Nonfiction Books

- All About Food Chains
- Animals Change and Grow
- Around the Forest
- Around the World
- Baby Animals in the Rain Forest
- Bees and Beekeepers
- The Dinosaur Detectives
- The Dinosaur Herds
- Fun in the Sun
- Honey
- In My Room
- Learn About Butterflies
- Learn About Worker Bees
- Let's Go to the Zoo
- Let's Visit a Butterfly Greenhouse
- Look at Dinosaurs
- A Mighty Oak Tree
- Monarchs Migrate South
- People Help the Forest
- The Seasons Change
- Seasons Come and Go
- What Animals Can You See?

Life Science

Fiction Books

- Bix the Dog
- Britton Finds a Kitten
- Carlos Picks a Pet
- Cary and the Wildlife Shelter
- Mac Can Do It!
- Mack and Zack
- Plans Change
- Sam
- The Sick Pets
- Time for Dinner
- What Brown Saw
- Which Animals Will We See?
- Which Fox?

Physical Science

Nonfiction Books

- The Inclined Plane
- Simple Machines at Work
- Simple Machines in Compound Machines

Grade 1 Leveled Readers

Social Studies

Citizenship

Nonfiction Books

- A Class
- A Garden for All
- Great Scientists: Detectives at Work
- Here in My Neighborhood
- A New Library
- Puppy Raiser
- The Story of the Kids Care Club
- Ways to Be a Good Citizen

Fiction Books

- The Art Show
- At Your Vet
- Big Wishes and Her Baby
- Double Trouble Twins
- Fly Away Owl!
- Grasshopper and Ant
- Hank's Song
- Let's Build a Park!
- Look at My Neighborhood
- My Little Brother Drew
- On the Farm
- Paul's Bed
- A Play
- Rules at School
- Space Star
- Squirrel and Bear
- That Cat Needs Help!

Culture

Nonfiction Books

- Cascarones Are for Fun
- My Babysitter
- Special Days, Special Food
- We Are a Family
- What Makes Buildings Special?

Fiction Books

- Go West!
- Grandma's Farm
- Gus the Pup
- Jamie's Jumble of Junk
- A New Baby Brother
- A Party for Pedro
- A Visit to the Ranch
- Where They Live

History

Nonfiction Books

- School: Then and Now
- Treasures of Our Country

Fiction Books

- Loni's Town

Government

Nonfiction Books

- America's Home
- Our Leaders

Fiction Books

- Mom the Mayor

Matching Books & Readers

Planning Teacher Study Groups

Adventurous teachers often have good ideas for lessons. A teacher study group is a great way to share ideas and get feedback on the best way to connect content and children. Working with other teachers can provide you with the support and motivation you need to implement new teaching strategies. A teacher study group offers many opportunities to collaborate, support each other's work, share insights, and get feedback.

Think About It

A weekly or monthly teacher study group can help support you in developing your expertise in the classroom. You and a group of like-minded teachers can form your own study group. What can this group accomplish?

- Read and discuss professional articles by researchers in the field of education.

- Meet to share teaching tips, collaborate on multi-grade lessons, and share resources.

- Develop lessons to try out new teaching strategies. Meet to share experiences and discuss how to further improve your teaching approach.

Let's Meet!

Forming a study group is easy. Just follow these four steps:

1. **Decide on the size of the group.** A small group has the advantage of making each member feel accountable, but make sure that all people can make the same commitment!

2. **Choose teachers to invite to join your group.** Think about whom you want to invite. Should they all teach the same grade? Can you invite teachers from other schools? Remember that the more diverse the group, the more it benefits from new perspectives.

3. **Set goals for the group.** In order to succeed, know what you want the group to do. Meet to set goals. Rank goals in order of importance and refer often to the goals to keep the group on track.

4. **Make logistical decisions.** This is often the most difficult. Decide where and when you will meet. Consider an online meeting place where group members can post discussion questions and replies if people are not able to meet.

What Will We Study? Use the goals you set to help determine what your group will study. Consider what materials are needed to reach your goals, and how long you think you will need to prepare for each meeting.

How Will It Work? Think about how you structure groups in your classroom. Use some of the same strategies.

- **Assign a group facilitator.** This person is responsible for guiding the meeting. This person comes prepared with discussion questions and leads the meeting. This could be a rotating responsibility dependent on experience with various topics. This person might be responsible for providing the materials.

- **Assign a recorder.** Have someone take notes during the meeting and record group decisions.

- **Use the jigsaw method.** Not everyone has time to be a facilitator. In this case, divide the text and assign each portion to a different person. Each person is responsible for leading the discussion on that particular part.

Meet Again Make a commitment to meet for a minimum number of times. After that, the group can reevaluate and decide whether or not to continue.

" Have some great teaching tips to share? Want to exchange ideas with your colleagues? Build your own professional community of teachers. **Customize Literacy** gets you started. "

Trial Lessons

Use your colleagues' experiences to help as you think about new ways to connect content and students. Use the following plan to create a mini-lesson. It should last twenty minutes. Get the support of your colleagues as you try something new and then reflect on what happened.

Be Creative! As you develop a plan for a mini-lesson, use these four words to guide planning: *purpose*, *text*, *resources*, and *routine*.

- **Purpose:** Decide on a skill or strategy to cover. Define your purpose for teaching the lesson.

- **Text:** Develop a list of the materials you could use. Ask your colleagues for suggestions.

- **Resources:** Make a list of the available resources, and consider how to use those resources most effectively. Consider using the leveled readers listed on pages CL16–CL17 and CL22–CL25 of Customize Literacy.

- **Routine:** Choose an instructional routine to structure your mini-lesson. See the mini-lessons in Customize Literacy for suggestions.

Try It! Try out your lesson! Consider audio- or videotaping the lesson for later review. You may wish to invite a colleague to sit in as you teach. Make notes on how the lesson went.

How Did It Go? Use the self-evaluation checklist on page CL29 as you reflect on your trial lesson. This provides a framework for later discussion.

Discuss, Reflect, Repeat Solicit feedback from your teacher study group. Explain the lesson and share your reflections. Ask for suggestions on ways to improve the lesson. Take some time to reflect on the feedback. Modify your lesson to reflect what you have learned. Then try teaching the lesson again.

Checklist for Teacher Self-Evaluation

How Well Did I ...

	Very Well	Satisfactory	Not Very Well
Plan the lesson?			
Select the appropriate level of text?			
Introduce the lesson and explain its objectives?			
Review previously taught skills?			
Directly explain the new skills being taught?			
Model the new skills?			
Break the material down into small steps?			
Integrate guided practice into the lesson?			
Monitor guided practice for student understanding?			
Provide feedback on independent practice?			
Maintain an appropriate pace?			
Assess student understanding of the material?			
Stress the importance of applying the skill as they read?			
Maintain students' interest?			
Ask questions?			
Handle student questions and responses?			
Respond to the range of abilities?			

Books for Teachers

Children aren't the only ones who need to read to grow. Here is a brief list of books that you may find useful to fill your reading teacher basket and learn new things.

A Professional Bibliography

Adams, M. J. "Alphabetic Anxiety and Explicit, Systematic Phonics Instruction: A Cognitive Science Perspective." *Handbook of Early Literacy Research.* The Guilford Press, 2001.

Adams, M. J. *Beginning to Read: Thinking and Learning About Print.* The MIT Press, 1990.

Afflerbach, P. "The Influence of Prior Knowledge and Text Genre on Readers' Prediction Strategies." *Journal of Reading Behavior,* vol. XXII, no. 2 (1990).

Armbruster, B. B., F. Lehr, and J. Osborn. *Put Reading First: The Research Building Blocks for Teaching Children to Read.* Partnership for Reading, Washington, D.C., 2001.

Bear, D. R., M. Invernizzi, S. Templeton, and F. Johnston. *Words Their Way.* Merrill Prentice Hall, 2004.

Beck, I., M. G. McKeown, and L. Kucan. *Bringing Words to Life: Robust Vocabulary Instruction.* The Guilford Press, 2002.

Biemiller, A. "Teaching Vocabulary in the Primary Grades: Vocabulary Instruction Needed." *Vocabulary Instruction Research to Practice.* The Guilford Press, 2004.

Blachowicz, C. and P. Fisher. "Vocabulary Instruction." *Handbook of Reading Research,* vol. III. Lawrence Erlbaum Associates, 2000.

Cunningham, P. M. and J. W. Cunningham. "What We Know About How to Teach Phonics." *What Research Says About Reading Instruction,* 3rd ed. International Reading Association, 2002.

Daniels, H. *Literature Circles.* 2nd ed. Stenhouse Publishers, 2002.

Dickson, S. V., D. C. Simmons, and E. J. Kame'enui. "Text Organization: Instructional and Curricular Basics and Implications." *What Reading Research Tells Us About Children with Diverse Learning Needs: Bases and Basics.* Lawrence Erlbaum Associates, 1998.

Diller, D. *Making the Most of Small Groups: Differentiation for All.* Stenhouse Publishers, 2007.

Duke, N. K., V. S. Bennett-Armistead, and E. M. Roberts. "Bridging the Gap Between Learning to Read and Reading to Learn." *Literacy and Young Children: Research-Based Practices.* The Guilford Press, 2003.

Duke, N. K. and C. Tower. "Nonfiction Texts for Young Readers." *The Texts in Elementary Classrooms.* Lawrence Erlbaum Associates, 2004.

Ehri, L. C. and S. R. Nunes. "The Role of Phonemic Awareness in Learning to Read." *What Research Has to Say About Reading Instruction.* 3rd ed. International Reading Association, 2002.

Fountas, I. C. and G. S. Pinnell. *Guided Reading: Good First Teaching for All Children.* Heinemann, 1996.

Fountas, I. C. and G. S. Pinnell. *Matching Books to Readers: Using Leveled Books in Guided Reading, K-3.* Heinemann, 1999.

Harvey, S. and A. Goudvis. *Strategies That Work: Teaching Comprehension to Enhance Understanding.* 2nd ed. Stenhouse Publishers, 2007.

Hiebert, E. H. and L. A. Martin. "The Texts of Beginning Reading Instruction." *Handbook of Early Literacy Research.* The Guilford Press, 2001.

Indrisano, R. and J. R. Paratore. *Learning to Write, Writing to Learn. Theory and Research in Practice.* International Reading Association, 2005.

Juel, C., G. Biancarosa, D. Coker, and R. Deffes. "Walking with Rosie: A Cautionary Tale of Early Reading Instruction." *Educational Leadership* (April 2003).

National Reading Panel. *Teaching Children to Read.* National Institute of Child Health and Human Development, 1999.

Pressley, M. *Reading Instruction That Works: The Case for Balanced Teaching,* 3rd ed. The Guilford Press, 2005.

Smith, S., D. C. Simmons, and E. J. Kame'enui. "Word Recognition: Research Bases." *What Reading Research Tells Us About Children with Diverse Learning Needs: Bases and Basics.* Lawrence Erlbaum Associates, 1998.

Snow, C., S. Burns, and P. Griffin, eds. *Preventing Reading Difficulties in Young Children.* National Academy Press, 1998.

Vaughn, S., P. G. Mathes, S. Linan-Thompson, and D. J. Francis. "Teaching English Language Learners at Risk for Reading Disabilities to Read: Putting Research into Practice." *Learning Disabilities Research & Practice,* vol. 20, issue 1 (February 2006).

Acknowledgments

Acknowledgments

Illustrations

Cover: Rob Hefferan
12 Amanda Haley
28–29, 49, 68, 108, 112 Anthony Lewis
32 Jamie Ho
39–43 Natalia Vasquez
50 Karen Stormer Brooks
52 Ron Lieser
58–63 Maria Mola
70–71 Martha Aviles
72 Stephen Lewis
79–85 Cale Atkinson
90 Ivanke & Lola
92 Jamie Smith
99–105 Dani Jones
110–111 Constanza Basaluzzo
119–125 Robbie Short
130–131 Cecilia Rebora

Photographs

Every effort has been made to secure permission and provide
appropriate credit for photographic material. The publisher deeply
regrets any omission and pledges to correct errors called to its attention
in subsequent editions.

Unless otherwise acknowledged, all photographs are the property of
Pearson Education, Inc.

Photo locators denoted as follows: Top (T), Center (C), Bottom (B),
Left (L), Right (R), Background (Bkgd)

10 (B) ©Ralf Gerard/Getty Images
30 (T) ©Digital Focus/Alamy
51 (T) ©Royalty-Free/Corbis
48 ©David R. Frazier Photolibrary, Inc./Alamy Images, ©Enigma/Alamy
Images, ©Visions of America, LLC/Alamy Images
88 ©David Young-Wolff/PhotoEdit, Inc., ©Jeff Greenberg/Alamy
Images, ©Tim Mantoani/Masterfile Corporation, ©Blend Images/
Jupiter Images
128 Frank Greenaway/©DK Images, Geoff Brightling/©DK Images, Tim
Ridley/©DK Images.

144

Teacher Editions

KWL Strategy: The KWL Interactive Reading Strategy was developed and is used by permission of Donna Ogle, National-Louis University, Skokie, Illinois, co-author of *Reading Today and Tomorrow*, Holt, Rinehart & Winston Publishers, 1988. (See also the *Reading Teacher*, February 1986, pp. 564–570.)

Understanding by Design quotes: Wiggins, G. & McTighe, J. (2005). *Understanding by Design.* Alexandria, VA: Association for Supervision and Curriculum Development.

Illustrations

Cover Rob Hefferan

Running Header Steven Mach

Photos

Every effort has been made to secure permission and provide appropriate credit for photographic material. The publisher deeply regrets any omission and pledges to correct errors called to its attention in subsequent editions.

Unless otherwise acknowledged, all photographs are the property of Pearson Education, Inc.